UNITED STATES
Road Atlas
Including Canada and Mexico

Contents

State Maps

City Maps

Mileage Chart

	Albany, NY	Albuquerque, NM	Amarillo, TX	Atlanta, GA	Austin, TX	Baltimore, MD	Billings, MT	Birmingham, AL	Boise, ID	Boston, MA	Brownsville, TX	Buffalo, NY	Charleston, SC	Charleston, WV	Charlotte, NC	Chicago, IL	Cincinnati, OH	Cleveland, OH	Columbia, SC	Columbus, OH	Dallas, TX	Daytona Beach, FL	Denver, CO	Des Moines, IA	Detroit, MI	El Paso, TX	Fargo, ND	Fort Lauderdale, FL	Fort Wayne, IN	Fort Worth, TX	Grand Rapids, MI	Greensboro, NC	Hartford, CT	Houston, TX	Indianapolis, IN	Jackson, MS	Jacksonville, FL	Kansas City, MO	Knoxville, TN	Las Vegas, NV	Lincoln, NE	Little Rock, AK
Albany, NY	0	2125	1825	1007	1882	332	2073	1112	2601	170	2007	292	932	639	795	795	729	496	823	657	1679	1209	1853	1193	690	2327	1463	1403	705	1682	710	661	106	1825	836	1320	1111	1279	836	2609	1336	1370
Albuquerque, NM	2125	0	300	1387	716	1881	1022	1260	970	2214	988	1801	1695	1583	1628	1346	1394	1606	1598	1468	673	1716	446	1013	1537	267	1314	1953	1410	632	1491	1677	2084	870	1289	1087	1678	811	1407	576	837	883
Amarillo, TX	1825	300	0	1087	485	1581	1037	965	1235	1914	784	1501	1517	1304	1338	1046	1094	1306	1298	1168	363	1467	454	806	1289	508	999	1670	1109	344	1191	1377	1822	608	989	787	1378	552	1107	876	596	607
Atlanta, GA	1007	1387	1087	0	884	669	1804	160	2252	1068	1175	912	300	495	251	695	438	692	211	543	805	446	1401	924	726	1453	1364	681	612	837	749	348	969	816	543	397	329	810	204	1947	1013	540
Austin, TX	1882	716	485	884	0	1550	1449	793	1716	1930	331	1566	1247	1251	1237	1100	1127	1371	1095	1233	203	1158	1009	897	1330	583	1333	1326	1200	192	1288	1281	1867	162	1111	519	1057	680	1051	1297	851	520
Baltimore, MD	332	1881	1581	669	1550	0	1875	804	2416	409	1825	352	567	339	430	697	510	355	513	405	1347	876	1692	997	511	1997	1339	1036	550	1379	624	346	308	1409	584	1006	770	1078	503	2408	1192	1037
Billings, MT	2073	1022	1037	1804	1449	1875	0	1759	586	2232	1771	1857	2222	1762	2027	1214	1479	1662	2075	1654	1395	2173	579	959	1579	1284	625	2466	1405	1406	1396	1958	2169	1739	1400	1743	2227	1078	1723	1060	836	1439
Birmingham, AL	1112	1260	965	160	793	804	1759	0	2101	1267	1065	941	460	539	411	669	468	722	359	584	637	505	1370	838	721	1304	1311	764	610	702	739	493	1058	676	497	251	472	724	255	1822	953	394
Boise, ID	2601	970	1235	2252	1716	2416	586	2101	0	2794	1921	2271	2503	2246	2408	1777	1983	2058	2289	2069	1610	2576	870	1402	2020	1241	1245	2820	1871	1598	1917	2408	2652	1854	1890	2091	2579	1476	2022	662	1205	1781
Boston, MA	170	2214	1914	1068	1930	409	2232	1267	2794	0	2255	454	989	728	828	965	875	632	928	738	1727	1257	1953	1305	795	2376	1623	1492	847	1761	908	739	105	1878	933	1395	1167	1435	871	2765	1500	1472
Brownsville, TX	2007	988	784	1175	331	1825	1909	1065	1921	2255	0	1865	1500	1479	1426	1430	1426	1670	1360	1533	526	1353	1251	1184	1694	806	1601	1542	1455	518	1585	1480	2094	357	1427	791	1264	1008	1320	1573	1216	819
Buffalo, NY	292	1801	1501	912	1566	352	1857	941	2271	454	1865	0	947	430	666	543	438	195	822	333	1363	1069	1602	867	366	2011	1185	1400	381	1395	419	641	397	1492	512	1119	1068	1007	671	2254	1057	1046
Charleston, SC	932	1695	1517	300	1247	567	2222	460	2503	989	1500	947	0	479	203	912	628	750	113	670	1164	351	1743	1185	874	1729	1557	586	740	1116	959	271	867	1027	743	702	248	1135	368	2247	1287	814
Charleston, WV	639	1583	1304	495	1251	339	1762	539	2246	728	1479	430	479	0	276	469	178	284	376	156	1134	726	1377	761	371	1672	1126	1004	284	1056	457	227	662	1246	328	790	676	777	284	2119	960	707
Charlotte, NC	795	1628	1338	251	1237	430	2027	411	2408	828	1426	666	203	276	0	738	446	543	100	453	1054	469	1548	1029	607	1710	1414	721	602	1061	791	89	763	1053	551	640	413	940	219	2173	1151	743
Chicago, IL	795	1346	1046	695	1100	697	1214	669	1777	965	1430	543	912	469	738	0	291	348	794	340	932	1096	1037	357	284	1435	649	1348	159	945	178	729	875	1160	186	762	999	543	537	1749	527	675
Cincinnati, OH	729	1394	1094	438	1127	510	1479	468	1983	875	1426	438	628	178	446	291	0	249	502	105	924	861	1199	583	260	1472	940	1086	184	956	357	458	746	1053	105	680	786	591	246	1921	715	608
Cleveland, OH	496	1606	1306	692	1371	355	1662	722	2058	632	1670	195	750	284	543	348	249	0	627	138	1168	952	1407	672	171	1716	997	1232	211	1200	284	486	539	1297	317	924	908	803	489	2059	867	851
Columbia, SC	823	1598	1298	211	1095	513	2075	359	2289	928	1360	822	113	376	100	794	502	627	0	513	1032	381	1616	1126	745	1668	1446	622	671	1057	858	188	836	1066	625	610	290	1025	267	2162	1199	759
Columbus, OH	657	1469	1168	543	1233	405	1654	584	2069	738	1533	333	670	156	453	340	105	138	513	0	1030	901	1270	657	195	1540	989	1126	150	1062	311	381	641	1159	179	786	850	665	351	1995	776	713
Dallas, TX	1679	673	363	805	203	1347	1395	637	1610	1727	526	1363	1164	1134	1054	932	924	1168	1032	1030	0	1123	806	714	1203	648	1131	1097	1030	33	1110	1122	1664	243	908	422	1005	511	820	1249	648	317
Daytona Beach, FL	1209	1716	1467	446	1158	876	2173	505	2576	1257	1353	1069	351	726	469	1096	883	952	381	901	1123	0	1823	1329	1103	1728	1714	227	1006	1126	1143	551	1138	952	880	688	97	1209	603	2316	1401	904
Denver, CO	1853	446	454	1401	1009	1692	579	1370	870	1953	1251	1602	1743	1377	1548	1037	1199	1407	1616	1270	806	1823	0	695	1321	705	915	2067	1186	773	1201	1621	1988	1060	1091	1246	1779	608	1341	743	507	992
Des Moines, IA	1193	1013	806	924	897	997	959	838	1402	1305	1184	867	1185	761	1029	357	583	672	1126	657	714	1329	695	0	600	1114	475	1581	516	747	502	1028	1283	930	478	846	1270	203	821	1399	203	562
Detroit, MI	690	1537	1289	726	1330	511	1579	721	2020	795	1694	366	874	371	607	284	260	171	745	195	1203	1103	1321	600	0	1701	922	1346	170	1240	162	567	701	1304	293	923	1046	791	506	2011	819	850
El Paso, TX	2327	267	508	1453	583	1997	1274	1304	1241	2376	806	2011	1729	1672	1710	1435	1372	1716	1668	1540	648	1728	705	1114	1701	0	1460	1869	1573	609	1554	1783	2263	743	1460	1070	1626	915	1488	722	946	960
Fargo, ND	1463	1314	999	1364	1333	1339	625	1311	1245	1625	1601	1185	1557	1126	1414	649	940	997	1446	989	1131	1714	915	475	922	1460	0	2007	808	1072	827	1412	1531	1334	835	1335	1704	609	1195	1535	451	1091
Fort Lauderdale, FL	1435	1953	1670	681	1326	1036	2466	764	2820	1492	1542	1400	586	1004	721	1348	1086	1232	622	1126	1097	227	2067	1581	1346	1869	2007	0	1271	1129	1342	786	1403	1191	1232	883	332	1459	860	2530	1670	1184
Fort Wayne, IN	705	1410	1109	612	1200	550	1405	610	1871	847	1455	381	740	284	602	159	184	219	671	150	1030	1006	1186	516	170	1573	808	1271	0	1053	172	551	768	1176	122	784	929	648	430	1878	686	711
Fort Worth, TX	1682	632	344	837	192	1379	1406	702	1598	1761	518	1395	1116	1056	1061	945	956	1200	1057	1062	33	1126	773	747	1236	609	1072	1129	1053	0	1121	1154	1696	264	912	446	1037	513	853	1203	648	349
Grand Rapids, MI	710	1491	1191	749	1288	624	1396	739	1917	908	1585	419	959	457	791	178	357	284	858	311	1110	1143	1201	502	162	1554	827	1342	172	1121	0	707	794	1196	263	957	1071	638	573	1889	699	799
Greensboro, NC	661	1677	1377	348	1281	346	1958	493	2408	739	1480	641	271	227	89	729	458	486	188	381	1122	551	1621	1028	567	1783	1412	786	551	1154	707	0	650	1167	563	770	483	1013	283	2237	1202	778
Hartford	106	2084	1822	969	1867	308	2169	1058	2652	105	2044	397	867	662	763	875	746	539	836	641	1664	1138	1988	1283	701	2263	1531	1403	768	1696	794	650	0	1773	805	1306	1071	1297	841	2675	1378	1344
Houston, TX	1825	870	608	816	162	1409	1639	676	1854	1878	357	1492	1027	1246	1053	1160	1053	1297	1066	1159	243	952	1060	930	1304	743	1334	1191	1176	264	1196	1167	1773	0	1041	406	891	754	922	1468	892	446
Indianapolis, IN	836	1289	989	543	1111	584	1400	497	1890	933	1427	512	743	328	551	186	105	317	625	179	908	980	1091	478	293	1460	835	1232	122	912	263	563	805	1041	0	681	867	486	351	1816	673	608
Jackson, MS	1320	1087	787	397	519	1006	1743	251	2091	1395	991	1119	702	790	640	762	680	924	610	786	422	688	1246	846	923	1070	1335	883	784	446	957	770	1306	406	681	0	591	716	506	1650	874	251
Jacksonville, FL	1111	1678	1378	329	1057	770	2227	472	2579	1167	1264	1068	248	676	413	999	786	908	290	850	1005	97	1779	1270	1046	1626	1704	332	929	1037	1071	483	1071	891	867	591	0	1110	555	2238	1321	843
Kansas City, MO	1279	811	552	810	680	1078	1078	724	1476	1435	1008	1007	1135	777	940	543	591	803	1025	665	511	1209	608	203	791	916	609	1459	648	513	638	1013	1297	754	486	716	1110	0	752	1345	211	409
Knoxville, TN	836	1407	1107	204	1051	503	1723	255	2022	871	1320	671	368	284	219	537	246	489	267	351	820	603	1341	821	506	1488	1195	860	430	872	573	283	841	922	351	506	555	752	0	1983	944	523
Las Vegas, NV	2609	576	876	1947	1297	2408	1060	1822	662	2765	1573	2254	2247	2119	2173	1749	1921	2059	2162	1995	1249	2316	743	1399	2011	722	1535	2530	1878	1203	1889	2237	2675	1468	1816	1650	2238	1345	1983	0	1224	1483
Lincoln, NE	1386	837	596	1013	851	1192	836	953	1205	1500	1216	1057	1287	960	1151	527	802	867	1199	776	648	1401	507	203	819	946	451	1670	686	648	699	1202	1378	892	673	874	1321	211	944	1224	0	616
Little Rock, AK	1370	883	607	540	520	1037	1439	394	1781	1472	819	1046	814	707	743	675	608	851	759	713	317	904	992	562	850	960	1091	1184	711	349	799	778	1344	446	608	251	843	409	523	1483	616	0
Los Angeles, CA	2911	823	1095	2197	1410	2676	1254	2067	837	2993	1678	2587	2521	2394	2617	1989	2164	2392	2426	2254	1401	2407	1009	1654	2270	818	1844	2704	2137	1361	2148	2478	2829	1581	2075	1880	2402	1589	2201	275	1476	1678
Louisville, KY	868	1332	1041	421	1022	608	1550	373	1908	976	1321	543	608	258	438	300	105	349	494	211	819	801	1127	591	365	1467	949	1078	222	851	373	462	867	948	129	575	729	519	246	1861	730	502
Memphis, TN	1232	1021	721	397	658	900	1557	239	1833	1379	957	908	689	653	604	551	469	713	612	575	455	749	1151	599	712	1103	1224	989	592	487	690	640	1209	584	470	211	697	470	385	1581	647	138
Miami, FL	1439	1994	1694	665	1338	1095	2580	788	2860	1516	1580	1524	630	1046	745	1338	1086	1264	658	1210	1321	259	2131	1582	1386	1958	1986	24	1326	1353	1356	810	1427	1207	1208	907	356	1475	859	2570	1673	1208
Milwaukee, WI	933	1443	1143	784	1203	794	1143	766	1777	1078	1530	640	1032	566	835	92	388	445	891	448	1013	1180	1070	365	389	1528	576	1443	256	1059	275	826	948	1155	283	884	1067	568	643	1752	560	772
Minneapolis, MN	1215	1256	1062	1105	1120	1105	812	1088	1488	1362	1456	948	1316	874	1143	405	696	753	1276	753	1013	1458	956	251	698	1520	244	1723	564	1001	583	1135	1257	1266	591	1123	1376	459	932	1630	409	881
Mobile, AL	1322	1265	965	340	656	990	1854	269	2343	1379	851	1184	607	825	575	908	745	989	555	834	592	502	1372	954	988	1236	1413	705	839	624	1006	681	1290	478	749	178	413	819	449	1841	1039	430
Montgomery, AL	1178	1345	1042	164	804	833	1836	93	2346	1232	1041	1076	464	632	405	762	561	815	379	707	677	458	1412	1311	814	1325	1521	671	686	701	819	512	1133	709	590	255	379	867	348	2015	975	470
Nashville, TN	993	1232	932	243	869	688	1640	195	2059	1062	1168	722	576	458	399	474	283	527	458	389	666	639	1167	712	536	1314	1136	900	385	698	534	429	973	795	302	422	592	590	174	1792	770	349
New Orleans, LA	1453	1187	875	493	535	1136	1820	352	2191	1526	730	1273	727	891	721	925	820	1078	701	940	530	632	1323	978	1077	1127	1494	843	916	519	1071	810	1436	367	857	193	551	857	607	1800	1114	430
New York City, NY	146	1995	1695	855	1728	201	1926	1019	2571	203	2002	390	786	524	625	794	628	446	715	551	1525	1054	1775	1070	620	2173	1450	1289	691	1557	706	561	101	1679	730	1192	957	1192	771	2520	1274	1235
Norfolk, VA	505	1905	1632	551	1403	237	2098	711	2551	660	1735	569	454	369	341	851	681	493	412	559	1359	702	1800	1202	711	1998	1581	964	709	1382	802	227	471	1362	669	948	632	1179	412	2534	1354	1025
Oakland, CA	2982	1134	1430	2488	1786	2864	1218	2321	671	3124	2034	2745	2788	2600	2755	2098	2317	2498	2703	2391	1803	2831	1223	1742	2350	1194	1870	3041	2257	1723	2308	2809	2909	1957	2212	2270	2771	1799	2509	582	1604	1984
Oklahoma City, OK	1523	559	267	863	414	1322	1168	701	1451	1659	680	1242	1176	1031	1069	804	835	1047	1091	909	211	1257	660	576	1030	708	989	1481	852	210	932	1118	1546	454	730	575	1181	373	847	1119	433	324
Omaha, NE	1308	905	754	989	847	1143	904	904	1274	1443	1249	1005	1303	899	1135	464	721	824	1283	795	693	1402	559	146	726	1256	464	1604	634	634	640	1208	1321	949	616	914	1305	195	930	1249	57	690
Orlando, FL	1249	1751	1451	446	1142	917	2277	545	2695	1297	2034	1306	401	814	559	1127	892	1046	440	997	1078	81	1896	1363	1143	1735	1826	208	1059	1110	1188	648	1208	964	989	697	138	1266	665	2311	1452	965
Philadelphia, PA	251	1922	1622	766	1630	97	2051	880	2488	327	1954	397	688	517	522	757	559	430	627	460	1427	914	1762	998	585	2075	1370	1127	604	1459	672	438	220	1581	624	1094	859	1134	646	2449	1260	1110
Phoenix, AZ	2512	446	746	1810	1030	2311	1220	1700	1022	2644	1289	2269	2222	2045	2061	1776	1808	2045	2025	1907	1013	2101	802	1497	2019	438	1791	2244	1831	983	1906	2099	2523	1110	1719	1500	2100	1277	1845	284	1236	1379
Pittsburgh, PA	471	1654	1354	712	1412	245	1681	778	2203	584	1713	219	778	211	504	470	291	128	572	186	1209	859	1475	770	304	1833	1112	1216	336	1241	397	438	486	1345	349	965	882	851	515	2181	965	899
Portland, Or	2869	1378	1636	2763	2059	2765	867	2571	439	3149	2468	2677	2952	2615	2757	2140	2474	2416	2972	2478	2051	3018	1283	1816	2368	1661	1484	3204	2299	2003	2251	2823	2877	2369	2335	2518	3042	1809	2550	991	1641	2270
Providence, RI	178	2156	1856	1027	1898	356	2238	1189	2701	41	2222	454	956	699	785	924	790	600	888	713	1695	1201	1961	1256	746	2335	1566	1459	799	1727	859	706	73	1849	892	1362	1127	1378	935	2683	1451	1395
Raleigh, NC	656	1759	1459	397	1355	324	2273	557	2560	713	1506	721	300	297	162	802	540	559	215	453	1152	559	1694	1123	643	1800	1485	794	603	1184	754	73	624	1233	635	815	486	1086	356	2319	1263	851
Reno, NV	2763	1056	1345	2411	1775	2562	1021	2363	404	2871	2068	2433	2765	2407	2570	1897	2221	2238	2626	2295	1731	2758	1030	1606	2190	1183	1660	3008	2056	1608	2067	2591	2749	1932	2116	2143	2716	1606	2363	478	1411	1986
Richmond, VA	482	1833	1533	527	1463	155	1655	699	2594	544	1646	552	462	251	280	788	356	583	390	498	1313	713	1904	1293	609	2023	1481	946	635	1333	722	191	455	2291	907	946	693	1205	440	2406	1249	963
Rochester,NY	219	1857	1557	1015	1623	300	1922	965	2352	381	1891	81	871	495	689	608	502	268	789	397	1420	1176	1637	932	424	2036	1249	1410	464	1452	499	600	324	1555	551	1183	1102	1062	710	2371	1135	1111
Saint Louis, MO	1028	1054	754	588	806	827	1381	539	1727	1184	1216	747	884	544	689	292	340	552	737	414	641	956	859	377	585	1238	872	1208	369	698	437	762	1030	835	251	495	859	251	497	1581	462	422
Saint Paul, MN	1215	1362	1062	1105	1120	1095	812	1118	1398	892	1565	948	1316	870	1143	405	696	753	1320	745	1013	1458	956	251	698	1541	244	1753	564	987	583	1138	1257	1266	591	1160	1376	459	951	1630	408	881
Salt Lake City, UT	2290	621	1324	1900	1341	2051	579	1825	349	2417	1775	1922	2254	1896	2059	1386	1710	1727	2115	1711	1287	2283	519	1085	1679	892	1172	2578	1527	1184	1556	2059	2238	1460	1605	1742	2286	1095	1766	413	900	1462
San Antonio, TX	1986	684	530	965	81	1646	1600	895	1709	2052	300	1638	1371	1419	1272	1208	1208	1443	1180	1305	284	1175	975	1022	1500	576	1402	1378	1269	283	1353	1321	1965	203	1200	649	1086	795	1150	1273	916	592
San Diego, CA	2855	787	1078	2174	1313	2714	1309	2034	1010	2992	1574	2613	2505	2402	2423	2335	2193	2334	2389	2277	1369	2418	1054	1760	2419	721	1934	2621	2189	1332	2269	2457	2944	1484	2067	1783	2329	1627	2269	349	1573	1743
San Francisco, CA	2966	1135	1396	2511	1776	2765	1239	2371	595	3133	2044	2403	2923	2616	2756	2108	2329	2408	2738	2461	1865	2827	1233	1832	2360	1184	1886	3073	2304	1735	2318	2740	3019	1947	2224	2183	2781	1869	2549	592	1614	1994
Seattle, WA	2855	1500	1805	2656	2157	2685	815	2475	524	2961	2521	2531	2960	2748	2765	2043	2334	2336	2971	2408	2203	3070	1371	1889	2299	1775	1440	3882	2202	2071	2221	2773	2918	2498	2229	2585	3090	1884	2553	1209	1636	2320
Shreveport, LA	1599	868	568	624	340	1229	1691	474	1912	1618	644	1265	945	899	885	916	826	1070	833	592	196	903	1112	827	1069	844	1229	1144	909	228	1018	937	1519	271	827	223	814	624	729	1468	727	219
Spokane, WA	2652	1346	1563	2367	1981	2417	541	2469	369	2693	2359	2263	2700	2503	2505	1775	2066	2068	2572	2115	1978	2811	1095	1556	2020	1686	1166	3014	1921	1978	1941	2503	2650	2222	1961	2205	2822	1727	2298	1119	1460	2092
Tallahassee, FL	1249	1508	1208	268	899	932	2306	302	2512	1312	1094	1155	364	868	559	957	706	949	408	828	835	259	1727	1216	957	1492	1598	462	871	867	1022	608	1223	721	818	421	170	1045	584	2068	1227	679
Tampa, FL	1281	1759	1459	476	1150	949	2143	553	2763	1329	1345	1346	479	903	584	1143	908	1091	497	1013	1086	141	1858	1460	1200	1743	1849	268	1092	1118	1219	673	1240	972	1069	672	195	1296	730	2319	1477	958
Toledo, OH	633	1526	1220	641	1315	454	1557	673	2020	742	1622	309	973	284	533	243	203	114	683	138	1112	1063	1272	567	65	1699	885	1289	105	1144	170	516	624	1249	243	876	989	717	449	1954	762	803
Tuscon, AZ	2442	486	656	1785	908	2246	1342	1621	1144	2571	1176	2166	2100	2039	1913	1711	1750	1971	2080	1833	964	1999	835	1484	1938	316	1897	2271	1783	932	1856	2059	2433	1079	1668	1378	2010	1281	1755	389	1246	1257
Tulsa, OK	1409	674	336	803	462	1208	1293	636	2020	1532	835	1128	1103	941	989	673	721	933	1018	795	259	1156	714	471	916	788	972	1409	738	305	818	1037	1411	504	616	510	1167	283	782	1224	416	259
Washington, DC	378	1864	1564	630	1509	41	2006	781	2441	430	1787	429	559	299	334	697	478	341	498	418	1306	802	1654	1054	506	1954	1322	1062	531	1338	608	309	341	1220	551	965	730	1046	554	2376	1184	832
West Palm Beach, FL	1396	1938	1638	632	1329	1046	2736	702	2942	1426	1524	1443	568	982	673	1289	1063	1192	586	1146	1265	195	2157	1646	1305	1922	2028	41	1157	1297	1476	737	1339	1151	1176	851	284	1052	806	2498	1598	1101
Youngstown, OH	462	1632	1346	719	1368	298	1632	738	2090	568	1695	190	709	251	502	413	275	74	561	170	1193	986	1421	737	239	1804	1038	1219	275	1225	340	482	470	1322	341	949	958	843	521	2124	923	876

Columns (left to right): Los Angeles, CA · Louisville, KY · Memphis, TN · Miami, FL · Milwaukee, WI · Minneapolis, MN · Mobile, AL · Montgomery, AL · Nashville, TN · New Orleans, LA · New York City NY · Norfolk, VA · Oakland, CA · Oklahoma City, OK · Omaha, NE · Orlando, FL · Philadelphia, PA · Phoenix, AZ · Pittsburgh, PA · Portland, OR · Providence, RI · Raleigh, NC · Reno, NV · Richmond, VA · Rochester, NY · Saint Louis, MO · Saint Paul, MN · Salt Lake City, UT · San Antonio, TX · San Diego, CA · San Francisco, CA · Seattle, WA · Shreveport, LA · Spokane, WA · Tallahassee, FL · Tampa, FL · Toledo, OH · Tucson, AZ · Tulsa, OK · Washington, DC · West Palm Beach, FL · Youngstown, OH

City (row)	LA	Lou	Mem	Mia	Mil	Min	Mob	Mon	Nas	NO	NYC	Nor	Oak	OKC	Oma	Orl	Phi	Phx	Pit	Por	Pro	Ral	Ren	Ric	Roc	StL	StP	SLC	SA	SD	SF	Sea	Shr	Spo	Tal	Tam	Tol	Tuc	Tul	DC	WPB	You
Albany, NY	2911	868	1232	1439	933	1215	1322	1178	993	1453	146	505	2982	1523	1308	1249	251	2512	471	2869	178	656	2763	482	219	1028	1215	2290	1986	2855	2966	2855	1599	2652	1249	1281	633	2442	1409	378	1396	462
Albuquerque, NM	823	1332	1021	1994	1443	1256	1265	1345	1232	1187	1995	1905	1134	559	905	1751	1922	446	1654	1378	2156	1759	1056	1833	1857	1054	1362	621	684	787	1135	1500	868	1346	1508	1759	1526	486	674	1864	1938	1646
Amarillo, TX	1095	1041	721	1694	1143	1062	965	1045	932	875	1695	1632	1430	267	754	1451	1622	340	1354	1636	1856	1458	1345	1533	1557	754	884	1316	345	1045	917	1390	1805	598	1563	1208	1459	1220	656	336	1564	1638
Atlanta, GA	2197	421	397	665	784	1105	340	164	243	493	855	551	2488	863	989	446	766	1810	712	2763	1027	397	2411	527	1015	588	1015	1900	965	2174	2511	2656	624	2367	268	476	641	2185	803	630	632	719
Austin, TX	1410	1022	658	1338	1203	1120	656	804	869	535	1728	1403	1786	414	847	1142	1630	1030	1442	2059	1898	1355	1775	1463	1623	806	1120	1311	81	1313	1776	2173	1341	1981	899	1150	1315	908	462	1503	1368	1255
Baltimore, MD	2676	608	900	1095	794	1105	990	833	688	1136	201	237	2864	1322	1143	917	97	2311	245	2765	356	324	2562	155	307	827	1095	2051	1646	2514	2765	2686	1229	2417	932	949	454	2246	1208	41	1046	298
Billings, MT	1254	1550	1557	2580	1143	812	1854	1836	1640	1820	1926	2098	1218	1168	904	2277	2051	1220	1681	867	2238	2273	1021	1655	1922	1381	812	579	1600	1309	1239	815	1691	541	2306	2143	1557	1342	1293	2006	2736	1632
Birmingham, AL	2067	373	239	788	766	1088	269	93	195	352	1019	711	2321	701	904	545	880	1700	778	2571	1189	557	2385	284	439	557	1118	1825	895	2034	2371	2475	414	2469	302	553	673	1621	636	781	702	738
Boise, ID	837	1908	1833	2860	1777	1488	2143	2346	2059	2191	2571	2551	671	1451	1274	2695	2498	1022	2203	439	2701	2560	404	2594	2352	1727	1398	349	1709	1010	595	524	1912	369	2512	2763	2020	1144	1582	2441	2492	2090
Boston, MA	2993	976	1379	1516	1078	1362	1379	1232	1062	1525	203	560	3124	1659	1443	1297	327	2644	584	3149	41	713	2871	544	381	1184	892	2417	2052	2992	3133	2961	1618	2693	1312	1329	742	2571	1532	430	1426	568
Brownsville, TX	1678	1321	957	1580	1530	1466	851	1041	1168	730	2002	1735	2034	680	1249	1034	1954	1289	1713	2468	2220	2068	1646	1891	1216	1565	1609	300	515	1444	1922	2506	1663	2506	644	1359	1094	1345	1622	1176	835	1787
Buffalo, NY	2587	543	908	1424	640	948	1184	1051	722	1273	390	569	2745	1242	1005	1306	397	2269	219	2677	454	231	2433	552	81	747	948	1922	1638	2613	2667	2531	1265	2363	1155	1345	309	2166	1325	429	1443	190
Charleston, SC	2521	668	844	576	907	1316	607	464	576	727	787	454	2788	1176	1303	401	688	2222	778	2952	906	300	2765	462	871	884	1316	2254	1371	2505	2923	2960	945	2700	364	479	973	2100	1103	559	568	709
Charleston, WV	2394	258	653	1046	566	632	638	437	458	891	534	891	2600	1031	899	814	517	2045	211	2615	699	297	2407	251	495	544	870	1896	1419	2402	2616	2748	899	2503	868	903	284	2039	941	369	982	251
Charlotte, NC	2417	438	592	604	835	1143	575	415	399	721	625	341	2755	1069	1135	559	522	2061	504	2757	785	162	2570	280	689	689	1143	2059	1272	2423	2756	2765	885	2505	559	584	583	1913	989	334	673	502
Chicago, IL	1989	300	551	1338	92	405	909	762	474	925	794	851	2098	804	454	1177	757	1776	470	2140	790	608	292	405	1386	262	408	1390	1200	2056	2134	2013	871	1844	959	991	244	1756	683	701	1199	416
Cincinnati, OH	2164	105	469	1086	388	696	712	561	283	810	628	601	2317	835	721	892	515	1808	290	2369	790	540	2201	500	346	696	696	1700	1305	2228	2390	2336	813	2066	706	908	203	1756	521	478	1051	275
Cleveland, OH	2392	349	713	1264	445	753	989	815	527	1078	446	693	2498	1047	824	1046	430	2045	128	2416	600	559	2238	583	268	552	753	1727	1443	2384	2408	2336	1070	2068	949	1091	144	1933	341	1192	74	—
Columbia, SC	2426	494	612	658	891	1276	555	379	458	701	715	412	2703	1091	1283	440	627	2025	572	2972	888	215	2696	389	789	737	1320	2115	1180	2389	2738	2971	833	2572	408	497	683	2080	1018	498	586	665
Columbus, OH	2254	211	575	1210	448	753	834	707	389	940	551	559	2391	910	795	997	460	1907	186	2478	713	453	2326	498	374	414	711	1711	1305	2277	2461	2408	592	2115	828	1513	138	1833	795	418	1146	170
Dallas, TX	1401	819	455	1301	1013	1013	592	723	693	1078	1552	1311	1713	206	641	1013	1287	1066	1286	2065	1803	211	1693	1378	1287	630	1013	1287	196	1978	836	2112	106	1113	964	1112	964	754	533	1255	1193	—
Daytona Beach, FL	2407	801	749	259	1180	1458	502	458	639	632	1054	702	2831	1257	1402	81	914	2102	859	3018	1201	550	2758	713	1176	956	1458	2827	1675	2493	2827	3018	903	2811	259	161	1063	1999	1156	802	195	986
Denver, CO	1009	1127	1151	2131	1070	956	1372	1412	1167	1323	1775	1800	1223	660	559	1896	1762	802	1475	1283	1961	1694	1030	1904	1637	839	956	519	975	1054	1133	1311	1112	1095	1727	1858	1272	835	714	1654	2157	1421
Des Moines, IA	1654	591	599	1582	365	251	954	1131	712	978	1072	1164	1527	492	132	576	146	1631	712	978	1072	932	937	251	1085	1022	1760	1832	1889	877	1556	1460	567	1484	471	1054	1646	737	—	—	—	—
Detroit, MI	2270	365	712	1386	389	698	988	814	536	1077	620	711	2350	1030	726	1143	585	2019	304	2368	746	643	2190	609	424	535	698	1679	1500	2419	2360	2299	1069	2020	957	1200	63	1938	916	506	1305	239
El Paso, TX	818	1461	1103	1958	1530	1194	1196	1128	1294	1036	2002	1954	1169	584	1043	1915	2036	434	2036	1238	1541	894	576	721	1184	1175	844	1686	1492	1743	1691	956	1161	1053	788	1954	1922	1804	—	—	—	—
Fargo, ND	1844	949	1224	1987	576	244	1413	1525	1138	1521	1450	1581	1870	989	464	1826	1370	1791	1112	1484	1566	1485	1660	1481	1249	917	244	1172	1402	1934	1886	1440	1229	1166	1598	1849	885	1897	972	1322	2028	1038
Fort Lauderdale	2704	1078	989	24	1443	1723	705	671	900	843	1289	964	3041	1481	1604	208	1127	2244	1216	3204	1459	794	3008	946	1410	1208	1753	2578	1378	2621	3073	3382	1144	3014	462	268	1289	2271	1409	1062	41	1219
Fort Wayne, IN	2137	222	592	1326	256	564	839	686	385	916	691	709	2287	852	634	959	604	1831	336	2290	703	603	2056	564	369	564	1269	2189	2304	2202	909	1921	871	1092	1092	1105	1138	738	531	1157	275	923
Fort Worth, TX	1361	851	497	1353	1059	1001	624	701	698	519	1557	1382	1723	210	634	1110	1459	924	2003	1727	1184	1608	1333	1452	698	987	1184	283	1332	1735	2011	228	1978	957	1144	932	896	432	1476	340	—	—
Grand Rapids, MI	2148	373	690	1356	275	583	1006	819	534	1071	706	802	2308	932	640	1188	672	1906	397	2251	859	754	2067	722	499	437	583	1556	1353	2269	2318	2221	1018	1941	1022	1219	170	1856	818	608	1476	340
Greensboro, NC	2478	468	810	826	1135	681	512	429	810	561	429	801	1739	1138	2059	1321	2457	2740	2773	937	2503	608	673	516	509	1037	309	737	482	—	—	—	—	—	—	—	—	—	—	—	—	—
Hartford, CT	2829	867	1209	1427	1155	1257	1290	1133	973	1436	101	471	2909	1546	1321	1208	220	2523	486	2877	73	624	2749	455	324	1030	1257	2238	1965	2944	3019	2918	1529	2656	1223	1240	654	2433	1411	341	1339	470
Houston, TX	1581	948	584	1207	1155	1266	478	709	795	367	1679	1362	1951	454	964	1581	1110	1345	2359	1849	1233	1912	907	1555	591	1591	605	2007	202	1484	1947	1498	271	2222	721	972	1249	1079	594	504	1420	1151	1322
Indianapolis, IN	2075	129	470	1208	285	591	749	590	285	834	709	669	2212	730	616	989	619	2116	290	2335	892	635	2116	907	551	591	605	591	1690	2147	2224	2229	827	1961	818	1069	243	668	670	576	1283	578
Jackson, MS	1880	575	211	907	884	1123	178	255	427	193	1192	948	2350	611	914	691	1094	1500	965	2518	1362	815	2143	946	1183	495	1160	1742	649	1783	2183	2585	223	2205	421	670	851	1378	510	965	851	949
Jacksonville, FL	2402	729	700	334	413	379	592	551	957	632	2771	1181	1305	138	859	2100	882	3030	1127	584	2716	693	1102	867	1374	2286	1086	2329	2781	3042	814	2822	170	195	989	2010	1167	730	284	958	—	—
Kansas City, MO	1589	519	470	1475	568	459	859	890	857	790	1217	1199	1799	349	195	1266	1134	1271	1801	1809	1378	1606	1205	1062	251	459	1095	795	1627	1869	1834	624	1727	1045	1296	717	1281	283	1052	144	843	—
Knoxville, TN	2201	246	385	909	543	843	449	348	174	607	753	412	2509	847	930	665	648	1845	515	2502	920	347	2378	435	1766	1150	2269	2459	729	2298	584	734	451	799	455	782	554	806	521	—	—	—
Las Vegas, NV	275	1861	1581	2570	1752	1630	1841	1805	1792	1800	2520	2534	582	1119	1249	2311	2449	281	2181	991	2683	2319	478	2406	2371	1581	1630	413	1273	349	592	1209	1468	1119	2068	2319	1954	389	1246	2376	2498	2104
Lincoln, NE	1476	730	647	1673	560	409	1039	975	770	1014	1274	1354	1604	433	57	1452	1260	1236	965	1641	1451	1263	1411	1249	1135	462	408	307	916	1573	1614	1630	727	1460	1227	1477	762	1246	416	1184	1598	923
Little Rock	1678	502	138	1208	772	811	488	430	470	443	1235	1025	1984	324	690	965	1341	1216	1368	2205	851	1986	661	1637	738	321	382	1159	1687	1606	2342	2576	2213	502	1459	2659	2772	679	958	803	1257	679	832
Los Angeles, CA	0	2136	1816	2828	2238	1905	2013	2035	2027	1883	2790	2790	372	1328	1508	2585	2717	389	2449	900	2902	2554	511	2641	2400	1849	1905	672	1378	121	382	1159	1687	1406	2342	2578	2213	502	1459	2659	2772	2424
Louisville, KY	2136	0	364	1102	397	705	626	466	178	729	707	607	2333	738	671	907	664	1782	381	2298	780	490	2173	525	349	247	705	1638	1103	2119	2388	2320	721	2075	664	915	300	1697	633	476	1094	373
Memphis, TN	1816	364	0	1013	613	849	393	383	211	391	1095	876	2030	455	690	752	949	1444	705	2427	1172	724	1891	875	939	300	949	1613	795	1600	1697	2506	357	2230	565	778	665	1367	397	901	738	738
Miami, FL	2828	1102	1013	0	1435	1743	729	695	900	867	1313	988	3087	1524	1670	227	1215	2448	1308	3366	1483	818	3032	988	1435	1231	1808	2602	1402	2645	3097	3406	1130	3138	486	292	1293	2326	1483	1086	65	1264
Milwaukee, WI	2238	397	613	1435	0	332	981	835	571	1045	851	908	2293	868	533	1274	834	1873	567	2002	1021	899	1305	899	1315	908	332	1554	1427	2299	2320	1970	1013	1702	1053	1240	332	1808	770	770	1386	510
Minneapolis, MN	1905	705	949	1743	332	0	1227	1312	932	1346	1160	1337	2065	803	381	1673	1677	1589	940	1678	1337	1449	1176	1237	1005	609	11	1475	1975	2075	1838	985	1370	1354	1589	641	1702	705	1078	1737	1794	949
Mobile, AL	2013	626	389	729	981	1227	0	176	462	146	1176	884	2351	786	1011	486	1078	1593	1050	2611	1346	738	2278	867	1273	673	1158	903	1971	2361	2710	401	2342	243	494	940	1542	713	949	673	1005	—
Montgomery, AL	2035	466	332	695	859	1281	176	0	288	322	1010	715	2295	790	978	632	789	1632	1191	561	1266	792	2189	614	770	323	892	1678	941	2002	2375	2384	669	2124	496	737	478	1581	608	632	875	841
Nashville, TN	2027	178	211	908	571	892	462	288	0	551	859	625	2374	673	715	689	761	1671	575	2376	1020	351	2189	614	770	320	892	1820	841	2067	2374	2579	528	2303	333	583	521	1797	601	638	632	606
New Orleans, LA	1883	729	397	867	1045	1346	146	322	551	0	1322	1054	2317	681	1026	624	1224	1540	1078	2505	1492	876	2278	1114	1362	681	1346	1842	551	1824	2327	2574	309	2409	381	632	1005	1419	657	1095	811	1095
New York, NY	2790	707	995	1313	851	1160	1176	1010	715	1322	0	389	2876	1458	1200	1094	101	2425	386	2882	186	520	2671	366	335	941	1160	2142	1832	2773	2886	2837	1415	2509	1109	1126	556	2360	1331	192	1223	436
Norfolk, VA	2809	607	876	988	948	1337	884	715	625	1054	389	0	2957	1349	1362	770	268	2393	365	2968	527	197	2789	96	535	941	1337	2262	1606	2669	2957	2837	1203	2790	802	822	592	2234	190	916	438	—
Oakland, CA	372	2333	2027	3087	2171	2065	2351	2295	2374	2317	2876	2957	0	1660	1596	2844	2913	744	2528	614	2974	2865	201	2988	2681	2003	2065	803	1511	478	1345	490	9	1844	1349	1660	0	—	—	—	—	—
Oklahoma City, OK	1354	738	462	1524	884	803	786	790	673	681	1436	1349	1660	0	495	1281	1363	998	1196	1946	1597	1364	1660	1662	1395	499	803	1151	478	1345	1641	1606	679	1403	1241	1395	1400	1078	1401	401	1151	1671	875
Omaha, NE	1508	671	705	1670	503	381	1110	1037	735	1026	1208	1362	1596	495	0	1421	1200	1427	908	1605	1394	1281	1395	1400	1078	381	947	949	1641	1606	1679	1403	1241	1395	1400	401	1151	1671	875	—	—	—
Orlando, FL	2585	907	770	227	1224	1673	486	452	689	624	1094	770	2844	1281	1421	0	1005	2205	1053	3123	1273	878	2913	900	1194	1070	1673	2402	1329	2408	2854	3163	920	2895	243	89	1086	2082	1248	872	194	1052
Philadelphia, PA	2717	664	989	1215	834	1126	1078	930	761	1224	101	268	2844	1281	1200	1005	0	2374	292	2853	259	412	2627	252	324	848	1126	2109	1734	2604	2923	2762	1209	2281	1484	1808	673	989	754	1492	1282	1962
Phoenix, AZ	389	1782	1444	2448	1873	1677	1593	1632	1671	1540	2425	2393	744	998	1427	2205	2374	0	2084	1322	2586	2172	754	2281	2281	1484	1808	673	989	357	754	1492	1282	1962	2213	1950	387	1387	2392	2061	—	—
Pittsburgh, PA	2449	381	795	1248	567	868	1050	843	575	1078	386	365	2528	1196	908	1053	292	2084	0	2538	593	433	2533	333	284	601	868	1468	1484	2441	2538	2513	1087	2190	932	998	227	2021	981	219	1111	65
Portland, OR	985	2298	2408	3366	2002	1670	2611	2632	2376	2505	2914	2968	614	1946	1605	3123	2830	1322	2538	0	3000	2903	616	3012	2676	2068	1670	764	2168	1078	624	170	2195	365	2880	3131	2311	1483	1987	2846	3310	2481
Providence, RI	2902	421	1531	1483	1021	1449	1346	1191	1020	1492	162	527	2974	1597	1394	1273	259	2586	593	3000	0	673	2814	511	381	1102	1322	2003	2002	2979	2984	2967	1585	2644	1288	1322	709	2457	1402	538	—	—
Raleigh, NC	2554	525	713	818	899	1241	738	561	502	876	510	197	2865	1200	1281	608	412	2172	519	2903	673	0	2716	170	608	851	1241	2205	1422	2529	2797	2971	538	2651	624	657	584	2124	1103	283	744	—
Reno, NV	511	2132	2124	3032	1930	1776	2278	2456	2189	2278	2635	2789	201	1662	1395	2789	2627	754	2335	616	2814	2716	0	2803	2489	1881	1776	511	1768	535	211	810	1927	770	2546	2797	2442	630	2425	1222	924	662
Richmond, VA	2641	686	875	988	941	1114	867	614	614	1114	366	96	2988	1662	1400	900	252	2281	333	3012	511	175	2803	0	455	976	1295	2235	1555	2643	2989	3029	1173	2794	827	630	2425	1222	398	141	924	—
Rochester, NY	2400	608	973	1435	697	1005	1273	1179	770	1320	335	535	2681	1298	1078	1090	324	2281	284	2676	381	600	2489	455	0	803	1005	1978	1686	2674	2676	2622	1361	2385	1238	381	2222	1398	341	1196	—	—
Saint Louis, MO	1849	290	320	1231	389	628	673	632	323	681	941	927	2003	495	381	1031	830	1484	601	2075	2076	624	1881	1295	795	1030	468	1476	887	1840	2075	2318	337	795	1242	1381	297	1548	383	832	1101	534
Saint Paul, MN	1905	705	949	1743	332	11	1158	1281	892	1346	1160	1337	2065	803	381	1551	1126	1808	868	1670	1227	627	1776	1237	1005	468	0	1475	1975	2075	1838	985	1702	705	1589	641	1702	705	1597	1794	794
Salt Lake City, UT	672	1638	1613	2602	1419	1475	1903	1905	1678	1842	2124	2262	545	1151	947	2359	2209	673	1824	764	2303	2205	511	2324	1978	1370	1475	0	1447	762	714	851	1563	706	2116	2318	1715	795	1223	2141	2490	1805
San Antonio, TX	1378	1103	740	1402	1427	1975	541	941	551	551	1832	1606	1832	478	1265	1441	1775	357	1274	2775	1287	876	535	1555	1403	2213	2464	2604	405	1403	2733	2072	2456	—	—	—	—	—	—	—	—	—
San Diego, CA	121	2119	1800	2645	2109	1975	1971	2127	2092	1824	2669	493	1345	1641	2402	2911	357	2441	1274	527	176	1565	1403	2213	2464	2604	405	1403	2733	2072	2456	—	—	—	—	—	—	—	—	—	—	—
San Francisco, CA	382	2388	2132	3097	2175	2075	2361	2464	2375	2327	2886	2967	9	1670	1606	2854	2923	754	2538	624	2984	2797	211	2989	2691	2075	2075	714	1774	527	0	787	2061	851	2611	2846	2415	868	1776	2949	3065	2569
Seattle, WA	1159	2342	2562	3138	1702	1370	2562	2562	2124	2505	2886	2984	787	1978	1606	2870	2913	1492	2513	1573	2984	2797	810	3029	2674	1840	1638	851	2061	1403	787	0	2335	274	2884	3131	2311	1583	1987	2846	3206	2481
Shreveport, LA	1687	721	357	1130	1013	985	401	478	669	309	1415	1203	2052	389	729	920	1270	1282	1255	1585	538	727	1173	1361	624	474	1565	2061	1223	0	2038	644	895	1099	1620	356	953	507	1081	—	—	—
Spokane, WA	1406	2075	2230	3138	1702	1370	2342	2562	2124	2409	2569	2700	979	1768	1403	2895	2512	1586	2190	365	2644	2651	770	2761	2384	1816	1370	706	2110	1403	852	274	2038	0	2652	2887	2100	1490	1240	2417	3196	2125
Tallahassee, FL	2342	664	565	486	1240	1589	243	496	333	381	1109	802	2601	1038	1241	243	1033	2213	932	2880	1288	624	2652	872	1240	1042	1589	2116	644	2652	2611	2920	356	2652	0	251	900	1840	1005	908	219	1088
Tampa, FL	2578	915	778	292	1240	1589	494	460	737	632	1126	827	2836	1395	1492	89	1037	2213	998	3131	1322	657	2797	1001	1589	1318	1151	2464	895	2887	251	0	1143	2076	1182	908	219	1088	—	—	—	—
Toledo, OH	2213	300	665	1233	332	641	940	766	478	1005	556	592	2295	961	705	1086	562	1950	227	2311	689	584	2133	630	141	297	283	1673	1387	2326	2415	2311	1099	2100	900	1143	0	2051	867	438	1254	77
Tucson, AZ	502	1697	1310	2326	1808	1702	1542	1633	1581	1419	2360	2271	878	908	1400	2083	2287	122	2013	1483	2525	2119	630	2222	1419	1702	705	955	1182	867	1038	251	1143	2076	0	1284	1167	964	—	—	—	—
Tulsa, OK	1459	633	397	1483	770	705	713	765	608	657	1331	1234	1766	105	401	1240	1249	981	1187	1483	1103	1702	1222	1398	381	705	1223	535	1403	1776	2034	356	1727	955	1182	867	1038	1284	0	1167	1167	964
Washington, DC	2659	633	901	1086	795	632	1095	252	190	2702	135	246	71	284	1341	195	6178	141	1605	2733	2949	2686	953	2417	891	908	438	2254	1167	0	1005	283	—	—	—	—	—	—	—	—	—	—
West Palm Beach, FL	2772	1094	957	65	1386	1737	673	639	867	811	1223	916	3055	1468	1671	194	1134	2392	1111	3310	1402	792	2976	924	1346	1167	1737	2490	1300	2072	3065	3206	507	3196	219	1248	1254	2260	1167	0	1167	—
Youngstown, OH	2424	373	738	1238	510	794	1005	831	543	1095	403	438	2463	1087	875	1052	357	2076	65	2481	527	535	2303	662	245	592	794	1877	1477	2432	2569	2456	1181	2125	1005	1088	170	2003	964	283	1167	0

1 • 2 • 3 • 4 • 5 • 6 • 7

A

BRITISH COLUMBIA Calgary **ALBERTA** Saskatoon
Vancouver Rocky Mtns. Preserve
Pacific Rim Nat'l Park Waterton-Glacier Int'l Peace Park
San Juan Island Nat'l Hist. Park Moose Jaw Regina **SASKATCHEWAN** **MANITOBA**
Olympic Nat'l Park CANADA Riding Mountain Nat'l Park
Ft. Vancouver Nat'l Hist. Site and Museum UNITED STATES Winnipeg
Seattle Tacoma Spokane Coeur d'Alene Ft. Union Nat'l Hist. Site Williston Lake Sakakawea Knife River Indian Village Nat'l Hist. Site

B

WASHINGTON Walla Walla Snake River Flathead Nat'l Forest Great Falls Missouri River Theodore Roosevelt Nat'l Park North Bismarck Fargo
Portland Columbia Lewis Nat'l Forest Helena **MONTANA** Theodore Roosevelt Nat'l Park South **NORTH DAKOTA**
Salem Mt. Hood Nat'l Forest Clearwater Nat'l Forest Nezperce Nat'l Forest Billings Yellowstone R.
Eugene John Day Fossil Beds Nat'l Mon. **IDAHO** Custer Nat'l Forest Custer Battlefield Nat'l Mon. **SOUTH DAKOTA**

C

OREGON Boise Challis Nat'l Forest Salmon Nat'l Forest Yellowstone Nat'l Park Bighorn Nat'l Forest Devil's Tower Nat'l Mon. Rapid City Pierre Lake Oahe
Crater Lake Nat'l Park Sawtooth Nat'l Forest Grand Teton Nat'l Park Thunder Basin Nat'l Grassland Mt. Rushmore Nat'l Mem. Badlands Nat'l Park Sioux Falls
Twin Falls Jackson Shoshone Nat'l Forest **BLACK HILLS** Wind Cave Nat'l Park Hot Springs

D

Redwood Nat'l Seashore **BLACK ROCK DESERT** Caribou Nat'l Forest **GREAT SALT LAKE** Fossil Butte Nat'l Mon. **WYOMING** Medicine Bow Nat'l Forest Laramie Nebraska Nat'l Forest Samuel R. McKelvie Nat'l Forest
Eureka Winnemucca Golden Spike Nat'l Hist. Site Wasatch Nat'l Forest Casper Scottsbluff Nebraska Nat'l Forest **NEBRASKA**
Lassen Volcanic Nat'l Park **NEVADA** Humboldt Salt Lake City Rock Springs Cheyenne N. Platte R. North Platte Lincoln

E

San Francisco San Jose Sacramento Oakland Carson City Reno Ely **UTAH** Provo Dinosaur Nat'l Mon. Rocky Mountain Nat'l Park Boulder Denver **COLORADO** **KANSAS**
Yosemite Nat'l Park Toiyabe Nat'l Forest Colorado Springs Wichita
Monterey Fresno Lehman Caves Nat'l Mon. Capitol Reef Nat'l Park Black Canyon of the Gunnison Pueblo Dodge City

F

Channel Islands Nat'l Park Bakersfield **MOJAVE DESERT** Cedar Breaks Nat'l Mon. Zion Nat'l Park Bryce Canyon Nat'l Park Mesa Verde Nat'l Park Durango Comanche Nat'l Grassland
Ventura Los Angeles Anaheim San Bernardino Lake Mead Grand Canyon Nat'l Park Rainbow Bridge Nat'l Mon. San Juan Nat'l Forest Aztec Ruins Nat'l Mon. Capulin Mtn. Nat'l Mon. **OKLAHOMA** Oklahoma City

G

PACIFIC OCEAN San Diego Tijuana Cabrillo Nat'l Mon. Cleveland Nat'l Forest Joshua Tree Nat'l Mon. **ARIZONA** Phoenix Flagstaff Petrified Forest Nat'l Park El Morro Nat'l Mon. Albuquerque Santa Fe Pecos Nat'l Mon. Amarillo Platt Nat'l Park
Mexicali **CALIFORNIA** Yuma Tucson Casa Grande Ruins Gran Quivira Nat'l Mon. **NEW MEXICO** Lubbock Wichita Falls

H

U.S.S.R. Arctic Ocean Prudhoe Bay Point Hope Barrow Organ Pipe Cactus Nat'l Mon. Coronado Nat'l Forest Nogales Douglas Chiricahua Nat'l Mon. Tumacacori Nat'l Mon. **BAJA CALIFORNIA** UNITED STATES MEXICO El Paso Ciudad Juarez White Sands Nat'l Mon. Carlsbad Caverns Lincoln Nat'l Forest Guadalupe Mtns. Nat'l Park Odessa Midland San Angelo Waco **TEXAS** Austin
Wainwright Nostak Nat'l Preserve Gates of the Arctic Nat'l Park & Preserve **SONORA** Santa Ana Old Ft. Davis Nat'l Hist. Site

J

Bering Sea Nome Fairbanks College Yukon-Charley Nat'l Preserve **ALASKA** Denali Nat'l Park and Preserve **YUKON** Nuevo Casas Grandes **CHIHUAHUA** Big Bend Nat'l Park San Antonio
Hooper Bay Anchorage Valdez Wrangell-St. Elias Nat'l Park Lahaina Wahiawa Pearl City Kaneohe Piedras Negras Nueva Rosita **COAHUILA**

K

Pacific Ocean Katmai Nat'l Park & Preserve Kodiak Island Kenai Fjords Nat'l Park Glacier Bay Nat'l Park Juneau **B.C.** **HAWAII** Honolulu Haleakala Nat'l Park Hilo Hawaii Volcanoes Nat'l Park City of Refuge Nat'l Hist. Park **NUEVO LEON** Monterrey Laredo Corpus Christi Padre Island Nat'l Seashore Brownsville **TAMAULIPAS**
Aleutian Islands Sitka Nat'l Hist. Park Ketchikan

1 • 2 • 3 • 4 • 5 • 6 • 7

8 · 9 · 10 · 11 · 12 · 13 · 14

USE ONLY FOR ORIENTATION TO NATIONAL PARKS AND LANDMARKS. FOR MORE DETAILED HIGHWAY INFORMATION, SEE INTERSTATE HIGHWAY MAP, PAGES 4-5, AND STATE MAP SECTION, PAGES 13-89.

A B C D E F G H J K

CENTRAL TIME ZONE
EASTERN TIME ZONE
EASTERN TIME ZONE
ATLANTIC TIME ZONE

Lake Winnipeg
Lake of the Woods
Kenora
Lake Nipigon
QUEBEC
Lake St. Jean
NEW BRUNSWICK
St. Lawrence River
Laurentides Prov. Park
Quebec

Voyageurs Nat'l Park
Thunder Bay
Pukaskwa Nat'l Park
Isle Royale Nat'l Park
Superior Nat'l Forest
Lake Superior
ONTARIO
La Verendrye Prov. Park
Mastigouche Prov. Park
Maurice Nat'l Park
Presque Isle
Roosevelt Campobello Int'l Park
MAINE
Bangor
Acadia Nat'l Park

Chippewa Nat'l Forest
Apostle Islands Nat'l Lakeshore
Pictured Rocks Nat'l Lakeshore
Sault Ste. Marie
Sudbury
North Bay
Ottawa River
Algonquin Prov. Park
Montreal
Ottawa
WHITE MTS. Nat'l Forest
Augusta
Portland
N.H.
Boston
Cape Cod Nat'l Seashore

Chequamegon Nat'l Forest
Ottawa Nat'l Forest
Hiawatha Nat'l Forest
Nicolet Nat'l Forest
Georgian Bay
Georgian Bay Is. Park
Peterborough
Toronto
Lake Ontario
Rochester
Syracuse
Albany
ADIRONDACK MTNS. Park
St. Lawrence Is. Nat'l Park
Champlain
VT. GREEN MTS. Nat'l Forest
Concord
MASS.
Providence
New Bedford
R.I.

MINNESOTA
St. Paul
Minneapolis
Manistee Nat'l Forest
Sleeping Bear Dunes Nat'l Lakeshore
Green Bay
WISCONSIN
Madison
Milwaukee
MICHIGAN
Grand Rapids
Lansing
Detroit
Windsor
London
Huron Nat'l Forest
Lake Huron
Lake Michigan
Lake Erie
Roosevelt Inaugural Nat'l Hist. Site
Buffalo
NEW YORK
Scranton
Allentown
Hartford
CONN.
New Haven
New York
Fire Island Nat'l Seashore
Statue of Liberty Nat'l Monument

Rochester
La Crosse
Wisconsin River
Sioux City
IOWA
Des Moines
Cedar Rapids
Rockford
Chicago
Gary
South Bend
Ft. Wayne
Toledo
Cleveland
Akron
Youngstown
Pittsburgh
Harrisburg
PENNSYLVANIA
Allegheny Nat'l Forest
Hopewell Village Nat'l Hist. Site
Trenton
NEW JERSEY
Philadelphia
Wilmington
Dover
DELAWARE

Omaha
Council Bluffs
Dodge House Nat'l Mon.
Davenport
Peoria
INDIANA
Indianapolis
Springfield
ILLINOIS
Victory & Int'l Peace Mem.
Ft. Wayne
OHIO
Columbus
Wheeling
WEST VIRGINIA
Charleston
Monongahela Nat'l Forest
Eisenhower Nat'l Hist. Site
Ft. Necessity Nat'l Battlefield
Baltimore
Washington D.C.
Annapolis
MARYLAND
Assateague Island Nat'l Seashore
Chesapeake Bay

Topeka
Kansas City
Columbia
MISSOURI
Jefferson City
St. Louis
Mound City Group Nat'l Mon.
Wayne Nat'l Forest
Cincinnati
Hoosier Nat'l Forest
Louisville
Frankfort
Lexington
Daniel Boone Nat'l Forest
Huntington
Richmond
VIRGINIA
George Washington's Birthplace Nat'l Mon.
George Washington Nat'l Forest
Jefferson Nat'l Forest
Lynchburg
Roanoke
Newport News
Norfolk
Petersburg Nat'l Battlefield

Springfield
Mark Twain Nat'l Forest
Shawnee Nat'l Forest
KENTUCKY
Mammoth Cave Nat'l Park
Kentucky Lake
Nashville
Cumberland Gap Nat'l Hist. Park
Andrew Johnson Nat'l Hist. Site
Great Smoky Mtns. Nat'l Park
Winston-Salem
Greensboro
Raleigh
NORTH CAROLINA
Uwharrie Nat'l Forest
Croatan Nat'l Forest
Wright Brothers Nat'l Memorial
Cape Hatteras Nat'l Seashore

Tulsa
Ozark Nat'l Forest
ARKANSAS
Little Rock
Pine Bluff
Ft. Smith
Ozark Nat'l Forest
Ouachita Nat'l Forest
Hot Springs Nat'l Park
Memphis
TENNESSEE
Chattanooga
Knoxville
Nantahala Nat'l Forest
Pisgah Nat'l Forest
Charlotte
Cowpens Nat'l Battlefield
SOUTH CAROLINA
Columbia
Sumter Nat'l Forest
Moore's Creek Nat'l Battlefield
Cape Lookout Nat'l Seashore

Texarkana
Holly Springs Nat'l Forest
Little River Nat'l Park
Tombigbee Nat'l Forest
Birmingham
Talladega Nat'l Forest
Atlanta
Oconee Nat'l Forest
Macon
Augusta
Chattahoochee Nat'l Forest
Kennesaw Mtn. Nat'l Battlefield Park
Congaree Swamp Nat'l Mon.
Francis Marion Nat'l Forest
ATLANTIC OCEAN
Ft. Sumter Nat'l Mon.

Tyler
Shreveport
Monroe
Delta Nat'l Forest
Bienville Nat'l Forest
Jackson
MISSISSIPPI
ALABAMA
Montgomery
Columbus
Ocmulgee Nat'l Mon.
GEORGIA
Savannah
Ft. Frederica Nat'l Mon.
Cumberland Island Nat'l Seashore

Sabine Nat'l Forest
Davy Crockett Nat'l Forest
Angelina Nat'l Forest
Sam Houston Nat'l Forest
Houston
LOUISIANA
Rocky Springs Nat'l Park
Homochitto Nat'l Forest
De Soto Nat'l Forest
Conecuh Nat'l Forest
Baton Rouge
Mobile
Pensacola
Panama City
Tallahassee
Apalachicola Nat'l Forest
Osceola Nat'l Forest
Jacksonville
Ft. Matanzas Nat'l Mon.
Ocala Nat'l Forest

Galveston
New Orleans
Lake Charles
Biloxi
Gulf Islands Nat'l Seashore
Daytona Beach
Canaveral Nat'l Seashore
John F. Kennedy Space Center
Orlando

GULF OF MEXICO
Tampa
St. Petersburg
FLORIDA
Desoto Nat'l Mon.
Lake Okeechobee
West Palm Beach
Ft. Myers
Ft. Lauderdale
Naples
Everglades Nat'l Park
Miami
Biscayne Nat'l Park

8 · 9 · 10 · 11 · 12 · 13 · 14

Index

Goose Bay .. C-12
Grand Falls .. C-14
Hebron .. C-11
Hopedale .. C-11
Labrador City .. D-11
Makkovik .. C-11
Marystown .. D-14
Northwest River .. C-12
Nutak .. C-11
Placentia .. C-14
St. Anthony .. C-13
St. John's .. C-14
St. Pierre (France) .. D-14
Stephenville .. D-13
Wabana .. C-14

N.W. TERRITORY
Aklavik .. C-2
Artic Bay .. A-6
Artic Red River .. D-2
Baker Lake .. D-6
Bathurst Inlet .. C-5
Cambridge Bay .. C-5
Cape Dorset .. C-8
Cape Dyer .. A-9
Chesterfield Inlet .. D-7
Clyde .. A-8
Colville Lake .. D-3
Coppermine .. D-4
Echo Bay (Port Radium) .. D-4
Ennadai .. E-6
Ft. Franklin .. D-3
Ft. Good Hope .. D-3
Ft. Laird .. F-3
Ft. McPherson .. C-2
Ft. Norman .. D-3
Ft. Providence .. E-4
Ft. Resolution .. E-4
Ft. Simpson .. E-3
Ft. Smith .. F-4
Frobisher Bay .. B-9
Gjoa Haven .. C-6
Hall Beach .. B-7
Hay River .. E-4
Holman .. C-4
Igloolik .. B-7
Inuvik .. C-2
Lac la Martre .. E-4
Lake Harbour .. B-9
Mould Bay .. A-4
Norman Wells .. D-3
Paulatuk .. C-3
Pangnirtung .. A-9
Pine Point .. F-4
Pond Inlet .. A-7
Rae .. E-4
Rankin Inlet .. D-7
Reliance .. E-5
Repulse Bay .. C-7
Resolute .. A-5
Resolution Island .. B-10
Sachs Harbour .. B-3
Snowdrift .. E-5
Spence Bay .. B-6
Trout Lake .. C-2
Tuktoyaktuk .. C-2
Wrigley .. E-3
Yellowknife .. E-4

NOVA SCOTIA
Amherst .. E-13
Bridgewater .. F-14
Canso .. E-14
Glace Bay .. E-14
Halifax .. F-14
Kentville .. F-13
New Glasgow .. E-14
Shelburne .. F-14
Sydney .. E-14
Truro .. F-13
Yarmouth .. F-13

ONTARIO
Armstrong .. G-9
Atikokan .. H-8
Barrie .. H-11
Belleville .. H-12
Blind River .. H-10
Brantford .. J-11
Brockville .. G-12
Chatham .. J-11
Cochrane .. G-10
Cornwall .. G-12
Deep River .. G-11
Favourable Lake .. G-8
Ft. Albany .. F-9
Ft. Frances .. H-8
Ft. Severn .. E-8
Geraldton .. H-9
Goderich .. J-11
Guelph .. H-11
Hamilton .. H-11
Hearst .. G-10
Kapuskasing .. G-10
Kenora .. H-8
Kingston .. H-12
Kirkland Lake .. G-10
Kitchener .. H-11
Lec Seul .. H-8
London .. J-11
Marathon .. H-9
Moosonee .. F-10
Niagara Falls .. H-12
Nipigon .. H-9
North Bay .. G-11
Oshawa .. H-11
Ottawa .. G-12
Owen Sound .. H-11
Parry Sound .. H-11
Pembroke .. G-11
Peterborough .. H-11
Pickle Lake .. G-9
Red Lake .. H-8
Renfrew .. G-12
St. Catharines .. H-12
St. Thomas .. J-11
Sault Ste. Marie .. H-10
Sioux Lookout .. H-8
Smith's Falls .. G-12
Sudbury .. H-10
Thunder Bay .. H-9
Timmins .. G-10
Toronto .. H-11
Trenton .. H-12
Wawa .. H-10
Windsor .. J-11
Winisk .. F-9

PRINCE EDWARD ISLAND
Charlottetown .. E-13
Summerside .. E-13

QUEBEC
Alma .. F-12
Amos .. G-11
Arvida .. G-12
Baie Comeau .. E-12
Belin (Payne) .. C-10
Cape Smith .. D-9
Chandler .. E-12
Chicoutimi .. F-12
Deception .. C-9
Desmaraisville .. F-11
Drummondville .. G-12
Eastmain .. F-10
Ft. Chimo .. C-10
Ft. George .. F-10
Ft. Rupert .. F-10
Gagnon .. E-11
Gaspe .. E-12
Granby .. G-12
Harve St. Pierre .. D-12
Hull .. G-11
Inoucdjouac (Port Harrison) .. D-9
Koartac .. C-9
La Tugue .. F-12
Lac-Allard .. D-12
Levis .. F-12
Manicougan .. E-12
Maniwaki .. G-11
Maricourt (Wakeham) C-9
Matagami .. F-10
Matane .. E-12
Mont-Laurier .. G-12
Montreal .. G-12
Nitchequon .. E-11
Noranda .. G-11
Nouveau-Quebec (George River) .. C-10
Port Alfred .. F-12
Port Cartier .. E-12
Poste-de-la-Baleine .. E-10
Povungnitak .. D-9
Quebec .. F-12
Rimouski .. E-12
Riviere-du-Loup .. F-12
Rouyn .. G-11
St. Hyacinthe .. G-12
St. Jean .. G-12
St. Jerome .. G-12
Ste. Anne-des-Monts .. E-12
Schefferville .. D-11
Senneterre .. G-11
Sept. Iles .. E-12
Shawinigan .. G-12
Sherbrooke .. G-12
Shibougamau .. F-11
Sorel .. G-12
Thetford Mines .. F-12
Trois-Rivieres .. G-12
Val-d'Or .. G-11

SASKATCHEWAN
Assiniboia .. J-6
Biggar .. H-5
Estevan .. J-7
La Loche .. G-5
La Rouge .. H-6
Lloydminster .. H-5
Meadow lake .. H-5
Melfort .. H-6
Missinipe .. G-6
Moose Jaw .. J-6
North Battleford .. H-5
Prince Albert .. H-6
Regina .. J-6
Saskatoon .. H-6
Stoney Rapids .. F-5
Swift Current .. J-5
Uranium City .. F-5
Weyburn .. J-6
Wollaston Lake .. F-6
Yorkton .. H-6

YUKON
Beaver Creek .. E-1
Carcross .. E-1
Carmacks .. E-1
Clinton Creek .. D-1
Dawson .. D-1
Elsa .. D-2
Faro .. E-2
Haines Jct. .. F-1
Mayo .. D-2
Old Crow .. C-1
Teslin .. F-2
Watson Lake .. F-2
Whitehorse .. E-2

CANADA

═══	EXPRESSWAYS	27	INTERSTATE HIGHWAYS
───	PRIMARY HIGHWAYS	277	U.S. HIGHWAYS
───	OTHER HIGHWAYS	31	CANADIAN HIGHWAYS
	TRANS-CANADA HIGHWAY		

MILES
0   100   200   300   400   500

KILOMETERS
0   160   320   480   640   800

© Creative Sales Corporation

UNITED STATES

ARIZONA
NEW MEXICO

Tijuana
Tecate
Mexicali
Yuma
San Luis
Ensenada
San Felipe
Puerto Penasco
Sonorita
Ajo
Tucson
Safford
Silver City
Alamogordo
Artesia
Hobbs
Las Cruces
Carlsbad
Midland
El Paso
Ciudad Juarez
Odessa
Pecos
Rankin
Alpine
Sanderson
Big Springs

BAJA CALIFORNIA
SONORA
CHIHUAHUA
COAHUILA

Nogales
Agua Prieta
Cananea
Douglas
Caborca
Altar
Magdalena
Santa Ana
Puerto de la Libertad
El Rosario
Bavispe
Janos
Nueva Casas Grandes
Villa Ahumada
Moctezuma
Buenaventura
Gallego
Ojinaga
Presidio
Boquillas del Carmen
La Cuesta

Hermosillo
Bahia Kino
Sahuaripa
Madera
Ciudad Guerrero
El Sauz
Chihuahua
Cuauhtemoc
Delicias
La Perla
Nacimiento
Sabinas
Ocampo

Guaymas
Empalme
Rosario
Ciudad Obregon
Navojoa
Tonichi
Yecora
Ciudad Camargo
Jimenez
Santa Barbara
Hidalgo del Parral
Escalon
La Cadena
Ocampo
San Pedro de las Colonias
Parras

San Ignacio
Santa Rosalia
Rosarito
El Fuerte
Sinaloa
Tameapa
Guasave
Los Mochis
Topolobampo
Culiacán
Altata
Eldorado
Cosalá
La Cruz
Gómez Palacio
TORREÓN
Cuencamé
Abasolo
Canatlán
Durango
El Salto
Sombrerete
Rio Grande
Concepción del Oro
Camacho

La Paz
Todos Santos
San Jose del Cabo
El Medano

Mazatlán
Villa Union
Rosario
Fresnillo
Zacatecas
Monte Escobedo
Aguascalientes
Jalpa
Moyahua
Lagos de Moreno
Tepatitlan

Tuxpan
Los Corchos
Tepic
Las Varas
Puerto Vallarta
El Tuito
GUADALAJARA
Tlaquepaque
Ocotlán
Salamanca
Irapuato
Sahuayu
Jiquilpan
Autlán
Sayula
Tomatlán
Ciudad Guzmán
Uruapan
Melaque
Colima
Apatzingán
Manzanillo
Arteaga
Playa Azul
Ixtapa

BAJA CALIFORNIA
BAJA CALIF SUR
DURANGO
ZACATECAS
NAYARIT
JALISCO
COLIMA
AGUASCALIENTES
SINALOA

Gulf of California
Pacific Ocean
Rio Grande

N
W E
S

MEXICO
EXPRESSWAYS
PRIMARY THROUGH ROUTES
OTHER THROUGH ROADS
OTHER ROADS
MEXICAN HIGHWAYS
INTERSTATE HIGHWAYS
U.S. HIGHWAYS
STATE HIGHWAYS

Approximate distances are shown between red markers on map.
Red numbers are kilometers, black numbers are miles.

0   100   200   300
MILES
0   160   320   480
KILOMETERS

© Creative Sales Corporation

MEXICO
Cities and Towns

City	Ref
Abasolo	D-5
Acambaro	F-6
Acapulco	G-6
Acatlan	F-7
Acayucan	F-8
Agua Prieta	A-3
Aguascalientes	E-6
Altar	A-3
Altata	D-4
Alvarado	F-8
Apatzingan	F-6
Arcelia	F-6
Arriga	G-9
Arteaga	F-6
Arlixco	F-7
Autlan	F-5
Bahia Kino	B-2
Bavispe	B-4
Becal	E-10
Boquillas de Carmen	B-6
Buenaventura	B-4
Caborca	A-2
Camacho	D-6
Campeche	E-10
Cananea	A-3
Canatlan	D-5
Cardenas	F-9
Celaya	E-6
Celestun	F-9
Champoton	F-10
Chetumal	F-11
Chihuahua	B-5
Chilpancingo	F-7
China	C-7
Ciudad Acuna	C-7
Ciudad Camargo	C-5
Ciudad Guerrero	B-4
Ciudad Guzman	F-5
Ciudad Juarez	A-4
Ciudad Madero	E-7
Ciudad Mante	D-7
Ciudad Victoria	D-7
Ciudad de Carmen	F-9
Ciudad de Valles	E-7
Ciudad del Maiz	E-7
Coatzacoalcos	F-9
Colima	F-5
Comitan	G-9
Conception de Oro	D-6
Cordoba	F-8
Cosala	D-4
Cuauhtemoc	B-4
Cuencame	D-5
Cuernavaca	F-7
Culiacan	D-4
Delicias	B-5
Durango	D-5
Dzilam de Bravo	E-10
Ejido Insurgentes	C-3
Eldorado	D-4
El Fuerte	C-4
El Medana	D-3
El Rosario	A-1
El Sauz	B-4
El Tuito	E-5
Empalme	B-3
Ensanada	A-1
Escalon	C-5
Escarcega	F-10
Fresnillo	D-5
Gallego	B-4
Gomez Palacio	C-5
Guadalajara	E-5
Guasave	C-4
Guaymas	B-3
Hermosillo	B-3
Hidalgo del Parral	C-5
Hopelchen	E-10
Huajuapan de Leon	F-7
Iguala	F-7
Irapuato	E-6
Iturbide	F-10
Jalapa	F-8
Jalpa	E-5
Janos	A-4
Jimenez	C-5
Juchitan	G-8
La Cruz	D-4
La Cadena	C-5
La Cuesta	B-6
La Paz	D-3
La Perla	B-5
La Pesca	D-7
La Piedad	E-6
Las Varas	E-5
Leon	E-6
Linares	D-7
Los Corchos	E-5
Los Mochis	C-3
Madera	B-4
Magdalena	A-2
Malpaso	G-9
Manuel	D-7
Manzanillo	F-5
Matamoros	C-7
Matehuala	D-6
Matias Romero	G-9
Mazatlan	D-4
Melaque	F-5
Merida	E-10
Mexicali	A-1
Mexico City	F-7
Miahuatlan	G-8
Mier	C-7
Minatitlan	F-8
Moctezuma	B-4
Molango	E-7
Moncloya	C-6
Monte Escobedo	E-5
Montemorelos	D-7
Monterrey	C-6
Morelia	F-6
Morelos	B-6
Moyahua	E-5
Nacimiento	C-6
Nautla	E-8
Navojoa	C-3
Nogales	A-3
Nueva Casas Grandes	B-4
Nueva Rosita	C-6
Nuevo Laredo	C-7
Oaxaca	G-8
Ocampo	C-6
Ocotlan	E-6
Ojinaga	B-5
Ometepec	G-7
Orizaba	F-7
Pachuca	E-7
Palenque	F-9
Papantla	E-7
Paraiso	F-9
Parras	C-6
Peto	E-10
Piedras Negras	B-6
Pijijiapan	G-9
Pinotepa Nacional	G-7
Piste	E-11
Playa Azul	F-6
Pochutla	G-8
Poza Pica	E-7
Progreso	E-10
Puebla	F-7
Puerto de la Libertad	B-2
Puerto Escondido	G-7
Puerto Juarez	E-11
Puerto Madero	G-9
Puerto Penasco	A-2
Punta Prieta	B-2
Queretaro	E-6
Rasarito	B-2
Reynosa	C-7
Rio Grande	D-6
Rio Lagartos	E-11
Rosario	C-3
Rosario	D-4
Sabinas	C-6
Sabinas Hidagalo	C-6
Sahuaripa	B-3
Salamanca	E-6
Salinas	C-6
Salina Cruz	G-8
Saltillo	C-6
San Andres Tuxtla	F-8
San Cristobal	G-9
San Felipe	A-2
San Fernando	D-7
San Ignacio	C-2
San Jose del Cabo	D-3
San Luis	A-2
San Luis Potosi	E-6
San Pedro de las Colonias	C-6
Santa Ana	A-3
Santa Barbara	C-5
Santa Rosalia	C-2
Sayula	F-5
Sinaloa	C-4
Sombrerete	D-5
Sonorita	A-2
Soto La Marina	D-7
Tameapa	C-4
Tampico	E-7
Tapachula	G-9
Tapanatepec	G-9
Taxco	F-7
Teapa	F-9
Tecate	A-1
Tehuacan	F-7
Tehuantepec	G-8
Temporal	E-7
Tepatitlan	E-6
Tepehuanes	D-5
Tepic	E-5
Ticul	E-10
Tijuana	A-1
Tiquicheo	F-6
Tlaciaco	G-7
Tlaxcala	F-7
Tlaxiaco	G-7
Todos Santos	D-3
Toluca	F-7
Tomatian	F-5
Tonichi	B-3
Topolobampo	C-3
Torreon	C-5
Totolapan	G-8
Tulancingo	F-7
Tulum	E-11
Tuxpan	E-5
Tuxpan	E-7
Tuxtepec	F-8
Tuxtla Gutierrez	G-9
Uruapan	F-6
Valladolid	E-11
Veracruz	F-8
Villa Ahumada	A-4
Villagran	D-7
Villahermosa	F-9
Villa Union	D-4
Xcan	E-11
Yecora	B-4
Zacatal	F-9
Zacatecas	E-6
Zamora	E-6
Zihuatanejo	F-6
Zimapan	E-7
Zitacuaro	F-6

STATE MAP LEGEND

ROAD CLASSIFICATIONS & RELATED SYMBOLS

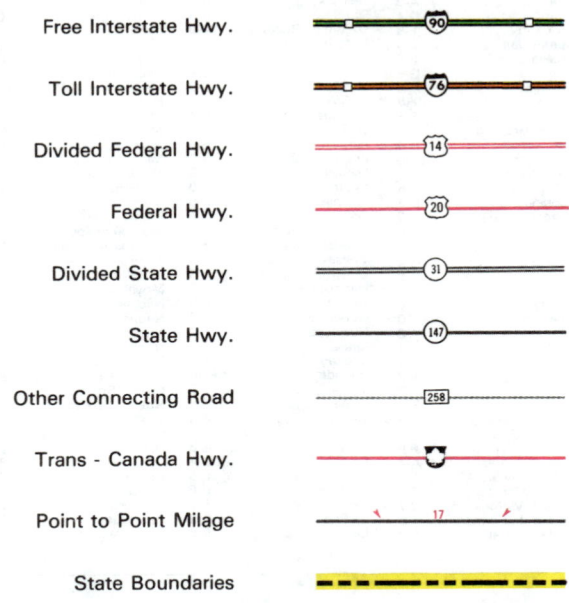

Free Interstate Hwy.

Toll Interstate Hwy.

Divided Federal Hwy.

Federal Hwy.

Divided State Hwy.

State Hwy.

Other Connecting Road

Trans - Canada Hwy.

Point to Point Milage

State Boundaries

LAND MARKS & POINTS OF INTEREST

Indian Reservation

National & State Forest or Wildlife Preserve

Military Installation

National & State Park or Recreation Area

Grassland

Desert

River, Lake, Ocean or other Drainage

Urban Area — **Denver**

Airport

State Capital

Park, Monument, University or other Point of Interest

Roadside Table or Rest Areas

ABBREVIATIONS

A.F.B. - Air Force Base
Hist. - Historical
Mem. - Memorial

Mgmt. - Management
Mon. - Monument
Nat. - Natural

Prov. - Province
Rec. - Recreation
Ref. - Refuge

S. F. - State Forest
St. Pk. - State Park
W.M.A. - Wildlife Management Area

CITIES & TOWNS - Type size indicates the relative population of cities and towns

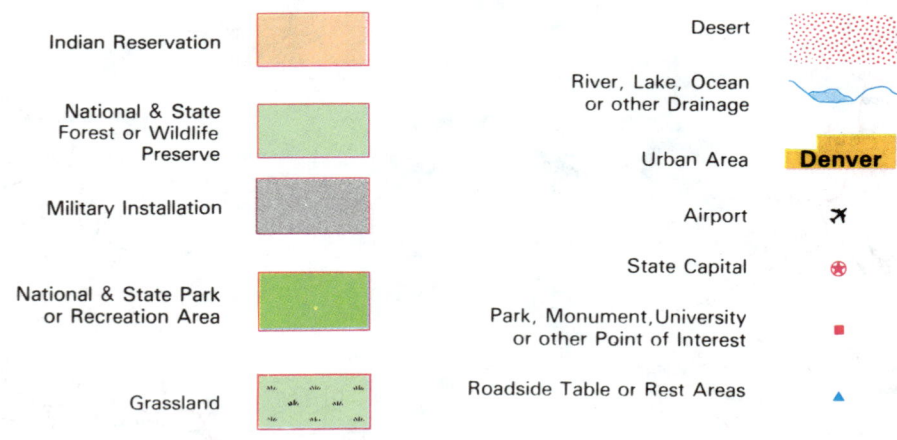

Mapleton	Kenhorst	Somerset	Butler	Auburn	Harrisburg	Madison	Chicago
under 1000	1000-5,000	5,000-10,000	10,000-25,000	25,000-50,000	50,000-100,000	100,000-500,000	500,000 and over

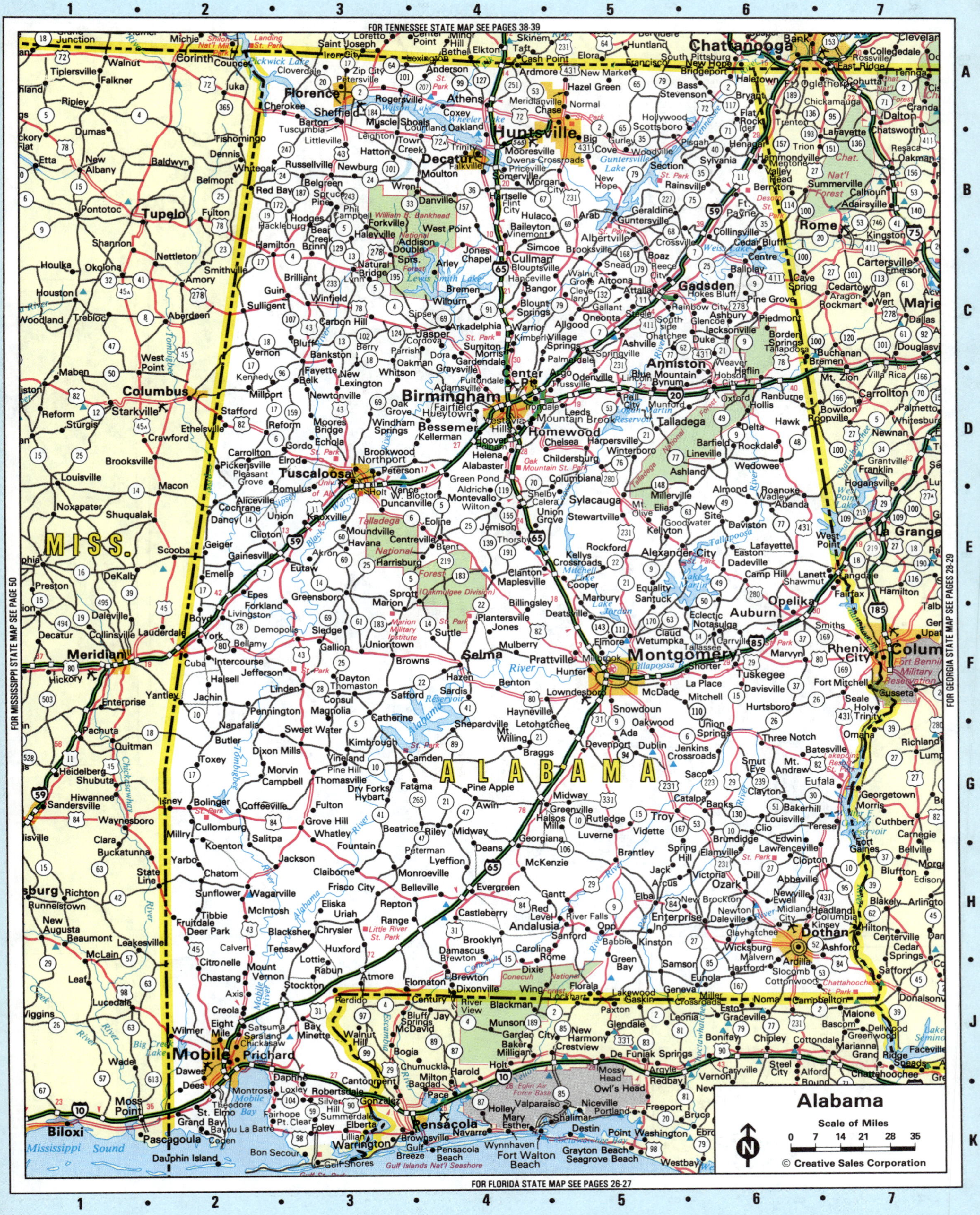
FOR TENNESSEE STATE MAP SEE PAGES 38-39
FOR FLORIDA STATE MAP SEE PAGES 26-27
FOR MISSISSIPPI STATE MAP SEE PAGE 50
FOR GEORGIA STATE MAP SEE PAGES 28-29
Alabama
Scale of Miles
0 7 14 21 28 35
N
© Creative Sales Corporation
ALABAMA
MISS.
Chattanooga
Huntsville
Florence
Sheffield
Decatur
Birmingham
Bessemer
Homewood
Tuscaloosa
Gadsden
Anniston
Talladega
Montgomery
Selma
Auburn
Opelika
Dothan
Mobile
Prichard
Pensacola
Tupelo
Columbus
Meridian
Rome
Biloxi
Pascagoula
Mississippi Sound
Dauphin Island
Gulf Islands Nat'l Seashore
William B. Bankhead National Forest
Talladega National Forest
Conecuh National Forest
Eglin Air Force Base
Fort Benning Military Reservation

ALASKA

N. W. TERR.

YUKON

B. C.

Canada
United States

Arctic Ocean
Beaufort Sea
Bering Sea
Bering Sea
Pacific Ocean
Gulf of Alaska
Norton Sound
Bristol Bay
Cook Inlet

Anchorage
Fairbanks
Juneau
Barrow
Nome
Whitehorse
Prudhoe Bay
Kotzebue
Bethel
Kodiak
Sitka
Ketchikan
Valdez
Seward
Homer
Kenai
Soldotna
Palmer
Wasilla
Cordova
McGrath
Dillingham
Unalaska
Dutch Harbor

Aleutian Islands
Near Islands
Andreanof Islands
Kodiak Island
Saint Lawrence Island
Pribilof Islands
Saint Matthew Island

Denali Nat'l Park and Preserve
Gates of the Arctic National Park & Preserve
Wrangell-St. Elias Nat'l Park & Preserve
Lake Clark Nat'l Park & Preserve
Katmai Nat'l Park & Preserve
Kenai Fjords Nat'l Park
Glacier Bay Nat'l Park & Preserve
Tongass National Forest
Chugach National Forest
Arctic Nat'l Wildlife Refuge
Yukon Flats Nat'l Wildlife Refuge
Kodiak Nat'l Wildlife Refuge
Togiak Nat'l Wildlife Refuge
Yukon Delta Nat'l Wildlife Refuge

Alaska
Scale of Miles
0 40 80 120 160 200
© Creative Sales Corporation

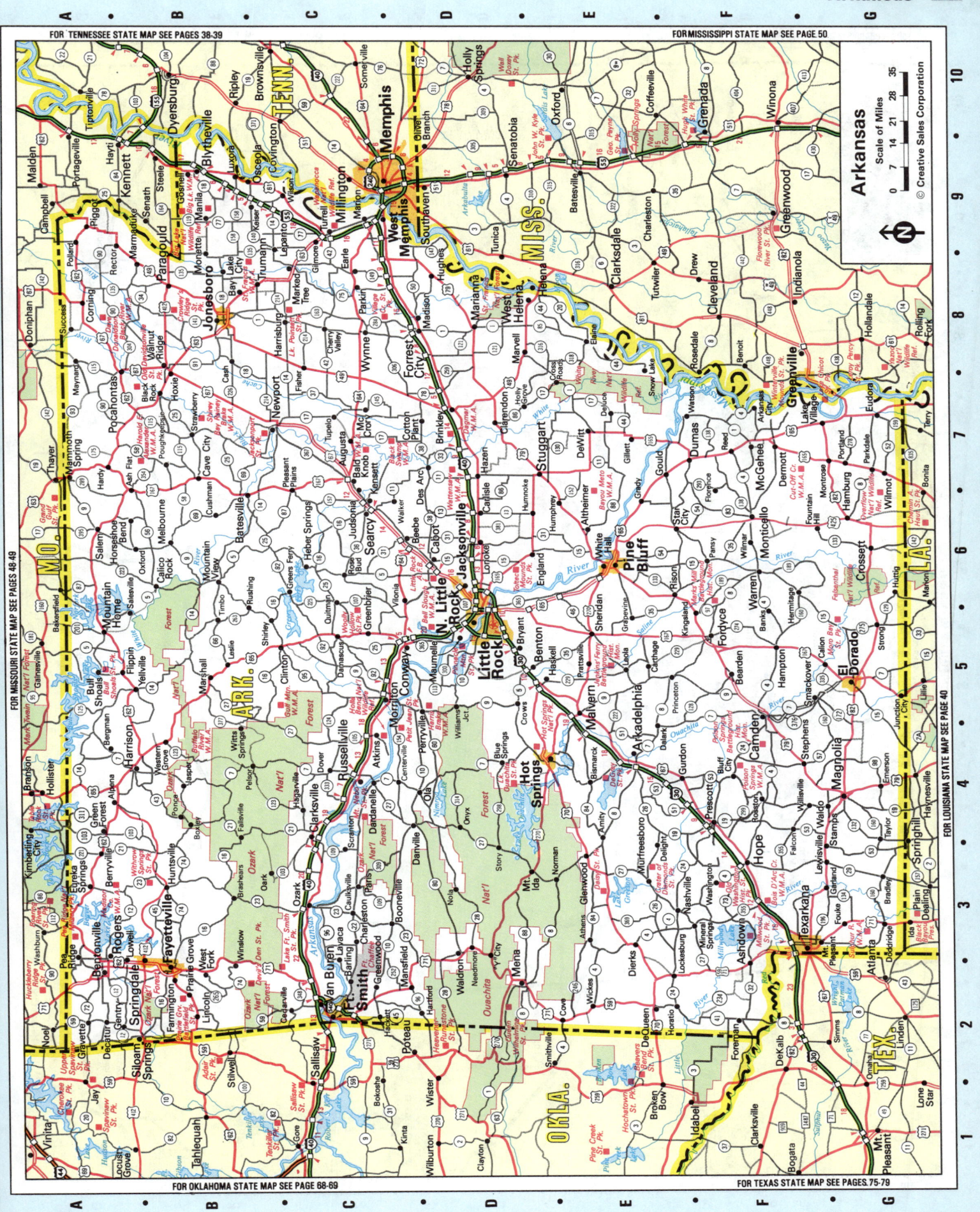

FOR TENNESSEE STATE MAP SEE PAGES 38-39
FOR MISSISSIPPI STATE MAP SEE PAGE 50
FOR MISSOURI STATE MAP SEE PAGES 48-49
FOR LOUISIANA STATE MAP SEE PAGE 40
FOR OKLAHOMA STATE MAP SEE PAGE 68-69
FOR TEXAS STATE MAP SEE PAGES 75-79

Arkansas

Scale of Miles

0 7 14 21 28 35

© Creative Sales Corporation

FOR COLORADO STATE MAP SEE PAGES 22-23
FOR NEW MEXICO STATE MAP SEE PAGE 62
FOR UTAH STATE MAP SEE PAGES 80-81
FOR NEVADA STATE MAP SEE PAGE 54

UTAH

NEVADA

ARIZONA

Manti-La Sal National Forest
Canyonlands National Park
Glen Canyon National Recreation Area
Dixie National Forest
Bryce Canyon Nat'l Park
Zion National Park
Grand Canyon National Park
Kaibab National Forest
Navajo Indian Reservation
Hopi Indian Reservation
Hualapai Indian Reservation
Havasupai Indian Reservation
Kaibab Indian Reservation
Lake Mead National Recreational Area
Lake Powell
Lake Mead
Petrified Forest National Park
Prescott National Forest
Coconino National Forest

La Sal, La Sal Jct., Summit Pt., Eastland, Monticello, Blanding, Bluff, Mexican Hat, Aneth, Montezuma Creek
Teec Nos Pos, Mexican Water, Tes Nez Iha, Rock Point, Round Rock, Many Farms, Tsaile, Chinle, Cross Canyon, St. Michaels, Window Rock, Lupton, Houck, Sanders, Navajo
Hanksville, Torrey, Grover, Boulder, Escalante, Henrieville, Tropic, Cannonville
Kayenta, Tsegi, Chilchinbito, Rough Rock, Cow Springs, Red Lake, Tonalea, Tuba City, Cedar Ridge, The Gap
Ganado, Greasewood, Kearns Canyon, Polacca, Old Oraibi, Oraibi, Second Mesa, Seba Dalkai, Indian Wells, Dilkon, Cedar Springs, Chambers
Holbrook, Joseph City, Sun Valley, Winslow, Angell, Winona, Leupp, Sunrise
Page, Marble Canyon, Jacob Lake, Fredonia, Colorado City, Kanab, Mt. Carmel, Glendale, Orderville, Kanarraville
Cameron, Gray Mountain, Desert View, North Rim, Grand Canyon, Moqui, Tusayan, Valle, Williams, Parks, Bellemont, Flagstaff, Mountainaire, Munds Park, Lake Montezuma, McGuireville
Cedar City, Hamilton Fort, Kanarraville, Hatch, Alton, Long Valley Jct.
Sedona, Cornville, Cottonwood, Clarkdale, Jerome, Chino Valley, Prescott Valley, Prescott, Paulden, Ash Fork, Seligman
Beaver, Greenville, Circleville, Paragonah, Parowan, Summit, Enoch
Peach Springs, Yampai, Nelson, Truxton, Valentine, Hackberry, Kingman, Hualapai Mtn. Park, Wikieup, Yucca
St. George, Washington, Santa Clara, Ivins, Hurricane, La Verkin, Toquerville, Leeds, Rockville, Springdale, Pintura, New Harmony, Central, Pine Valley, Veyo, Gunlock, Shivwits
Mesquite, Bunkerville, Littlefield, Beaver Dam, Meadview, Dolan Springs, Chloride, Golconda
Moapa, Glendale, Logandale, Overton, N. Las Vegas, E. Las Vegas, Henderson, Boulder City, Nelson, Willow Beach, Temple Bar, Cottonwood Cove, Katherine, Bullhead City, Oatman, Riviera, Golden Shores, Topock, Lake Havasu City, Needles, Laughlin
Alamo, Elgin, Caliente, Pioche, Panaca, Ursine, Minersville, Adamsville, Lund, Beryl, Zane, Newcastle, Uvada, Modena, Enterprise

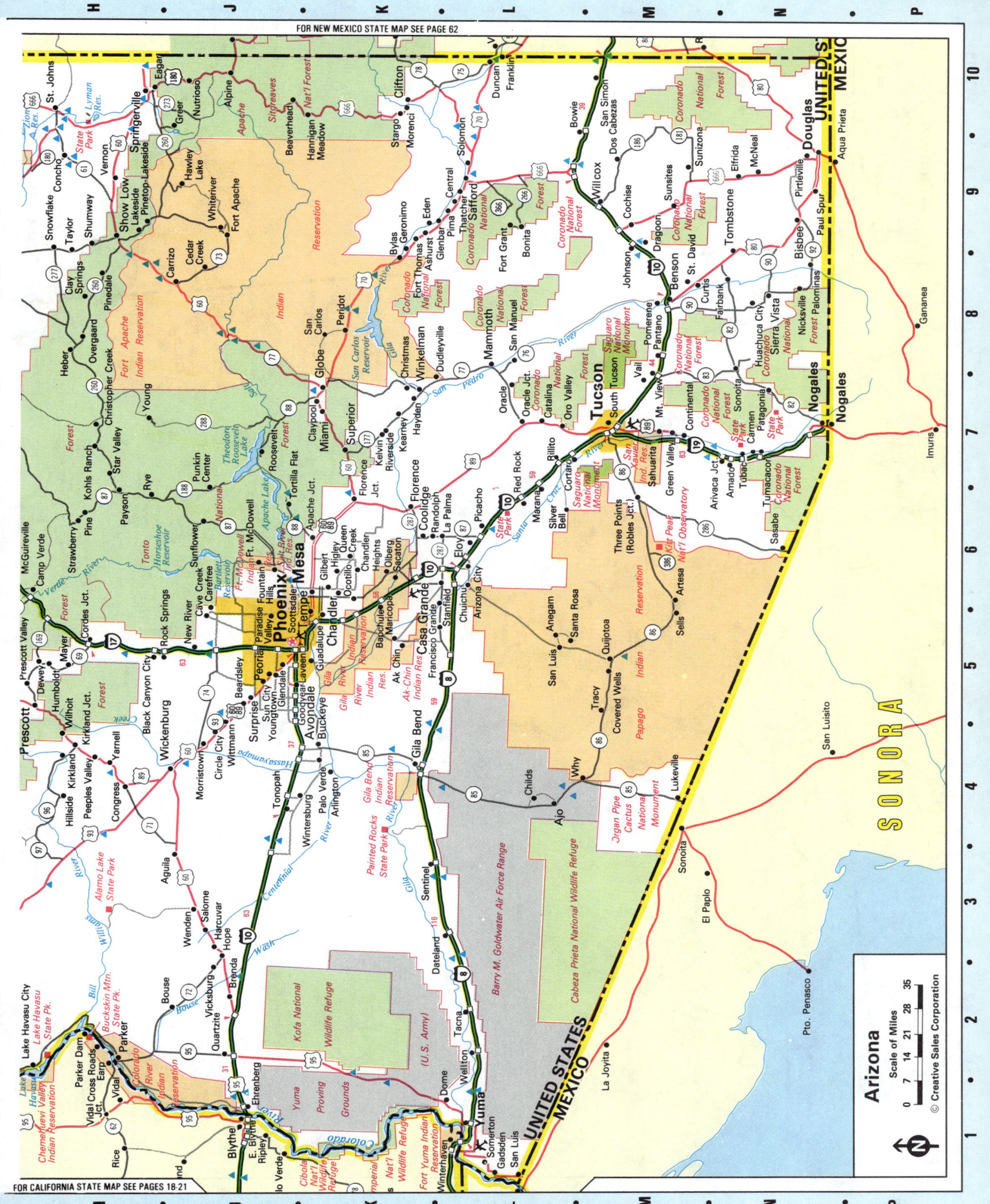

FOR NEVADA STATE MAP SEE PAGE 54

California
Scale of Miles
© Creative Sales Corporation
0 7 14 21 28 35

N

FOR OREGON STATE MAP SEE PAGES 70-71

NEVADA

OREGON

CALIFORNIA

Indian Reservation

Pyramid Lk.

Reno
Sparks
Carson City
Virginia City
Dayton
Silver Springs
Fernley
Fallon
Wadsworth
Nixon
Gerlach
Eagle Picher
Wabuska

Klamath Falls
Lakeview
Merrill
Bonanza
Tulelake
Newell
Macdoel
Dorris
Hornbrook
Yreka
Montague
Weed
Mt. Shasta
McCloud
Dunsmuir
Castella

Redding
Anderson
Cottonwood
Red Bluff
Corning
Orland
Chico
Paradise
Oroville
Marysville
Yuba City
Linda
Grass Valley
Nevada City
Colfax
Truckee
Tahoe City
Kings Beach

Alturas
Canby
Adin
Likely
Cedarville
Eagleville
Madeline
Termo
Ravendale
Susanville
Westwood
Chester
Greenville
Quincy
Portola
Loyalton
Sierraville
Downieville

Crescent City
Smith River
Brookings
Ft. Dick
Klamath
Orick
Trinidad
Arcata
Eureka
Fortuna
Scotia
Ferndale
Rio Dell
Petrolia
Redcrest
Weott
Miranda
Redway
Garberville
Leggett
Laytonville
Willits
Ukiah
Ft. Bragg
Mendocino
Willow Creek
Hoopa
Weaverville
Hayfork
Junction City
Douglas City
Covelo
Clearlake
Lakeport
Kelseyville
Potter Valley
Redwood Valley

Lassen Volcanic Nat'l Park

Redwood Nat'l Park

Shasta Nat'l Forest
Klamath Nat'l Forest
Trinity Nat'l Forest
Modoc Nat'l Forest
Lassen Nat'l Forest
Plumas Nat'l Forest
Tahoe Nat'l Forest
Mendocino Nat'l Forest
Six Rivers Nat'l Forest

Sacramento River
Eel River
Trinity River
Klamath River
Russian River

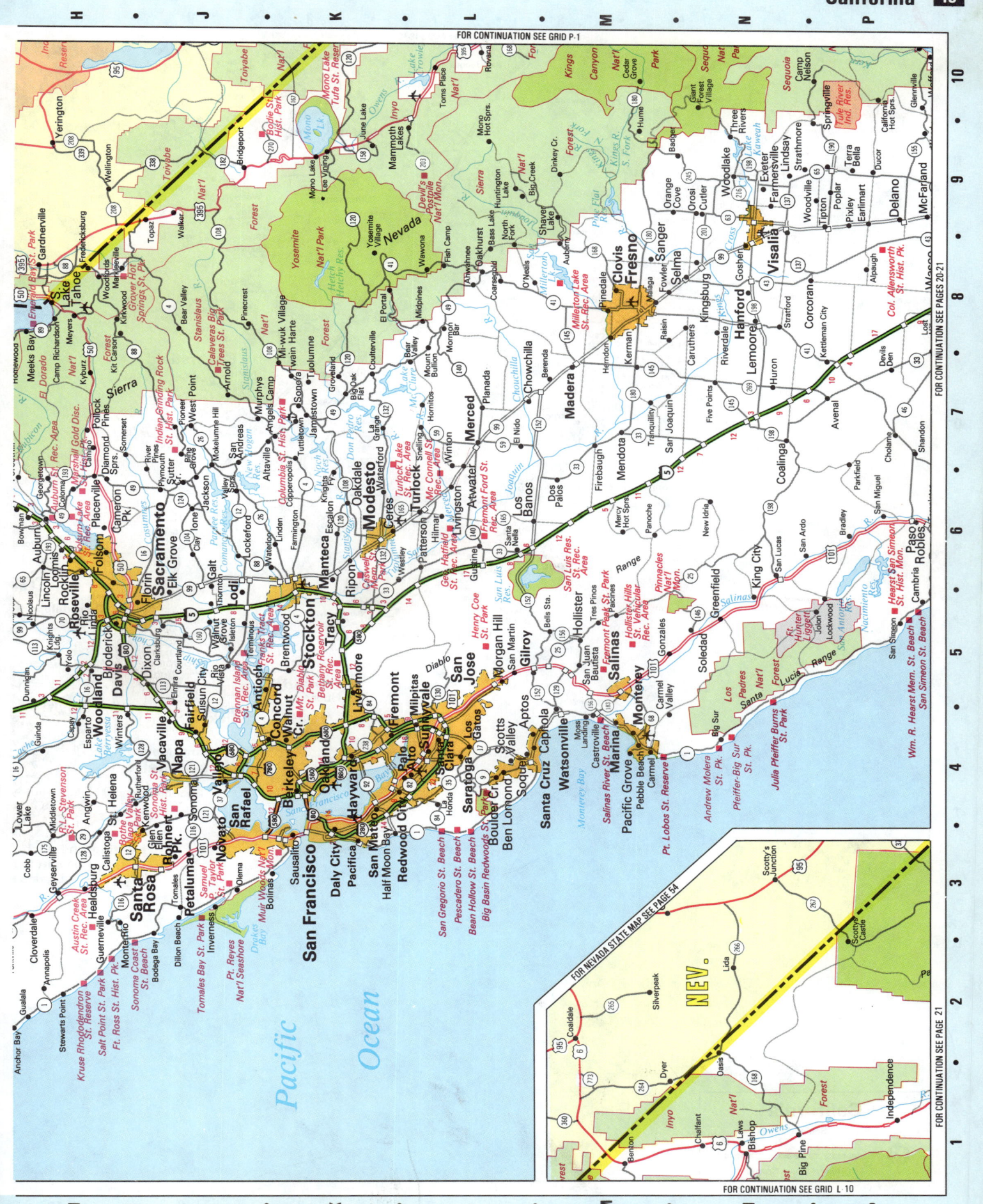

FOR CONTINUATION SEE PAGES 18-19

Pacific

Ocean

California

Scale of Miles

0   7   14   21   28   35

N

© Creative Sales Corporation

FOR NEVADA STATE MAP SEE PAGE 54

NEVADA

CALIFORNIA

ARIZONA

MEXICO

Grid numbers top/bottom: 11 12 13 14 15 16 17
Grid letters right: N O P Q R S T U V

Lone Pine
Keeler
136
Owens Lk.
395
Cartago
Olancha
Darwin
Panamint Sprs.
Stovepipe Wells
Furnace Cr. Ranch
Death Valley Jct.
190
Panamint Range
Death Valley Nat'l Monument
Salt Cr.
127
Shoshone
178
Tecopa
Amargosa R.
Armagosa Valley
Mercury
Indian Springs
373
160
Pahrump
372
157
156
Toyabe Nat'l Forest
168
93
Mesquite
Glendale
Bunkerville
Overton
15
3
Virgin R.

Haiwee Res.
Little Lake
China Lake
178
Inyokern
14
Ridgecrest
Johannesburg
Randsburg
Red Mountain
Red Rock Canyon St. Park
Cantil
California City
Mojave
U.S. Naval Weapons Sta.
Ft. Irwin Military Res.
Avawatz Mtns.
127
Goodsprings
161
Jean
160
Nelson
Las Vegas
North Las Vegas
Henderson
146
Boulder City
Willow Beach
Lake Mead
Temple Bar
Lake Mead Nat'l Rec. Area
95
23
164
Cottonwood Cove
Searchlight
Nipton
Cima
163
Laughlin
Bullhead City
68
Kingman
McConnico
93
Chloride
Yucca
Black Mtns.
Mohave

Boron
North Edwards
58
Hinkley
Barstow
Yermo
Lenwood
Daggett
Helendale
Edwards Air Force Base
Mojave R.
42
Cady Mtns.
Newberry Sprs.
40
Ludlow
Kelso
Providence Mtns. St. Rec. Area
Providence Mtns.
Goffs
Fenner
Essex
Amboy
Sheep Hole Mtns.
Old Woman Mtns.
Sacramento Mtns.
Needles
Golden Shores
Topock
95
Lake Havasu City
Hualapai Mtns.
95
Lake Havasu State Pk.

Lancaster
Pearblossom
Adelanto
Victorville
Apple Valley
Hesperia
Lucerne Valley
Saddleback Butte St. Pk.
Oro Grande
138
247
Bullion Mtns.
Twentynine Palms Marine Corps Base
330
Silverwood Lake St. Rec. Area
San Bernardino Nat'l Forest
Fawnskin
Big Bear Lake
Yucca Valley
Joshua Tree
Twentynine Palms
Morongo Valley
62
Granite Mtns.
Rice
177
Vidal
Parker Dam
Earp
Parker
Buckskin Mtn. State Pk.
Poston
Big Maria Mtns.
Bouse
72
Quartzsite
Vicksburg
60

Wrightwood
Phelan
15
138
Los Angeles
Angeles Nat'l Forest
39
Glendora
Pomona
Fullerton
Ontario
Riverside
San Bernardino
Yucaipa
38
Beaumont
Banning
Cabazon
Desert Hot Sprs.
243
Palm Sprs.
Thousand Palms
Joshua Tree Nat'l Mon.
Desert Center
Chuckwalla Mtns.
10
45
Blythe
Ehrenberg
Ripley
Palo Verde
Chocolate Mtns.
Dome Rock Mtns.
95
95

Anaheim
Santa Ana
Corona
71
91
Perris
Sun City
San Jacinto
Hemet
Idyllwild
111
Palm Desert
Indio
La Quinta
Coachella
Mecca
Salton Sea St. Rec. Area
Salton Sea
Niland
Calipatria
78
Cibola Nat'l Wildlife Refuge
Imperial Nat'l Wildlife Refuge
Stone Cabin
Martinez Lake
Picacho St. Rec. Area
Imperial Dam

Lake Mathews
Lake Elsinore
74
Murrieta
Temecula
79
Pauma Valley
Palomar Mtn.
371
Cahuilla Ind. Res.
Santa Rosa Ind. Res.
Santa Rosa Mtns.
Anza-Borrego
Borrego Sprs.
Desert Shores
Salton City
Ocotillo Wells St. Vehicular Rec. Area
Westmorland
Brawley
86
Alamorio
Glamis
Beaumont

El Toro
San Juan Capistrano
San Clemente
San Clemente St. Beach
San Onofre St. Beach
Fallbrook
Camp Pendleton
Pala
Oceanside
Carlsbad
Carlsbad St. Beach
Vista
San Marcos
Escondido
Santa Ysabel
Julian
Ramona
76
78
79
Cuyamaca Rancho St. Park
Mt. Laguna
Pine Valley
Cleveland Nat'l Forest
St. Park
Ocotillo
Niland

Leucadia
Encinitas
Del Mar
Poway
67
Santee
La Jolla
San Diego
Coronado
El Cajon
Alpine
Jamul
Cabrillo Nat'l Mon.
Silver Strand St. Beach
Imperial Beach
Border Field St. Park
Chula Vista
Dulzura
94
Barrett L.
Campo
Boulevard
Tecate
2
Jacumba
Seeley
Imperial
El Centro
Heber
Calexico
98
Mexicali
Algodones
Winterhaven
Dome
Yuma
Wellton
Tacna
Somerton
8
Tijuana
Rosarito
Metamuco
La Rumorosa
Colonia Progreso
Hermosillo
San Luis Rio Colorado
Galeana

U.S. MEXICO

FOR WYOMING STATE MAP SEE PAGES 88-89

WYOMING

Saratoga
Medicine Bow
Centennial
Albany
Riverside
Encampment
Woods Landing
Mountain Home
Baggs Dixon Savery
Medicine Bow Nat'l Forest
Cowdrey
Routt
Lake John
State Forest National
Walden
Roosevelt National Forest
Rustic
Estes Park
Rocky Mountain National Park
Deer Ridge
Grand Lake
Raymond

Carter
Little America
Green River
Quealy Creek
Fort Lyman
Urie Mountain View
Robertson
Lonetree Burntfork
McKinnon
Manila
Green Lake
Ashley
Oak Park Res.
National
Forest State Park
Steinaker Res.
Whiterocks
Monarch Neola Maeser Vernal Naples
Lapoint Jensen
Altamont Cedarview Gusher
Bluebell
Mt. Emmons Upalco Fort Duchesne Leota
Arcadia Ioka Roosevelt Leota
Bridgeland Myton Ouray
Duchesne
Ashley National Forest

Hiawatha
Sunbeam Maybell Craig Milner Steamboat Sprs. Gould
Lay Hayden Coalmont Rand
Hamilton Oak Creek Phippsburg Hot Sulphur Springs
Blue Mountain Elk Springs
Dinosaur National Monument
Yampa River
Routt National Forest
Arapaho National Forest
Grand Lake
Meeker Buford Yampa
Toponas Parshall
Rio Blanco Kremmling Tabernash Fraser
Rangely White River McCoy Bond State Bridge
National Rollinsville
Winter Park
Dotsero Gypsum Wolcott Silverthorne Georgetown Empire
New Castle Eagle Edwards Avon Vail Frisco Echo Lake
Silt Dowd Gilman Dillon
Rifle Glenwood Sprs. Red Cliff Breckenridge
Parachute Carbondale Climax Blue River
Basalt Snowmass Jefferson
DeBeque Redstone Woody Creek Alma Como
Collbran Molina Aspen Malta Fairplay
Mesa Marble Leadville Garo Park
Cameo Skyway Snowmass Village Granite
Palisade Grand Mesa National Forest Twin Lakes
Mack Loma Fruita Clifton Cedaredge Bowie Somerset Crested Butte Buena Vista
Whitewater Austin Paonia Johnson Village
Grand Junction Orchard City Hotchkiss Mount Princeton Hot Springs Nathrop
Colorado National Monument Delta Lazear Crawford Almont
Gateway Olathe Maher Gunnison Garfield Salida
Uncompahgre National Forest Montrose Cimarron Sapinero Parlin Poncha Springs
Paradox Bedrock Nucla Black Canyon of the Gunnison National Monument Doyleville Sargents Howard
Moab Redvale Norwood Ridgway Blue Mesa Res. Coaldale
La Sal Jct. La Sal Vancorum Naturita Ouray Curecanti National Recreation Area Villa Grove
Slick Rock Placerville Saw Pit Lake City Powderhorn Saguache
Egnar Telluride Ophir Red Mountain Creede Center Hooper
Summit Pt. Dunton Gladstone Silverton Wagon Wheel Gap Del Norte Mosca
Monticello Rico South Fork Spar City Homelake
Eastland Cahone Stoner Rockwood Monte Vista
Fry Canyon Pleasant View Dolores Hermosa Summitville Platoro Alamosa
Blanding Yellow Jacket Mancos Capulin
Lewis Arriola Durango Chimney Rock Pagosa Sprs. San Acacio
Bluff Cortez Hesperus Bayfield La Jara Romeo Sanford
Montezuma Creek Towaoc Fort Lewis Breen Kline Oxford Chromo Conejos Antonito
Mexican Hat Mesa Verde National Park Marvel Ignacio Arboles Monero Chama
Aneth Ute Mountain Ute Indian Reservation Redmesa Allison Dulce Lumberton

Mineral Hot Springs Moffat
Great Sand Dunes National Monument
Rio Grande National Forest
San Juan National Forest
Uncompahgre National Forest
Gunnison National Forest
San Isabel National Forest
Pike National Forest
White River National Forest

UTAH
Sunnyside East Carbon City
Woodside
Green River Thompson Cisco
Crescent Jct.
Arches National Park
Canyonlands National Park
Glen Canyon National Recreation Area
Manti-La Sal National Forest
Hovenweep Nat'l Monument
Natural Bridges Nat'l Monument

FOR UTAH STATE MAP SEE PAGE 80-81

Colorado
Scale of Miles
0 7 14 21 28 35
N
© Creative Sales Corporation

La Plata Cedar Hill
Beklabito Aztec Turley Archuleta
Flora Vista Kirtland Blanco Bloomfield La Puente Tierra Amarilla
Shiprock **Farmington** Los Ojos Rutheron Ensenada Tres Piedras
Navajo Lake State Park
Jicarilla National Forest
Carson National Forest

FOR NEW MEXICO STATE MAP SEE PAGE 62

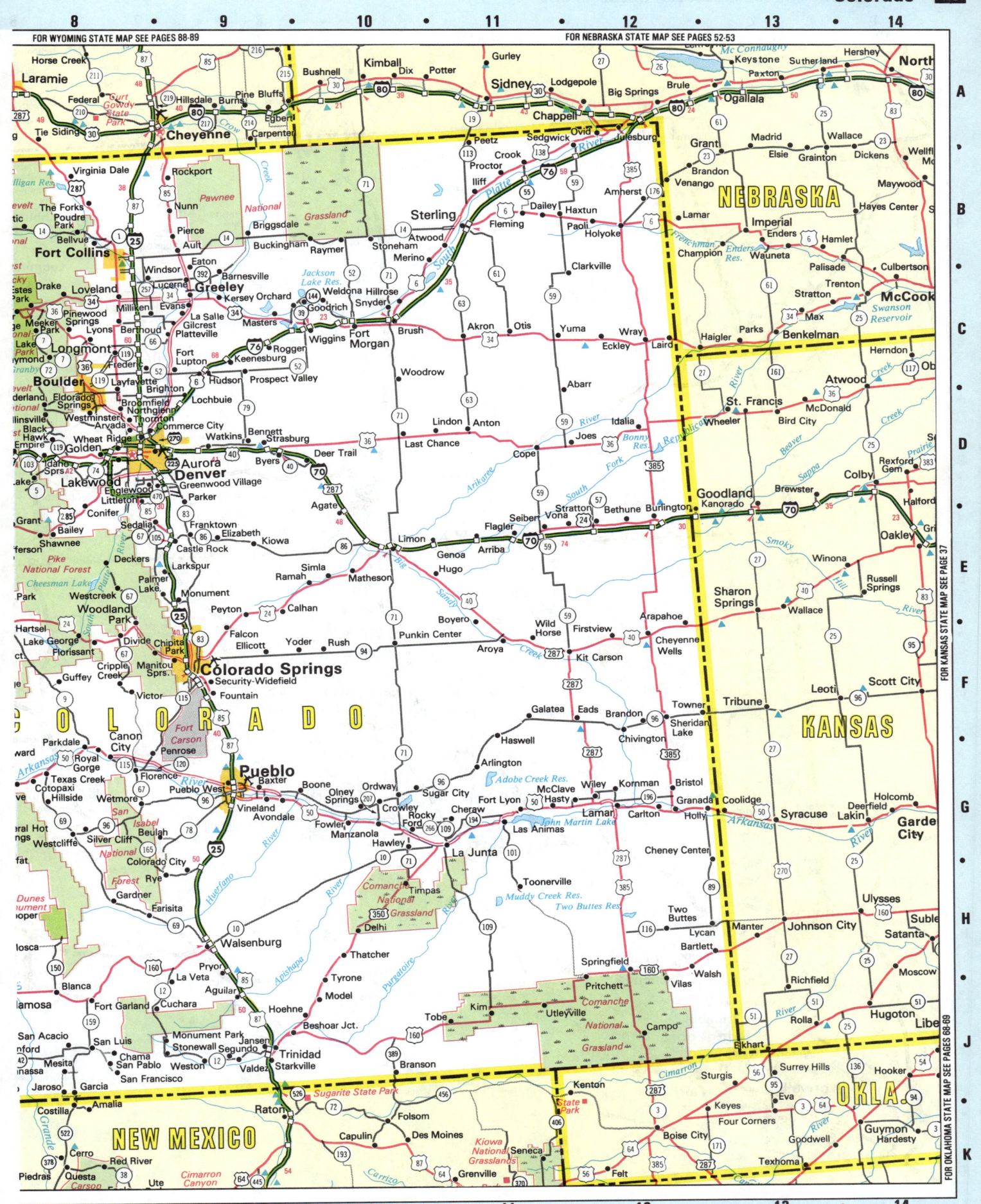

FOR VERMONT STATE MAP SEE PAGE 55

FOR NEW YORK STATE MAP SEE PAGES 58-61

VT. N.H. MASS. CONN. N.Y.

Troy · Albany · Rensselaer · Nassau · Pittsfield · Chatham · Hudson · Hillsdale

Williamstown · North Adams · Adams · Cheshire · Dalton · Hinsdale · Peru · Lenox · Richmond · West Stockbridge · Stockbridge · Great Barrington · Sheffield · Monterey · New Marlborough · Sandisfield · Otis

Wilmington · Whitingham · Stamford · Readsboro · Pownal · Clarksburg · Florida · Savoy · Hawley · Plainfield · Cummington · Worthington · Chesterfield · Middlefield · Washington · Becket · Chester · Westhampton · Huntington · Russell · Montgomery · Blandford · Tolland · Westfield

Guilford · Winchester · Northfield · Warwick · Greenfield · Deerfield · Shelburne · Conway · Ashfield · Buckland · Charlemont · Colrain · Heath · Leyden · Gill · Bernardston · Millers Falls · Montague · Sunderland · Leverett · Amherst · Hadley · Northampton · Easthampton · South Hadley · Holyoke · Granby · Three Rivers · Chicopee · Springfield · West Springfield · Agawam · Longmeadow · East Longmeadow · Hampden · Monson · Wales · Holland · Wilbraham · Palmer · Brimfield · Sturbridge · Southbridge · Dudley · Webster

Swanzey · Troy · Fitzwilliam · Rindge · Jaffrey · Greenville · Ashby · Ashburnham · Winchendon · Royalston · Athol · Orange · Baldwinville · Fitchburg · Gardner · Leominster · Westminster · Templeton · Petersham · Princeton · Barre · Hardwick · Gilbertville · New Braintree · Oakham · Rutland · West Boylston · Holden · Worcester · Paxton · Leicester · Spencer · North Brookfield · West Brookfield · Brookfield · Ware · Warren · Charlton · Oxford · Webster

Salisbury · Canaan · Norfolk · Colebrook · Hartland · East Hartland · Granby · East Granby · Suffield · Enfield · Somers · Stafford · Union · Woodstock · Pomfret · Putnam · Eastford · Ashford · Willington · Tolland · Westford · Windsor · Windsor Locks · Melrose · Ellington · Vernon · Storrs · Mansfield · Chaplin · Hampton · Brooklyn · Killingly

Sharon · Cornwall · Goshen · Torrington · Winsted · Barkhamsted · New Hartford · Canton · Simsbury · Bloomfield · Avon · South Windsor · East Hartford · Manchester · Hartford · West Hartford · Coventry · Columbia · Lebanon · Windham · Scotland · Canterbury · Plainfield · Sterling

Kent · Warren · Litchfield · Harwinton · Burlington · Farmington · Bristol · Plymouth · Thomaston · Terryville · Bethlehem · Washington · Watertown · Wolcott · Newington · Wethersfield · Glastonbury · Rocky Hill · New Britain · Berlin · Cromwell · Marlborough · Hebron · Colchester · Franklin · Bozrah · Norwich

New Milford · Woodbury · Southbury · Waterbury · Naugatuck · Middlebury · Cheshire · Meriden · Southington · Middletown · Middlefield · Durham · Haddam · East Hampton · Westchester · Salem · Oakdale

Danbury · Brookfield · New Fairfield · Bethel · Newtown · Monroe · Oxford · Seymour · Derby · Ansonia · Shelton · Hamden · Woodbridge · North Haven · Wallingford · North Branford · Guilford · Madison · Clinton · Westbrook · Old Saybrook · Essex · Deep River · Chester · Killingworth · Haddam · East Haddam

New Canaan · Norwalk · Westport · Weston · Wilton · Ridgefield · Redding · Georgetown · Trumbull · Bridgeport · Stratford · Fairfield · Milford · West Haven · New Haven · East Haven · Branford

Stamford · Greenwich · Darien

New London · Waterford · Groton · Mystic · Stonington · Pawcatuck · Ledyard · North Stonington · Old Lyme · East Lyme

Long Island Sound · Fishers Island · Gardiners Island · Shelter Island · Greenport · Southold · Montauk · Peconic

Quabbin Res. · Candlewood Lake

FOR NEW HAMPSHIRE STATE MAP SEE PAGE 55

Atlantic

Ocean

Merrimack
Wilton
Milford
Nashua
Hudson
Methuen
Derry
Londonderry
Windham
Litchfield
Hampstead
Atkinson
Amesbury
Merrimac
West Newbury
Salisbury
Salisbury Beach St. Res.
Newburyport
Newbury
Parker River Nat'l Wildlife Ref.
Haverhill
Groveland
Georgetown
Rowley
Plum Is. St. Pk.
Lawrence
Andover
Boxford
Ipswich
Topsfield
Essex
Rockport
Townsend
Tyngsborough
Dracut
North Reading
Wenham
Hamilton
Manchester
Gloucester
Pepperell
Groton
Westford
Tewksbury
Lynnfield
Danvers
Beverly
Salem
Lunenburg
Shirley
Littleton
Ayer
Chelmsford
Billerica
Wilmington
Reading
Peabody
Saugus
Marblehead
Swampscott
Harvard
Acton
Carlisle
Bedford
Concord
Wakefield
Woburn
Lexington
Lynn
Nahant
Sterling
Clinton
Bolton
Stow
Maynard
Lincoln
Cambridge
Revere
Chelsea
Winthrop
Northborough
Marlborough
Hudson
Wayland
Newton
Boston
Massachusetts Bay
Shrewsbury
Cochituate
Wellesley
Hull
Westborough
Natick
Framingham
Milton
Quincy
Grafton
Hopkinton
Westwood
Dedham
Hingham
Scituate
Millbury
Upton
Medfield
Norwood
Canton
Braintree
Randolph
Weymouth
Norwell
Northbridge
Milford
Hopedale
Medway
Millis
Walpole
Holbrook
Avon
Rockland
Hanover
Marshfield
Whitinsville
Mendon
Norfolk
Sharon
Stoughton
Abington
Hanson
Pembroke
Uxbridge
Bellingham
Wrentham
Foxborough
Easton
Brockton
Whitman
East Bridgewater
Duxbury
Blackstone
N. Attleborough
Mansfield
Bridgewater
Halifax
Kingston
Plympton
Woonsocket
Norton
Raynham
Carver
Plymouth
Slatersville
Harrisville
Pascoag
Attleboro
Taunton
Middleborough
Nasonville
Mapleville
Chepachet
Berkley
Dighton
Freetown
Wareham
Harmony
Pawtucket
Rehoboth
Fall River
Buzzards Bay
Sagamore
Sandwich
Provincetown
Truro
N. Scituate
Providence
Seekonk
Somerset
Swansea
Acushnet
Bourne
Barnstable
Wellfleet
Cape Cod Nat'l Seashore
Foster Center
Cranston
East Providence
Auburn
Warren
Bristol
Marion
Centerville
Eastham
Orleans
Brewster
Vernon
R.I.
Hope
Fiskeville
Barrington
Mattapoisett
Fairhaven
New Bedford
Dartmouth
Falmouth
East Falmouth
Hyannis
Osterville
South Yarmouth
West Dennis
Dennis Port
Dennis
Yarmouth
Harwich
Chatham
Warwick
East Greenwich
Westport
Buzzards Bay
Nantucket Sound
Monomoy Island
West Greenwich Center
Nooseneck
Exeter
Wickford
Homestead
Narragansett
Tiverton
Portsmouth
Little Compton
Millville
Saunderstown
Middletown
Jamestown
Newport
Gay Head
Chilmark
West Tisbury
North Tisbury
Tisbury
Vineyard Haven
Oak Bluffs
Edgartown
Martha's Vineyard
Chappaquiddick Island
Nantucket
Nantucket Island
Hope Valley
Kingston
Woodville
Carolina
Wakefield
Narragansett Pier
Rhode Island Sound
Charlestown
Westerly
Block Island
Elizabeth Islands
Cape Cod Bay

Connecticut
Massachusetts
Rhode Island

Scale of Miles
0 3 6 9 12 15

© Creative Sales Corporation

Florida
Scale of Miles
0 7 14 21 28 35
© Creative Sales Corporation

N

Atlantic Ocean

Gulf of Mexico

GEORGIA

Tallahassee
Jacksonville
Gainesville
Ocala
Orlando
Tampa
St. Petersburg
Clearwater
Lakeland
Daytona Beach
St. Augustine
Valdosta

FOR GEORGIA STATE MAP SEE PAGES 28-29

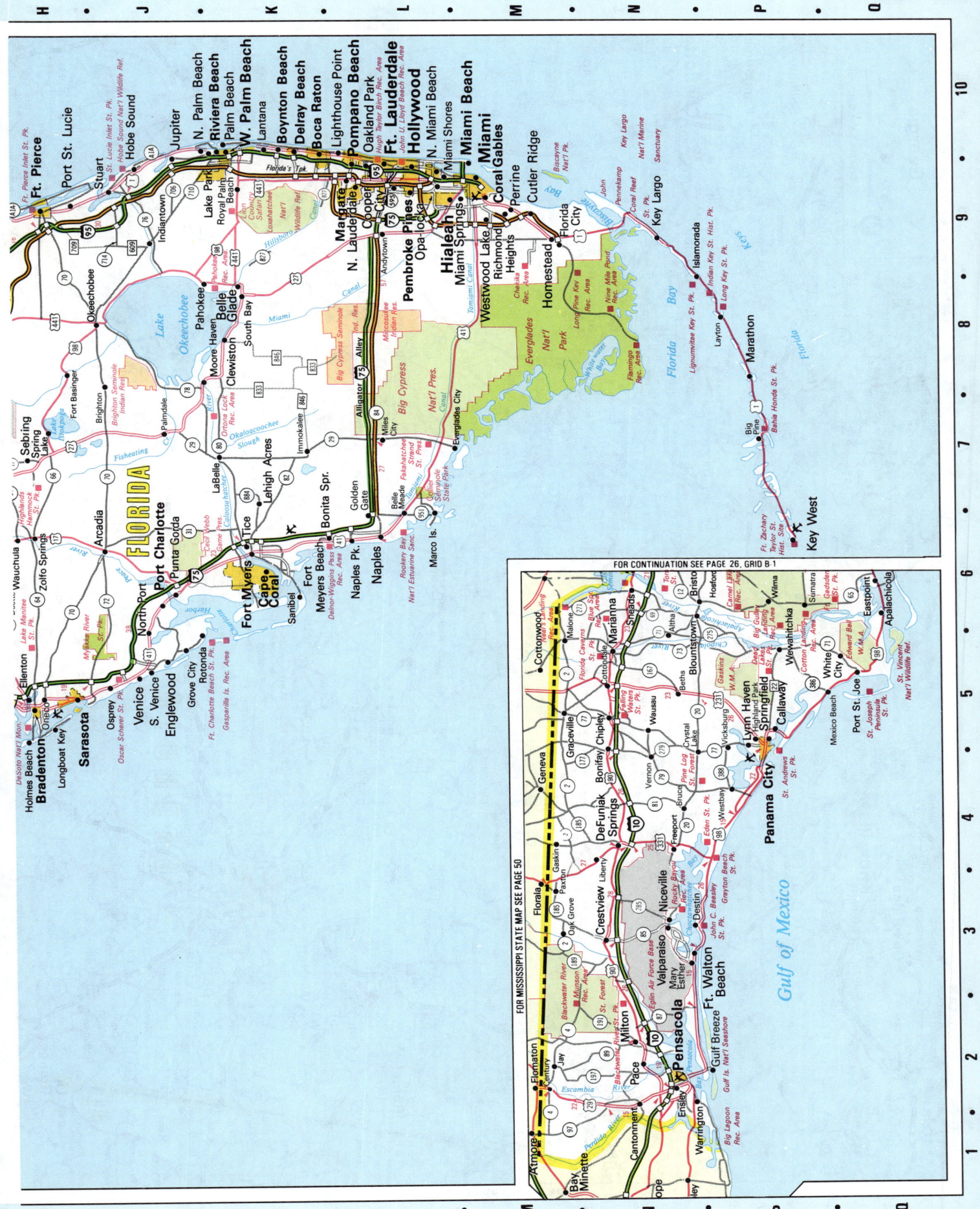

FOR CONTINUATION SEE PAGE 26, GRID B-1

FOR MISSISSIPPI STATE MAP SEE PAGE 50

Gulf of Mexico

FLORIDA

Lake Okeechobee

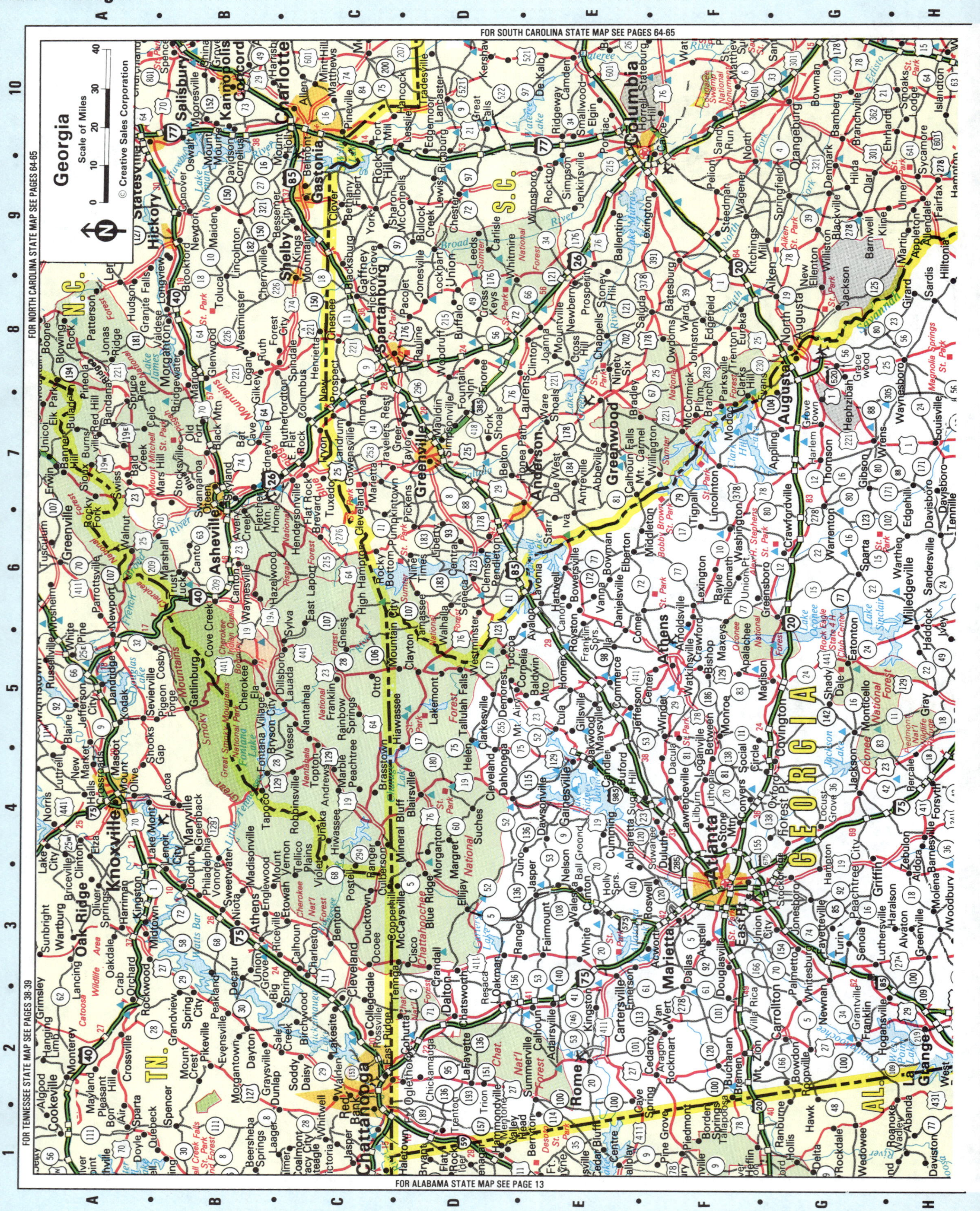
FOR NORTH CAROLINA STATE MAP SEE PAGES 64-65
FOR SOUTH CAROLINA STATE MAP SEE PAGES 64-65
FOR TENNESSEE STATE MAP SEE PAGES 38-39
FOR ALABAMA STATE MAP SEE PAGE 13
Georgia
Scale of Miles
0 10 20 30 40
© Creative Sales Corporation
N.C.
S.C.
TN.
AL.
GEORGIA
Atlanta
Athens
Augusta
Chattanooga
Knoxville
Asheville
Greenville
Spartanburg
Charlotte
Columbia
Anderson
Greenwood
Gastonia
Rome
Marietta
Gainesville
Oak Ridge
Hickory
Salisbury
Statesville
Shelby
LaGrange
Carrollton
Dalton

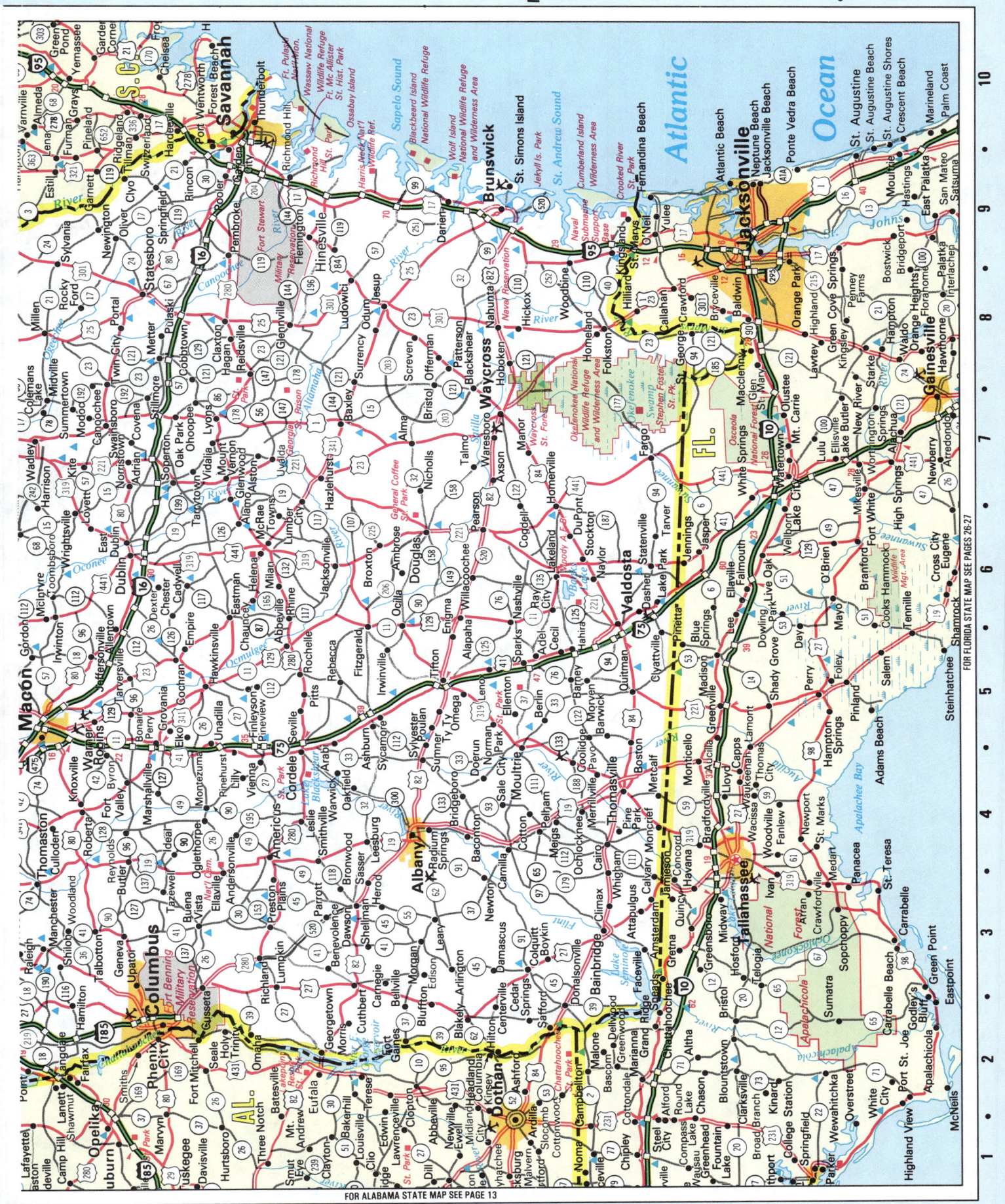

Hawaii

Scale of Miles
0 4 8 12 16 20

© Creative Sales Corporation

N

Maui (inset)

Kalahu Pt.
Waianapanapa St. Pk.
Mokuea Pt.
Hana
Kipahulu
Haleakala Crater
Haleakala Nat'l Park
Kaupo
Apole Pt.
Cape Hanamanioa
Keoneoio
Ulupalakua
Keokea
Makena
Wailea
Kihei
Kamaole Beach Park
Puunene
Kirei
Nukuele Pt.
31
Spreckelsville
37
378
377
Makawao
Haiku
Paia
36
Pauwela Pt.
Kahului
Wailuku
Iao Valley
340
30
Puunene
Maalaea
Olowalu
Hekili Pt.
Mopua
Waikapu
Lahaina
Honokahua
30
Nakalele Pt.
Kahakuloa Pt.
Waihee Pt.
Kahului Bay
Waiehu
Maluaea Bay
Pukalani

Maui
Pacific Ocean
Miles 0 2 4

Alenuihaha Channel

Molokai (inset)

Cape Halawa
Halawa
Waialua
Lamaloa Head
Kikipua Pt.
Pauwalu
Pukoo
Ujapue
Kamalo
450
Kaunakakai
Kamiloloa
Kualapuu
Kalae
Kalaupapa
Makanalua Pen.
Kahiu Pt.
460
Mauna Loa
Kolo
Lilo Pt.
Laau Pt.

Molokai
Pacific Ocean
Miles 0 2 4

Pailolo Channel
Kalohi Channel

Niihau (inset)

Kauai
Anahola
56
Lihue
Haena
Waiarea
Mana
Lawai
50

Niihau (Private)
Puuwai

Pacific Ocean
Kaulakahi Channel

Oahu (small inset)

Kahuku
83
Kahana
Kaneohe
Kailua
Pearl City
2
Honolulu
Waikiki
1
Haleiwa
Makaha
Nanakuli
Oahu

Pacific Ocean

Honolulu Co.
Maui Co.
Kaui Co.

Molokai/Lanai/Maui (center)

Halawa
Kualapuu
Kamalo
460
Kamalo
Koele
Lanai City
Lanai
Kaunolu
Kalohi Channel
Keomuku
Kaka Pt.
Kahoolawe
Kealaikahiki Channel
Auau Channel
Pailolo Channel

Halawa
Hana
360
Haleakala Nat'l Park
Ulupalakua
36
37
31
Kahului
Honokohau
Lahaina
30
Maui

HAWAII

Pailolo Channel

Hawaii (Big Island)

Waiakea
Pohoiki
Honohina
Papaikou
Hakalau
Hilo
Rainbow Falls
Keaau
130
Kaimu
Kaena Pt.
Pahoa
Kurtistown
Mountain View
Glenwood
Hawaii Volcanoes National Park
Apua Pt.
Punaluu Black Sand Beach
Honuapo
Naalehu
Kaalualu
Ka Lae
11
Waiohinu
Hookena
Honaunau
Napoopoo
Captain Cook
Kealakekua
Kainaliu
Kalaoa
19
Kailua
Keauhou
Keahole Pt.
Honokohau
Kukio
Kaupulehu
Puako
Kawaihae
250
270
Mahukona
Upolo Pt.
Hawi
Niulii
Kapaau
Kukuihaele
Honokaa
Paauilo
Ookala
Laupahoehoe
Papaaloa
190
200
Mauna Kea 13,796 ft.
Mauna Loa 13,680 ft.
Waimea
Waika
Waiki
Pepeekeo
Papaikou
Paukaa
Pahala
11
Hawaii

Oahu (large inset)

Mokapu Pt.
Kaneohe Marine Air Station
Kaneohe Bay
Kailua
Waimanalo
3
Kailua
72
Makapuu Pt.
Koko Head
Hawaii Kai
Sea Life Park
Waimanalo Bay
61
Pali Lookout
63
Kaneohe
Diamond Head
Waikiki
92
Honolulu
78
Aiea
99
Pearl City
Waipahu
Ewa
95
1
Barbers Pt.
Makakilo City
750
780
Range
Mililani Town
Schofield Barracks
Wahiawa
99
2
Waialua
Haleiwa
Sunset Beach
83
Kahuku
Laie
Polynesian Cultural Center
Hauula
Punaluu
Kahana
Sacred Falls
Koolau
Range
Kualoa Pt.
Kaaawa
Kahaluu
Kaena Pt.
Waianae
Maili
Nanakuli
Makaha
Kepuhi Pt.
Dillingham Air Force Base
930
Barbers Pt. Naval Air Sta.
Honolulu Int'l Airport

Oahu
Pacific Ocean
Kaena Pt.
Kaiwi Channel
Miles 0 2 4

Kauai (large inset)

Anahola
Moloaa
Kealia
Kapaa
Wailua
56
Hanamaulu
Lihue Airport
Nininí Pt.
Lihue
Nawiliwili
580
583
Puhi
50
Koloa
Poipu
Koheo Pt.
Makahuena Pt.
Lawai
Eleele
Kalaheo
Port Allen
Hanapepe
Waimea
Kekaha
550
Waimea Canyon
Kokee State Park
Kalalau
Mt. Waialeale 5243 ft.
Hanalei
Kilauea
Haena
Haena
Mana
Kaumakani
56

Kauai
Pacific Ocean
Miles 0 2 4

Idaho

Scale of Miles

0 20 40 60

© Creative Sales Corporation

N

Lake Michigan

FOR WISCONSIN STATE MAP SEE PAGES 86-87

WIS. IA. ILL. IND.

Kenosha · Winthrop Harbor · Zion · Waukegan · Lake Forest · Highland Park · Winnetka · Evanston · Skokie · Chicago · Hammond · Gary · Portage · Merrillville · Hebron

Antioch · Fox Lake · McHenry · Crystal Lake · Palatine · Schaumburg · Elgin · St. Charles · Wheaton · Elmhurst · Oak Park · Downers Gr. · Bolingbrook · Naperville · Aurora · Joliet · Chicago Heights · Crete · Bradley · Kankakee · Bourbonnais · Danville · Urbana · Champaign

Beloit · South Beloit · Machesney Park · Rockford · Belvidere · Woodstock · Marengo · Sycamore · De Kalb · Hinckley · Sandwich · Plano · Yorkville · Morris · Ottawa · Streator · Pontiac · Normal · Bloomington · Decatur · Springfield

Dubuque · East Dubuque · Galena · Freeport · Mount Morris · Dixon · Rock Falls · Sterling · Princeton · Peru · La Salle · Spring Valley · Mendota · Eureka · Washington · East Peoria · Pekin · Morton · Peoria · Lincoln

Cedar Rapids · Clinton · Bettendorf · Davenport · Rock Island · Moline · Silvis · Milan · Geneseo · Kewanee · Galesburg · Knoxville · Monmouth · Macomb · Canton · Havana · Petersburg · Jacksonville

Iowa City · Muskatine · Burlington · Ft. Madison · Keokuk · Carthage · Nauvoo · Warsaw · Hamilton · Quincy

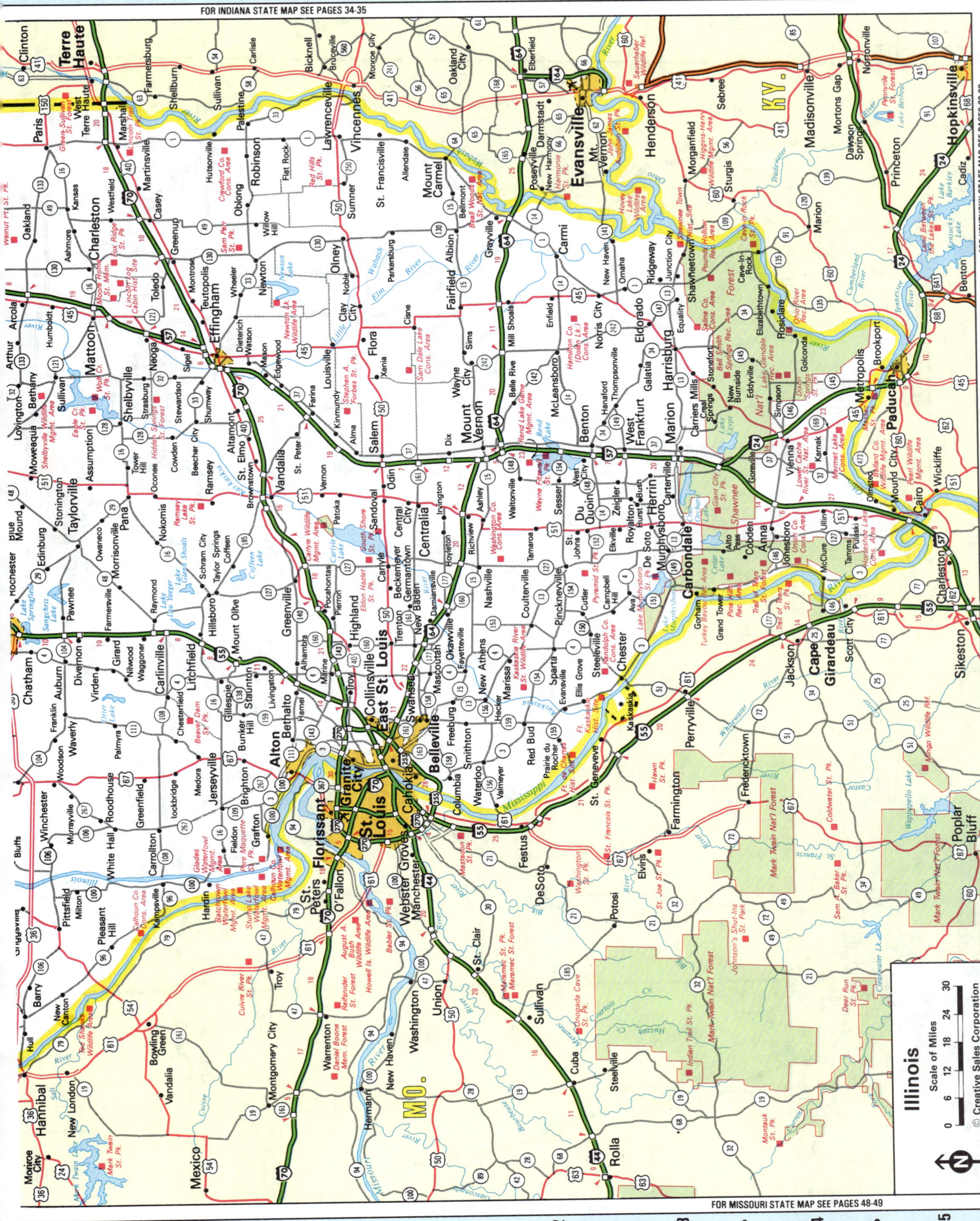

FOR INDIANA STATE MAP SEE PAGES 34-35

FOR KENTUCKY STATE MAP SEE PAGES 38-39

KY.

MO.

Illinois
Scale of Miles
0 6 12 18 24 30

© Creative Sales Corporation

N

Terre Haute · Clinton · Paris · Charleston · Mattoon · Effingham · Vandalia · Centralia · Mount Vernon · Fairfield · Carmi · Evansville · Henderson · Madisonville · Hopkinsville · Princeton · Cadiz · Salem · Flora · Olney · Lawrenceville · Vincennes · Robinson · Mount Carmel · Albion · Grayville · New Harmony · Harrisburg · Marion · Eldorado · Metropolis · Paducah · Cairo · Carbondale · Anna · Cape Girardeau · Chester · Sparta · Pinckneyville · Du Quoin · Benton · West Frankfort · Herrin · Murphysboro · Sikeston · Poplar Bluff · Rolla · Sullivan · Washington · Festus · De Soto · Farmington · Perryville · Ste. Genevieve · Belleville · East St. Louis · St. Louis · Granite City · Alton · Collinsville · Edwardsville · Litchfield · Carlinville · Jacksonville · Hannibal · Shelbyville · Pana · Taylorville · Hillsboro · Greenville · Highland · Mascoutah · Waterloo · Columbia

Mark Twain Nat'l Forest · Shawnee Nat'l Forest · Mississippi River · Ohio River · Wabash River · Kaskaskia River

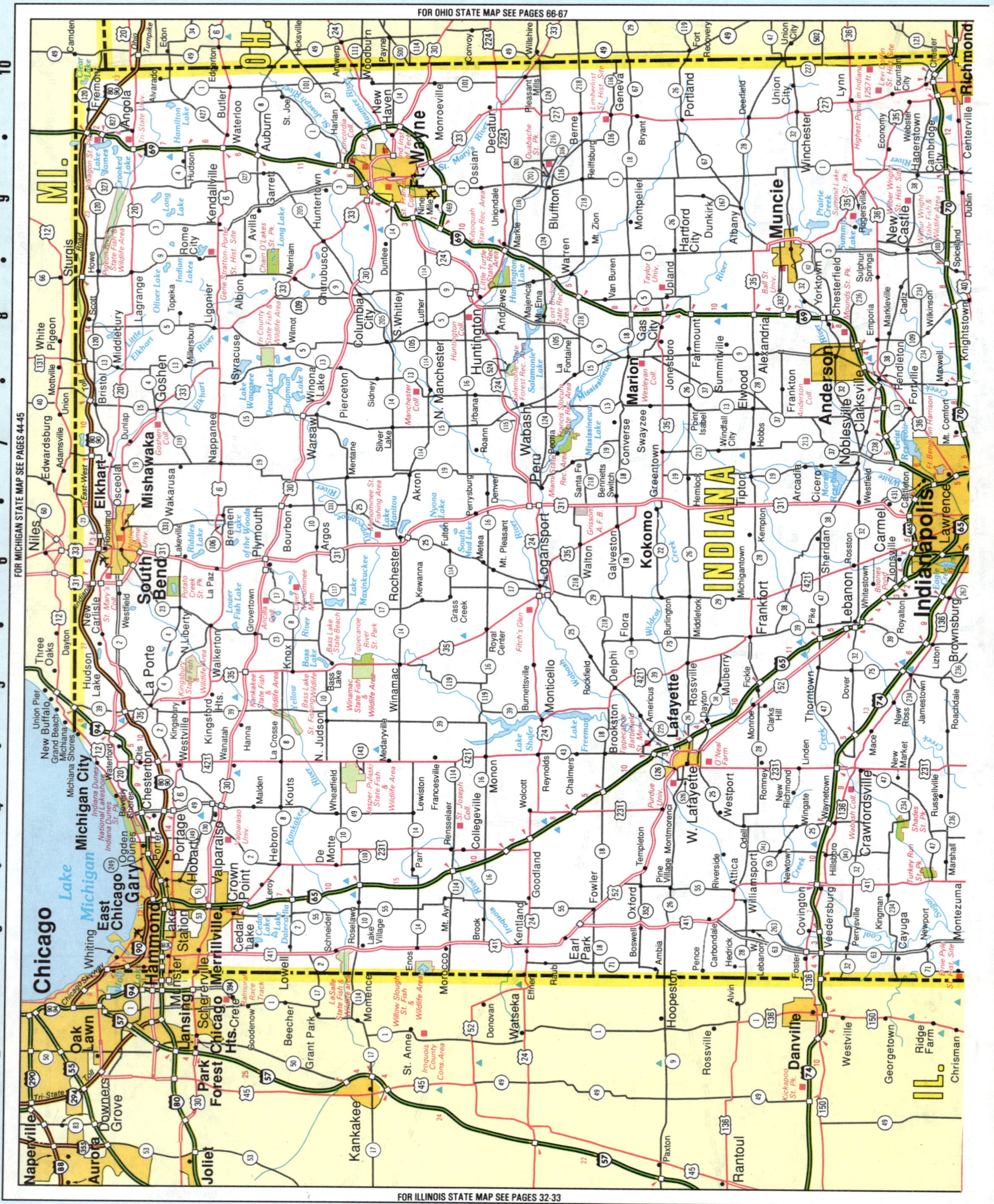

FOR OHIO STATE MAP SEE PAGES 66-67

FOR MICHIGAN STATE MAP SEE PAGES 44-45

FOR ILLINOIS STATE MAP SEE PAGES 32-33

OH

MI.

IL

INDIANA

Lake Michigan

Chicago

Fort Wayne

South Bend

Mishawaka

Elkhart

Muncie

Anderson

Indianapolis

Lafayette

W. Lafayette

Kokomo

Marion

Peru

Logansport

Wabash

Huntington

Warsaw

Columbia City

Richmond

New Castle

Danville

Michigan City

Gary

Hammond

East Chicago

Valparaiso

Crown Point

Portage

Hobart

Merrillville

Naperville

Aurora

Joliet

Oak Lawn

Park Forest

Downers Grove

Goshen

Angola

Auburn

Decatur

Bluffton

Portland

Winchester

Union City

Hartford City

Noblesville

Carmel

Lebanon

Crawfordsville

Monticello

Rochester

Plymouth

La Porte

Rensselaer

Kankakee

Watseka

Hoopeston

FOR OHIO STATE MAP SEE PAGES 66-67

Indiana
Scale of Miles
0 5 10 15 20
© Creative Sales Corporation

KY.

FOR KENTUCKY STATE MAP SEE PAGES 38-39

FOR ILLINOIS STATE MAP SEE PAGES 32-33

Connersville, Rushville, Greenfield, Greenwood, Speedway, Beech Grove, Southport, Mooresville, Whiteland, Franklin, Shelbyville, Columbus, Bloomington, Martinsville, Spencer, Greencastle, Brazil, Terre Haute, Sullivan, Vincennes, Washington, Bedford, Bloomfield, Linton, Mitchell, Paoli, Salem, Orleans, French Lick, Jasper, Huntingburg, Petersburg, Princeton, Evansville, Owensboro, Henderson, Mt. Vernon, Tell City, Cannelton, Corydon, New Albany, Jeffersonville, Louisville, Charlestown, Madison, Versailles, Batesville, Greensburg, Brookville, Liberty, Oxford, Lawrenceburg, Rising Sun, Vevay, Frankfort, Shelbyville, New Castle, Bardstown, Radcliff

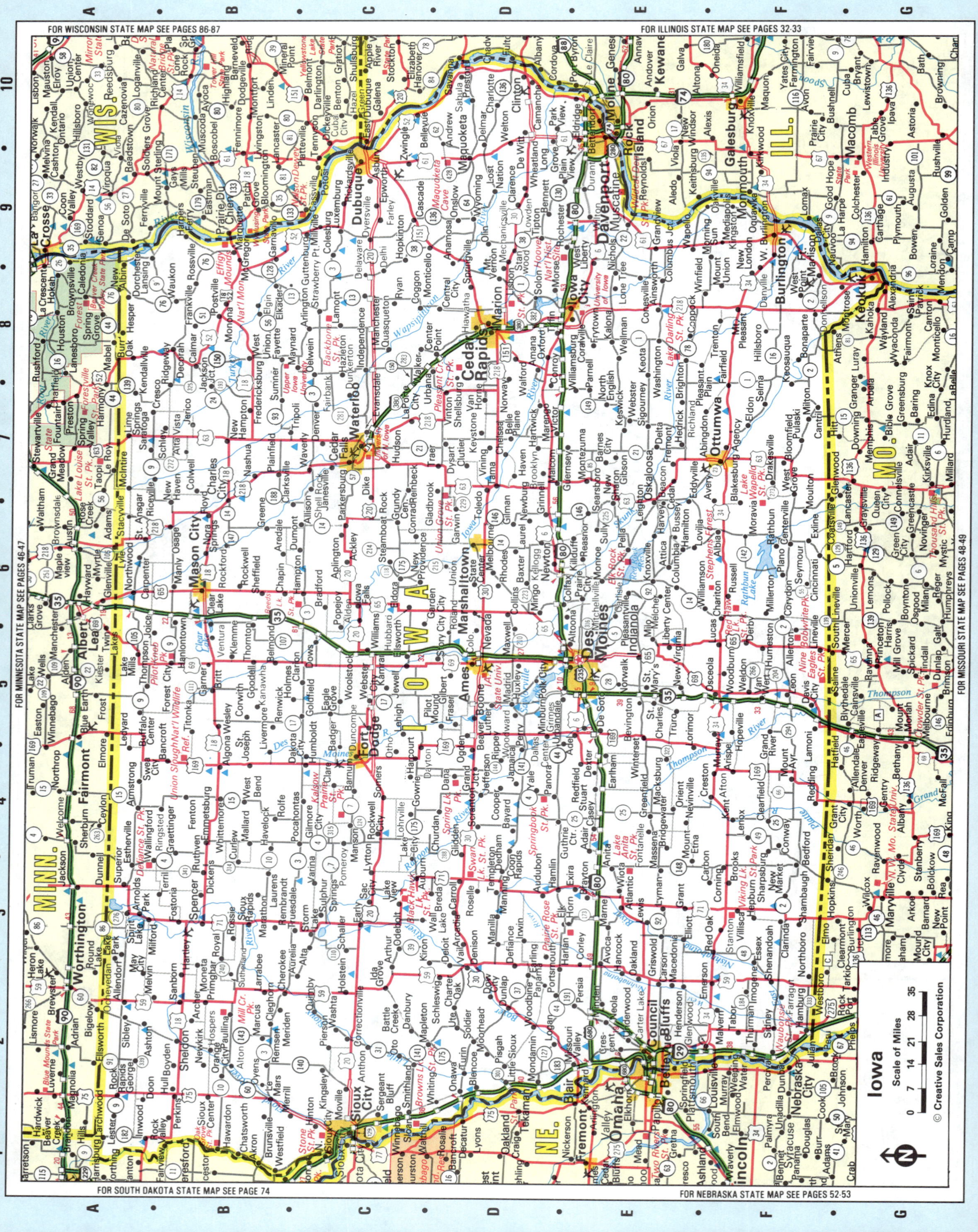
FOR WISCONSIN STATE MAP SEE PAGES 86-87
FOR ILLINOIS STATE MAP SEE PAGES 32-33
FOR MINNESOTA STATE MAP SEE PAGES 46-47
FOR MISSOURI STATE MAP SEE PAGES 48-49
FOR SOUTH DAKOTA STATE MAP SEE PAGE 74
FOR NEBRASKA STATE MAP SEE PAGES 52-53
MINN.
WIS.
ILL.
MO.
NE.
IOWA
Des Moines
Cedar Rapids
Davenport
Waterloo
Dubuque
Sioux City
Council Bluffs
Iowa City
Ames
Mason City
Fort Dodge
Ottumwa
Burlington
Marshalltown
Clinton
Keokuk
Iowa
Scale of Miles
0 7 14 21 28 35
© Creative Sales Corporation

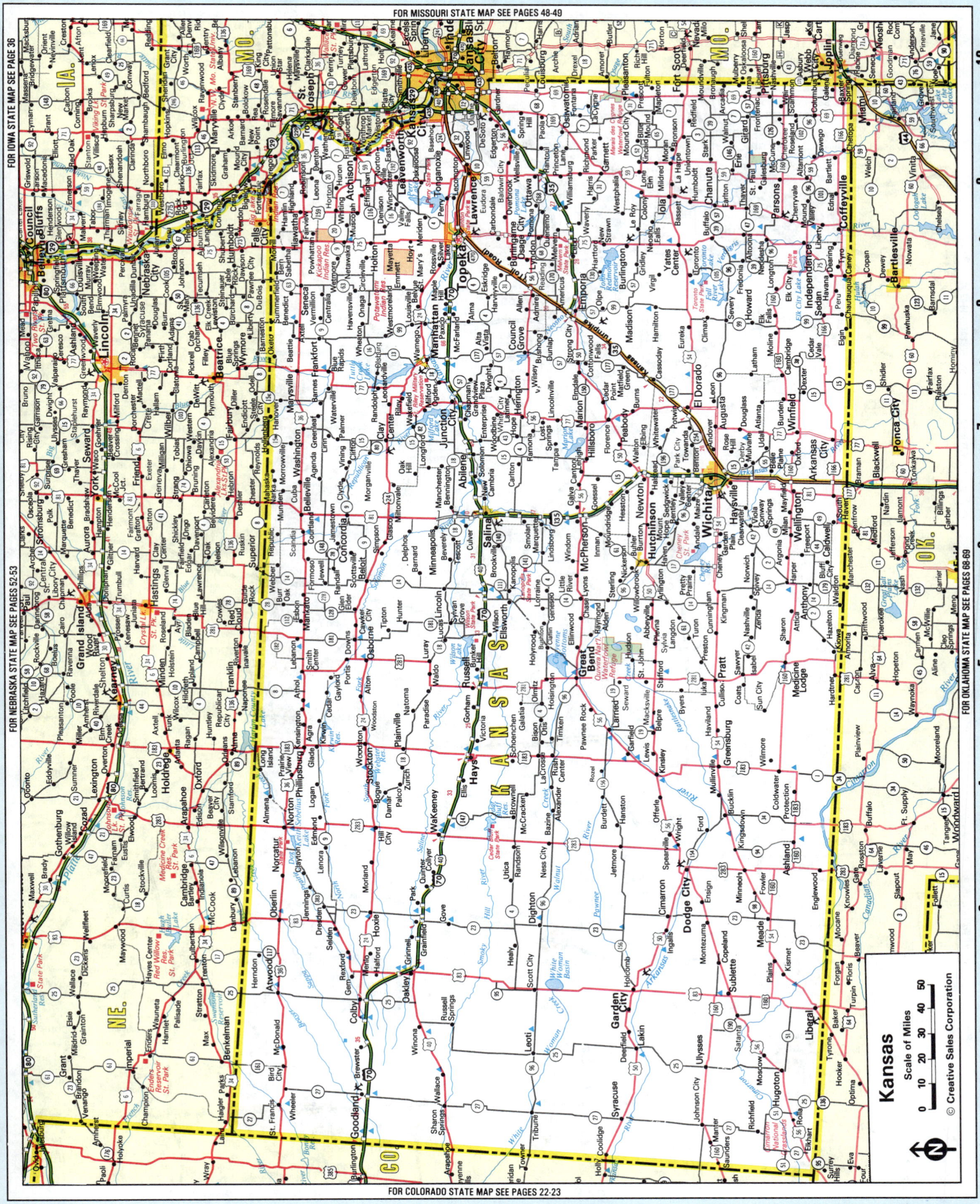

FOR IOWA STATE MAP SEE PAGE 36

FOR MISSOURI STATE MAP SEE PAGES 48-49

FOR NEBRASKA STATE MAP SEE PAGES 52-53

FOR OKLAHOMA STATE MAP SEE PAGES 68-69

FOR COLORADO STATE MAP SEE PAGES 22-23

Kansas

Scale of Miles

0 10 20 30 40 50

© Creative Sales Corporation

IA MO NE CO OK

Council Bluffs · St. Joseph · Kansas City · Leavenworth · Lawrence · Topeka · Atchison · Hiawatha · Falls City · Beatrice · Lincoln · Manhattan · Junction City · Abilene · Salina · Emporia · Council Grove · Ottawa · Chanute · Parsons · Coffeyville · Bartlesville · Independence · Winfield · Arkansas City · Ponca City · Wichita · Hutchinson · Newton · McPherson · Wellington · Great Bend · Hays · Russell · Dodge City · Garden City · Liberal · Colby · Goodland · Grand Island · Hastings · Kearney · McCook

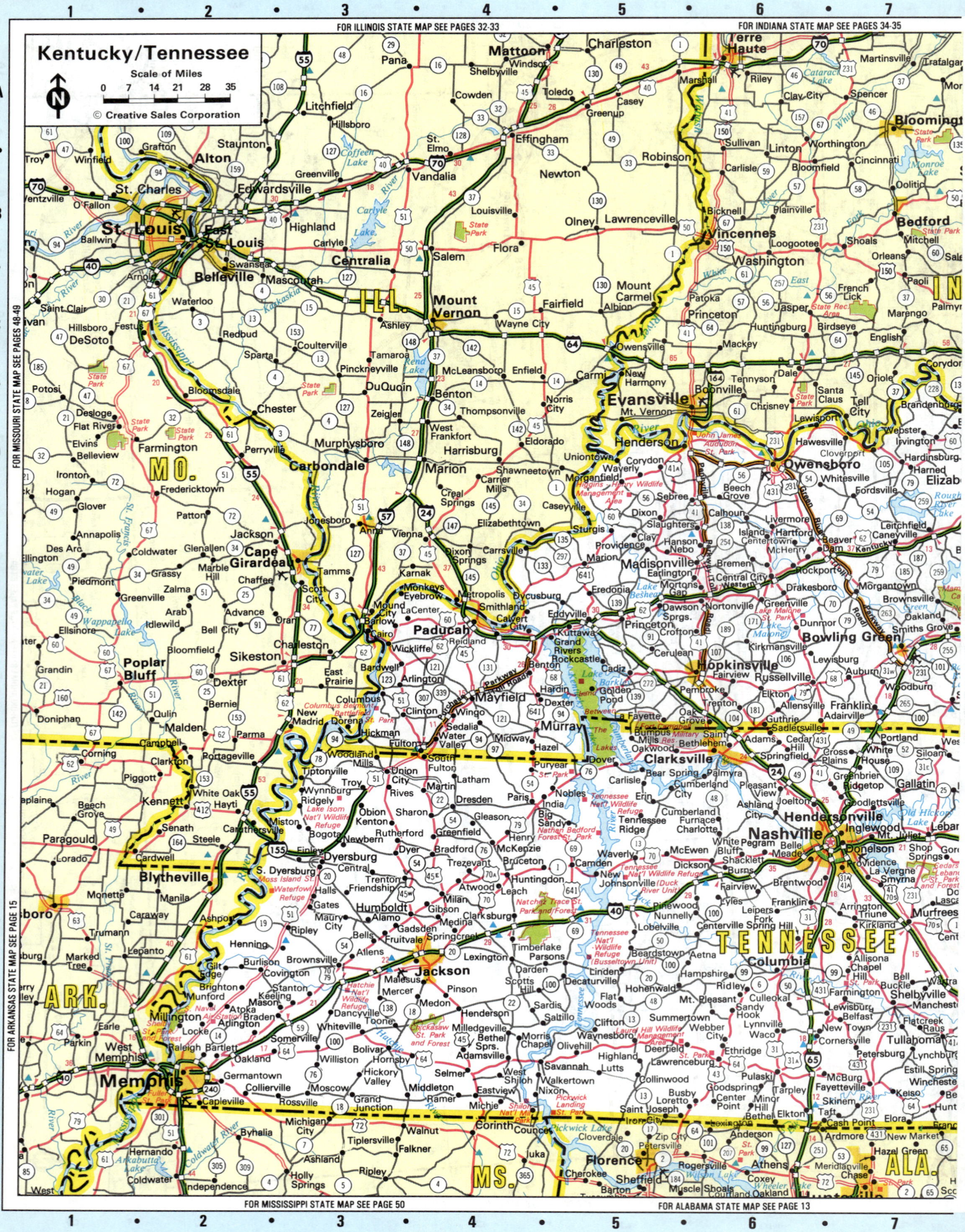
Kentucky/Tennessee
Scale of Miles
0 7 14 21 28 35
© Creative Sales Corporation
FOR ILLINOIS STATE MAP SEE PAGES 32-33
FOR INDIANA STATE MAP SEE PAGES 34-35
FOR MISSOURI STATE MAP SEE PAGES 48-49
FOR ARKANSAS STATE MAP SEE PAGE 15
FOR MISSISSIPPI STATE MAP SEE PAGE 50
FOR ALABAMA STATE MAP SEE PAGE 13
ILL.
MO.
IN
ARK.
MS.
ALA.
TENNESSEE
St. Louis
East St. Louis
Belleville
Alton
St. Charles
Centralia
Mount Vernon
Carbondale
Marion
Paducah
Evansville
Henderson
Owensboro
Hopkinsville
Bowling Green
Clarksville
Nashville
Murfreesboro
Columbia
Jackson
Memphis
Cape Girardeau
Poplar Bluff
Sikeston
Blytheville
Dyersburg
Murray
Mayfield
Vincennes
Terre Haute
Mattoon
Charleston
Effingham
Florence
Huntsville

FOR OHIO STATE MAP SEE PAGES 66-67

FOR WEST VIRGINIA STATE MAP SEE PAGES 82-83

FOR VIRGINIA STATE MAP SEE PAGES 82-83

FOR VIRGINIA STATE MAP SEE PAGES 64-65

FOR NORTH CAROLINA STATE MAP SEE PAGES 64-65

FOR SOUTH CAROLINA STATE MAP SEE PAGES 64-65

FOR ALABAMA STATE MAP SEE PAGE 13

FOR GEORGIA STATE MAP SEE PAGES 28-29

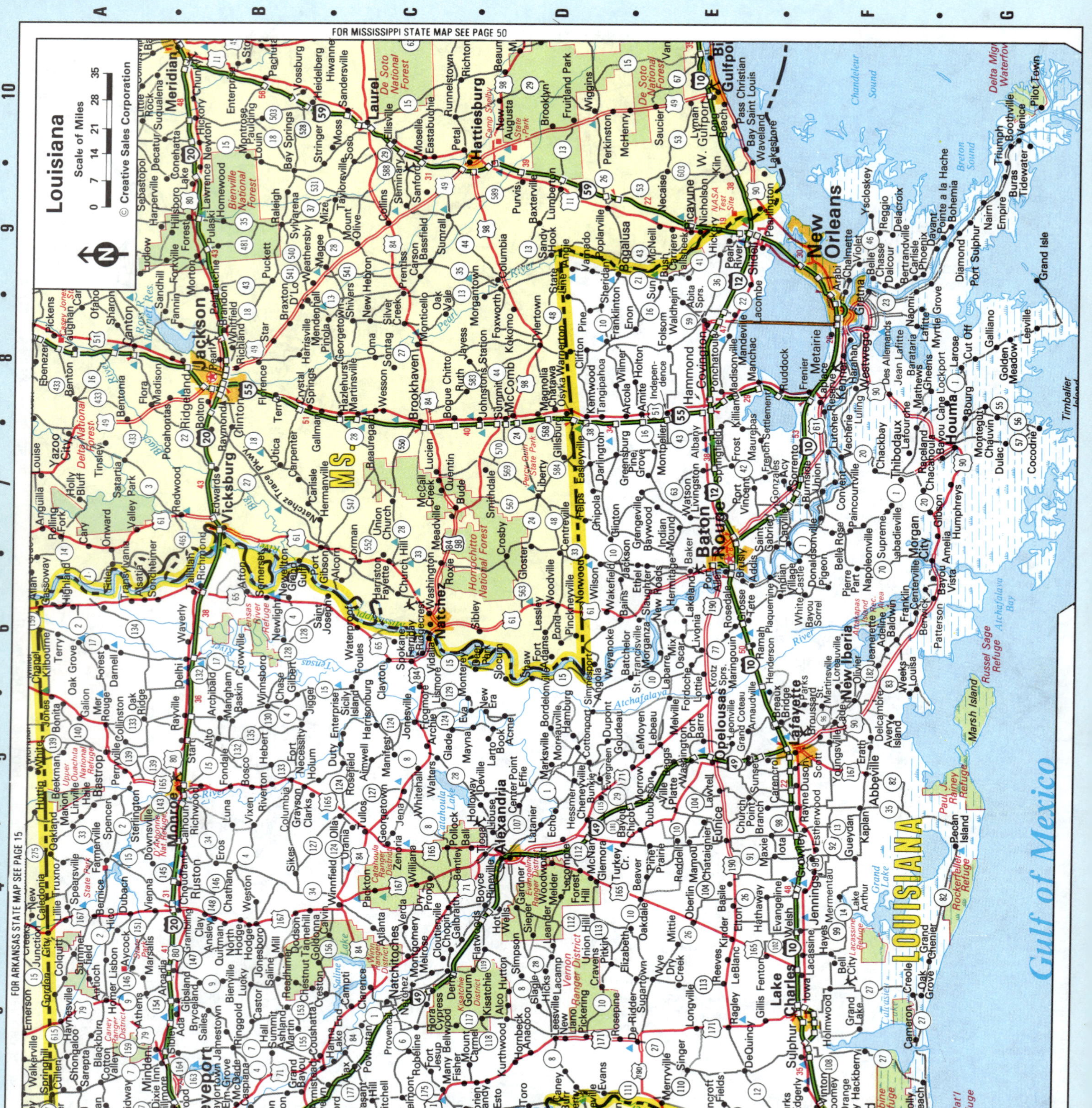

FOR MISSISSIPPI STATE MAP SEE PAGE 50
FOR ARKANSAS STATE MAP SEE PAGE 15
FOR TEXAS STATE MAP SEE PAGES 75-79
Louisiana
Scale of Miles
0 7 14 21 28 35
© Creative Sales Corporation
LOUISIANA
MS
TEX
Gulf of Mexico
Shreveport
Monroe
Alexandria
Lafayette
Baton Rouge
New Orleans
Lake Charles
Natchez
Vicksburg
Jackson
Hattiesburg
Meridian
Laurel
Gulfport
Beaumont
Port Arthur
Houma
Opelousas
Natchitoches
New Iberia
Ruston
Bastrop
Orange
Chandeleur Sound
Breton Sound
Marsh Island
Atchafalaya Bay
Kisatchie National Forest
De Soto National Forest
Homochitto National Forest
Bienville National Forest
Sabine National Forest
Angelina National Forest
Delta National Forest

Maine

Scale of Miles

0 7 14 21 28 35

N

© Creative Sales Corporation

Atlantic Ocean

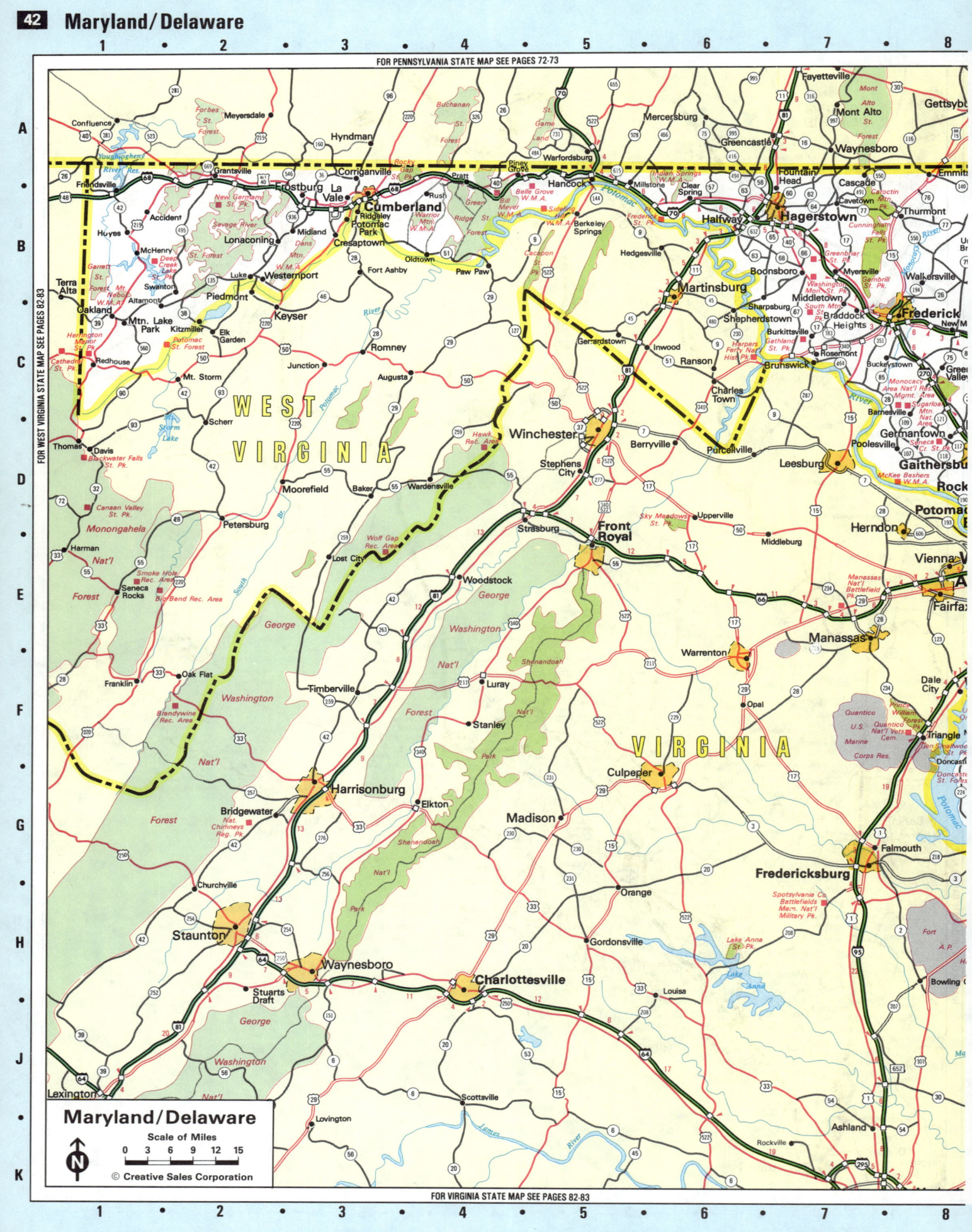

FOR PENNSYLVANIA STATE MAP SEE PAGES 72-73

FOR WEST VIRGINIA STATE MAP SEE PAGES 82-83

WEST VIRGINIA

VIRGINIA

Maryland/Delaware

Scale of Miles

0 3 6 9 12 15

N

© Creative Sales Corporation

FOR VIRGINIA STATE MAP SEE PAGES 82-83

FOR PENNSYLVANIA STATE MAP SEE PAGE 72-73

FOR NEW JERSEY STATE MAP SEE PAGES 56-57

FOR VIRGINIA STATE MAP SEE PAGES 82-83

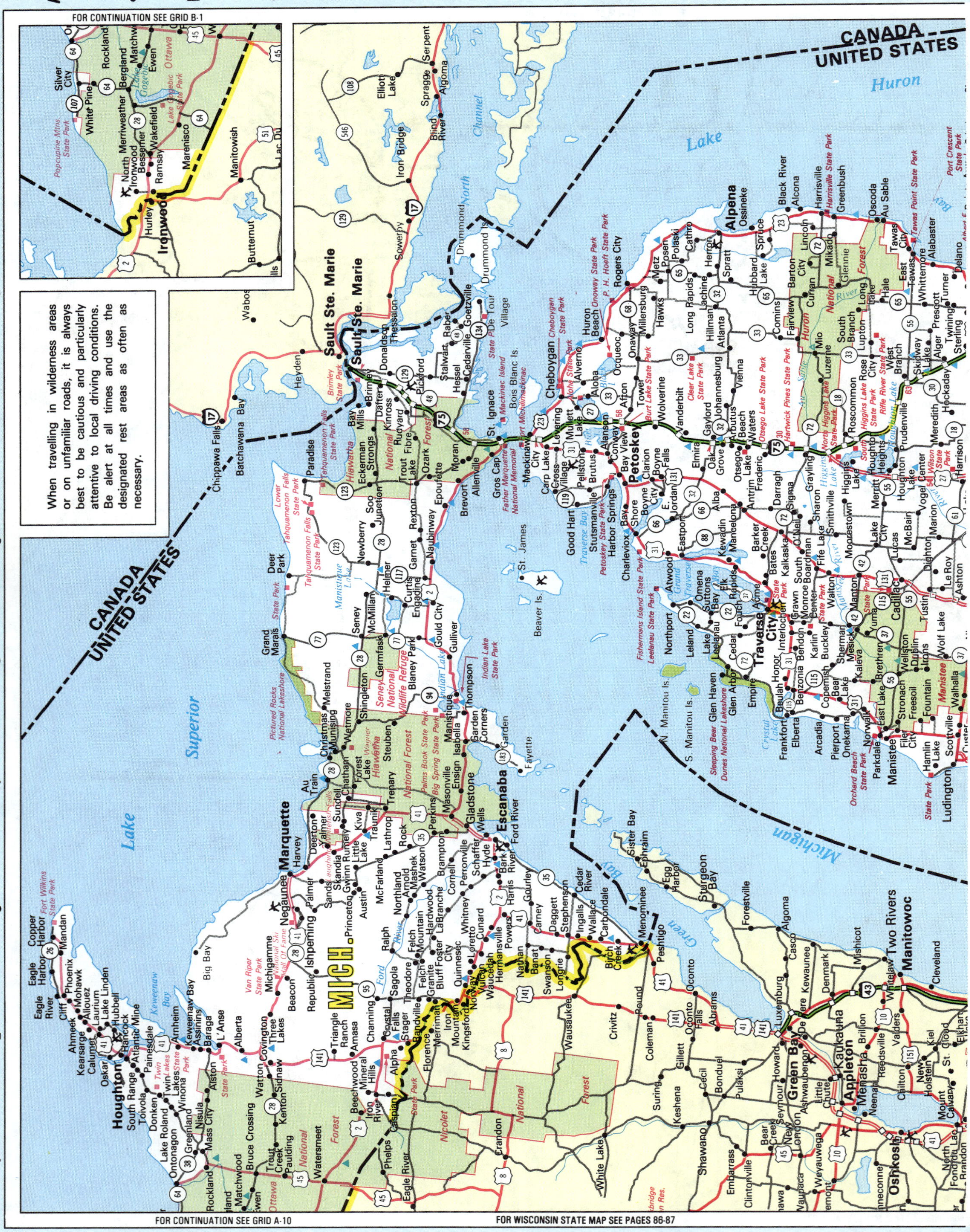

FOR CONTINUATION SEE GRID B-1
FOR CONTINUATION SEE GRID A-10
FOR WISCONSIN STATE MAP SEE PAGES 86-87
When travelling in wilderness areas or on unfamiliar roads, it is always best to be cautious and particularly attentive to local driving conditions. Be alert at all times and use the designated rest areas as often as necessary.
CANADA
UNITED STATES
Lake Superior
Lake Huron
Lake Michigan
Green Bay
North Channel
MICH.
Sault Ste. Marie
Marquette
Escanaba
Petoskey
Traverse City
Cheboygan
Alpena
Cadillac
Ironwood
Houghton
Green Bay
Appleton
Oshkosh
Manitowoc
Two Rivers
Hiawatha National Forest
Ottawa National Forest
Huron National Forest
Manistee National Forest
Nicolet National Forest
Seney National Wildlife Refuge
Pictured Rocks National Lakeshore
Sleeping Bear Dunes National Lakeshore

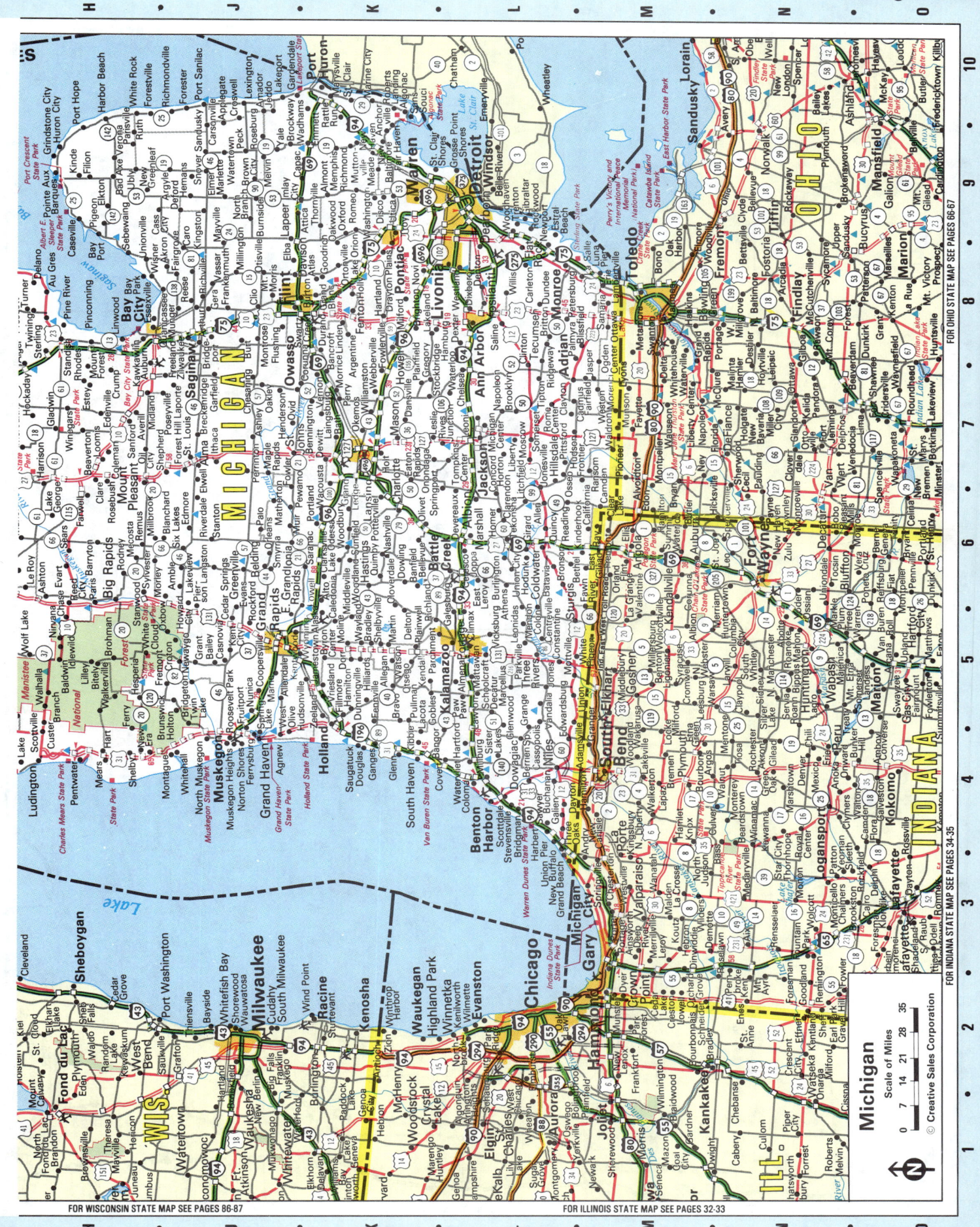

Michigan

Scale of Miles

© Creative Sales Corporation

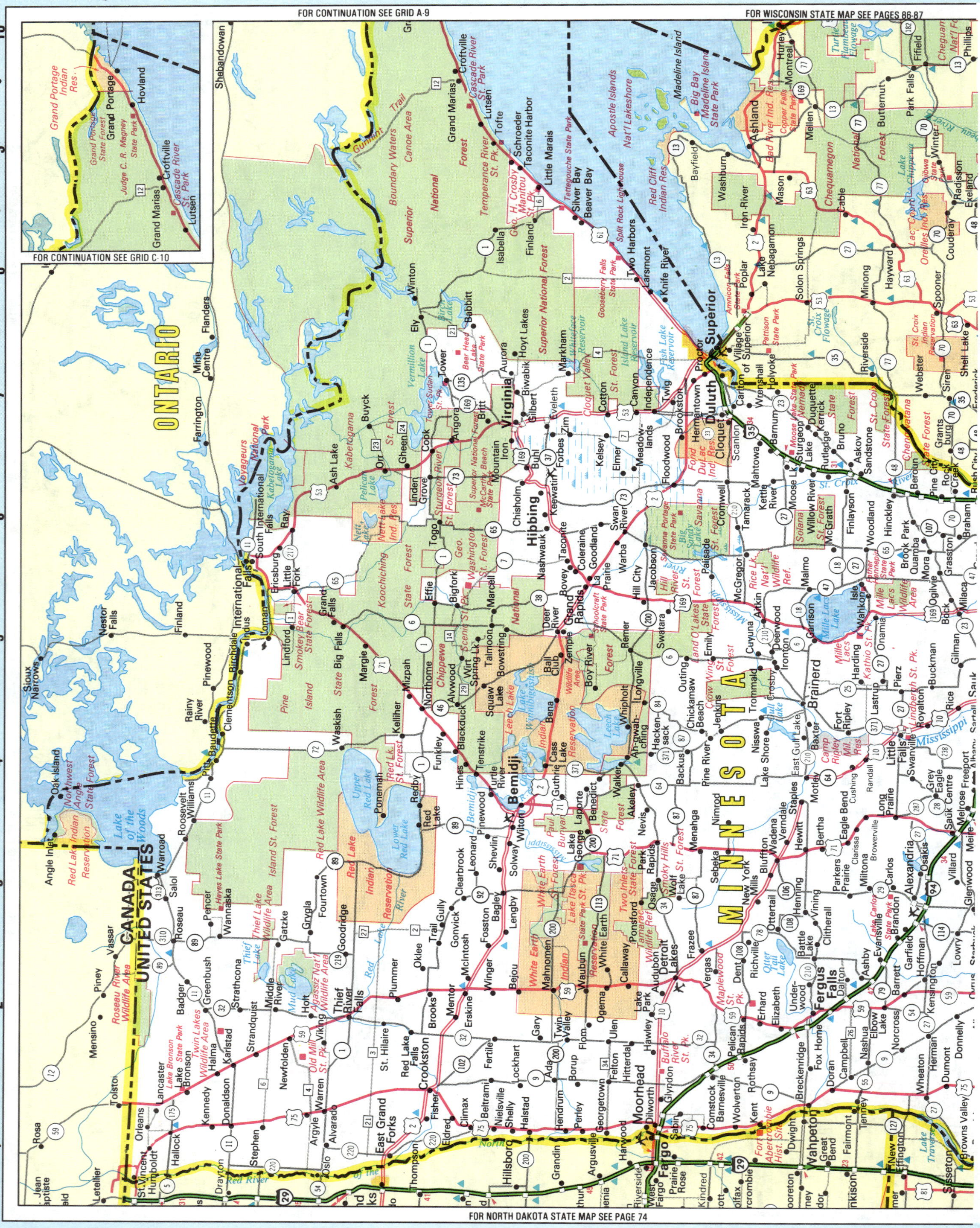
FOR CONTINUATION SEE GRID A-9
FOR WISCONSIN STATE MAP SEE PAGES 86-87
FOR CONTINUATION SEE GRID C-10
FOR NORTH DAKOTA STATE MAP SEE PAGE 74
ONTARIO
CANADA
UNITED STATES
MINNESOTA
Lake of the Woods
Upper Red Lake
Lower Red Lake
Mille Lacs Lake
Grand Portage
Grand Marais
Lutsen
Duluth
Superior
Cloquet
Virginia
Hibbing
Grand Rapids
Bemidji
International Falls
Thief River Falls
Crookston
East Grand Forks
Moorhead
Fargo
Detroit Lakes
Fergus Falls
Wahpeton
Alexandria
Brainerd
Ashland
Roseau
Warroad
Baudette
Ely
Two Harbors
Boundary Waters Canoe Area
Superior National Forest
Chippewa National Forest
Voyageurs National Park

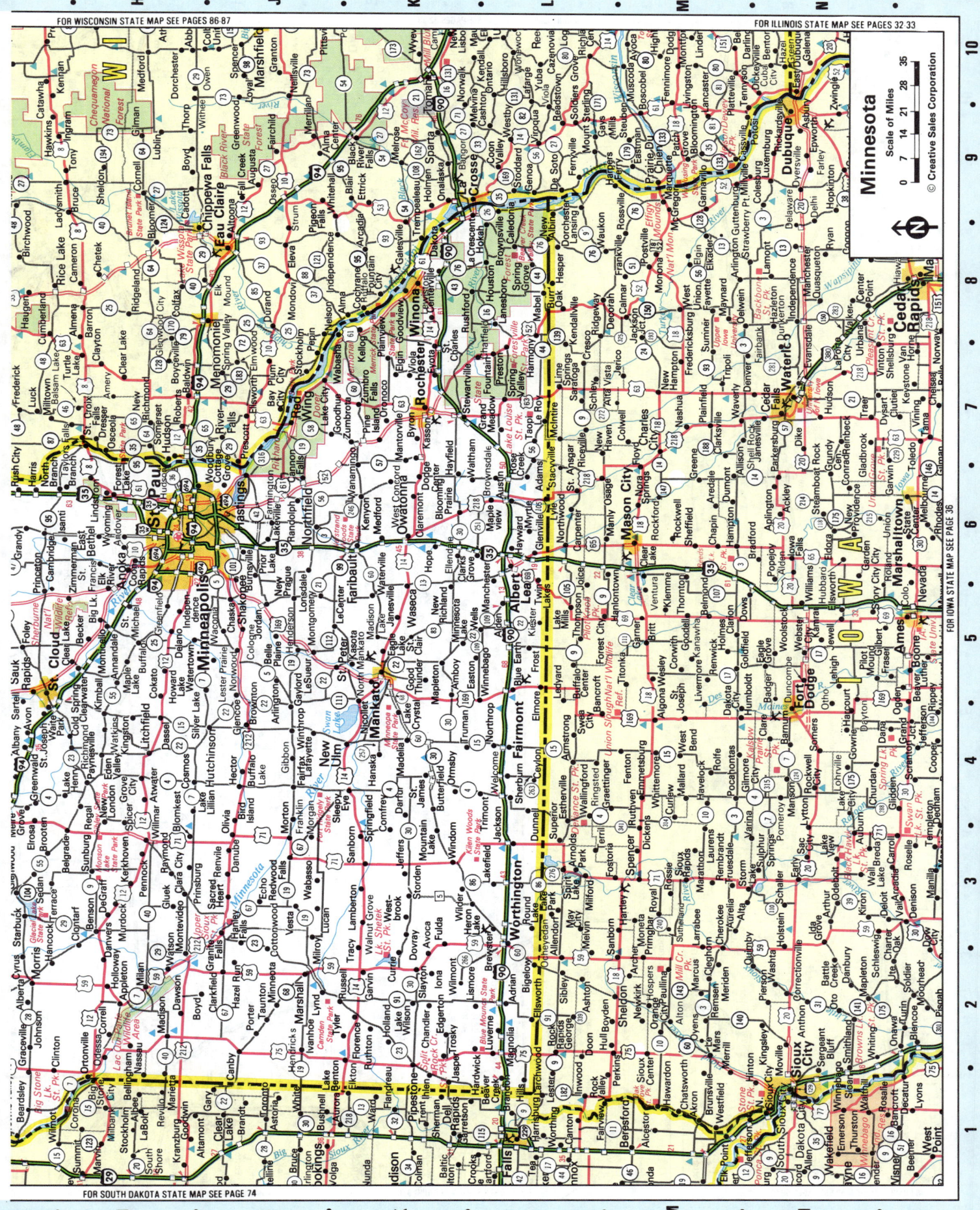

FOR WISCONSIN STATE MAP SEE PAGES 86-87
FOR ILLINOIS STATE MAP SEE PAGES 32-33
FOR SOUTH DAKOTA STATE MAP SEE PAGE 74
FOR IOWA STATE MAP SEE PAGE 36

Minnesota

Scale of Miles

0   7   14   28   35

© Creative Sales Corporation

FOR ILLINOIS STATE MAP SEE PAGES 32-33

FOR CONTINUATION SEE GRID D-1

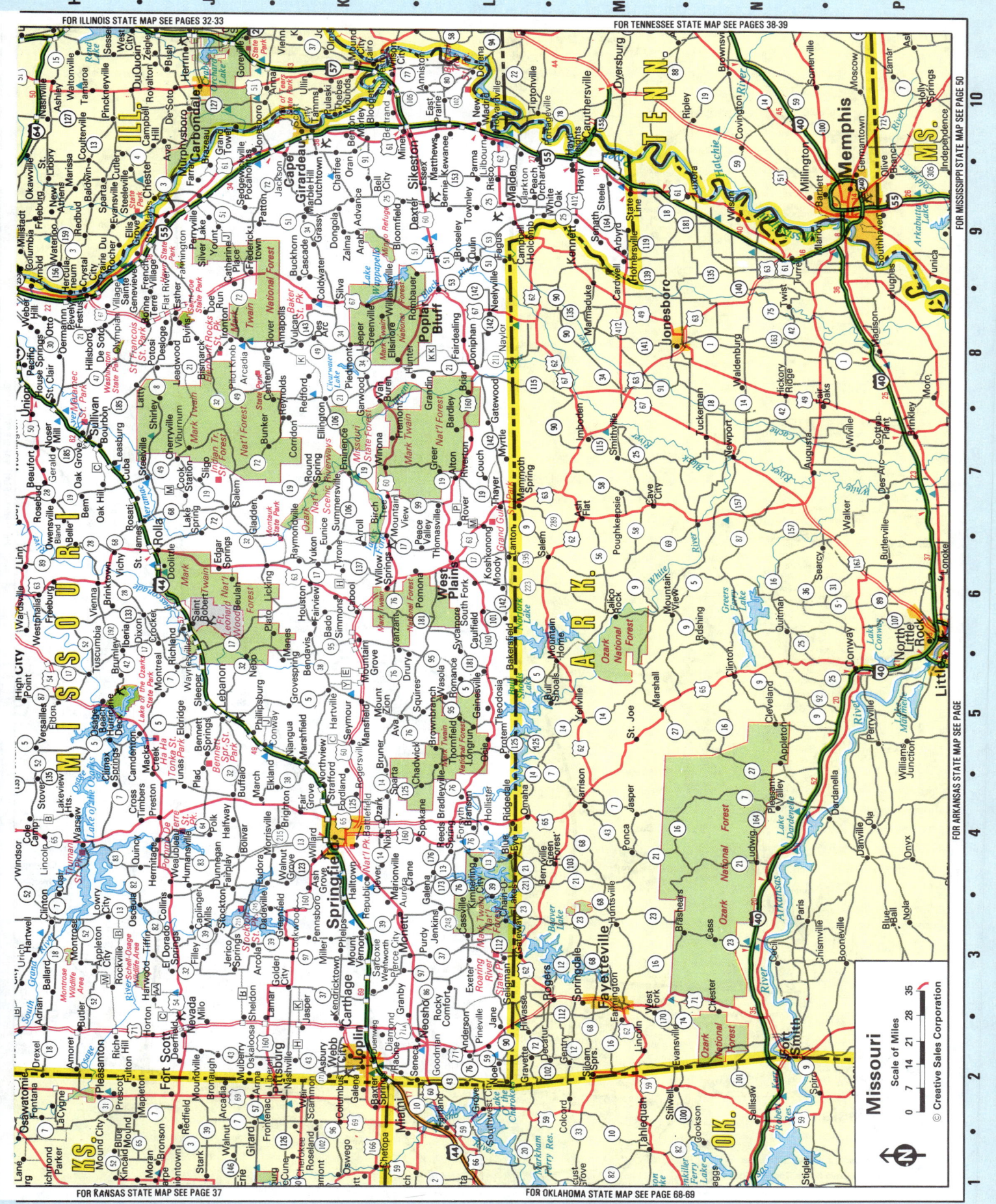

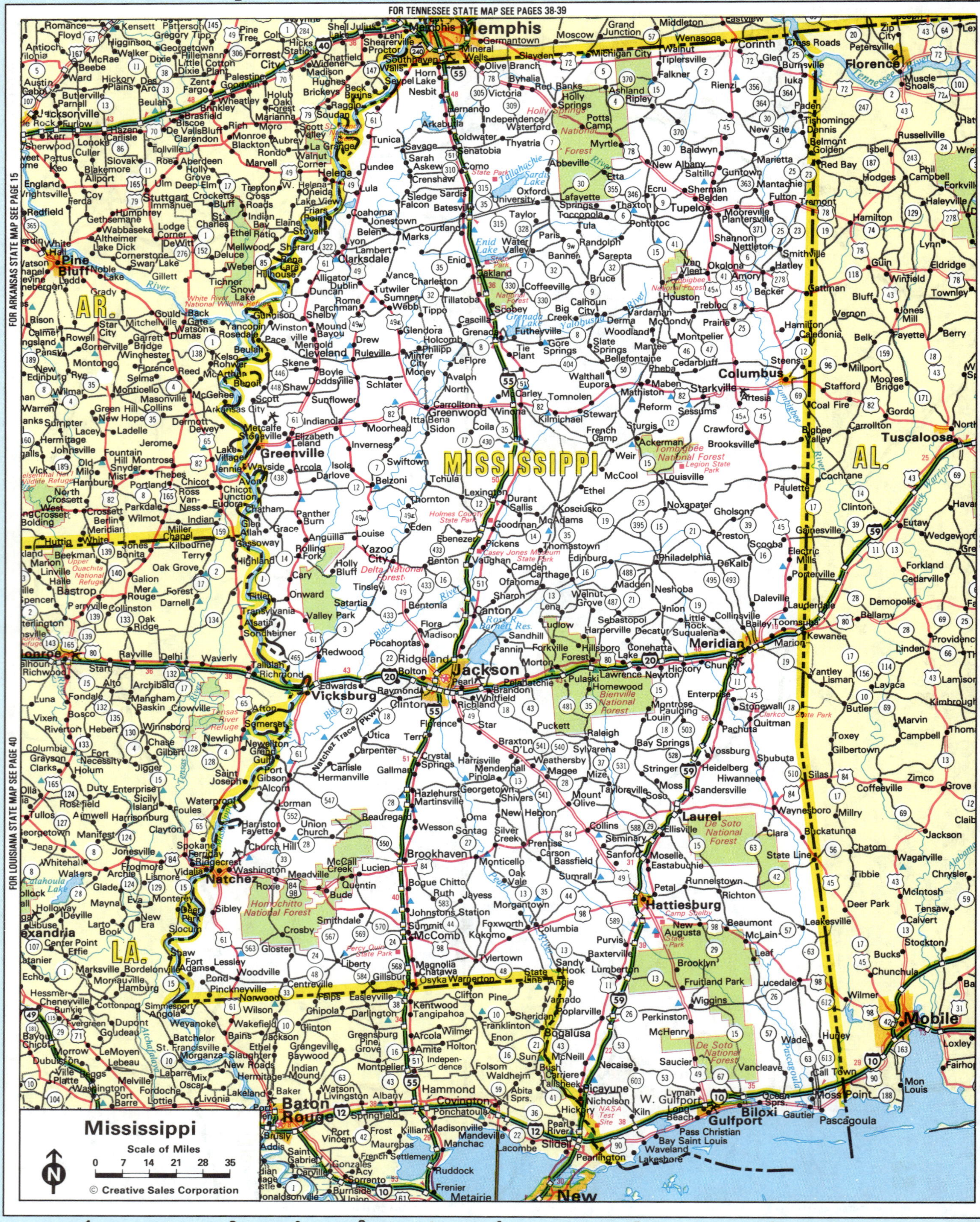
FOR TENNESSEE STATE MAP SEE PAGES 38-39
FOR ARKANSAS STATE MAP SEE PAGE 15
FOR LOUISIANA STATE MAP SEE PAGE 40
FOR ALABAMA STATE MAP SEE PAGE 13
MISSISSIPPI
AR.
AL.
LA.
Memphis
Jackson
Vicksburg
Greenville
Natchez
Meridian
Columbus
Tupelo
Hattiesburg
Laurel
Gulfport
Biloxi
Pascagoula
Mobile
Tuscaloosa
Baton Rouge
Pine Bluff
Corinth
Florence
Oxford
Greenwood
Clarksdale
Brookhaven
McComb
Starkville
Mississippi
Scale of Miles
0 7 14 21 28 35
N
© Creative Sales Corporation

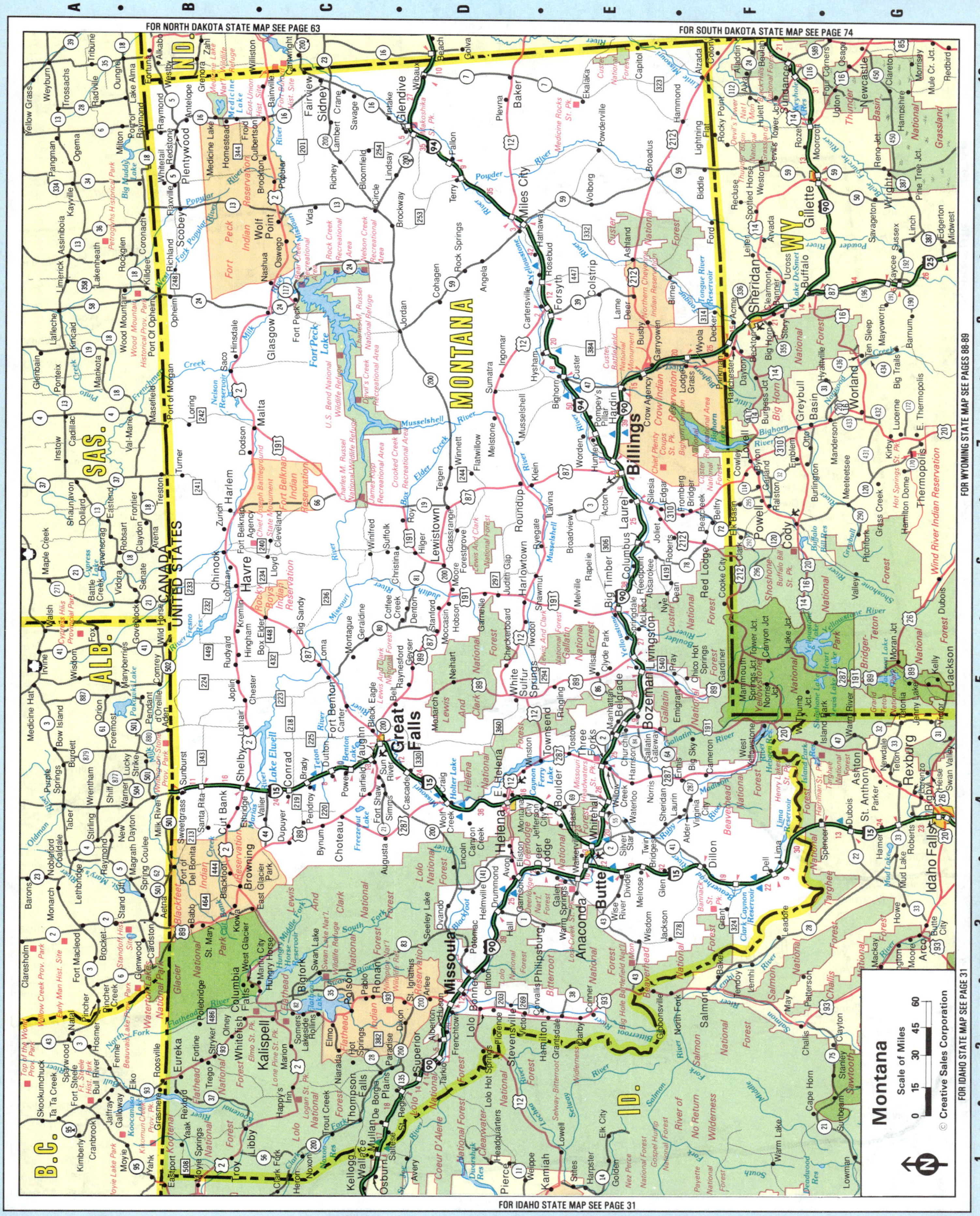

FOR NORTH DAKOTA STATE MAP SEE PAGE 63

FOR SOUTH DAKOTA STATE MAP SEE PAGE 74

FOR WYOMING STATE MAP SEE PAGES 88-89

FOR IDAHO STATE MAP SEE PAGE 31

MONTANA

CANADA
UNITED STATES

B.C. ALB. SAS.

N.D.

WY.

ID.

Major cities: Billings, Great Falls, Missoula, Butte, Helena, Bozeman, Kalispell, Havre, Glendive, Sidney, Miles City, Forsyth, Hardin, Livingston, Anaconda, Dillon, Glasgow, Wolf Point, Lewistown, Shelby, Conrad, Cut Bank, Browning, Polson, Whitefish, Columbia Falls, Bigfork, Deer Lodge, Red Lodge, Laurel, Columbus, Big Timber, Three Forks, Townsend, White Sulphur Springs, Roundup, Circle, Baker, Broadus, Colstrip, Ashland, Sidney, Fairview

Fort Peck Indian Reservation
Fort Belknap Indian Reservation
Rocky Boys Indian Reservation
Blackfeet Indian Reservation
Flathead Indian Reservation
Crow Indian Reservation
Northern Cheyenne Indian Reservation

Glacier National Park
Yellowstone National Park
Flathead National Forest
Lolo National Forest
Bitterroot National Forest
Gallatin National Forest
Custer National Forest
Helena National Forest
Beaverhead National Forest
Lewis And Clark National Forest
Kootenai National Forest

Fort Peck Lake
Flathead Lake

Missouri River
Yellowstone River
Milk River

Scale of Miles
0 15 30 45 60

© Creative Sales Corporation

Montana

FOR SOUTH DAKOTA STATE MAP SEE PAGE 74

WY

Mule Cr. Jct.
Lance Creek
Redbird
Edgemont
Gap
Hot Springs
Cheyenne
Pine Ridge
Indian Reservation
Kyle
Long Valley
White River
Wood

Provo
Buffalo Gap National Grassland
Angostura Res.
Oelrichs
Oglala
Wounded Knee
Wounded Knee Battle Site
Allen
Martin
Batesland
Rosebud
Parmelee
Okreek Mission

Manville
Lusk
Node
Oglala National Grasslands
Pine Ridge
Saint Francis
Rosebud Indian Reservation

Van Tassell
Harrison
Whitney
Chadron
Merriman
Eli
Cody
Nenzel
Kilgore
Crookston
Sparks
Norder

Jay Em
Fort Robinson State Park
Crawford
Rushville
Clinton
Gordon
Cottonwood Lake St. Pk.
Valentine
Ft. Niobrara Nat'l Wildlife Refuge
Niobrara

Fort Laramie
Lingle
Chandron St. Park
Hay Springs
Nebraska Nat'l Forest
Walgren Lake St. Pk.
Box Butte Res. St. Pk.
Samuel R. McKelvie Nat'l Forest
Merritt Res.
Wood Lake
Johnst

Agate Fossil Beds Nat'l Mon.
Marsland
Niobrara
Snake
River
Valentine Nat'l Wildlife Ref.
Ainsworth

Torrington
Huntley
Yoder
Morrill
Mitchell
Scottsbluff
Hemingford
Alliance
North Platte Nat'l Wildlife Ref.
Antioch
North
Brownlee
Elsmere
Purdum
Halsey

Hawk Sprs.
Terrytown
Gering
Minatare
Bayard
Angora
Lakeside
Ellsworth
Bingham
Hyannis
Whitman
Mullen
Seneca
Thedford
N E B R

La Grange
Melbeta
McGrew
Ashby
Dunning
Nebraska National Forest

Albin
Harrisburg
Bridgeport
Broadwater
Crescent Lake National Wildlife Refuge
Arthur
Loup

Egbert
Bushnell
Kimball
Dix
Potter
Dalton
Gurley
Lisco
North Platte River
Oshkosh
Tryon
Stapleton
Gandy
Anselmo
Victo
Arnold

Oliver Res. St. Pk.
Sidney
Lodgepole
Lewellen
Ash Hollow St. Hist. Pk.
LeMoyne
Lake McConaughy State Park
Buffalo Bill St. Hist. Pk.
Arnold Lake St. Pk.
Brok

Chappell
Big Springs
Brule
Ogallala
Lake C.W. McConaughy
Keystone
Paxton
Sutherland
North Platte
Callawa

Sedgwick
Ovid
Julesburg
Crook
Sutherland Res.
Hershey
Maxwell
Brady
Gothenburg

Proctor
Sterling Res.
Grant
Elsie
Wallace
Moorefield
Willow Island
Cozad

Briggsdale
Buckingham
Raymer
Stoneham
Willard
Fleming
Haxtun
Paoli
Amherst
Brandon
Venango
Madrid
Grainton
Dickens
Wellfleet
Maywood
Farnam
Eustis
Johnsom St. Pk.

Jackson Lake Res.
Weldona
Snyder
Menno
Holyoke
Imperial
Moorefield
Curtis
Stockville
Elwood

Orchard
Log Lane Village
Clarkville
Champion
Enders
Wauneta
Hayes Center
Red Willow Res. St. Pk.
Hugh Butler Lake
Medicine Creek Res. St. Pk.
Smit

Wiggins
Fort Morgan
Brush
Akron
Otis
Enders Reservoir St. Park
Hamlet
Palisade
Cambridge
Bartley
Arapaho

Woodrow
Yuma
Eckley
Wray
Max
Stratton
Culbertson
Indianola
McCook
Edison
Beaver City

Last Chance
Lindon
Anton
Laird
Haigler
Parks
Benkelman
Swanson Reservoir
Trenton
Danbury
Wilsonville
Lebanon
Stamfor

COL.

Cope
Joes
Idalia
St. Francis
Bird City
McDonald
Atwood
Herndon
Oberlin
Norcatur
Almena

River Bend
Limon
Arriba
Seibert
Vona
Stratton
Burlington
Goodland
Colby
Gem
Rexford
Jennings
Clayton
Keith Sebelius Lake
Norton
Phil

Hugo
Genoa
Brewster
Menlo
Halford
Hoxie
Morland

Republican River
South Fork
Arikaree River
Bonny Res.
Beaver
Sappa
Prairie Dog
North Fork
South

FOR WYOMING STATE MAP SEE PAGES 88-89
FOR COLORADO STATE MAP SEE PAGES 22-23

FOR SOUTH DAKOTA STATE MAP SEE PAGE 74
FOR MINNESOTA STATE MAP SEE PAGES 46-47
FOR IOWA STATE MAP SEE PAGE 36
FOR KANSAS STATE MAP SEE PAGE 37
Nebraska
Scale of Miles
0 7 14 21 28 35
© Creative Sales Corporation
N
S.D.
IOWA
KANSAS
R A S K A
Mitchell
Sioux Falls
Yankton
Sioux City
Norfolk
Columbus
Fremont
Omaha
Council Bluffs
Bellevue
Lincoln
Grand Island
Kearney
Hastings
Beatrice
Concordia
Niobrara State Park
Santee Indian Res.
Winnebago Ind. Res.
Long Pine St. Pk.
Atkinson Lk. St. Pk.
Pibel Lake State Park
Ft. Hartsuff St. Hist. Pk.
Sherman Res. St. Park
Crystal Lk. St. Pk.
Two Rivers St. Pk.
Alexandria Lks.St.Pk.
Harlan County Lake
Kickapoo Indian Res.
Sac and Fox Indian Res.
Waubonsie St. Pk.
Stone St. Pk.
Lewis and Clark Lake
Lake Francis Case
Lake Andes
Elkhorn River
Cedar River
Loup River
Platte River
Big Blue River
Little Blue River
Republican River
Niobrara River
8 9 10 11 12 13
B C D E F G H J

FOR OREGON STATE MAP SEE PAGES 70-71

FOR IDAHO STATE MAP SEE PAGE 31

OR.

ID.

CA.

UT.

AZ.

NEVADA

FOR CALIFORNIA STATE MAP SEE PAGES 18-21

FOR UTAH STATE MAP SEE PAGES 80-81

FOR ARIZONA STATE MAP SEE PAGES 16-17

Riddle, Three Creek, Rogerson, Sawtooth National Forest, Jackpot, Owyhee, Duck Valley Indian Reservation, Mountain City, Jarbridge, Contact, Thousand Springs, Montello, Oasis, Wells, Deeth, Halleck, Elko, Lamoille, Lee, Jiggs, Ruby Valley, Currie, Shantytown, Cherry Creek, Lage's, Goshute Indian Reservation, McGill, Ely, East Ely, Ruth, Kimberly, Copper Pit, Preston, Lund, Currant, Duckwater, Nyala, Adaven, Baker, Garrison, Gandy, Trout Cr., Wendover, Wendover Range, Desert Test Center, Dugway Proving Grounds

McDermitt, Ft. McDermitt Indian Reservation, Humboldt National Forest, Orovada, Paradise Valley, Midas, Tuscarora, Jack Creek, Winnemucca, Golconda, Valmy, Battle Mountain, Beowawe, Beowawe Geysers, Carlin, Crescent Valley, Te-Moak Indian Res., Sulphur, Rye Patch State Rec. Area, Rye Patch Reservoir, Imlay, Mill City, Unionville, Gerlach, Empire, Black Rock Desert, Eagle Picher Mine, Lovelock, Oreana, Austin, Eureka

Cedarville, Eagleville, Forest, Modoc, Alkali Lake, Massacre Lake, Antelope Range, Charles Sheldon, Summit Lake Indian Reservation, High Rock Canyon, Smoke Creek Desert, Honey Lake, Pyramid Lake, Pyramid Lake Indian Reservation, Herlong, Doyle, Sutcliffe, Nixon, Wadsworth, Reno, Sparks, Fernley, Virginia City, Silver Springs, Carson City, Carson Lake, Fallon, U.S. Naval Air Station, Cold Springs, Middle Gate, Frenchman, Toiyabe National Forest, Ione, Carver's, Round Mountain, Gabbs, Berlin-Ichthyosaur State Park, Warm Springs, Weed Heights, Yerington, Wellington, Topaz, Walker, Hawthorne, Walker Lake, Luning, Mina, Coaldale, Tonopah, Goldfield, Silver Peak, Lida, Gold Point, Scotty's Junction, Beatty

Squaw Valley, Tahoe City, Lake Tahoe, Carson City, Meyers, Camp Richardson, Bear Valley, Bridgeport, Mono Lake, Lee Vining, Benton, Dyer, June Lake, Mammoth Lakes, Tom's Place, Round Valley, Bishop, Laws, Oasis, Big Pine, Independence, Lone Pine, Keeler, Fresno, Clovis, Tulare, Visalia, Hanford, Delano, Lost Hills, Oildale, Bakersfield, Sequoia National Park, Kings Canyon National Park, Death Valley, Panamint Springs, Death Valley Jct., Shoshone, Tecopa, China Lake Naval Weapons Center, Fort Irwin Military Reservation, Barstow, Yermo, Baker, Cima, Searchlight, Nipton, Jean, Sandy, Goodsprings, Blue Diamond, Las Vegas, N. Las Vegas, Henderson, Boulder City, Mead, Hoover Dam, Lake Mead, Nellis Air Force Range, Nevada Test Site, Mercury, Cactus Springs, Indian Springs, Rachel, Hiko, Alamo, Ash Springs, Caliente, Elgin, Carp, Glendale, Moapa, Mesquite, Bunkerville, Overton, Valley of Fire State Park, Kingman, Grand Canyon National Park, Hualapai Indian Reservation

Piochel, Caselton, Panaca, Ursine, Uvada, Beryl, Lund, Pioche, Cathedral Gorge State Park, Echo Canyon Rec Area, Kershaw-Ryan State Rec Area, Spring Valley State Park, Dixie National Forest, Shivwits

Nevada

Scale of Miles

0   20   40   60

N

© Creative Sales Corporation

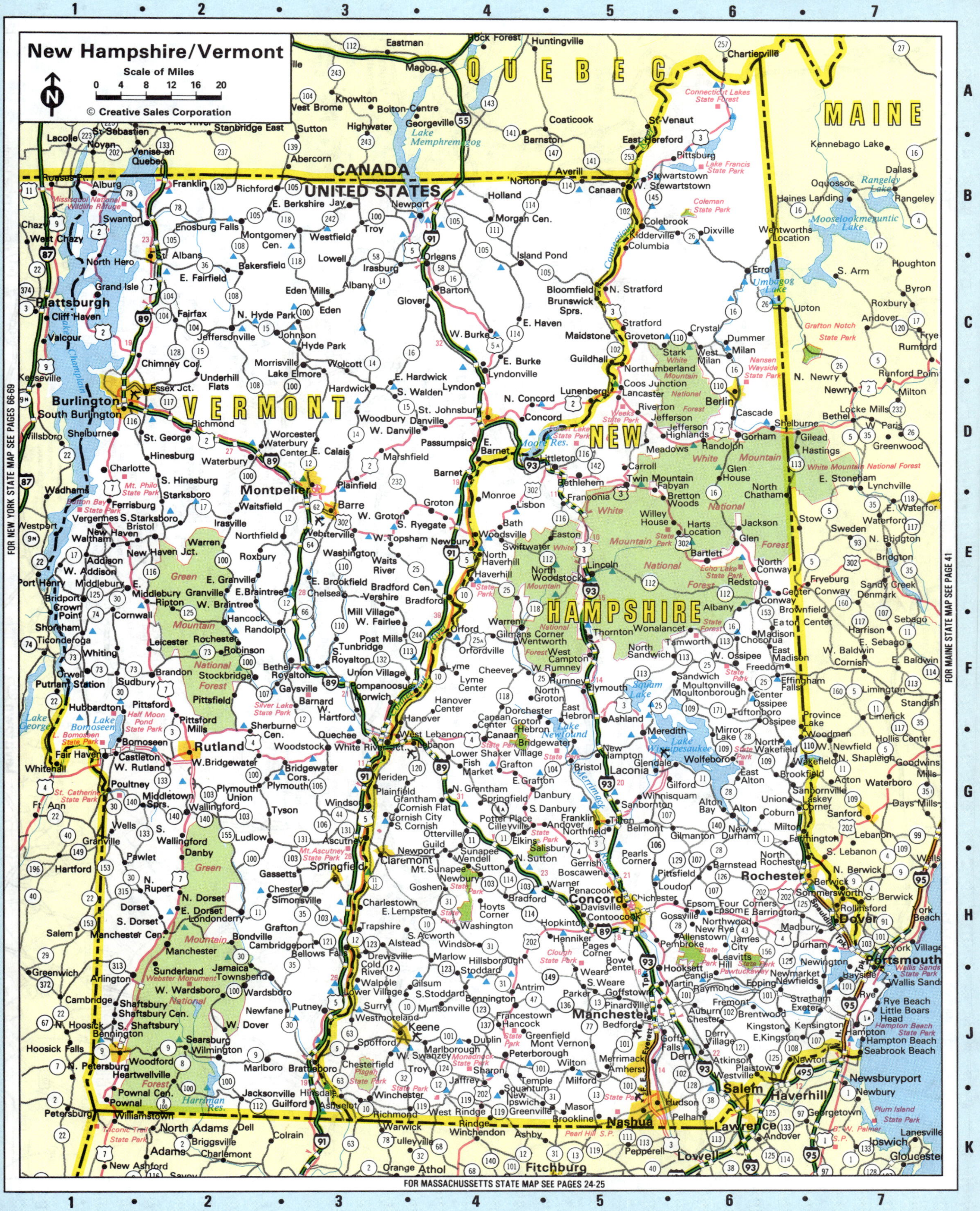

New Hampshire/Vermont

Scale of Miles
0 4 8 12 16 20

© Creative Sales Corporation

N

FOR NEW YORK STATE MAP SEE PAGES 66-69

FOR MAINE STATE MAP SEE PAGE 41

FOR MASSACHUSSETTS STATE MAP SEE PAGES 24-25

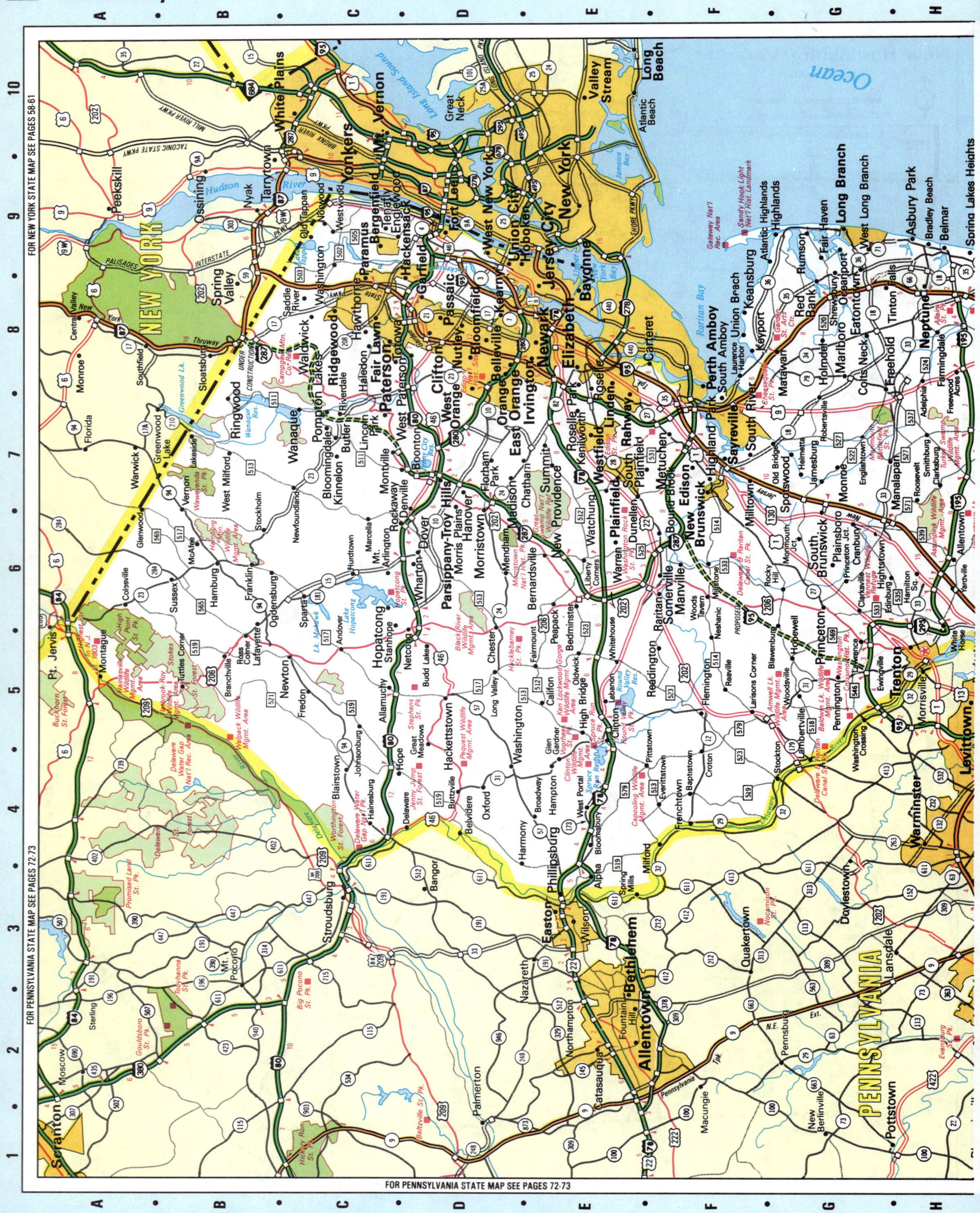

FOR NEW YORK STATE MAP SEE PAGES 58-61

FOR PENNSYLVANIA STATE MAP SEE PAGES 72-73

FOR PENNSYLVANIA STATE MAP SEE PAGES 72-73

NEW YORK

PENNSYLVANIA

Ocean

Long Island Sound

Hudson River

White Plains
Yonkers
Mt. Vernon
New York
Jersey City
Newark
Elizabeth
Paterson
Clifton
Passaic
Hackensack
Englewood
Fort Lee
Bayonne
Perth Amboy
Long Branch
Asbury Park
Neptune
Freehold
Red Bank
Keansburg
Matawan
New Brunswick
Princeton
Trenton
Somerville
Flemington
Morristown
Dover
Hackettstown
Phillipsburg
Easton
Bethlehem
Allentown
Scranton
Stroudsburg
Pottstown
Doylestown
Lansdale
Warminster
Levittown
Pt. Jervis
Montague
Newton
Sussex
Franklin
Hamburg
Vernon
Warwick
Monroe
Peekskill
Ossining
Tarrytown
Nyack
Spring Valley
Ridgewood
Pompton Lakes
Wanaque
Butler
Boonton
Parsippany-Troy Hills
Summit
Westfield
Plainfield
Metuchen
Edison
South Amboy
Sayreville
South River
Manville
Raritan
Bound Brook
Hopewell
Pennington
Lambertville
Woodstown

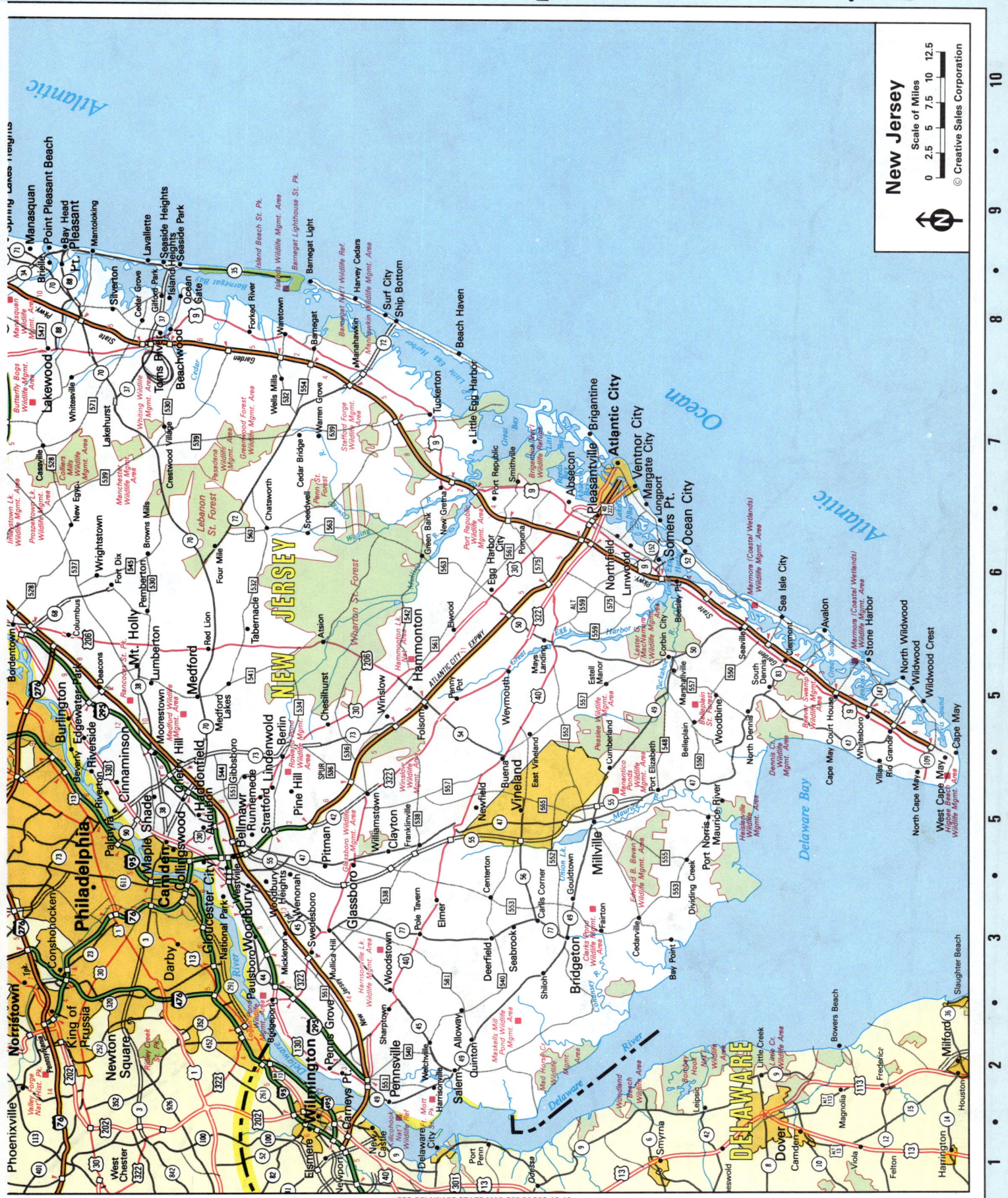

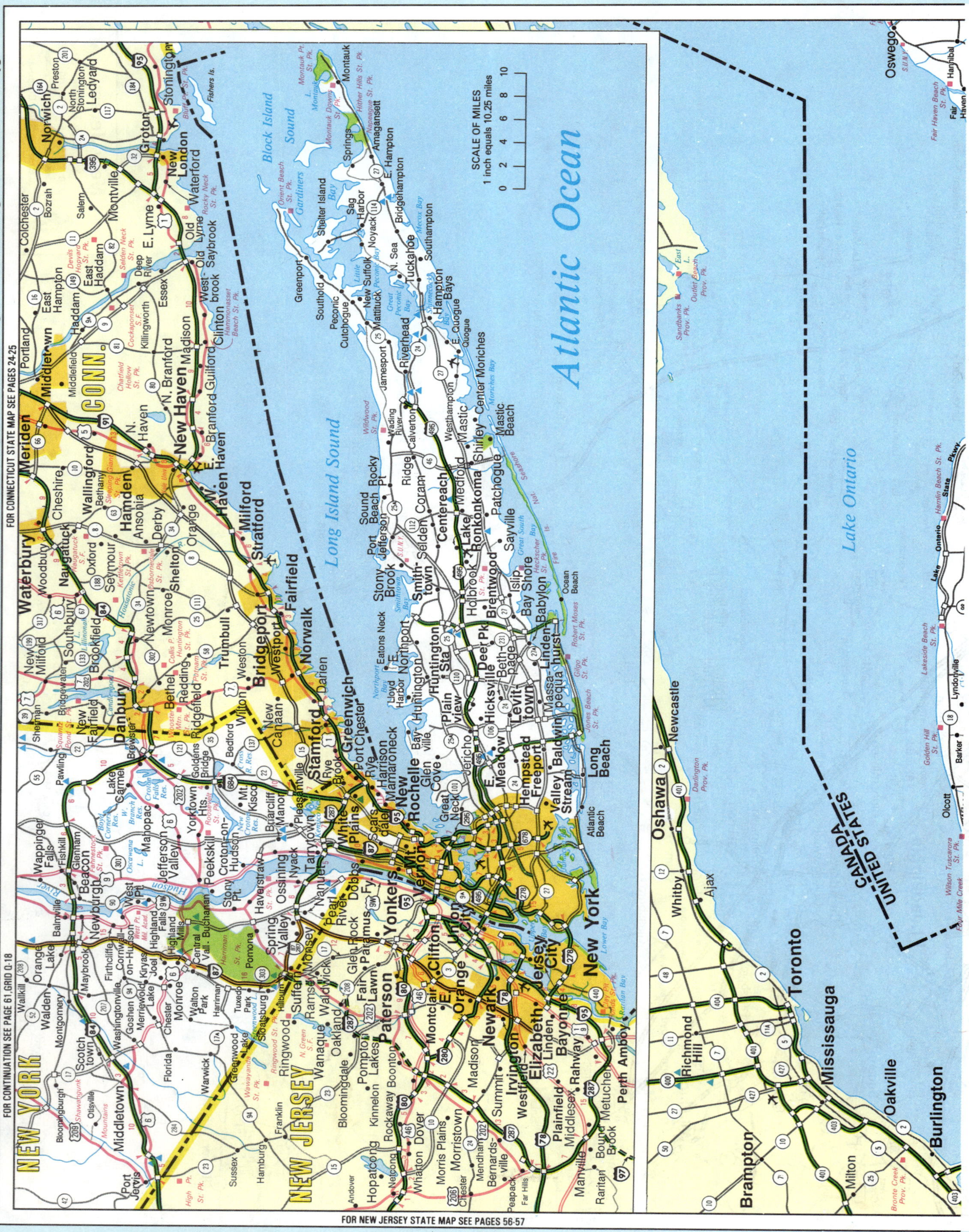

NEW YORK

CONN.

NEW JERSEY

Atlantic Ocean

Long Island Sound

Block Island Sound

Lake Ontario

CANADA
UNITED STATES

SCALE OF MILES
1 inch equals 10.25 miles
0 2 4 6 8 10

FOR CONTINUATION SEE PAGE 61, GRID 0-18
FOR CONNECTICUT STATE MAP SEE PAGES 24-25
FOR NEW JERSEY STATE MAP SEE PAGES 56-57

New York
Newark
Jersey City
Yonkers
Paterson
Clifton
New Rochelle
White Plains
Stamford
Greenwich
Norwalk
Bridgeport
Fairfield
New Haven
Meriden
Waterbury
Danbury
Newburgh
Long Beach
Hempstead
Freeport
Levittown
Hicksville
Huntington
Bay Shore
Islip
Patchogue
Riverhead
Southampton
Montauk
Greenport
Toronto
Mississauga
Oshawa
Whitby
Ajax
Brampton
Burlington
Oakville
Oswego

FOR CONTINUATION SEE PAGE 61

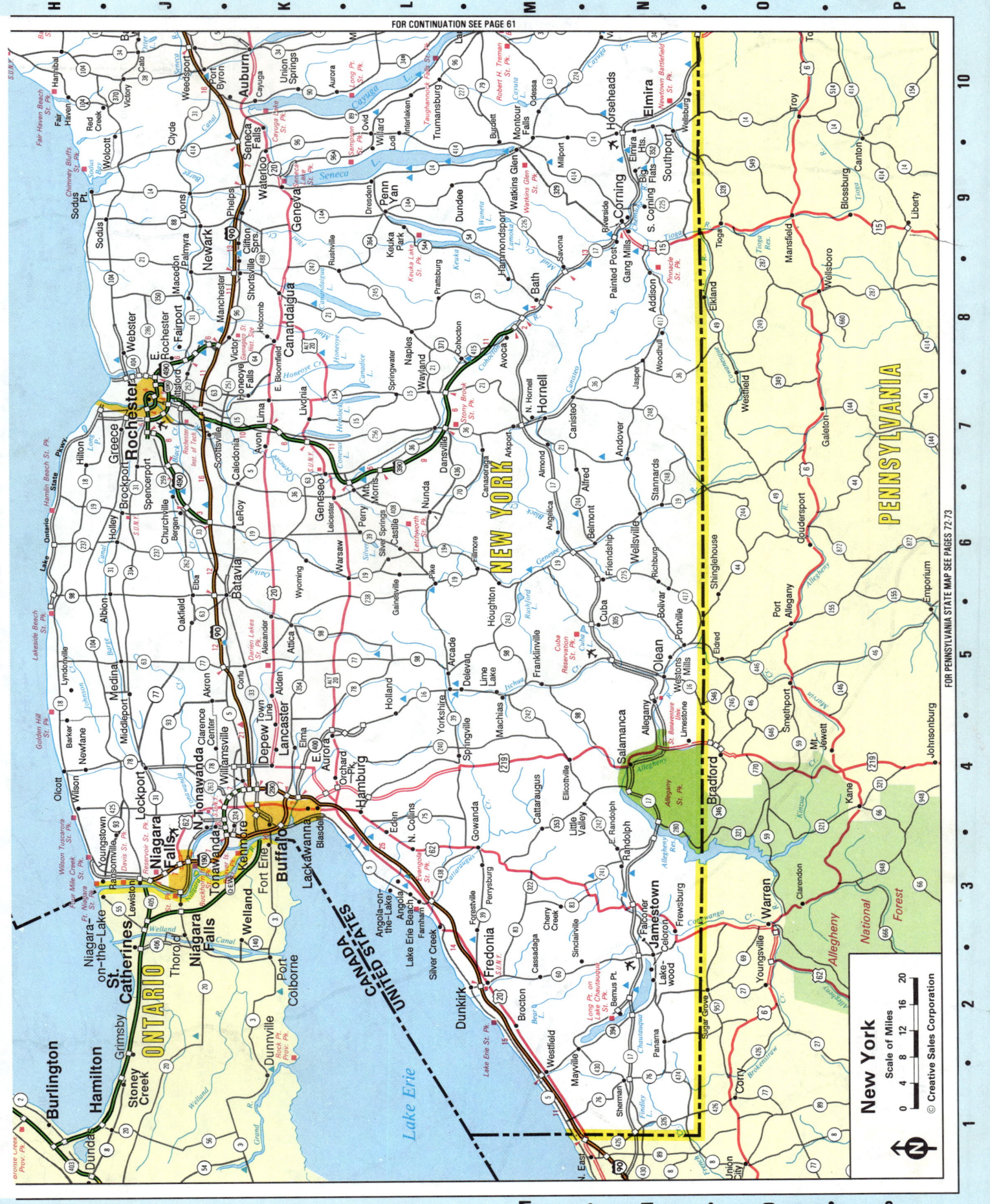

NEW YORK

PENNSYLVANIA

ONTARIO

CANADA
UNITED STATES

Lake Erie

FOR PENNSYLVANIA STATE MAP SEE PAGES 72-73

New York
Scale of Miles
0 4 8 12 16 20

© Creative Sales Corporation

FOR VERMONT STATE MAP SEE PAGE 55

VERMONT

QUEBEC

CANADA

UNITED STATES

ONTARIO

NEW YORK

Adirondack Park

Lake Champlain

New York

Scale of Miles

0 4 8 12 16 20

© Creative Sales Corporation

N

St. Albans · Swanton · Colchester · Burlington · Winooski · Shelburne · Hinesburg · Bristol · New Haven · Middlebury · Vergennes · Ferrisburg · Charlotte · Essex Jct.

Plattsburgh · Champlain · Rouses Pt. · Lacolle · Morrisonville · W. Plattsburgh · Keeseville · Peru · Westport · Port Henry · Witherbee · Ticonderoga · Crown Pt.

Malone · Chateaugay · Burke · Brushton · Moira · Bombay · Fort Covington · Hogansburg

Massena · Brasher Falls · Norfolk · Winthrop · Norwood · Unionville · Potsdam · Canton · Hermon · Edwards

Saranac Lake · Lake Placid · Bloomingdale · Tupper Lake · Star Lake · Mt. Marcy Elev. 5344 Highest Pt. in N.Y.

Ogdensburg · Prescott · Morristown · Hammond · Alexandria Bay · Clayton · Cape Vincent · Chaumont · Brownville · Watertown · Dexter · Sackets Harbor · Adams · Mannsville · Lacona · Pulaski

Gouverneur · Rensselaer Falls · Richville · Antwerp · Philadelphia · Theresa · Evans Mills · Fort Drum Military Reserve · Black River · Carthage · West Carthage · Copenhagen · Castorland · Lowville · Turin · Boonville

Glens Falls · Lake George · Warrensburg · Lake Luzerne · Hadley · Corinth · Hudson Falls · Ft. Edward · S. Glens Falls

Northville · Speculator · Old Forge · Atwell · Remsen · Prospect · Barneveld · Poland · Holland Patent · Camden · Central Square · Constantia · Mexico · Fulton · Minetto · Oswego

Kingston · Gananoque · Brockville · Smiths Falls · Merrickville · Kemptville · Winchester · Iroquois · Morrisburg · Cornwall

Lake Ontario

St. Lawrence River

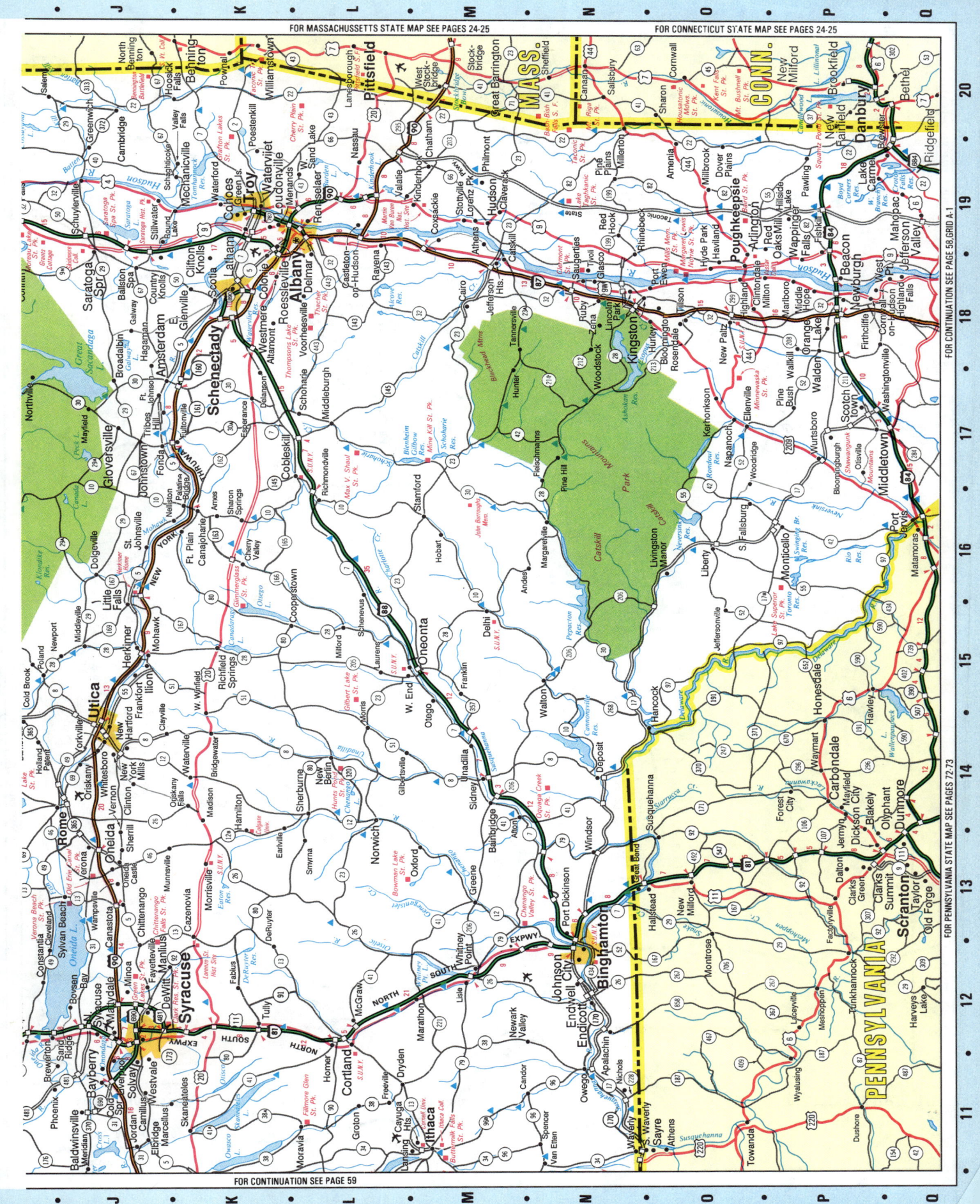

FOR MASSACHUSSETTS STATE MAP SEE PAGES 24-25

FOR CONNECTICUT STATE MAP SEE PAGES 24-25

FOR CONTINUATION SEE PAGE 58; GRID A-1

FOR PENNSYLVANIA STATE MAP SEE PAGES 72-73

FOR CONTINUATION SEE PAGE 59

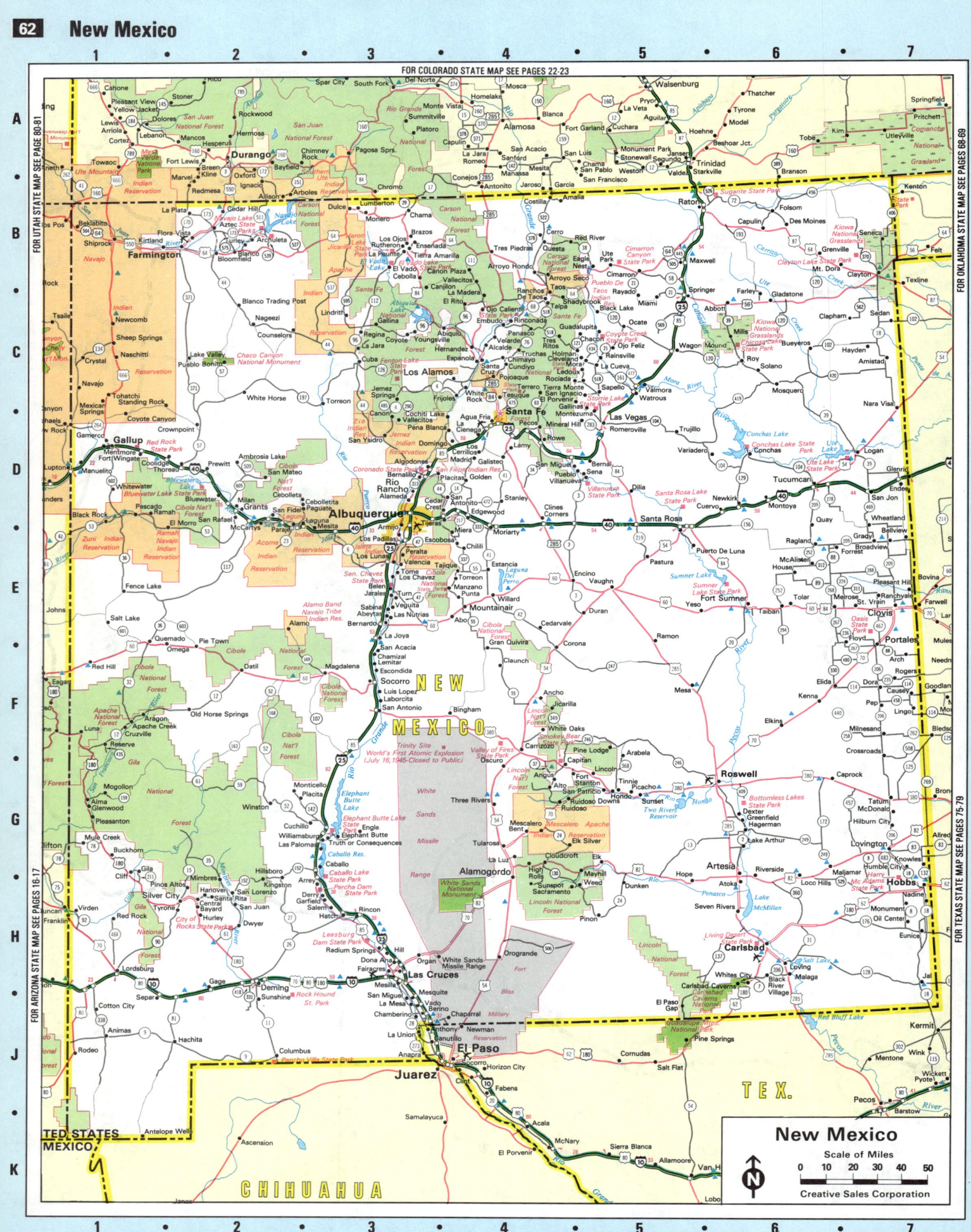

New Mexico

Scale of Miles

0 10 20 30 40 50

Creative Sales Corporation

FOR MINNESOTA STATE MAP SEE PAGES 46-47

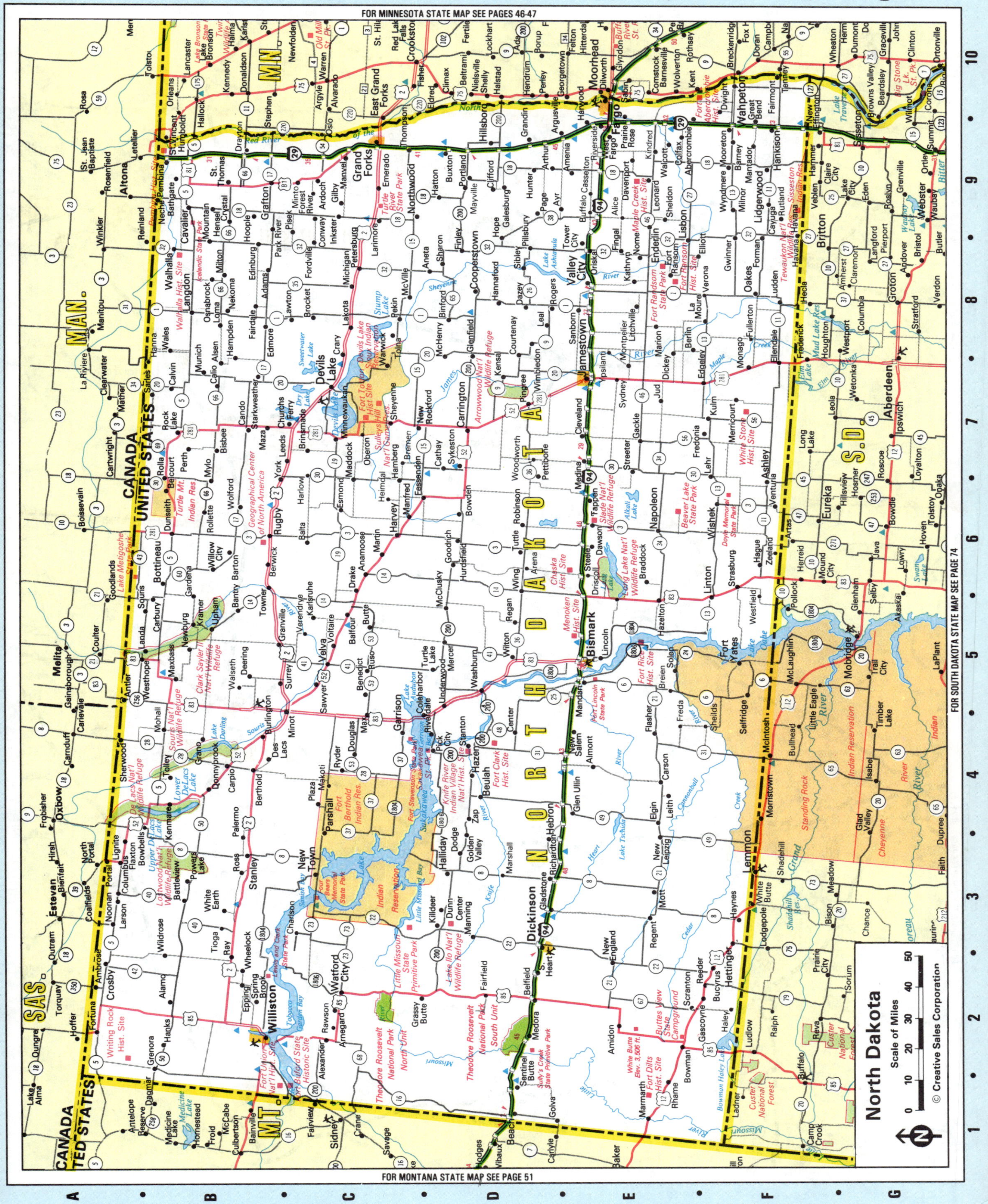

North Dakota

Scale of Miles

0 10 20 30 40 50

© Creative Sales Corporation

FOR SOUTH DAKOTA STATE MAP SEE PAGE 74

FOR MONTANA STATE MAP SEE PAGE 51

CANADA — UNITED STATES

MAN.
SAS.
MT.
S.D.
MN

Red River

Williston Minot Bismarck Dickinson Jamestown Valley City Fargo Grand Forks Devils Lake Aberdeen Wahpeton Moorhead

Theodore Roosevelt National Park

Standing Rock Indian Reservation

Fort Berthold Indian Reservation

Lake Sakakawea

Lake Oahe

White Butte Elev. 3,506 ft.

Geographical Center of North America

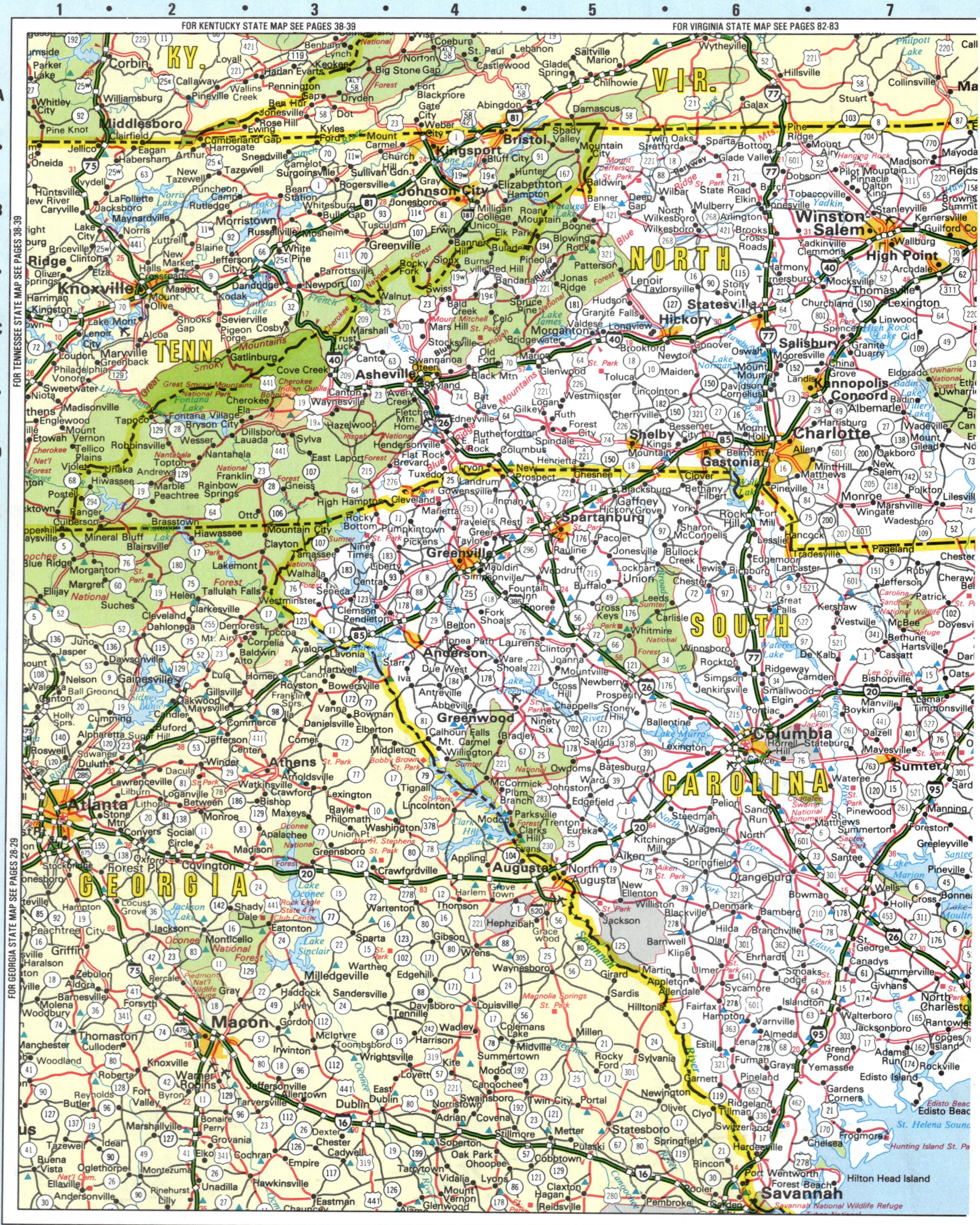

FOR KENTUCKY STATE MAP SEE PAGES 38-39
FOR VIRGINIA STATE MAP SEE PAGES 82-83
FOR TENNESSEE STATE MAP SEE PAGES 38-39
FOR GEORGIA STATE MAP SEE PAGES 28-29

KY.

VIR.

TENN.

NORTH

SOUTH

CAROLINA

GEORGIA

Major cities: Knoxville, Asheville, Winston-Salem, High Point, Statesville, Hickory, Salisbury, Kannapolis, Concord, Charlotte, Gastonia, Shelby, Spartanburg, Greenville, Anderson, Greenwood, Columbia, Sumter, Augusta, Atlanta, Athens, Macon, Savannah, Kingsport, Johnson City, Bristol, Corbin, Middlesboro

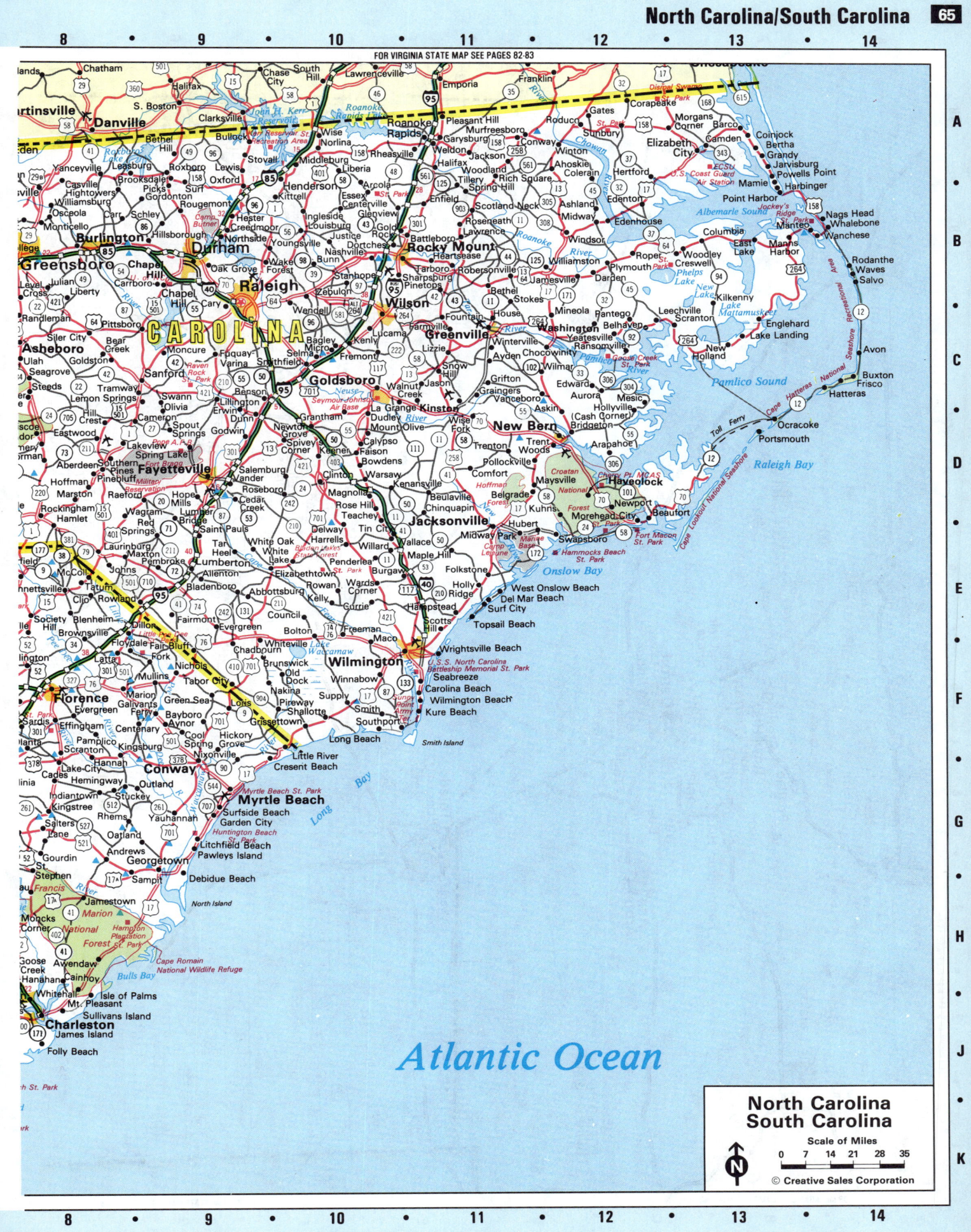

Atlantic Ocean

North Carolina
South Carolina

Scale of Miles

0 7 14 21 28 35

© Creative Sales Corporation

FOR PENNSYLVANIA STATE MAP SEE PAGES 72-73

FOR MICHIGAN STATE MAP SEE PAGES 44-45

FOR MICHIGAN STATE MAP SEE PAGES 44-45

FOR INDIANA STATE MAP SEE PAGES 34-35

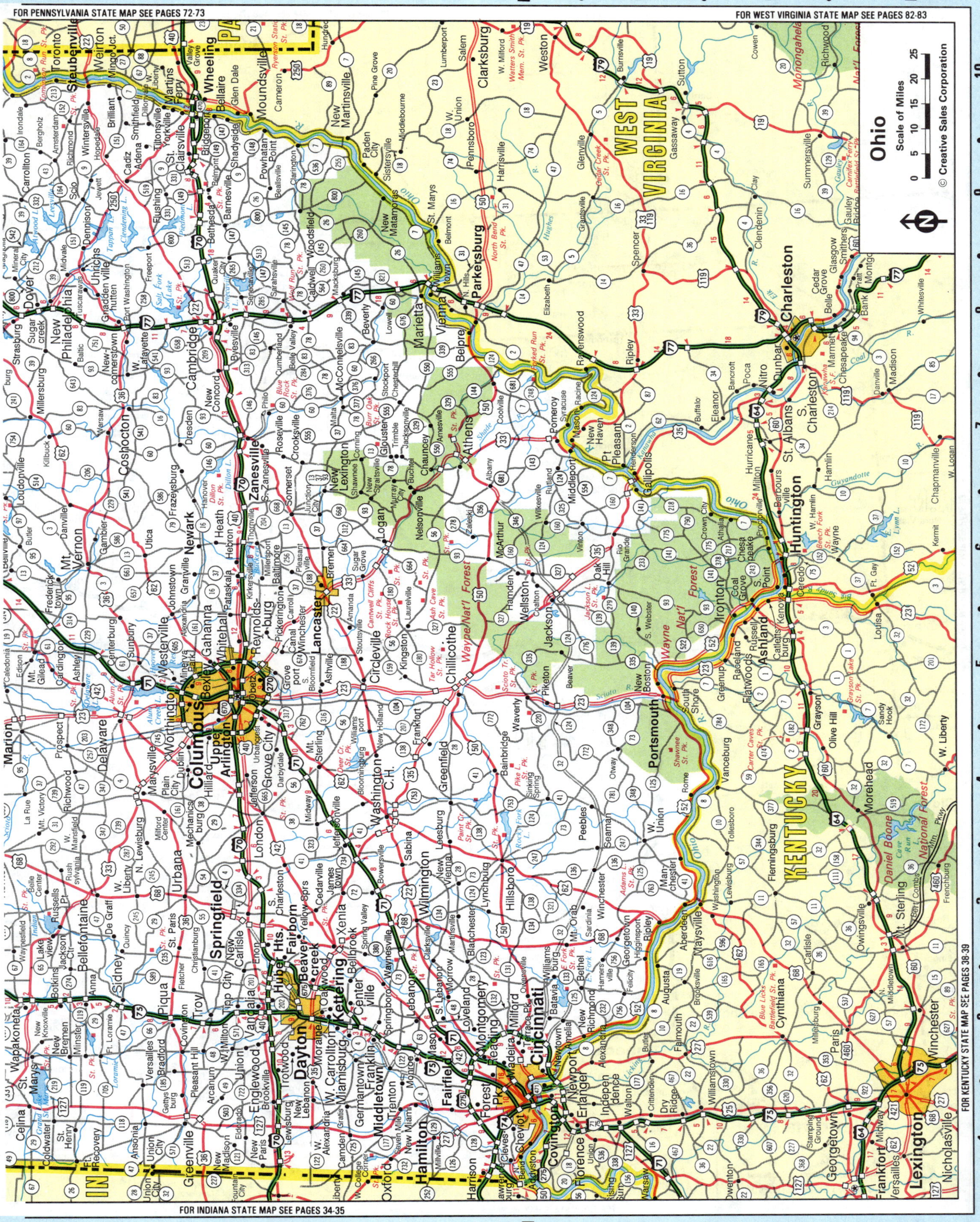

FOR PENNSYLVANIA STATE MAP SEE PAGES 72-73
FOR WEST VIRGINIA STATE MAP SEE PAGES 82-83

Ohio
Scale of Miles
0 5 10 15 20 25
© Creative Sales Corporation

WEST VIRGINIA

KENTUCKY

IN

FOR INDIANA STATE MAP SEE PAGES 34-35
FOR KENTUCKY STATE MAP SEE PAGES 38-39

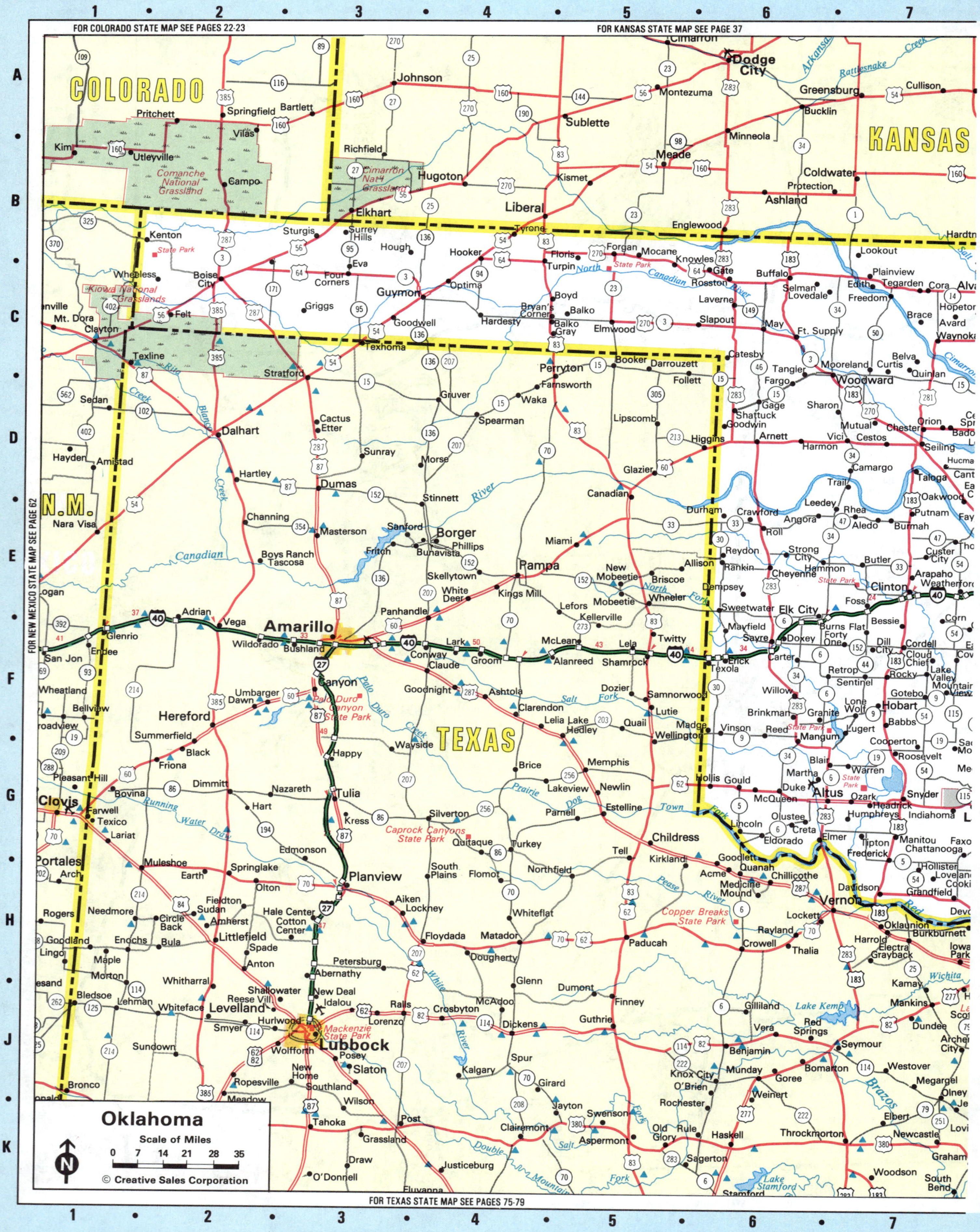

FOR COLORADO STATE MAP SEE PAGES 22-23

FOR KANSAS STATE MAP SEE PAGE 37

FOR NEW MEXICO STATE MAP SEE PAGE 62

FOR TEXAS STATE MAP SEE PAGES 75-79

COLORADO

KANSAS

N.M.

TEXAS

Dodge City

Amarillo

Lubbock

Clovis

Liberal

Guymon

Woodward

Clinton

Elk City

Altus

Vernon

Oklahoma

Scale of Miles

0 7 14 21 28 35

N

© Creative Sales Corporation

FOR KANSAS STATE MAP SEE PAGE 37

When travelling on highways in states where there are long stretches of open space, it is important to watch your speed. The 65 mile per hour speed limit applies only to rural areas where it is clearly marked. Drivers should always observe the posted speed limit. Remember, speed kills, so take it easy.

FOR MISSOURI STATE MAP SEE PAGES 48-49

FOR ARKANSAS STATE MAP SEE PAGE 15

FOR TEXAS STATE MAP SEE PAGES 75-79

Pacific

Ocean

FOR WASHINGTON STATE MAP SEE PAGES 84-85

WASH.

OREGON

CAL.

FOR CALIFORNIA STATE MAP SEE PAGES 18-21

Astoria, Seaside, Cannon Beach, Manzanita, Nehalem, Wheeler, Rockaway, Garibaldi, Bay City, Tillamook, Oceanside, Netarts, Pacific City, Cloverdale, Neskowin, Otis, Lincoln City, Kernville, Gleneden Beach, Lincoln Beach, Depoe Bay, Otter Rock, Newport, S. Beach, Toledo, Siletz, Waldport, Yachats, Florence, Glenada, Dunes City, Siltcoos, Reedsport, Winchester Bay, Gardiner, Lakeside, North Bend, Coos Bay, Charleston, Eastside, Sumner, Coquille, Riverton, Bandon, Myrtle Point, Langlois, Denmark, Sixes, Port Orford, Ophir, Wedderburn, Gold Beach, Agness, Brookings, Harbor, Smith River, Fort Dick, Crescent City, Klamath

Longview, Kelso, Kalama, Vancouver, Portland, Hillsboro, Gresham, Beaverton, Tigard, Tualatin, Oregon City, Newberg, McMinnville, Sheridan, Dallas, Monmouth, Independence, Salem, Silverton, Stayton, Mill City, Albany, Corvallis, Philomath, Lebanon, Sweet Home, Junction City, Springfield, Eugene, Creswell, Cottage Grove, Oakridge, Westfir, Drain, Sutherlin, Roseburg, Winston, Myrtle Creek, Canyonville, Glendale, Wolfcreek, Grants Pass, Merlin, Central Point, Medford, Jacksonville, Phoenix, Talent, Ashland, Cave Junction, Williams

Yakima, Toppenish, Granger, Goldendale, White Salmon, Bingen, Hood River, The Dalles, Dufur, Maupin, Moro, Grass Valley, Condon, Fossil, Antelope, Madras, Culver, Metolius, Redmond, Sisters, Terrebonne, Bend, Sunriver, La Pine, Gilchrist, Crescent, Chemult, Prineville, Post, Brothers, Hampton, Christmas Valley, Silver Lake, Summer Lake, Paisley, Valley Falls, Lakeview, Adel

Warm Springs Indian Reservation, Crater Lake Nat'l Park, Klamath Falls, Fort Klamath, Chiloquin, Beatty, Bly, Bonanza, Merrill, Malin, Tulelake, Yreka

FOR WASHINGTON STATE MAP SEE PAGES 84-85

A B C D E F G H J K

8 9 10 11 12 13 14

Vernita · U.S. Dept. of Energy · Basin City · Connell · Penawawa · Pullman · 270 · Deary · Troy

Hanford Site · Mesa · Ringold · Kahlotus · Hooper · Hay · Illia · Wawawai · Almota · Joel · 8 · Kendrick · Juliaetta · Genesee · Cavendish · Ahsahka · Headquarters · National Forest · Dworshak Reservoir

Outlook · Sunnyside · West Richland · Benton City · Glade · Page · Eltopia · Clyde · Eureka · Riparia · Ayer · Starbuck · Dodge · Gould City · Pomeroy · Pataha · Uniontown · Colton · Spalding · Lenore · Myrtle · Gifford · Reck · Orofino · Greer · Grangemont · Pierce · Selway-Bitterro · Crags · Wilderness

Prosser · Kiona · Richland · Kennewick · Pasco · Burbank · 124 · Prescott · Dayton · 126 · Waitsburg · Clarkston · Asotin · Cloverland · Waha · Reubens · Mohler · Craigmont · Ferdinand · Nezperce · Kamiah · Clearwater Mountains · Nezperce · Moose Rid

Paterson · Plymouth · Umatilla · McNary · Hermiston · Stanfield · Touchet · College Place · Walla Walla · Milton-Freewater · Rogersburg · Anatone · 129 · Greencreek · Keuterville · Cottonwood · Kooskia · Harpster · Lowell · Selway · National

Irrigon · Umapine · Helix · Adams · Weston · Athena · 11 · Flora · Troy · Fenn · Grangeville · Mount Idaho · Golden · Elk City · Forest

Boardman · National Wildlife Refuge · Echo · Pendleton · Mission · Umatilla Indian Res. · Gibbon · Meacham · Minam · Wallowa · Imnaha · White Bird · 14 · Orogrande

Ione · Lexington · Heppner · Pilot Rock · Kamela · Elgin · Summerville · Imbler · Lostine · Enterprise · Lucile · Dixie · Salmon River Breaks Primitive Area

Ukiah · Alicel · Island City · LaGrande · Cove · Joseph · Riggins · Payette · Gospel Hump Wilderness · Idaho Primitive Area

Union · Telocaset · Medical Springs · Homestead · Cuprum · Pollock · Burgdorf · Warren

Ritter · Monument · Long Creek · Granite · Sumpter · North Powder · Haines · Halfway · New Bridge · Tamarack · New Meadows · Meadows · Stibnite

Fox · Greenhorn · Austin · Baker · Richland · Starkey · Fruitvale · McCall · Lake Fork · Yellow Pine

Dayville · Whitney · Prairie City · Hereford · Pleasant Valley · Durkee · Cambridge · Council · Donnelly · Warm Lake

Mount Vernon · John Day · Canyon City · Unity · Bridgeport · Midvale · Mesa · Casacade

Seneca · Ironside · Brogan · Huntington · Weiser · Ola · Crouch · Garden Valley · Lowman · Cape Horn · Sunbeam · Clayto

Jamieson · Willow Creek · Vale · Ontario · Payette · Fruitland · New Plymouth · Banks · Gardena · Centerville · Placerville · Pioneerville · Stanley

Westfall · Harper · Nyssa · Letha · Montour · Sweet · Horse Shoe Bend · Idaho City · Atlanta

Burns · Hines · Riley · Lawen · Crane · Drewsey · Drinkwater Pass · Juntura · Owyhee · Parma · Notus · Middleton · Eagle · Pearl · Garden Valley

Warm Springs Valley · New Princeton · Roswell · Adrian · Wilder · Caldwell · Star · Meridian · Boise · Mayfield · Pine

Diamond · Homedale · Nampa · Kuna · Bowmont · Melba · Orchard · Corral · Hill City · Fairfield

Frenchglen · Marsing · Reynolds · Murphy · Mountain Home · Fairfield

Sheaville · The Craters · Jordan Valley · Silver City · Oreana · Hammett · King Hill · Shosh

Arock · Lava Beds · Grand View · Bruneau · Glenns Ferry · Bliss · Good · Tuttle · Wend

Rome · Triangle · Bruneau Hot Sprs. · Hagerman · Hollister · Rogerson · Twin F

Burns Jct. · Andrews · Fields · Grasmere · Castleford · Buhl · Filer

Alvord · Riddle · Denio · Denio Junction · Fort McDermitt Indian Reservation · McDermitt · Duck Valley · Owyhee

Oregon
Scale of Miles
0 7 14 21 28 35
© Creative Sales Corporation

NV.

IDAHO

FOR NEVADA STATE MAP SEE PAGE 54

FOR IDAHO STATE MAP SEE PAGE 31

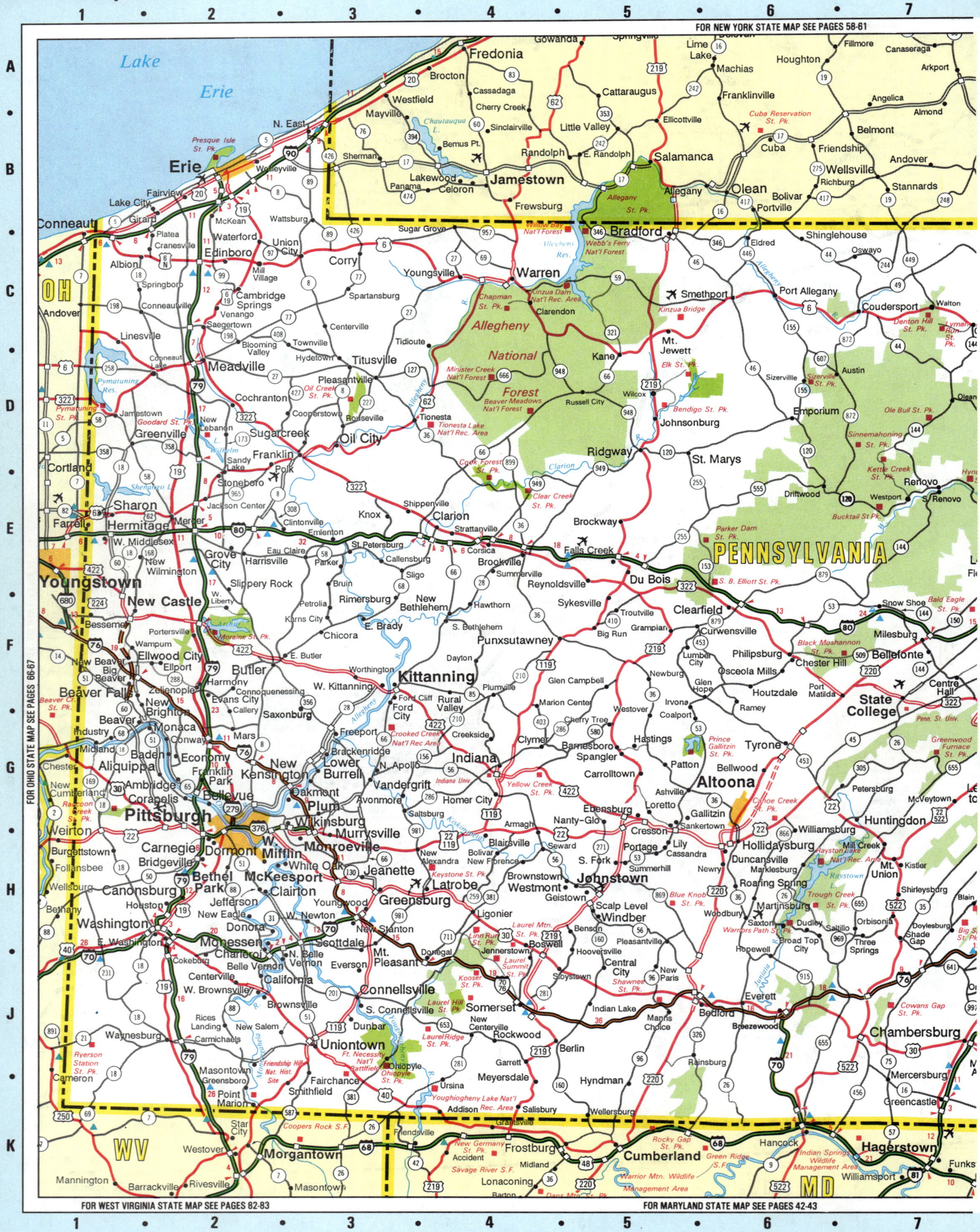

FOR NEW YORK STATE MAP SEE PAGES 58-61

Lake Erie

PENNSYLVANIA

OH

WV

MD

Allegheny National Forest

FOR OHIO STATE MAP SEE PAGES 66-67

Erie, Fairview, Lake City, Conneaut, Girard, Albion, Springboro, Conneautville, Linesville, Andover, Meadville, Cambridge Springs, Saegertown, Venango, Townville, Centerville, Blooming Valley, Hydetown, Titusville, Corry, Youngsville, Warren, Clarendon, Kane, Mt. Jewett, Smethport, Port Allegany, Coudersport, Eldred, Shinglehouse, Bradford, Olean, Salamanca, Allegany, Wellsville, Andover, Friendship, Bolivar, Portville

Sharon, Hermitage, Farrell, Greenville, Jamestown, Mercer, Grove City, Slippery Rock, Franklin, Oil City, Polk, Stoneboro, Clarion, Knox, Clintonville, Emlenton, St. Petersburg, Callensburg, Sligo, New Bethlehem, Brookville, Summerville, Reynoldsville, Sykesville, Du Bois, Falls Creek, Brockway, Ridgway, St. Marys, Johnsonburg, Emporium, Renovo, Driftwood, Westport, Snow Shoe, Clearfield, Curwensville, Philipsburg, Osceola Mills, Houtzdale, Ramey, Bellefonte, Milesburg, State College, Centre Hall, Huntingdon

Youngstown, New Castle, Beaver Falls, Ellwood City, Zelienople, Harmony, Butler, Saxonburg, Kittanning, Ford City, Rural Valley, Indiana, Clymer, Cherry Tree, Barnesboro, Spangler, Carrolltown, Patton, Altoona, Hollidaysburg, Tyrone, Bellwood, Williamsburg, Martinsburg, Roaring Spring, Woodbury, Saxton

Pittsburgh, Aliquippa, Ambridge, Coraopolis, Carnegie, Bridgeville, Canonsburg, Washington, Monroeville, Murrysville, Jeannette, Greensburg, Latrobe, Ligonier, Johnstown, Windber, Ebensburg, Nanty-Glo, Cresson, Portage, Gallitzin, Duncansville, Mt. Union, Everett, Bedford, Breezewood, Chambersburg, Mercersburg, Greencastle, Hagerstown

Uniontown, Connellsville, Brownsville, California, Masontown, Point Marion, Morgantown, Waynesburg, Carmichaels, Somerset, Meyersdale, Berlin, Salisbury, Addison, Frostburg, Cumberland, Hancock

FOR WEST VIRGINIA STATE MAP SEE PAGES 82-83

FOR MARYLAND STATE MAP SEE PAGES 42-43

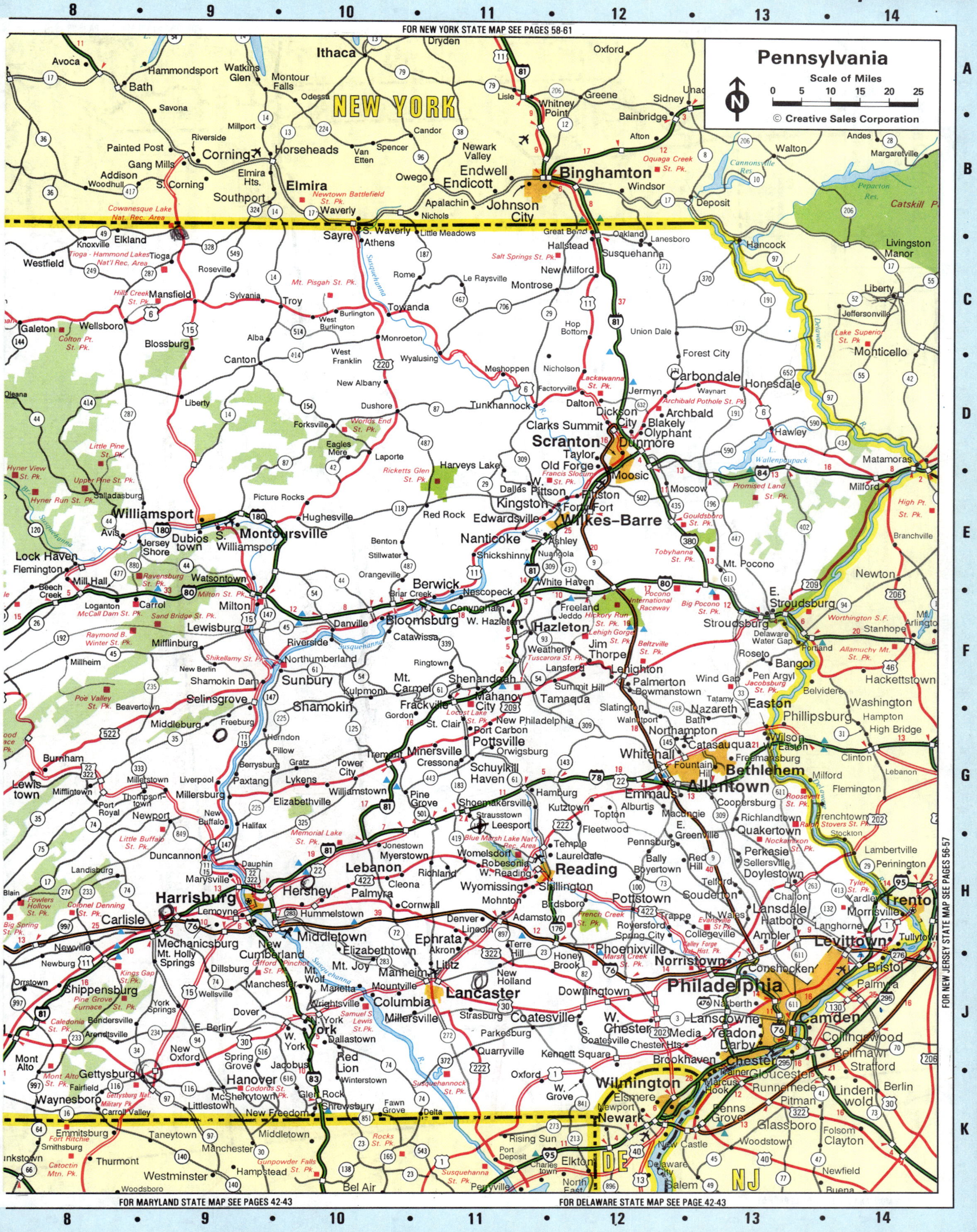

Pennsylvania
Scale of Miles
0 5 10 15 20 25
© Creative Sales Corporation

N

FOR NEW YORK STATE MAP SEE PAGES 58-61

NEW YORK

Binghamton

Elmira
Corning

Scranton
Dunmore
Wilkes-Barre

Williamsport
Montoursville

Hazleton

Lock Haven

Bloomsburg
Sunbury
Shamokin

Pottsville

Stroudsburg
E. Stroudsburg

Easton
Phillipsburg
Bethlehem
Allentown
Emmaus

Reading
Wyomissing

Lebanon
Hershey

Harrisburg
Carlisle

Lancaster
Columbia

York

Gettysburg
Hanover
Waynesboro

Norristown
Philadelphia
Conshohocken

Trenton
Levittown
Bristol
Camden

Wilmington
Newark

Chester

NJ

MD

FOR NEW JERSEY STATE MAP SEE PAGES 56-57

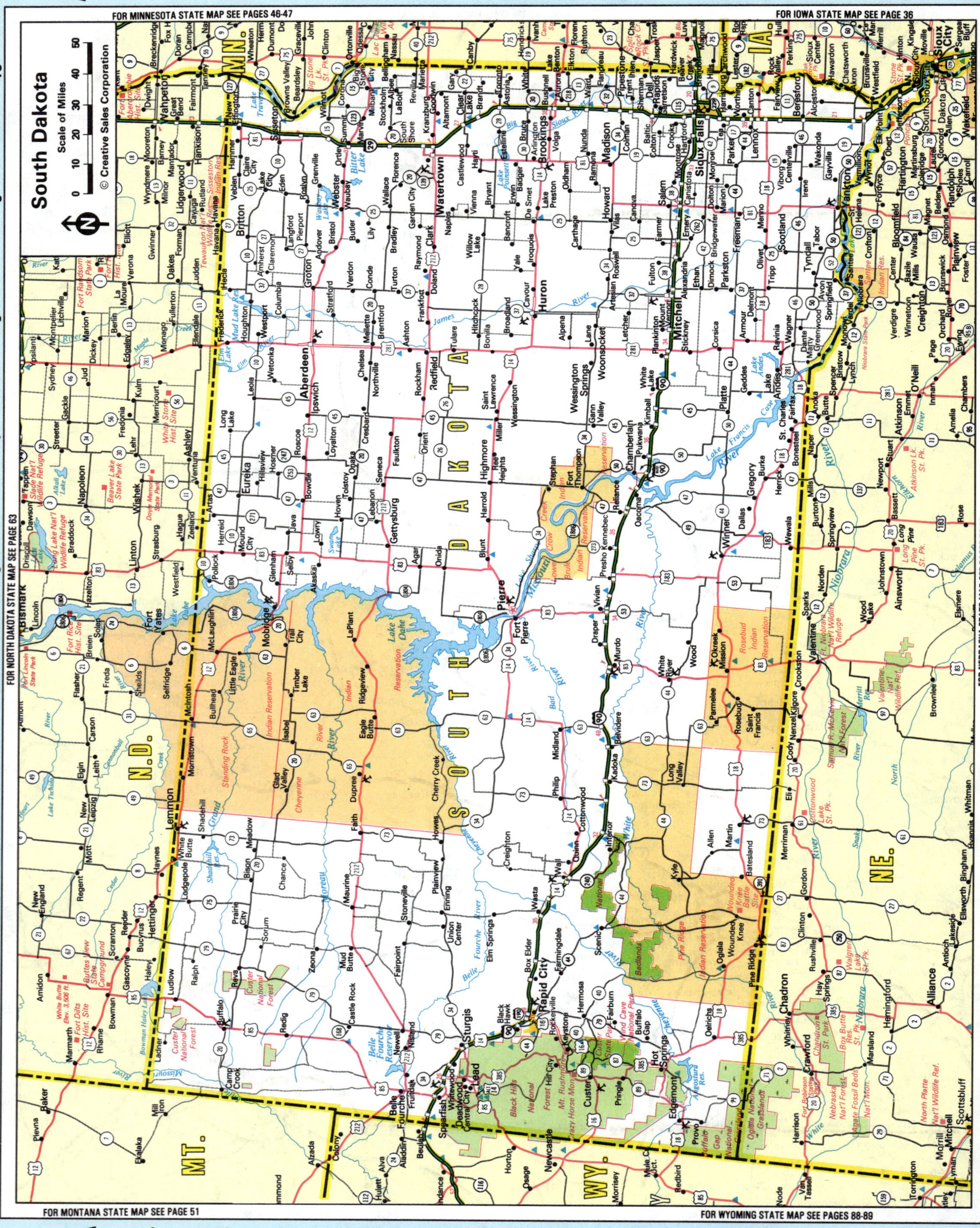

South Dakota

Scale of Miles

0 10 20 30 40 50

© Creative Sales Corporation

N

FOR MINNESOTA STATE MAP SEE PAGES 46-47
FOR IOWA STATE MAP SEE PAGE 36
FOR NORTH DAKOTA STATE MAP SEE PAGE 63
FOR NEBRASKA STATE MAP SEE PAGES 52-53
FOR MONTANA STATE MAP SEE PAGE 51
FOR WYOMING STATE MAP SEE PAGES 88-89

SOUTH DAKOTA

N.D. MN IA NE. MT. WY.

Selected cities and towns: Sioux Falls, Brookings, Watertown, Aberdeen, Mitchell, Huron, Pierre, Rapid City, Sturgis, Deadwood, Lead, Spearfish, Belle Fourche, Hot Springs, Custer, Mobridge, Chamberlain, Yankton, Vermillion, Madison, Redfield, Webster, Milbank, Sisseton, Britton, Groton, Clark, De Smet, Miller, Highmore, Gettysburg, Eagle Butte, Faith, Lemmon, Philip, Kadoka, Wall, Murdo, Winner, Gregory, Platte, Parkston, Freeman, Scotland, Tyndall, Wagner, Gregory, Martin, Pine Ridge, Kyle, Mission, Rosebud, Valentine.

Standing Rock Indian Reservation
Cheyenne River Indian Reservation
Lower Brule Indian Reservation
Crow Creek Indian Reservation
Rosebud Indian Reservation
Pine Ridge Indian Reservation

Lake Oahe, Lake Sharpe, Lake Francis Case, Lake Andes, Missouri River, James River, Big Sioux River, White River, Cheyenne River, Belle Fourche River, Grand River, Moreau River, Bad River, Niobrara River

Badlands National Park
Black Hills National Forest
Custer National Forest
Wind Cave National Park
Mt. Rushmore National Memorial
Crazy Horse Memorial
Wounded Knee Battle Site

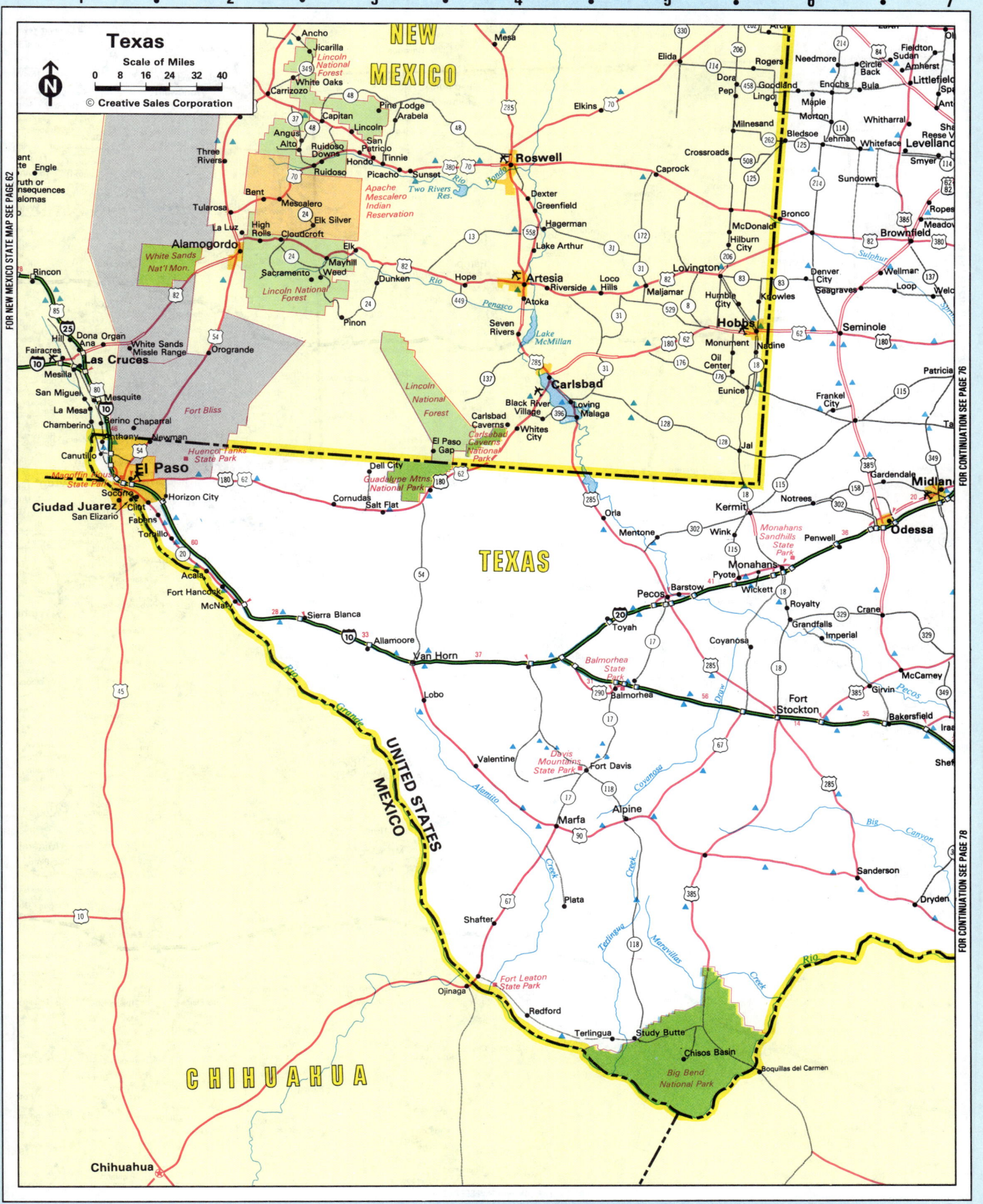

Texas
Scale of Miles
0 8 16 24 32 40
© Creative Sales Corporation

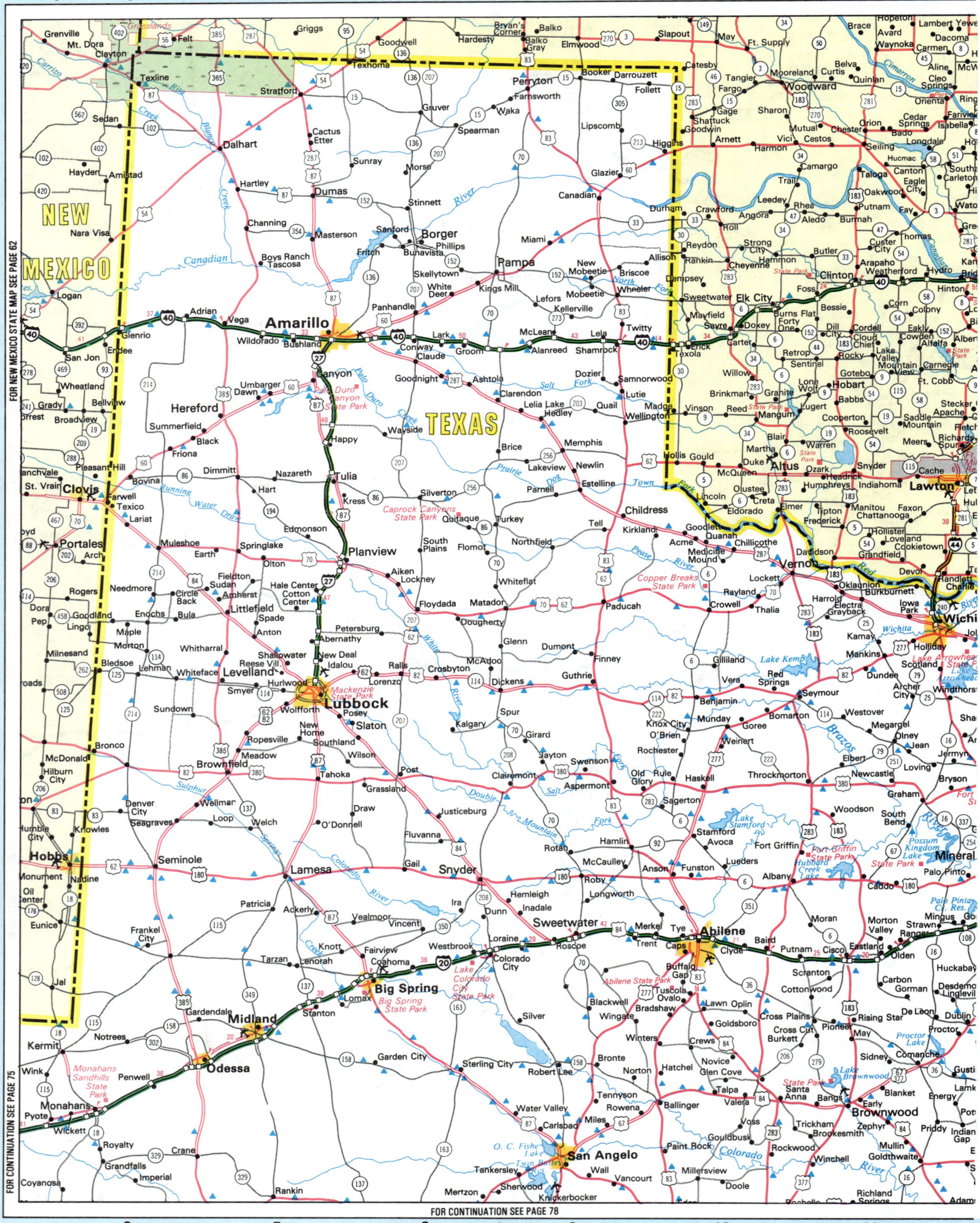

NEW MEXICO

TEXAS

FOR NEW MEXICO STATE MAP SEE PAGE 62

FOR CONTINUATION SEE PAGE 75

FOR CONTINUATION SEE PAGE 78

Texas
Scale of Miles
0 8 16 24 32 40
© Creative Sales Corporation

FOR OKLAHOMA STATE MAP SEE PAGES 68-69

FOR ARKANSAS STATE MAP SEE PAGE 15

FOR LOUISIANA STATE MAP SEE PAGE 40

FOR CONTINUATION SEE PAGE 79

OKLAHOMA
ARKANSAS
TEXAS
LA.

FOR CONTINUATION SEE PAGE 76

FOR CONTINUATION SEE PAGE 75

6 • 7 • 8 • 9 • 10 • 11

J

McCamey Big Lake Barnhart Christoval Melvin Rochelle Springs Lometa Adamsv
Girvin Pecos Eden Brady San Saba Cop
Fort Stockton Bakersfield Iraan Knickerbocker Calf Creek Voca Fredonia Cherokee Lampas
Sheffield Ozona Eldorado Fort McKavett Menard Hext Katemcy Pontotoc Valley Spring Bluffton Tow Buchanan Lake In
Fort Lancaster State Park Sonora Fort McKavett State Park Fort McKavett London Grit Mason Llano Kingsland Marble Falls Buchan Spicev

K

Sanderson Big Canyon River Roosevelt Junction Segovia Harper Doss Cherry Spring Willow City Round Mountain Lake Lyndon B. Johnson State Park
Dryden Juno Telegraph Fredericksburg Enchanted Rock State Park Johnson City Stonewall Lyndon B. Johnson State Par Blanco

L

Langtry Rio Grande Seminole Canyon State Park Comstock Loma Alta Rocksprings Mountain Home Hunt Ingram Kerrville Luckenbach Blanco State Park Spring Branch N Bra
Basin Boquillas del Carmen Devils Lake Amistad National Recreation Area Lake Walk Carta Valley Barksdale Camp Wood Kerrville State Park Camp Verde Comfort Sisterdale Medina Vanderpool Lost Maples State Park

M

Del Rio Ciudad Acuna Fort Clark Springs Brackettville Uvalde Knippa Sabinal Hondo Castle Hills Leon Valley San Martinez Elme
Spofford Dabney Blewett Natalia Lytle Somerset
Quemado Normandy Frio Town Moore Bigfoot Poteet Leming

N

COAHUILA Nueva Rosita Eagle Pass Piedras Negras La Pryor Batesville Pearsall Dilley Charlotte Christine Pleasan
Crystal City Brundage Millett Big Wells Woodward Los Angeles Fowlerton Tilden Three Rivers
Carrizo Springs Asherton Cotulla Calliham George W

P

UNITED STATES MEXICO Catarina Artesia Wells Encinal Freer San Diego Ben
Rio Grande TEXAS Nueces Benavides

Q

Monclova Nuevo Laredo Laredo Oilton Bruni Realitos Concepcio Ramirez
San Ygnacio Escobas Randado Mirando City Hebbronville Enci

R

Sabinas Hidalgo Falcon Res. Bustamante Lopeno Falcon La Gloria Santa Ele San Isidr
Nuevo Guerrero Falcon State Park El Sauz La Reforma
Cd. Mier Roma Rio Grande City

S

NUEVO LEON Cd. Camargo La Grulla Edinbur La Joya Mission
San Pedro de las Colonias Presa De El Azucar Bentsen Rio Grande Valley State Park Sullivan City Hidalgo Reynosa Monterrey

6 • 7 • 8 • 9 • 10 • 11

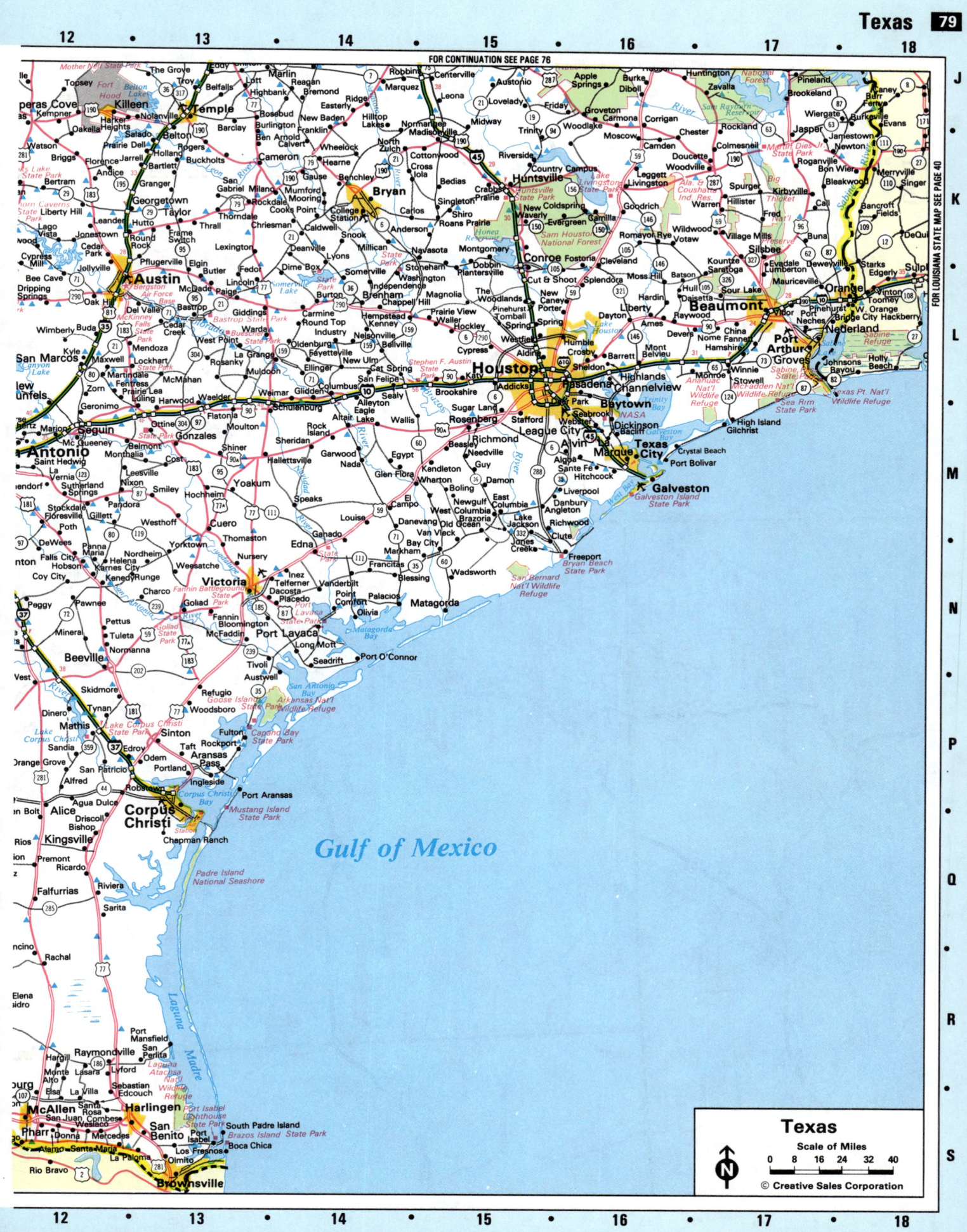

FOR CONTINUATION SEE PAGE 76

FOR LOUISIANA STATE MAP SEE PAGE 40

Gulf of Mexico

Texas

Scale of Miles

0   8   16   24   32   40

N

© Creative Sales Corporation

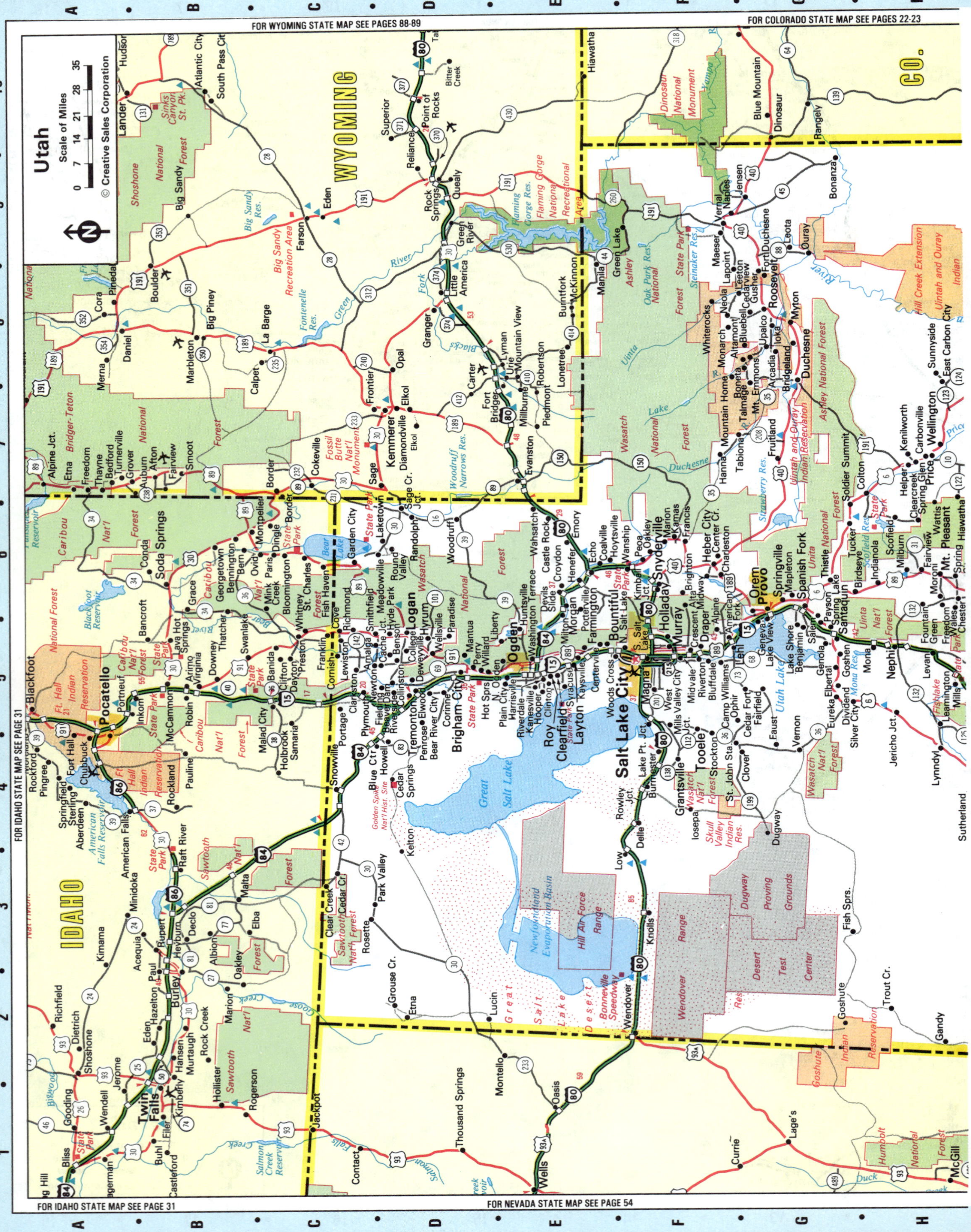

FOR WYOMING STATE MAP SEE PAGES 88-89
FOR COLORADO STATE MAP SEE PAGES 22-23
FOR IDAHO STATE MAP SEE PAGE 31
FOR IDAHO STATE MAP SEE PAGE 31
FOR NEVADA STATE MAP SEE PAGE 54

Utah
Scale of Miles
0 7 14 21 28 35
© Creative Sales Corporation
N

WYOMING
IDAHO
COLO.
NEVADA

Salt Lake City
Provo
Orem
Ogden
Logan
Pocatello
Blackfoot
Twin Falls
Brigham City
Layton
Clearfield
Roy
Bountiful
Tooele
Wendover
Vernal
Roosevelt
Duchesne
Nephi
Price
Helper
Rock Springs
Green River
Evanston
Kemmerer
Lander
Pinedale
Big Piney
Soda Springs
Montpelier

Great Salt Lake
Utah Lake
Bear Lake
Strawberry Res.
Flaming Gorge National Recreational Area
Dinosaur National Monument
Fossil Butte Nat'l Monument
Uinta National Forest
Wasatch National Forest
Ashley National Forest
Caribou National Forest
Sawtooth National Forest
Uintah and Ouray Indian Reservation
Ft. Hall Indian Reservation
Goshute Indian Reservation
Skull Valley Indian Res.
Dugway Proving Grounds
Desert Test Center
Hill Air Force Range
Wendover Range
Bonneville Speedway
Great Salt Lake Desert
Newfoundland Evaporation Basin
Bridger-Teton National Forest
Shoshone National Forest

FOR COLORADO STATE MAP SEE PAGES 22-23
FOR NEW MEXICO STATE MAP SEE PAGE 62
FOR ARIZONA STATE MAP SEE PAGES 16-17

UTAH

N. M.

ARIZONA

NEVADA

Grand Junction, Fruita, Loma, Mack, Cisco, Thompson, Crescent Jct., Green River, Woodside, East Carbon City, Woodside, Cleveland, Elmo, Huntington, Castle Dale, Clawson, Molen, Ferron, Orangeville, Moore, Emery, Fremont Jct.

Moab, La Sal Jct., La Sal, Paradox, Bedrock, Gateway, Uravan, Vancorum, Naturita, Nucla, Slick Rock, Egnar, Dove Creek, Cahone, Summit Pt., Eastland, Monticello, Blanding, Bluff, Mexican Hat, Montezuma Creek, Aneth

Dolores, Cortez, Lewis, Arriola, Pleasant View, Yellow Jacket, Lebanon, Towaoc, Teec Nos Pos, Tes Nez Iha, Mexican Water, Dinnehotso, Kayenta, Tsegi

Farmington, Kirtland, Newcomb, Sheep Springs, Naschitti, Tohatchi, Standing Rock, Shiprock, Beclabito, Crystal, Navajo, Mexican Springs, Rock Point, Many Farms, Chinle, Round Rock, Tsaile, Canyon DeChelly Nat'l Mon., Rough Rock, Chilchinbito, Cow Springs, Red Lake, Tonalea, Tuba City, Cameron, Moenkopi, Tusayan, Old Oraibi, Oraibi, Second Mesa, Polacca, Keams Canyon, Gray Mountain

Manti-La Sal National Forest, Arches National Park, Canyonlands National Park, Glen Canyon National Recreation Area, Lake Powell, Natural Bridges Nat'l Monument, Rainbow Bridge Nat'l Monument, Hovenweep Nat'l Monument, Dead Horse Point State Park, Goosenecks State Park, Edge of the Cedars State Park

Price, Mt. Pleasant, Spring City, Pigeon Hollow Jct., Ephraim, Manti, Sterling, Mayfield, Freedom, Wales, Chester, Fountain Green, Fayette, Gunnison, Centerfield, Axtell, Salina, Redmond, Aurora, Sigurd, Glenwood, Richfield, Venice, Elsinore, Central, Annabella, Monroe, Burrville, Koosharem, Greenwich, Angle, Antimony, Kingston, Junction, Circleville, Marysvale, Sevier, Joseph, Austin, Greenwich

Leamington, Lynndyl, Oak City, Scipio, Holden, Fillmore, Meadow, Kanosh, Delta, Deseret, Oasis, Hinckley, Sutherland, Abraham, Flowell, Greenwood, Black Rock, Cove Fort, Beaver, Greenville, Manderfield, Minersville, Adamsville, Milford, Beryl, Zane, Lund, Newcastle, Enterprise, Modena, Uvada, Garrison, Baker

Fishlake National Forest, Dixie National Forest, Fremont, Loa, Bicknell, Teasdale, Lyman, Torrey, Grover, Boulder, Escalante, Henrieville, Cannonville, Tropic, Bryce, Bryce Canyon Nat'l Park, Widtsoe Jct., Hanksville, Hatch, Panguitch, Paragonah, Parowan, Summit, Enoch, Cedar City, Hamilton Fort, Kanarraville, New Harmony, Pintura, Toquerville, Leeds, La Verkin, Hurricane, Virgin, Springdale, Rockville, Washington, St. George, Santa Clara, Ivins, Shivwits, Gunlock, Central, Pine Valley, Veyo

Capitol Reef National Park, Fry Canyon, Paria, Kanab, Fredonia, Colorado City, Glendale, Mt. Carmel, Mt. Carmel Jct., Orderville, Zion National Park, Long Valley Jct., Alton, Brian Head, Cedar Breaks Nat'l Monument, Kaibab Indian Reservation, Kaibab National Forest, Jacob Lake, Marble Canyon, Page, North Rim, Grand Canyon National Park, Desert View

McGill, Garrison, Ursine, Panaca, Pioche, Caliente, Elgin, Carp, Mesquite, Bunkerville, Littlefield, Beaver Dam Mtns. Wilderness Area, Lake Mead National Recreation Area, Logandale, Overton, Glendale, Meadview, Willow Beach, Hualapai Indian Reservation, Havasupai Indian Reservation, Glen Canyon, Colorado River

Navajo Indian Reservation, Hopi Indian Reservation

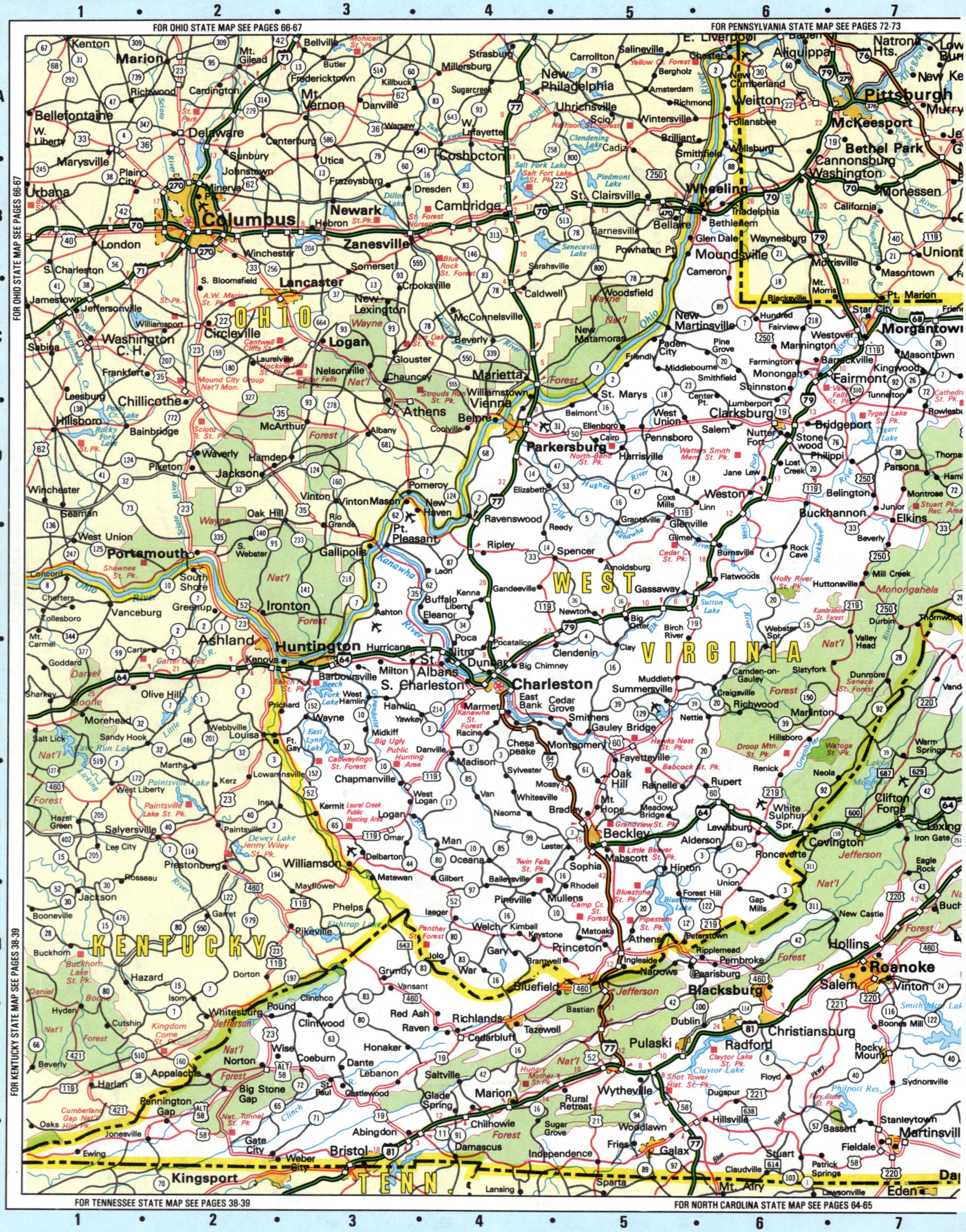
FOR OHIO STATE MAP SEE PAGES 66-67
FOR PENNSYLVANIA STATE MAP SEE PAGES 72-73
FOR OHIO STATE MAP SEE PAGES 66-67
FOR KENTUCKY STATE MAP SEE PAGES 38-39
FOR TENNESSEE STATE MAP SEE PAGES 38-39
FOR NORTH CAROLINA STATE MAP SEE PAGES 64-65
OHIO
WEST VIRGINIA
KENTUCKY
TENN.
Columbus
Zanesville
Newark
Cambridge
Lancaster
Chillicothe
Portsmouth
Huntington
Ashland
Charleston
Parkersburg
Marietta
Wheeling
Pittsburgh
Weirton
Morgantown
Fairmont
Clarksburg
Beckley
Bluefield
Blacksburg
Roanoke
Salem
Christiansburg
Radford
Pulaski
Wytheville
Bristol
Kingsport
Martinsville
Williamson
Logan
Elkins
Buckhannon
Lewisburg
Covington

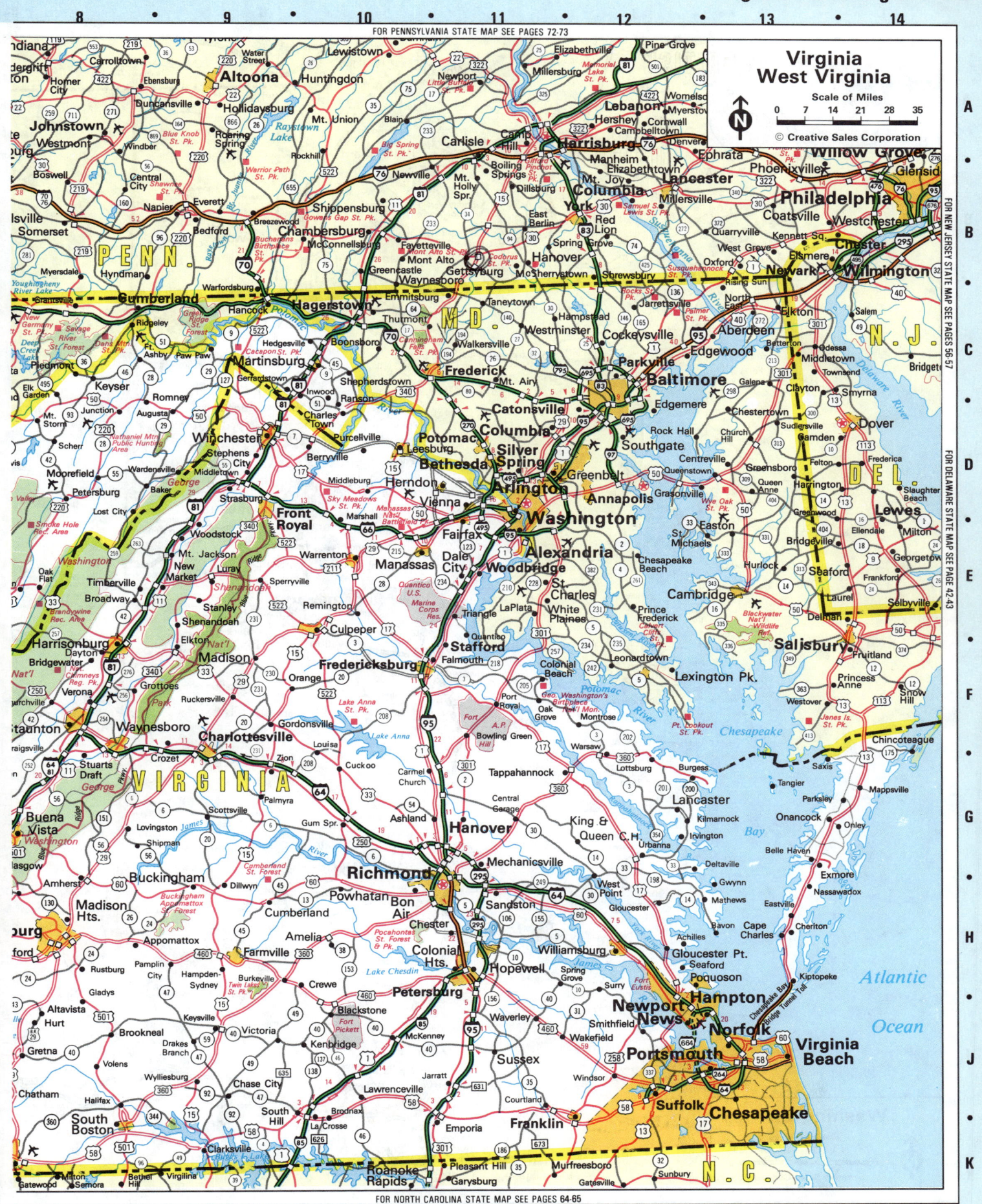

Virginia
West Virginia
Scale of Miles
0   7   14   21   28   35
© Creative Sales Corporation

WASHINGTON

BC
CANADA
U.S.
OREGON
IDAHO

Manning Prov. Pk.
Cathedral Prov. Pk.
Osoyoos Lake
Greenwood
Grand Forks
Rossland
Trail
Montrose
Osoyoos
Oroville
Similkameen Dam
Danville
Northport
Boundary
Boundary Dam
Colville
Orient
Pasayten Wilderness
Ross Lake
Okanogan
Tonasket
Wauconda
Republic
Curlew Lk. St. Pk.
Marcus
Kettle Falls
Bossburg
Ione
Metaline
Metaline Falls
Nordman
Kaniksu
Priest Lake
Sandpoint
Conconully
Riverside
Colville National Forest
Addy
Gifford
Chewelah
Priest Lake St. Pk.
Priest River
Winthrop
Twisp
Omak
Okanogan
Disautel
Keller
Springdale
Deer Park
Clayton
Newport
Round Lake St. Pk.
Pend Oreille
Bayview
Athol
Farragut St. Pk.
Brewster
Methow
Pateros
Bridgeport
Chief Joseph Dam
Grand Coulee Dam
Coulee Dam
Elmer City
Electric City
Grand Coulee
Wilbur
Creston
Davenport
Reardan
Spokane
Millwood
Mt. Spokane St. Pk.
Spirit Lake
Twin Lakes
Rathdrum
Post Falls
Coeur D'Alene
Hayden Lake
Manson
Chelan
Lake Chelan Dam
Mansfield
Withrow
Banks Lake
Dry Falls
Coulee City
Hartline
Almira
Medical Lake
Cheney
Spangle
Rockford
Fairfield
Waverly
Plummer
Coeur D'Alene Lake
Coeur D'Alene Indian Res.
Telma
Chelan
Waterville
Sun Lakes St. Pk.
Summer Falls St. Pk.
Harrington
Edwall
Latah
Rosalia
Tekoa
Oakesdale
Leavenworth
Cashmere
Wenatchee
East Wenatchee
Rocky Reach Dam
Rock Island
Rock Island Dam
Lenore Lake
Lake Lenore Caves St. Pk.
Soap Lake
Wilson Creek
Krupp
Odessa
Sprague
Lamont
St. John
Steptoe Butte St. Pk.
Garfield
Palouse
Farmington
Appleyard
Wenatchee Hts.
Squilchuck St. Pk.
Ephrata
Quincy
Soap Lake
Ritzville
Steptoe
Endicott
Colfax
Potlatch
Roslyn
Cle Elum
Crescent Bar
Winchester Res.
Moses Lake
Moses Lake Dam
George
Lind
Albion
Moscow
Ellensburg
Kittitas
Vantage
Potholes Res.
O'Sullivan Dam
Warden
La Crosse
Dusty
Pullman
Naches
Tieton
Selah
Wanapum St. Pk.
Frenchman Hills Lakes
Potholes St. Pk.
Royal City
Othello
Hatton
Washtucna
Palouse Falls St. Pk.
Lyons Ferry St. Pk.
Lower Granite Dam
Clarkston
Lewiston
Yakima
Union Gap
Moxee City
Priest Rapids Dam
Yakima Sportsman's St. Pk.
Saddle Mtn. Nat'l Wildlife Refuge
Mattawa
Connell
Mesa
Kahlotus
Little Goose Dam
Dodge
Pomeroy
Starbuck
Uniontown
Colton
Genesee
Wapato
Zillah
Sunnyside Dam
Hanford Site
U.S. Dept. of Energy
Juniper Dunes Wilderness
Lower Monumental Dam
Harrah
Toppenish
Granger
Sunnyside
West Richland
Benton City
Richland
Pasco
Kennewick
Eureka
Prescott
Waitsburg
Asotin
White Swan
Grandview
Mabton
Prosser
Wallula
Wallula
Walla Walla
College Place
Umatilla Nat'l Forest
Wenaha
Fields Spring St. Pk.
Goldendale
Bickleton
McNary Dam
Whitman Mission Nat'l Hist. Site
Milton-Freewater
Roosevelt
Boardman
Hermiston
Stanfield
Athena
Wallowa-Whitman Nat'l Forest
John Day Dam
Arlington
Wasco
Moro
Ione
Lexington
Heppner
Pilot Rock
Pendleton
Umatilla Indian Res.
Elgin
Wallowa
Enterprise
Joseph
Hells Canyon Nat'l Rec. Area

FOR IDAHO STATE MAP SEE PAGE 31

FOR MICHIGAN STATE MAP SEE PAGES 44-45

Canadian Citizens Visiting the United States

Passports or visas are not required of Canadian citizens or British subjects residing in Canada entering the United States for a period of six months or less, however, evidence of citizenship is required. Check with customs officials for complete regulations and requirements.

United States Citizens Visiting Canada

All persons entering Canada must report to the Canadian Immigration and Customs Office at the Port of Entry and secure required permits for admission for their person and possessions. The transportation of plants and produce is rigidly controlled. Check with customs officials for complete regulations and requirements.

The Interstate Highway System in and around the Chicago area is confusing to many people. It is helpful to remember that, in most cases, Interstate Highways running north and south have odd numbers, and Interstate Highways running east and west have even numbers

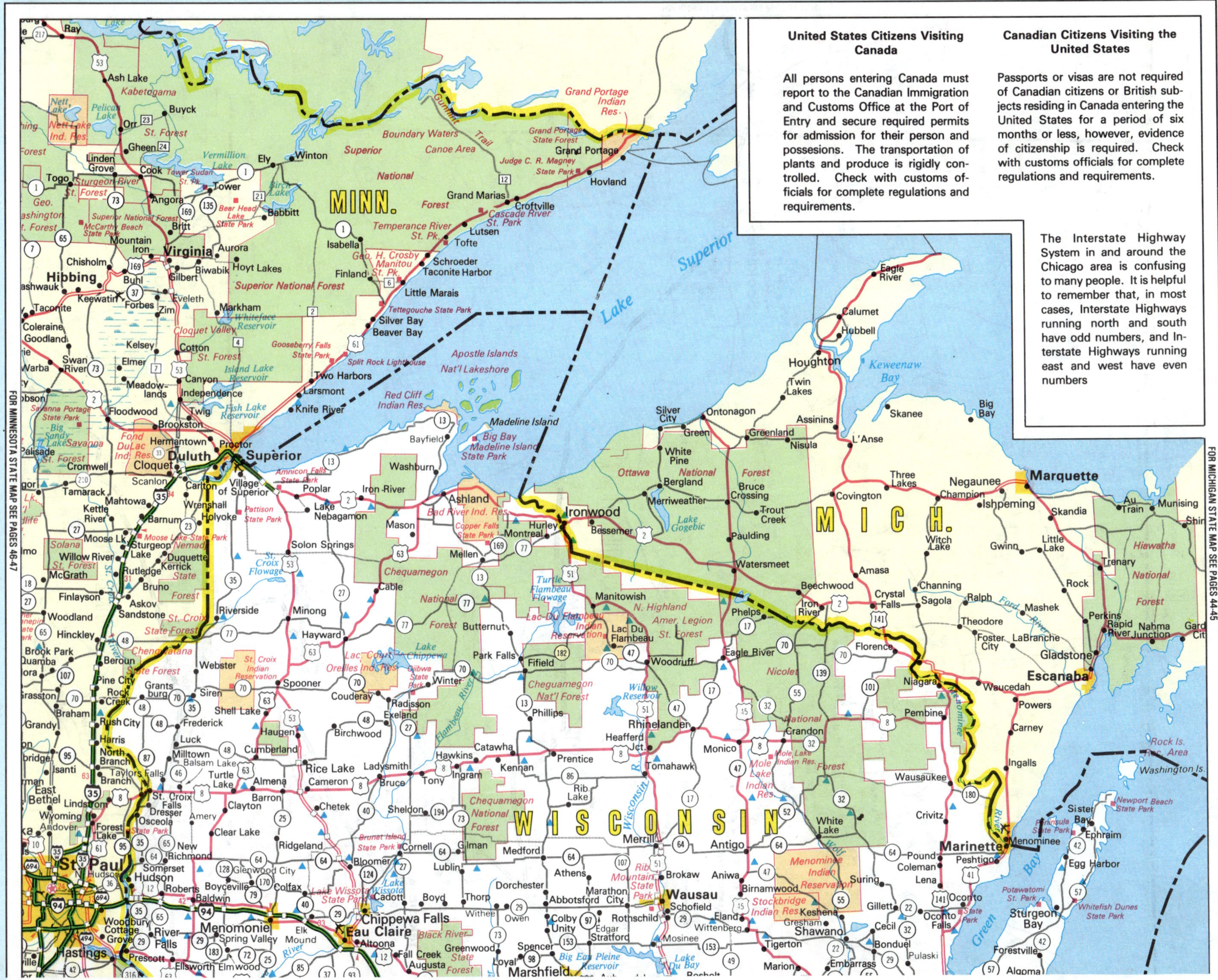

MICH.

WISCONSIN

MINN.

Lake Superior

Keweenaw Bay

Green Bay

Marquette

Escanaba

Marinette

Wausau

Eau Claire

Menomonie

Superior

Duluth

Virginia

Hibbing

Chippewa Falls

St. Paul

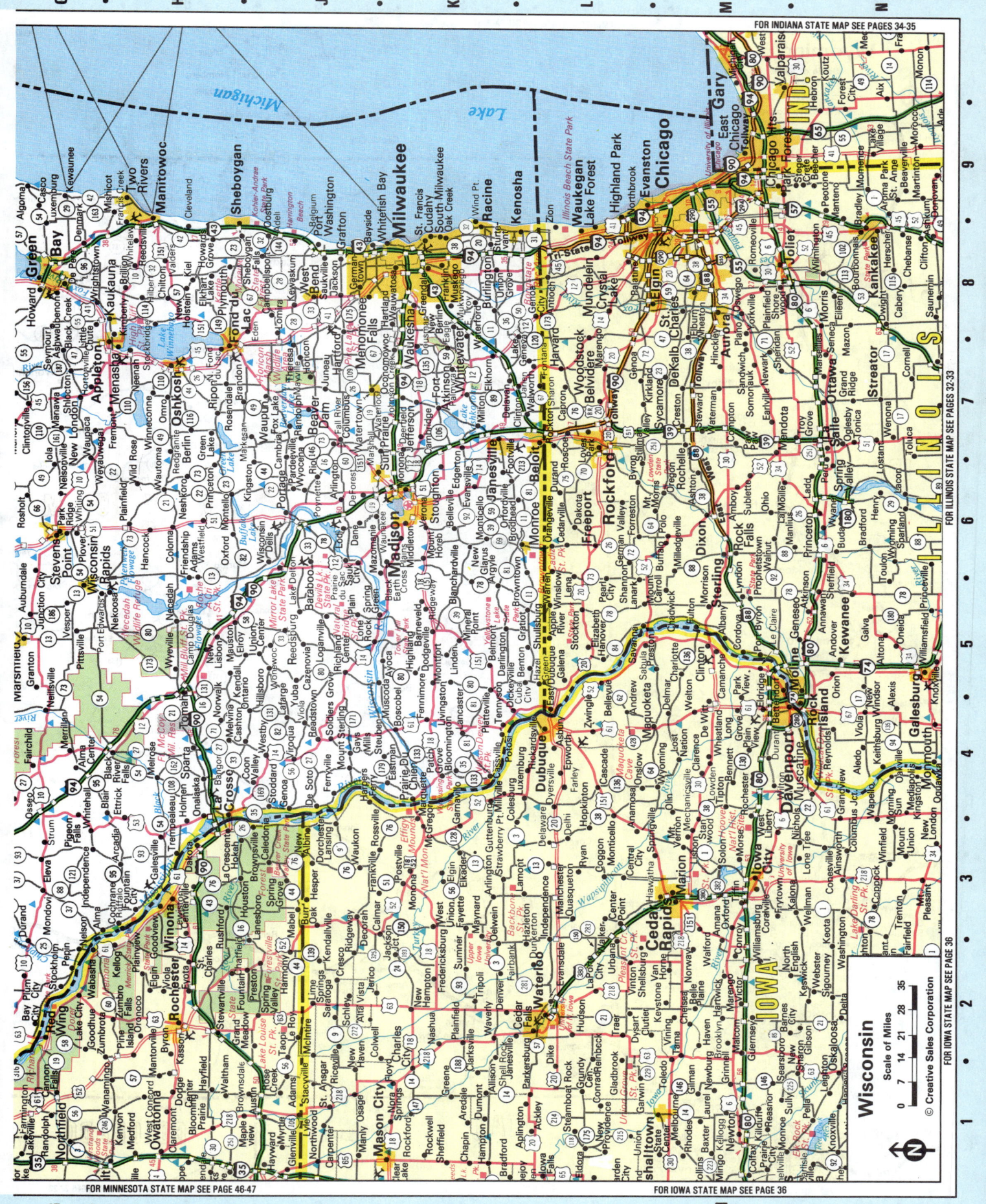

FOR INDIANA STATE MAP SEE PAGES 34-35

FOR ILLINOIS STATE MAP SEE PAGES 32-33

Wisconsin

Scale of Miles

0 7 14 21 28 35

© Creative Sales Corporation

FOR IOWA STATE MAP SEE PAGE 36

Wyoming

Scale of Miles
0 7 14 21 28 35

© Creative Sales Corporation

N

FOR MONTANA STATE MAP SEE PAGE 51
FOR IDAHO STATE MAP SEE PAGE 31
FOR UTAH STATE MAP SEE PAGES 80-81
FOR COLORADO STATE MAP SEE PAGES 22-23

MT.

IDAHO

WYOMING

UTAH

COLORADO

Emigrant, Pray, Chico Hot Springs, Big Sky, Cameron, Gardiner, Nye, Dean, Fishtail, Joliet, Boyd, Edgar, Roberts, Fromberg, Bridger, Bearcreek, Red Lodge, Cooke City, Belfry, Frannie, Deaver, Cowley, Clark, Elk Basin, Garland, Byron, Lovell, Powell, Ralston, Burgess

Grant, Dell, Lima, Lima Reservoir, Blue Dome, Spencer, Dubois, Ashton, Warm River, St. Anthony, Parker, Chester, Newdale, Sugar City, Teton, Rexburg, Lorenzo, Tetonia, Driggs, Heise, Victor, Swan Valley, Irwin, Moose, Teton Village, Kelly, Wilson, Jackson, Hoback Jct., Alpine Jct., Etna, Freedom, Thayne, Bedford, Turnerville, Grover, Auburn, Afton, Fairview, Smoot

Mammouth Springs Jct., Tower Jct., Norris Jct., Canyon Jct., Madison Jct., Lake Jct., Old Faithful, W. Thumb Jct., Shoshone Lake, Lewis Lake, Heart Lake, Jackson Lake, Jenny Lake, Moran Jct., Cody, Buffalo Bill Reservoir, Valley, Pitchfork, Meeteetse, Emblem, Shell, Greybull, Basin, Burlington, Otto, Manderson, Worland, Grass Creek, Hamilton Dome, Kirby, Lucerne, Thermopolis, E. Thermopolis

Dubois, Burris, Crowheart, Morton, Pavillion, Kinnear, Ethete, Fort Washakie, Riverton, Shoshoni, Lysite, Moneta, Hudson, Lander, Arapahoe, St. Stephens, Atlantic City, South Pass City

Merna, Cora, Pinedale, Daniel, Boulder, Marbleton, Big Piney, Calpet, La Barge, Big Sandy, Farson, Eden, Reliance, Superior, Point of Rocks, Rock Springs, Green River, Granger, Little America, Carter, Fort Bridger, Lyman, Mountain View, Robertson, Lonetree, Burntfork, McKinnon, Manila, Green Lake, Hiawatha

Kemmerer, Diamondville, Elkol, Opal, Frontier, Sage, Cokeville, Border, Montpelier

IDAHO FALLS, Pocatello, Blackfoot, Shelley, Firth, Basalt, Moreland, Rockford, Pingree, Fort Hall, Chubbuck, Portneuf, Inkom, McCammon, Arimo, Downey, Thatcher, Grace, Bancroft, Soda Springs, Lava Hot Springs, Conda, Georgetown, Bennington, Bern, Ovid, Paris, Dingle, Fish Haven, Garden City, Laketown

Malad City, Holbrook, Samaria, Clifton, Dayton, Preston, Whitney, Franklin, Cove, Richmond, Lewiston, Cornish, Fish Haven, St. Charles, Bloomington

Snowville, Portage, Plymouth, Clarkston, Newton, Smithfield, Amalga, Cache Jct., Meadowville, Hyde Park, Benson, Logan, Hyrum, Wellsville, Paradise, Woodruff, Randolph

Brigham City, Perry, Willard, Mantua, Liberty, Huntsville, Eden, Roy, Clearfield, Layton, Kaysville, Ogden, N. Ogden, Pleasant View, Harrisville, Riverdale, Farmington, Bountiful, Salt Lake City, Holladay, Snyderville

FOR MONTANA STATE MAP SEE PAGE 51

FOR SOUTH DAKOTA STATE MAP SEE PAGE 74

FOR NEBRASKA STATE MAP SEE PAGES 52-53

FOR COLORADO STATE MAP SEE PAGES 22-23

MT.

SOUTH DAK.

NEBRASKA

CO.

Northern Cheyenne Indian Reservation

Custer National Forest

Custer National Forest

Crow Indian Reservation

Thunder Basin Nat'l Grassland

Devils Tower Nat. Monument

Black Hills Nat'l Forest

Black Hills National Forest

Big Horn National Forest

Thunder Basin National Grassland

Medicine Bow National Forest

Pathfinder Reservoir

Seminoe Reservoir

Medicine Bow Nat'l Forest

Buffalo Gap National Grassland

Badlands National Park

Wind Cave National Park

Oglala National Grasslands

Nebraska National Forest

Roosevelt National Forest

Pawnee National Grassland

Pine Ridge Indian Reservation

Belle Fourche Reservoir

Keyhole Res.

Glendo Res.

Wheatland Res. No. 2

Angostura Reservoir

Lake DeSmet

Carryowen, Crow, Lodge Grass, Wyola, Parkman, Ranchester, Dayton, Beckton, Big Horn, Banner, Story, Sheridan, Acme, Decker, Leiter, Clearmont, Arvada, Ucross, Buffalo, Hyattville, Ten Sleep, Big Trails, Mayoworth, Kaycee, Sussex, Barnum, Linch, Midwest, Edgerton, Lost Cabin, Arminto, Waltman, Hiland, Powder River, Natrona, Casper, Mills, Evansville, Glenrock, Bar Nunn, Boxelder, Alcova, Shirley Basin, Bairoil, Lamont, Rawlins, Sinclair, Walcott, Elk Mountain, Arlington, Saratoga, Riverside, Encampment, Dixon, Savery, Cowdrey, Walden, Hanna, Elmo, Medicine Bow, Rock River, McFadden, Bosler, Centennial, Albany, Woods Landing, Mountain Home, Laramie, Federal, Tie Siding, Virginia Dale

Broadus, Birney, Ford, Biddle, Hammond, Recluse, Spotted Horse, Rockypoint, Lightning Flat, New Haven, Weston, Oshoto, Hulett, Alva, Aladdin, Colony, Belle Fourche, Newell, Nisland, Fruitdale, Spearfish, Sundance, Beulah, Devil's Tower Jct., Gillette, Rozet, Moorcroft, Upton, Four Corners, Osage, Newcastle, Wright, Reno Jct., Rochelle, Hampshire, Clareton, Morrisey, Mule Cr. Jct., Bill, Pine Tree Jct., Savageton, Edgemont, Redbird, Igloo, Provo, Lance Creek, Manville, Lusk, Node, Keeline, Shawnee, Orin, Douglas, Orpha, Lost Springs, Glendo, Guernsey, Fort Laramie, Lingle, Torrington, Wheatland, Slater, Chugwater, Hawk Sprs., Yoder, Veteran, La Grange, Albin, Hillsdale, Burns, Pine Bluffs, Egbert, Carpenter, Cheyenne, Horse Creek, Iron Mountain, Jay Em, Sunrise, Hartville, Van Tassel

Zeona, Hoover, Mud Butte, Maurine, Castle Rock, Fairpoint, Stoneville, Red Owl, Union Center, Whitewood, Sturgis, Deadwood, Lead, Pluma, Central City, Rochford, Deerfield, Silver City, Hill City, Keystone, Hisega, Rapid City, Box Elder, New Underwood, Caputa, Farmingdale, Hermosa, Custer, Game Lodge, Fairburn, Elm Springs, Crazy Horse Mon., Mt. Rushmore Nat'l Mon., Blue Bell, Pringle, Buffalo Gap, Hot Springs, Oral, Smithwick, Manderson, Oelrichs, Ardmore, Chadron, Rushville, Whitney, Crawford, Hay, Harrison, Marsland, Hemingford, Alliance, Antioch, Morrill, Mitchell, Scottsbluff, Gering, Terrytown, Lyman, Huntley, Minatare, Bayard, Bridgeport, Melbeta, McGrew, Harrisburg, Dalton, Gurley, Kimball, Dix, Potter, Sidney, Bushnell, Sterling, Crook, Proctor, Iliff, Peetz, Fleming, Atwood, Stoneham, Raymer, Buckingham, Ault, Pierce, Briggsdale, Nunn, Rockport, The Forks, Poudre Park, Rustic, Bellvue, Fort Collins

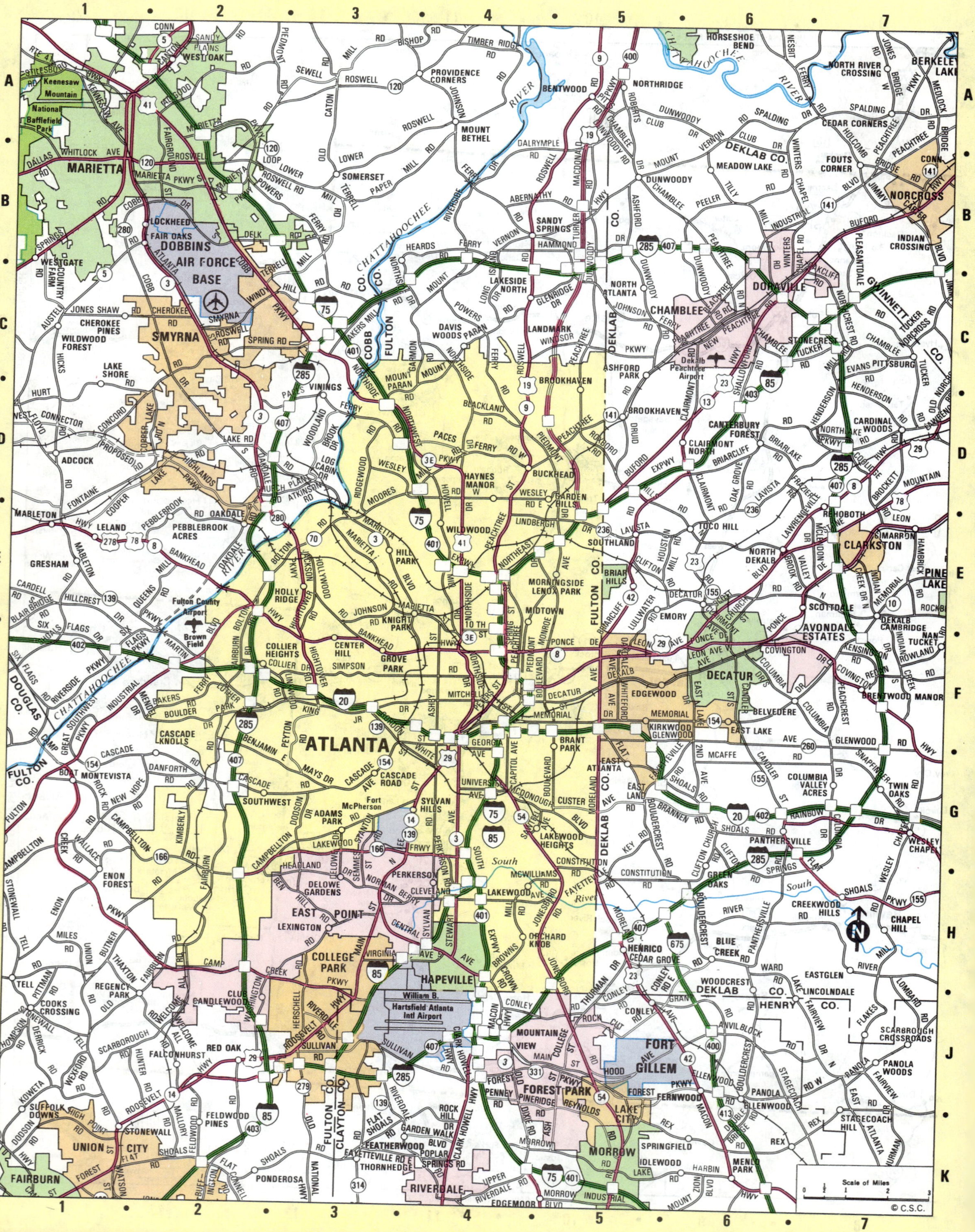
ATLANTA
MARIETTA
SMYRNA
DOBBINS AIR FORCE BASE
Keenesaw Mountain National Battlefield Park
VININGS
SANDY SPRINGS
DUNWOODY
CHAMBLEE
DORAVILLE
NORCROSS
BROOKHAVEN
BUCKHEAD
DECATUR
CLARKSTON
AVONDALE ESTATES
EAST POINT
COLLEGE PARK
HAPEVILLE
William B. Hartsfield Atlanta Intl Airport
FOREST PARK
FORT GILLEM
LAKE CITY
MORROW
RIVERDALE
UNION CITY
FAIRBURN
Fulton County Airport Brown Field
Dekalb Peachtree Airport
CHATTAHOOCHEE RIVER
South River
DEKALB CO.
FULTON CO.
COBB CO.
DOUGLAS CO.
CLAYTON CO.
HENRY CO.
Scale of Miles
© C.S.C.

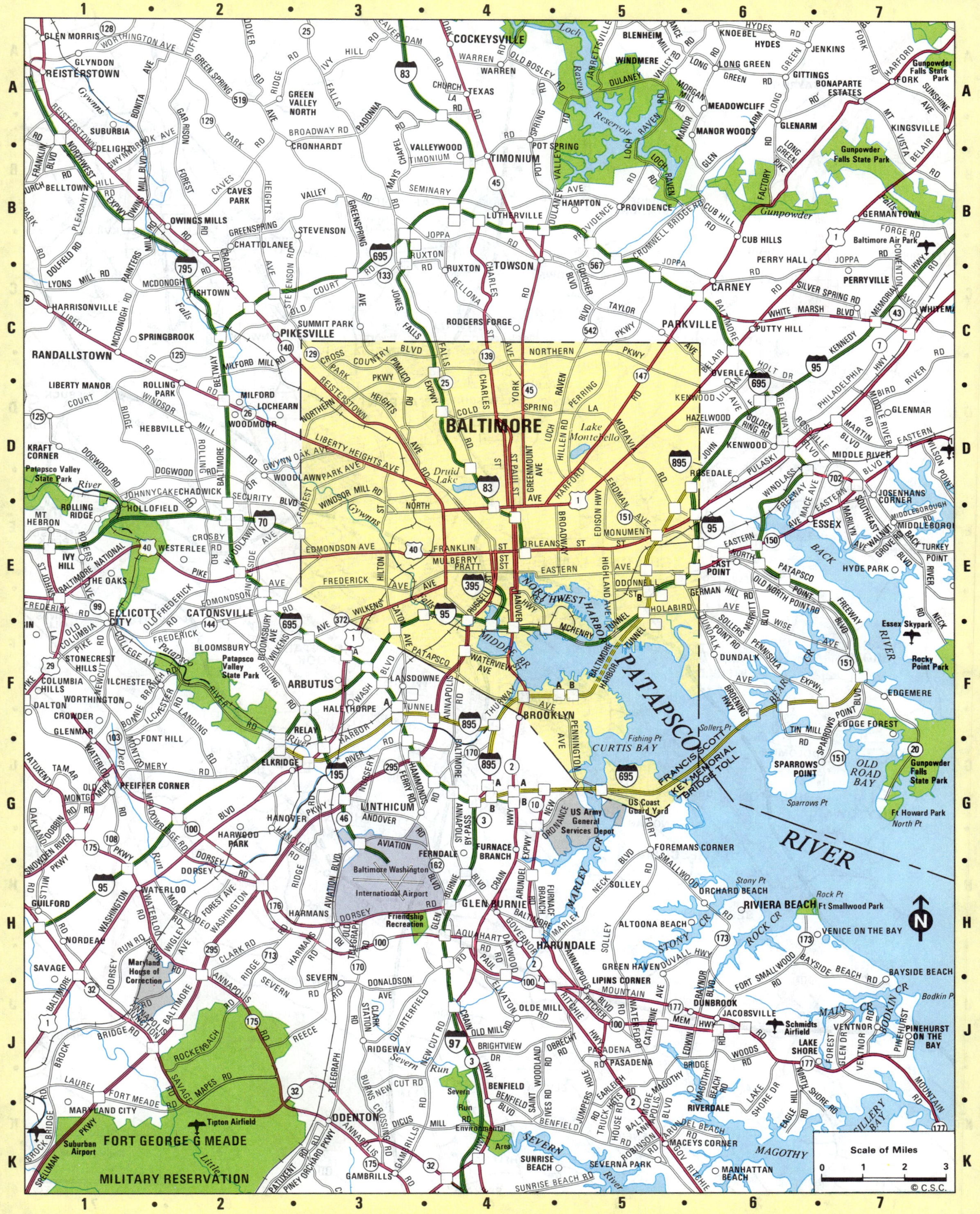

BALTIMORE

PATAPSCO

RIVER

OLD ROAD BAY

MAGOTHY

COCKEYSVILLE
REISTERSTOWN
GLEN MORRIS
GLYNDON
SUBURBIA
DELIGHT
BELLTOWN
OWINGS MILLS
CAVES PARK
CHATTOLANEE
STEVENSON
SPRINGBROOK
PIKESVILLE
RANDALLSTOWN
LIBERTY MANOR
ROLLING PARK
MILFORD
LOCHEARN
WOODMOOR
KRAFT CORNER
HEBBVILLE
DOGWOOD
ROLLING RIDGE
MT HEBRON
IVY HILL
THE OAKS
WESTERLEE
HOLLOFIELD
JOHNNYCAKE
CHADWICK
ELLICOTT CITY
CATONSVILLE
BLOOMSBURY
STONECREST HILLS
COLUMBIA HILLS
WORTHINGTON
DALTON
CROWDER
GLENMAR
FONT HILL
ARBUTUS
HALETHORPE
RELAY
ELKRIDGE
LANSDOWNE
LINTHICUM
ANDOVER
HANOVER
HARWOOD PARK
AVIATION
DORSEY
HARMANS
FERNDALE
FURNACE BRANCH
GLEN BURNIE
HARUNDALE
LIPINS CORNER
PASADENA
GUILFORD
NORDEAC
SAVAGE
WATERLOO
MARYLAND HOUSE OF CORRECTION
ANNAPOLIS JUNCTION
ROCKENBACH
MARYLAND CITY
TIPTON AIRFIELD
SUBURBAN AIRPORT
FORT GEORGE G MEADE
MILITARY RESERVATION
ODENTON
GAMBRILLS
RIDGEWAY
SEVERN
DONALDSON
BENFIELD
BRIGHTVIEW
SUNRISE BEACH
SEVERNA PARK
MANHATTAN BEACH
MACEYS CORNER
RIVERDALE
LAKE SHORE
JACOBSVILLE
VENTNOR
PINEHURST ON THE BAY
DUNBROOK
GREEN HAVEN
ALTOONA BEACH
ORCHARD BEACH
RIVIERA BEACH
VENICE ON THE BAY
BAYSIDE BEACH
FORT SMALLWOOD
FT SMALLWOOD PARK
SPARROWS POINT
FT HOWARD PARK
GUNPOWDER FALLS STATE PARK
ROCKY POINT PARK
ESSEX SKYPARK
EDGEMERE
LODGE FOREST
HYDE PARK
ESSEX
MIDDLE RIVER
JOSENHANS CORNER
MIDDLEBOROUGH
GLENMAR
MARTIN
ROSEDALE
DUNDALK
SOLLERS POINT
HOLABIRD
US ARMY GENERAL SERVICES DEPOT
US COAST GUARD YARD
CURTIS BAY
FISHING PT
FRANCIS SCOTT KEY MEMORIAL BRIDGE TOLL
BROOKLYN
WATERVIEW
FORT McHENRY
EAST POINT
PARKVILLE
OVERLEA
CARNEY
HAZELWOOD
ROSSVILLE
KENWOOD
GERMANTOWN
PERRY HALL
WHITE MARSH BLVD
PERRYVILLE
WHITEMA...
KINGSVILLE
BELAIR
GITTINGS
BONAPARTE ESTATES
GLENARM
MEADOWCLIFF
MANOR WOODS
WINDMERE
BLENHEIM
KNOEBEL
JENKINS
LONG GREEN
CUB HILL
CUB HILLS
DULANEY
PROVIDENCE
HAMPTON
TOWSON
RUXTON
LUTHERVILLE
RODGERS FORGE
TIMONIUM
VALLEYWOOD
POT SPRING
GREEN VALLEY NORTH
CRONHARDT
SUMMIT PARK
LAKE MONTEBELLO
DRUID LAKE
Reservoir
Loch Raven
Gunpowder
Gunpowder Falls State Park
Patapsco Valley State Park
Baltimore National

Baltimore Air Park
Baltimore Washington International Airport
Friendship Recreation
Schmidts Airfield
Lake Shore

NORTHWEST HARBOR
MIDDLE BR

Scale of Miles
0   1   2   3

© C.S.C.

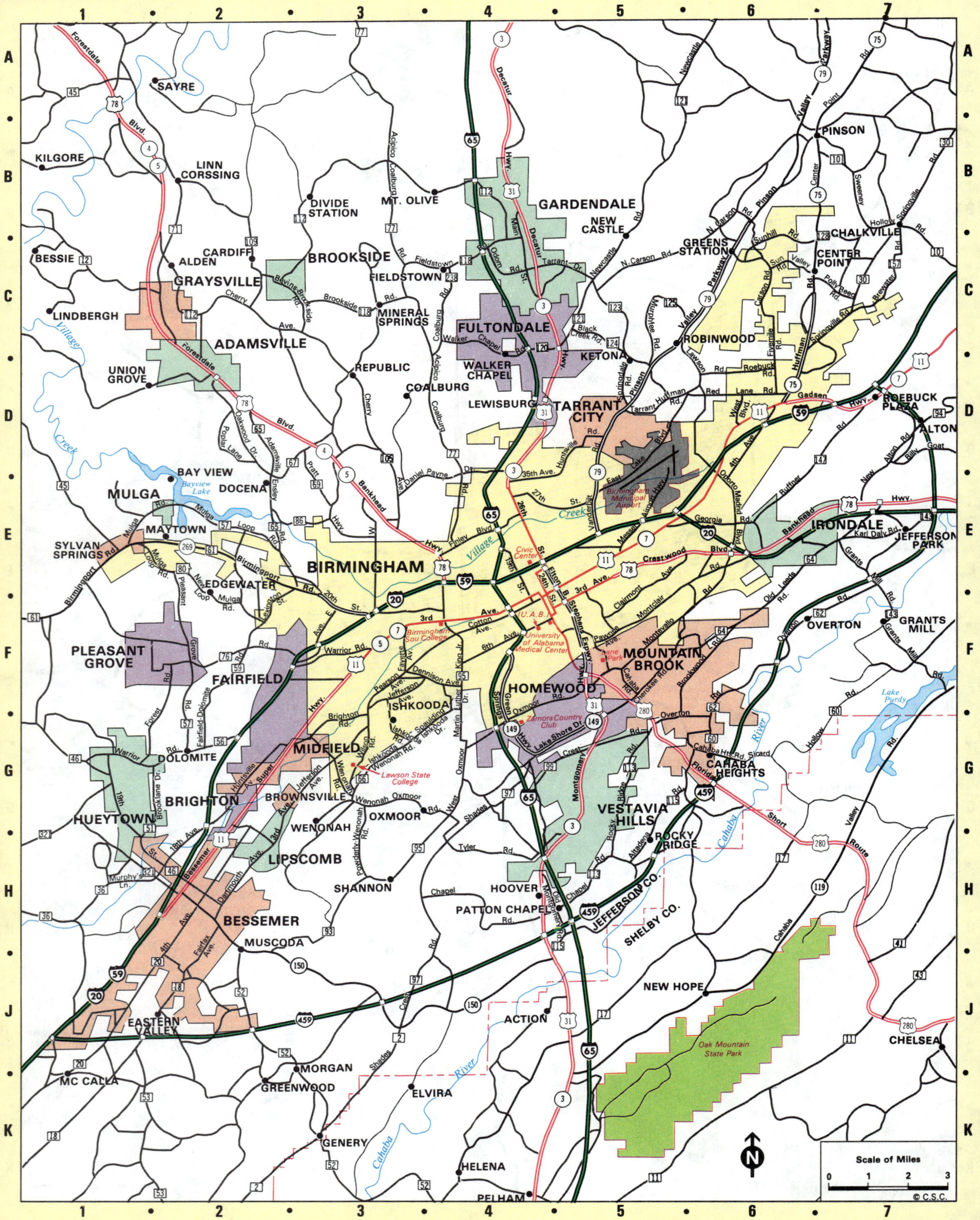

SAYRE
KILGORE
LINN CORSSING
BESSIE
ALDEN
CARDIFF
GRAYSVILLE
LINDBERGH
ADAMSVILLE
UNION GROVE
DIVIDE STATION
MT. OLIVE
BROOKSIDE
FIELDSTOWN
MINERAL SPRINGS
REPUBLIC
COALBURG
GARDENDALE
NEW CASTLE
FULTONDALE
WALKER CHAPEL
KETONA
LEWISBURG
TARRANT CITY
PINSON
CHALKVILLE
CENTER POINT
GREENS STATION
ROBINWOOD
ROEBUCK PLAZA
ALTON
BAY VIEW
Bayview Lake
DOCENA
MULGA
MAYTOWN
SYLVAN SPRINGS
EDGEWATER
BIRMINGHAM
Birmingham Municipal Airport
Civic Center
U.A.B.
Birmingham Sou. College
University of Alabama Medical Center
IRONDALE
JEFFERSON PARK
OVERTON
GRANTS MILL
PLEASANT GROVE
FAIRFIELD
ISHKOODA
HOMEWOOD
Zamora Country Club
MOUNTAIN BROOK
Lane Park
Lake Purdy
MIDFIELD
Lawson State College
DOLOMITE
BRIGHTON
BROWNSVILLE
HUEYTOWN
WENONAH
OXMOOR
VESTAVIA HILLS
CAHABA HEIGHTS
ROCKY RIDGE
LIPSCOMB
SHANNON
HOOVER
PATTON CHAPEL
BESSEMER
MUSCODA
JEFFERSON CO.
SHELBY CO.
NEW HOPE
ACTION
EASTERN VALLEY
Oak Mountain State Park
CHELSEA
MORGAN
MC CALLA
GREENWOOD
ELVIRA
GENERY
HELENA
PELHAM
Village Creek
Cahaba River
Scale of Miles
0 1 2 3
N
© C.S.C.

Billerica · Wilmington · Lynnfield · Reading · Peabody · Salem · Burlington · Bedford · Woburn · Wakefield · Stoneham · Lynn · Swampscott · Lexington · Winchester · Melrose · Saugus · Medford · Malden · Revere · Everett · Chelsea · Nahant · Arlington · Belmont · Somerville · Waltham · Watertown · Cambridge · Charlestown · Winthrop · Weston · Boston · Brookline · Newton · Roxbury · Wellesley · Needham · Dedham · Milton · Quincy · Dover · Westwood · Norwood · Hyde Park · Mattapan · Hingham · Hull · Braintree · Weymouth · Canton · Randolph

MASSACHUSETTS BAY · BROAD SOUND · BOSTON HARBOR · QUINCY BAY · HINGHAM BAY · NAHANT BAY

Logan International Airport

Scale of Miles
0 1 2 3

© Arrow Map, Inc.

1 2 3 4 5 6 7

A B C D E F G H J K

NIAGARA FALLS
Hyde Park G.C.
Pine
Packard
Echota
Ferry
Convention Center
Erie
Buffalo
NIAGARA FALLS
LA SALLE

BERKHOLTZ
Niagara Falls International Airport
Oppenheim Zoo
ST. JOHNSBURG
Niagara Falls
NASHVILLE
BEACH RIDGE
Loveland
Moyer
Killian
Steig
Ernst
Shawnee
HOFFMAN
SAWYER
Rule
Shultz
WURLITZER PARK
Ward
Nash
Walck Erie
Oliver
MARTINSVILLE
E. Robinson
French
NORTH TONAWANDA
Ellicott Cr. Park
Sweeney

WENDELVILLE
Bear
Tonawanda
Campbell
Schoelles
Meyer
Ridge
Sauer Home Rd.
PENDLETON
RAPIDS
MILLERSPORT
Steffen Airport
Amherst Airport
ELSERS CORNERS
SWORMVILLE
GETZVILLE
EAST AMHERST
CLARENCE CENTER

CHIPPAWA
Chippawa Battle Monument
SANDY BEACH
PEACH HAVEN
Huth
EDGEWATER
Ransom
Buckhorn State Park
Navy Is.
Long
Point
Bedell

Big Six Mile Creek Park
Whitehaven
Grand Island
Staley
Section
Love
Fix
Bush
GRANDYLE VILLAGE
West River Pkwy
TONAWANDA
Youngmann
190
KENMORE
Sheridan Park
Sheridan
Englewood
NORTH BAILEY
AMHERST
Brighton
Expwy
S.U.N.Y. Buffalo
Heim
Hopkins
Klein
Paradis
Transit
Clarence
Roll
Maple
Park C.C.
Ayer
Sheridan
Shimerville
Thompson
Greiner
HARRIS HILL

SNYDER
Netherby
Queen
Niagara
Beaver Island State Park
FERRY VILLAGE
River
Parkway
Kenmore
Military
Amherst
Hertel
Delaware
Colvin
Englewood
Parker
EGGERTSVILLE
SNYDER
S.U.N.Y. Buffalo
Bailey
Evans
WILLIAMSVILLE
New York
State Thruway
90
Genesee
33
BOWMANSVILLE
Pleasant
View

STEVENSVILLE
Eagle
Summit
Arcadia St.
Elizabeth
Bowen
Fort Erie Airport
FORT ERIE NORTH
198
Scajaquada Expwy
Delaware Park
Buffalo Zoo
SUNY Coll Buffalo
384
Main
Kensington
E. Delavan
33
Kensington Expwy
Buffalo International Airport
George
Urban
DEPEW
Walden
LANCASTER
130
Broadway
Cemetery

POINT ABINO
RIDGEWAY
Dominion
Bernard Av.
Ridge
Store
Mill Rd.
Rose Hill Rd.
Garrison
Ridgemount
Petit
FORT ERIE
Fort Erie Race Track
Ferry
Porter
Elmwood
Delaware
Michigan
Niagara
Best
Buffalo Museum of Science
E. Ferry
Genesee
War Mem. Stadium
Broadway
William
SLOAN
90
CHEEKTOWAGA
BELLEVUE
Como Park
Lossen
William
BLOSSOM
ELMA
354

THUNDER BAY
Thunder Bay Rd.
CRESCENT PARK
Thompson
Fort Erie
ERIE BEACH
Erie Beach
Waverly Beach
Crescent Beach
Airport
Swan
South
Seneca
Clinton
Bailey
190
354
Aurora
400
French
Borden
Buffalo Air Park
Clinton
GARDENVILLE
20
78
Indian
Church
ELMA CENTER
Rice

CRYSTAL BEACH
Crystal Beach
Buffalo Harbor
BUFFALO
Tifft
Park
Abbott
240
16
Cazenovia
62
Ridge
Botanical Gardens
5
WEST SENECA
EAST SENECA
Seneca
EBENEZER
Fisher
Leydecker
Angle
SPRINGBROOK
Davis
422
400

Lake Erie
LACKAWANNA
BLASDELL
South
Park
Orchard Creek
Michael
Orchard Park Airport
16
Proner Airport
78

CANADA UNITED STATES
ONTARIO NEW YORK
WELLAND CO. ERIE CO.
WOODLAWN
BAY VIEW
Bayview
WINDOM
Mile
Webster Cors.
WEBSTER CORNERS
Willochita
Knox

ATHOL SPRINGS
LOCKSLEY PARK
South Shore C.C.
75
Southwestern
Sowles
Big Tree
EAST HAMBURG
20A
ORCHARD PARK
277
Orchard Park C.C.
Jewett-Holmwood
Transit
20A

MT. VERNON
WANAKAH
CARNEGIE
Rogers
Amsdell
20
SCRANTON
Clark
ARMOR
Erie Co. Fairgrounds
Powers
219
DUELLS CORNERS
Freeman
ELLICOTT
240
ELLICOTT HEIGHTS
Blake

CLIFTON HEIGHTS
PINEHURST
Pleasant
Chestnut Ridge Park
Gartman
Schurr
JEWETTVILLE
Mill
GRIFFINS MILLS
Falls

HIGHLAND-ON-THE-LAKE
LAKE VIEW
View
Heitz
HAMBURG
WATER VALLEY
Lakeview Airport
Eighteen Mile Creek
Lake
Smith
391
WEST FALLS
West
Behm
Cole

NORTH EVANS
Wisconsin
Versailles
Bauer
62
Eden
EAST EDEN
Boston
NORTH BOSTON
277
Ridge
Cole

JERUSALEM CORNERS
DERBY
Point
Derby
Ferry
Southwestern
EDEN VALLEY
North
Hardt
Eckhardt
Mayer
Zimmerman
Black Creek

ANGOLA-ON-THE-LAKE
EVANS
90
75
Church
EAST EDEN
219
391
PATCHIN

N

Scale of Miles
0 1 2 3

© C.S.C.

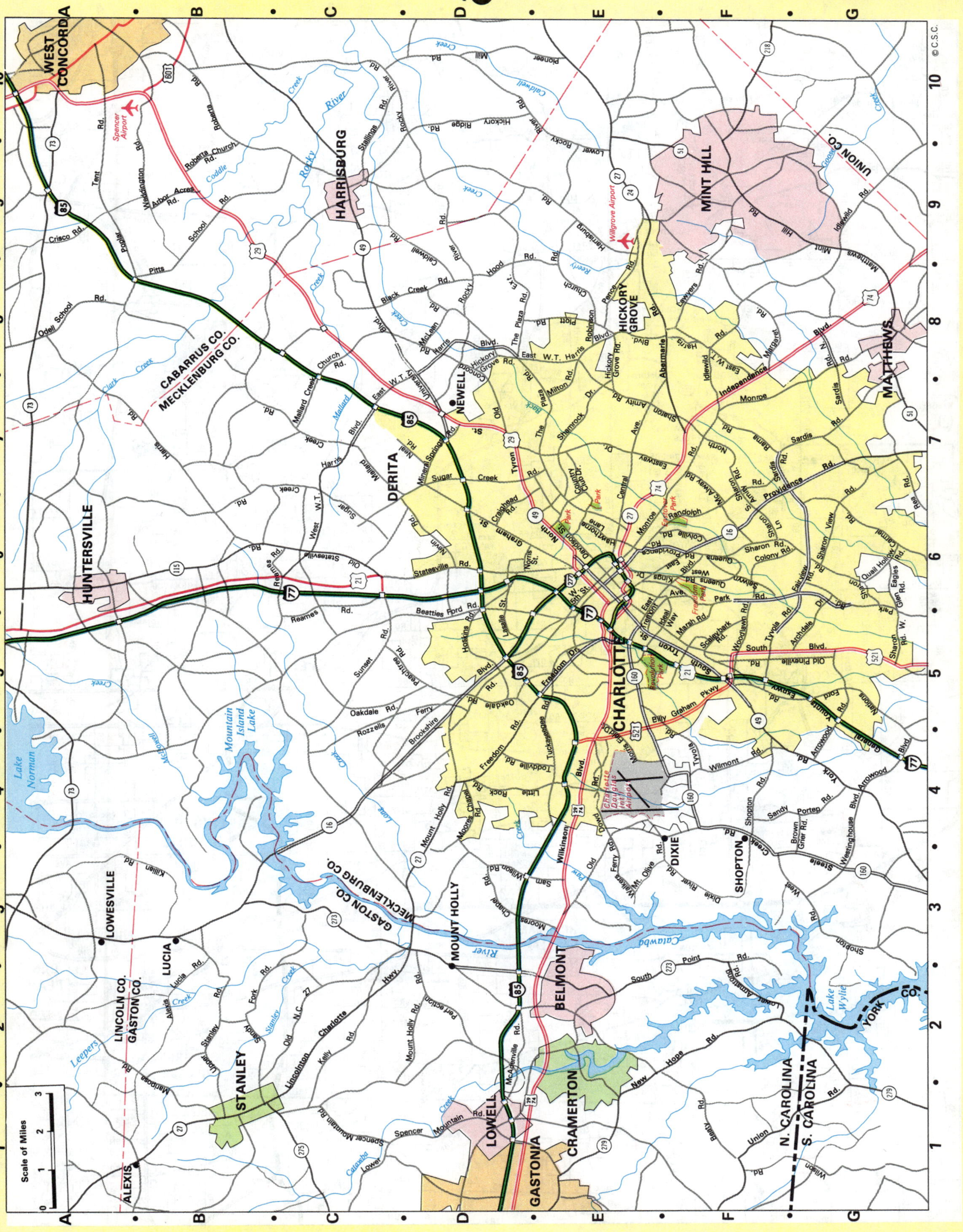

© C.S.C.

WEST CONCORDA

HARRISBURG

MINT HILL

UNION CO.

CABARRUS CO.
MECKLENBURG CO.

NEWELL

HICKORY GROVE

MATTHEWS

HUNTERSVILLE

DERITA

Spencer Airport

Willgrove Airport

Lake Norman

Mountain Island Lake

CHARLOTTE

Charlotte Douglas Int'l Airport

DIXIE

SHOPTON

Freedom Park

LOWESVILLE

LUCIA

LINCOLN CO.
GASTON CO.

GASTON CO.
MECKLENBURG CO.

STANLEY

MOUNT HOLLY

BELMONT

Catawba River

Lake Wylie

N. CAROLINA
S. CAROLINA

YORK CO.

LOWELL

GASTONIA

CRAMERTON

Scale of Miles
0 1 2 3

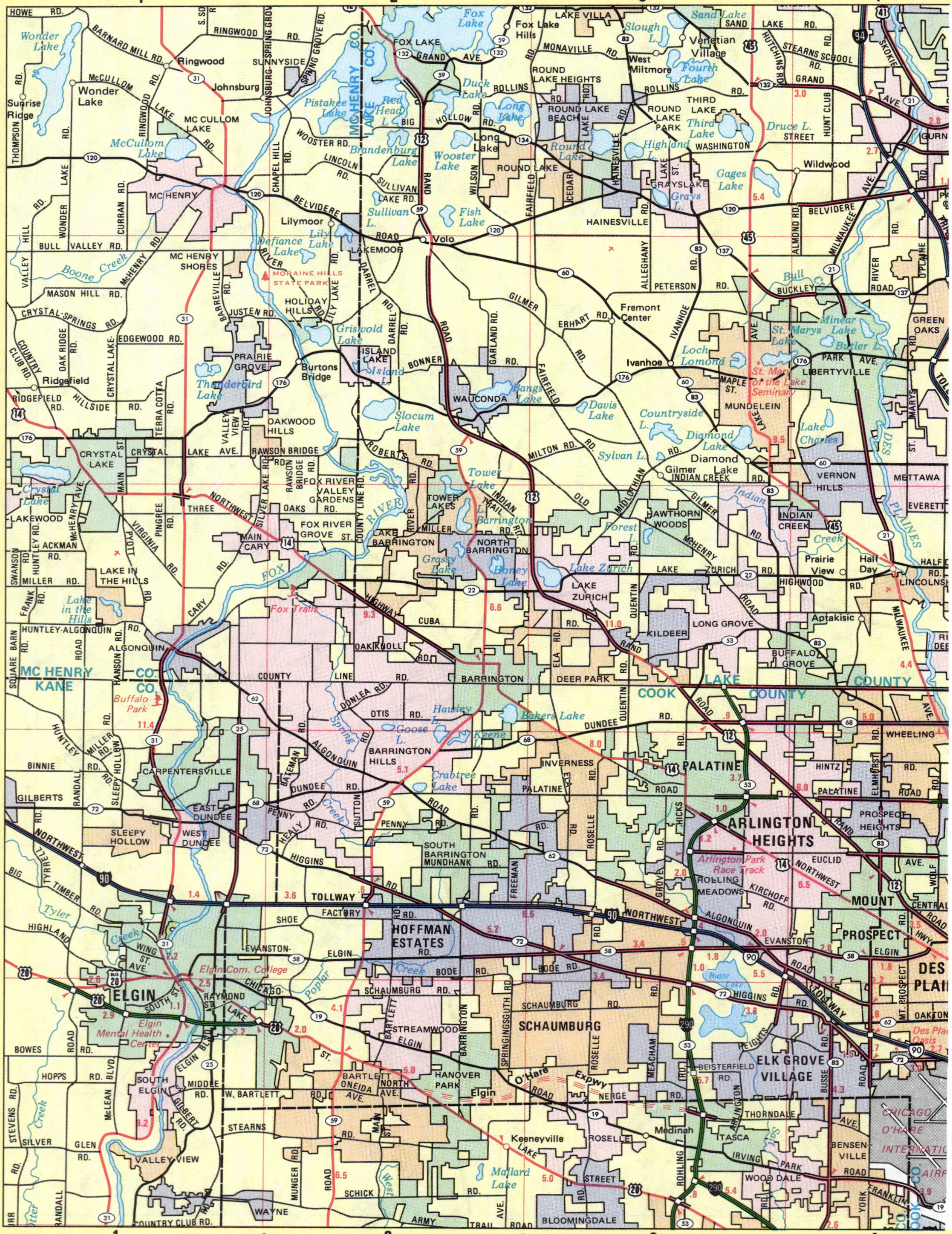

Fox Lake
Fox Lake Hills
Lake Villa
Sand Lake
Venetian Village
Round Lake Heights
Round Lake Beach
Round Lake Park
Round Lake
Third Lake
Grayslake
Hainesville
Gurnee
Wildwood
Wonder Lake
Ringwood
Johnsburg
Sunnyside
McCullom Lake
McHenry
Lilymoor
Lakemoor
Volo
Long Lake
Sunrise Ridge
McHenry Shores
Moraine Hills State Park
Holiday Hills
Burtons Bridge
Prairie Grove
Island Lake
Wauconda
Ridgefield
Oakwood Hills
Crystal Lake
Rawson Bridge
Fox River Valley Gardens
Fox River Grove
Tower Lakes
Lake Barrington
North Barrington
Cary
Lakewood
Lake in the Hills
Fremont Center
Ivanhoe
Mundelein
Libertyville
Green Oaks
Diamond Lake
Vernon Hills
Mettawa
Indian Creek
Prairie View
Half Day
Lake Zurich
Hawthorn Woods
Long Grove
Kildeer
Aptakisic
Buffalo Grove
Wheeling
Algonquin
Barrington
Deer Park
Barrington Hills
Inverness
Palatine
Arlington Heights
Prospect Heights
Mount Prospect
Des Plaines
Carpentersville
East Dundee
West Dundee
Sleepy Hollow
Gilberts
South Barrington
Hoffman Estates
Schaumburg
Elgin
South Elgin
Streamwood
Hanover Park
Bartlett
Keeneyville
Roselle
Medinah
Elk Grove Village
Bensenville
Wood Dale
Itasca
Valley View
Bloomingdale
Wayne
Chicago O'Hare International Airport
McHenry Co.
Lake Co.
Kane Co.
Cook County
Lake County

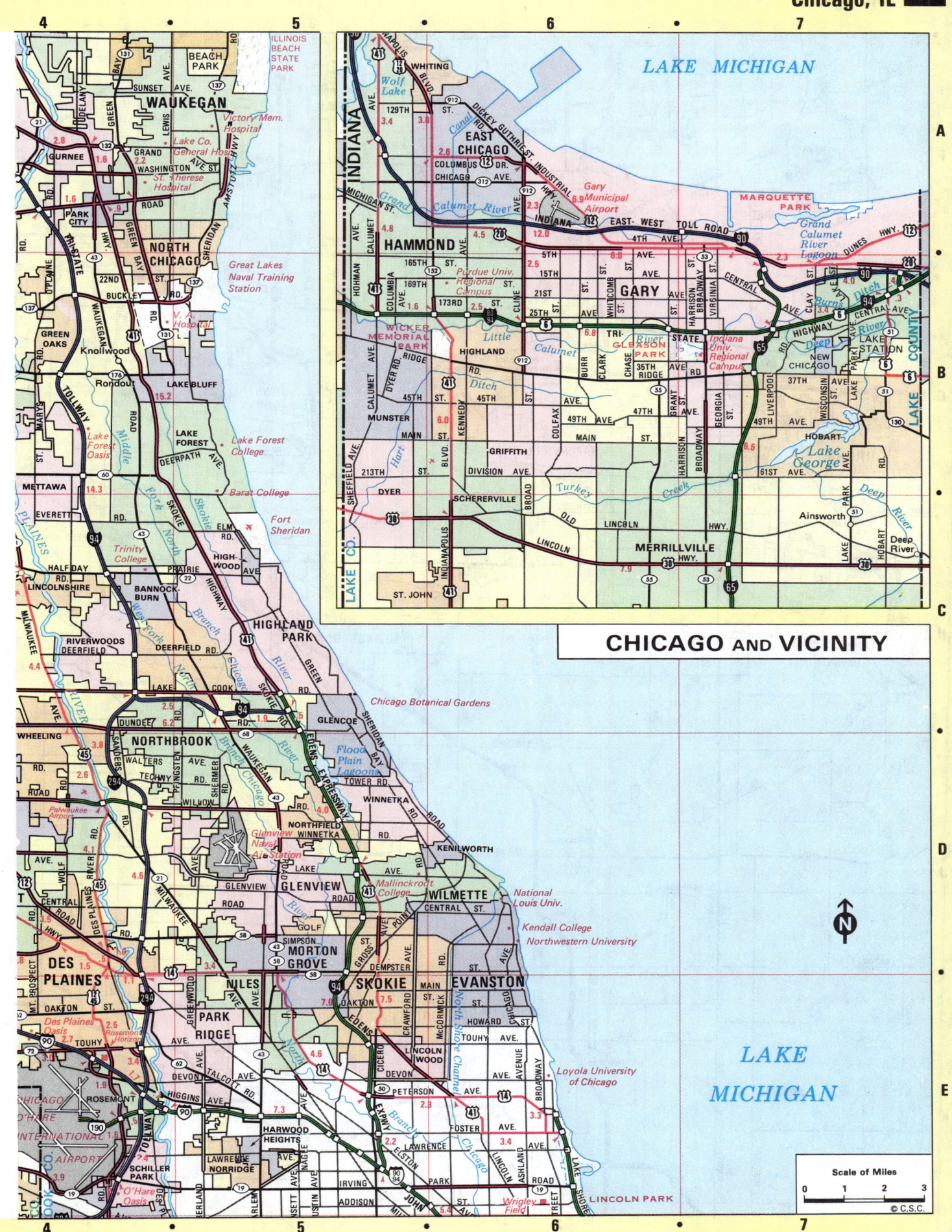

CHICAGO AND VICINITY

NATIONAL ACCELERATOR LABORATORY

ARGONNE NATIONAL LABORATORY

St. Dominic College
St. Charles
Geneva
Hawthorne
West Chicago
Batavia
Mooseheart
North Aurora
Marywood
Aurora
Aurora College
Indian Trail
Montgomery
Oswego
Normantown
Plainfield
Caton Farm
Shorewood
Joliet
Joliet Jr. College
College of St. Francis
Rockdale
Crest Hill
Theodore St.
South Lockport
Fairmont
Lockport
Romeoville
Romeoville
Bolingbrook
Woodridge
Naperville
North Central College
Illinois Benedictine College
Lisle
Warrenville
Wheaton
Wheaton College
Maryknoll Seminary
College of DuPage
Glen Ellyn
Carol Stream
Cloverdale
Glendale Heights
Bloomingdale
Addison
Lombard
Villa Park
Elmhurst
Elmhurst College
Oakbrook Terrace
Oakbrook
Hinsdale
Clarendon Hills
Westmont
Downers Grove
Darien
Willow Brook
Burr Ridge
Morton Arboretum
Chicago Coll. of Osteopathic Medicine
Herrick Lake
Flowerfield
York Center
Highland Hills
Lewis University
Stateville Correctional Center
Illinois Crime Lab.
New Lenox
Marley
Ingalls Park
Washington
Preston Heights
Sag Bridge
Hastings
Lemont
Goodings Grove
Fox River
Du Page River
Des Plaines River
Illinois River
Illinois & Michigan Canal
Kress Creek
Aux Sable Creek
E. Aux Sable Creek
Waubonsee Creek
Spring Brook
Rock Run
Hickory Creek
Long Run
Fraction Run
Mink Creek
Lily Cache Creek
Kane Co.
Du Page Co.
Will County
Kendall County
Cook Co.
Du Page County
Will County

Scale of Miles
0 1 2 3
© C.S.C.

This is a map of Cincinnati, OH.

Grid coordinates run 1–6 horizontally across the top and bottom, and A–G vertically on the left and right sides.

Places and features labeled on the map:

Dunlap, FOREST PARK, Springdale, E. Kemper, Hauck, Greenhills, Glendale, Sharonville, Woodlawn, EVENDALE, BLUE ASH, Dry Ridge Rd, Belvis, Lincoln Hts., Mt. Healthy, WYOMING, Lockland, Reading, Deer Park, Barnsburg, W. North, College Hill, Arlington Hts., AMBERLEY, Silverton, Belmont, Elmwood Pl. Township, Golf Manor, Madeira, Mt. Airy Forest, St. Bernard, NORWOOD, Cheviot, Westwood, Zoological Gardens, Univ. of Cincinnati, Fairfax, Mariem, Bridgetown, University, CINCINNATI, Observatory, Ault Park, Potters Field, Rapid Run Park, Mt. Echo Park, Art Museum, Eden Park, Daytona, Bellevue, Lunken Airport, Ludlow, COVINGTON, Newport, Ft. Thomas, Constance, Park Hills, Southgate, GREATER CINCINNATI AIRPORT, Villa Hills, Ft. Wright, Wilders, Crescent Springs, Kenton Vale, Ft. Mitchell, Lakeview, Highland Hts., Cold Spring, Silver G., Erlanger, Lakeside Park, Crestview Hills

KENTUCKY, OHIO, Ohio River, Little Miami River, Licking River

Scale of Miles: 0 1 2 3

© C.S.C.

Lake Erie
CLEVELAND
LAKEWOOD
ROCKY RIVER
FAIRVIEW PARK
BROOKLYN
BROOKLYN HEIGHTS
BROOK PARK
BEREA
MIDDLEBURG HEIGHTS
PARMA HEIGHTS
PARMA
SEVEN HILLS
INDEPENDENCE
VALLEY VIEW
GARFIELD HEIGHTS
MAPLE HEIGHTS
BEDFORD
BEDFORD HTS.
SOLON
NORTH ROYALTON
BRECKSVILLE
BROADVIEW HEIGHTS
STRONGSVILLE
N. ROYALTON
SAGAMORE HILLS
MACEDONIA
TWINSBURG
BOSTON HEIGHTS
HUDSON
BRUNSWICK
HINCKLEY
RICHFIELD
PENINSULA
EVERETT
ABBEYVILLE
WEYMOUTH
REMSEN CORNERS
GRANGER
BATH
BATH CENTER
GHENT
BOTZUM
STOW
EUCLID
WICKLIFFE
HIGHLAND HEIGHTS
RICHMOND HEIGHTS
BRATENAHL
SOUTH EUCLID
EAST CLEVELAND
LYNDHURST
MAYFIELD HEIGHTS
CLEVELAND HEIGHTS
UNIVERSITY HEIGHTS
SHAKER HEIGHTS
BEECHWOOD
PEPPER PIKE
WARRENSVILLE HEIGHTS
EMERY
ORANGE
MORELAND HILLS
CUYAHOGA CO.
SUMMIT CO.
CUYAHOGA CO.
MEDINA CO.
Burke Lakefront Airport
Cleveland Municipal Stadium
City Hall
Edgewater Yacht Club
Cleveland State University
Grace Hosp.
Cleveland Zoological Park
Case Western Reserve University
Institute of Art
John Carroll University
Cleveland Hopkins Int'l Airport
Holy Cross Cem.
Midtown S. C.
Parma Comm. Hosp.
Valley Forge H. S.
Normandy H. S.
Cuyahoga Community College
Rocky River Reservation
Bedford Reservation
Hawthornden St. Hosp.
Northfield Sq. S. C.
Four Points Airport
Strongsville Airport
Golf Course
Metropolitan Rocky River Reservation
Brecksville Reservation
Brecksville V. A. Hosp.
Briarwood Golf Course
U.S. Military Res.
Furnace Run Park
Hinckley Res.
Virginia Kendall Park
Welcome Airport
Macedonia H. S.
Cleveland Boys Sch
Crown Hill Cem.
Richmond Mall
Cuyahoga County Airport
Country Club
Ursuline College
Pepper Pike Country Club
South Chagrin Reservation
Scale of Miles
0 1 2 3
© C.S.C.

1 2 3 4 5 6 7

A
Moore
Hyatts
Shanahan
North Platt
Hollenback
GALENA
Vans Valley
605
37
745
257
Duffy
Merchant
Home
Taggart
Columbus
Rome Corners
Trenton
Woodtown
RATHBONE
HYATTS
LEWIS CENTER
Lewis Center
Lewis Center
Jaycox
Miller-Paul
CENTER VILLAGE
Center Village
Cook
Harriott
Concord
315
AFRICA
Africa-Kenyon
Big Walnut
Freeman
Sunbury
HARLEM
Gorsuch
Robins
Fancher
JEROME

B
SHAWNEE HILLS
Powell
750
POWELL
Jewett
Powell
Columbus
23
Hanawalt
71
Maxtown
Smothers
Tussic Street
Red Bank
Green-Cook
Bevelheimer
33
257
DELAWARE
FRANKLIN
Summit View
Brand
MOUNT AIR
FLINT
Park
WESTERVILLE
Otterbein College
Walnut
Schrock
Walnut
Cubbage
Schott
New Albany-Condit
Peter Hoover

C
161
KILEVILLE
Post
Indian Run
Snouffer
Worthington Galena
710
WORTHINGTON
Schrock
Hoover Dam
Central College
605
Plain City
745
DUBLIN
161
LINWORTH
Dublin-Granville
R.R. Museum
HUBER RIDGE
New Albany
62
Shier Rings
Avery
Rings
Tuttle
RIVERLEA
MINERVA PARK
161
Minerva Lake Rd.
GOULD PARK
AMLIN

D
HAYDEN
Hayden Run
33
CLINTON
Morse
Cooke
3
270
Thompson
Morse
161
NEW ALBANY
Bethel
Henderson
High
Ferris
Karl
McCutcheon
Headley
Clark
Havens
Davidson
McCoy
Highland
Maize
Oakland Park
N. Broadway
McCutcheon

E
HILLARD
Hillard-Cam
UPPER ARLINGTON
Fishinger
270
COLUMBUS
315
Weber
Hudson
Indianola
Agler
Mock
GAHANNA
62
Haven's Corner
MUDSOCK
SAN MARGHERITA
Dublin
Tremont
Lane
Ohio History Museum
Ohio State Univ
Seventeenth
Ohio Dominican College
Columbus-Millersburg
Port Columbus International Airport
317
BLACKLICK
16

F
MARBLE CLIFF
McKinley
GRANDVIEW HEIGHTS
670
Leonard
40
Broad
BEXLEY
WHITEHALL
REYNOLDSBURG
70
VALLEYVIEW
33
State Capitol
Main
33
Capital University
40
ALTON
NEW ROME
40
Broad
Sullivant Ave.
71
23
Livingston
James
256
National

G
Georgesville
3
62
BRIGGSDALE
Frank
Marion
Champion
Lockbourne
Refugee
270
BRICE
GALLOWAY
Alkire
104
Winchester
EDGEWATER PARK
GEORGEVILLE
Pike
URBANCREST
Home Rd.
Gantz Rd.
Williams
Groveport
317
33
Noe-Bixby
Shannon
Wright

H
Alkire
Johnson
GROVE CITY
Stringtown
White
OBETZ
Bixby
GROVEPORT
Groveport
DARBYDALE
665
PLEASANT CORNERS
London-Groveport
Columbus St.
Rensch
REESE
CANAL WINCHESTER
Lithopolis
WATERLOO
674

J
Orders
Holton
SHADEVILLE
317
London-Groveport
U.S. Military Res. Rickenbacker Air Force Base
LITHOPOLIS
71
HARRISBURG
ORIENT
FRANKLIN
PICKAWAY
104
LOCKBOURNE
Rowe
Vause
Lancaster
62
3
762
23

K

Scale of Miles
0 1 2 3

© C.S.C.

MARSHALL SUPERIOR

McCastlin Blvd.

BROOMFIELD

BOULDER COUNTY
ADAMS COUNTY

W. 128th Ave.
EASTLAKE
E. 128th Ave.
HENDERSON

128
287
120th Ave.

BOULDER COUNTY
JEFFERSON COUNTY

NORTHGLENN

W. 112th Ave.
E. 112th Ave.

U.S. Atomic Energy Commission
(Rocky Flats Plant)

104th Ave.

121

100th Ave.

THORNTON

96th Ave.

96th Ave.

WESTMINSTER

92nd

FEDERAL HEIGHTS

Standley Lake

88th Ave.

DUPONT

Rocky Mountain Arsenal

Coal 72 Creek Canyon Rd.

84th

W. 82nd Ave.

80th Ave.

80th Ave.

EL DORADO ESTATES

WELBY

72nd Ave.

ARVADA

Indiana

Wadsworth

Sheridan

Federal

Pecos

70th Ave.

COMMERCE CITY

64th

64th Ave.

64th Ave.

Ralston Rd.

Mayborn Lake

58th

56th Ave.

52nd Ave.

Ridge Rd.

ADAMS COUNTY
DENVER COUNTY

Stapleton International Airport

GOLDEN

44th Ave.

MOUNTAIN VIEW

Smith Rd.

40th Ave.

58

38th Ave.

WHEAT RIDGE

32nd

City Park Zoo & Ave.

Park Hill G.C.

32nd

Camp George West (National Guard)

26th Ave.

29th Ave.

31st St.

23rd

Montview

PLEASANT VIEW

Colfax

Golden Rd.

EDGEWATER

DENVER

AURORA

6

20th

State Capitol

Botanic Garden

8th

6th

Apex County Park

Federal Ctr.

Simms

Kipling

Garrison

Carr

1st

Colfax

Lowry Air Force Base

6th Ave.

Alameda

LAKEWOOD

Alameda

Pulaski Park

Alameda Ave.

Mississippi

GLENDALE

Mississippi

Jefferson Co. Park

Florida

Washington Park

Leetsdale Dr.

IDLEDALE

Jewell

Iliff

Evans Ave.

MORRISON

Bear Creek Canyon Rd.

Bear Creek Lake

Federal Correctional Institute

Denver University

Yale

Havana

Peoria

Iliff

Yale

ENGLEWOOD

INDIAN HILLS

Mount Falcon County Park

SHERIDAN

CHERRY HILL VILLAGE

Quincy

Cherry Creek Park

Quincy

Quincy Ave.

Marston Lake

Belleview

DENVER COUNTY
ARAPAHOE COUNTY

Cherry Creek Reservoir

Airline Rd.

TINY TOWN

W. Belleview Ave.

BOW MAR

GREENWOOD VILLAGE

Smoky Hill Rd.

TWIN FORKS

Summit St.

Bowles

LITTLETON

Littleton Blvd.

Littleton Blvd.

Orchard Ave.

Belleview

FENDERS

Ken Caryl Rd.

COLUMBINE

Coal Mine

Arapahoe

Arapahoe

Dry Creek Rd.

Arapahoe County Airport

Windermere

Ridge Rd.

Stelle

Holly

Colorado

Quebec

ARAPAHOE COUNTY
DOUGLAS COUNTY

HOMEWOOD PARK

County Line

GRANDVIEW ESTATES

PHILLIPSBURG

Deer Creek Canyon Rd.

Chatfield Lake

McClellan Rd.

RIVERSIDE

DEERMONT

CHATFIELD ACRES

N

Scale of Miles
0 1 2 3

© C.S.C.

Newark

DENTON COUNTY
TARRANT COUNTY

Flower Mound

Roanoke

Westlake

Grapevine Lake

EAGLE MOUNTAIN NATIONAL GUARD BASE

AVONDALE-HASLET RD.

KELLER-

Haslet

HASLET-ROANOKE RD.

NORTHWEST PKWY.

Grapevine

BLUE MOUND RD.

HASLET RD.

Southlake

1709

KELLER-HICKS RD.

SKEET RICHARDSON RD.

HICKS RD.

1709

Big

Keller

Bear

Creek

North Car Rental & Return Area for: Metro Flight Braniff Ozark Frontier & Texas Internat'l.

PARK DR.

BOWMAN-ROBERTS RD.

HALSTON-BAILEY-BOSWELL RD.

Little

Colleyville

Hotel

Fort Worth Nature Center and Refuge

Saginaw Airfield

Saginaw

SAGINAW RD.

Watauga

North Richland Hills

Bear

Creek

Return Area for: American, Continental, Delta & Eastern

Eagle Mountain Lake

DECATUR RD.

156

Blue Mound

WATAUGA

SMITHFIELD RD.

1938

Harwood

JACKSBORO HWY.

AIRPORT

DAVIS HWY.

Bedford

121

Euless

Lakeside

Lake Worth

AZLE AVE.

Meacham Field

820

FREEWAY

26

PIPELINE

EDLISS

157

360

Sansom Park

GLENVIEW

Hurst

River Oaks

CARSWELL A.F.B.

28TH ST.

183

MIDWAY

Richland Hills

10

Haltom City

FT. WORTH

White Settlement

Westworth

BELKNAP ST.

RIVERSIDE

26

River

MILL LN.

Collins

Arlington Stadium

Westover Hills

BOWIE BLVD.

E. 1ST ST.

RANDOL

LAMAR

30

RANDOL MILL

WEST FRWY.

CAMP

180

80

7TH ST.

Lancaster

Oakland

820

Cooks

Village

DIVISION

E. ABRAM ST.

VICKERY

University

Trinity

Texas Christian Univ.

8TH AVE.

S. MAIN

ROSEDALE AVE.

PIONEER

Lake Arlington

303

Pantego

Arlington

Collins AVE.

Watson PKWY.

Clear

BERRY ST.

RIVERSIDE DR.

MITCHELL

VAUGHN

287

ARKANSAS

Univ. of Texas at Arlington

Benbrook

SEMINARY DR.

35W

Wichita

POLY FRWY.

LITTLE

Dalingworth Gardens

Cooper ST.

Matlock

Benbrook Lake

OLD GRANBURY

JAMES ST.

SOUTH

Edgecliff

731

MANSFIELD HWY.

Forest Hill

Arlington Municipal Airfield

MC KNIGHT RD.

Fish

DIRKS RD.

CLEBURNE RD.

SCHOOL RD.

OAK GROVE

FOREST HILL

ANGLIN

Kennedale

EDEN RD.

HARRIS RD.

WEBB RD.

SYCAMORE

Everman

287

Watsonville

157

MANSFIELD

Mansfield

CROWLEY RD.

RENDON RD.

Crowley

MAIN ST.

1187

Rendon

287

TARRANT COUNTY
JOHNSON COUNTY

Burleson

731

WILSHIRE

174

35W

Retta

917

2738

287

Lewisville • Hebron • Plano • Plano • Murphy

COLLIN COUNTY / DALLAS COUNTY

Renner • Renner RD. • 15th St. • 14th St. • Sachse

Coppell • Carrollton • Addison • Richardson • Arapaho • Belt Line Rd. • Buckingham • Garland

Farmers Branch • Forest Ln. • Lyndon B. Greenville Expwy • Buckingham • Miller

North Lake • Valley View • Royal • Walnut Hill • Inwood • Central Ave. • North Star • Glenbrook • Lavon

DALLAS FT. WORTH REGIONAL AIRPORT

North Control Plaza • Ozark Frontier & Texas Internat'l. • Eastern & American • Continental & Delta • South Car Rental & Return Area • Airport

Univ. of Dallas • Texas Stadium • Northwest Hwy • Harry Hines • Marsh Ln. • Marsh • Hill • Denton Dr. • Lemmon • Love Field • Southern Methodist Univ. • Lovers Ln. • White Rock Lake • Skillman • Garland Rd. • Saturn • Centerville • Broadway

Irving • Shady Grove • O'Conner • Nursery • Irving Blvd. • Cedar Springs • Maple • Oak Lawn • University Park • Highland Park • Greenville • Abrams • Ave. • White Rock Lake • Buckner • Mesquite • Sunnyvale

DALLAS • Singleton Blvd. • Commerce • Trinity River • Ross • Elm St. • Haskell • Gaston • Grand • Ferguson • Thornton • Scyene • Military

Grand Prairie • Hunter • Ferrell • Davis • Jefferson • Hampton • Westmoreland • Zang • Illinois • Corinth • Cedar Crest Blvd. • Scyene • Second • Cotton Bowl • Bruton • Lake June • Augustine • Balch Springs • Kleburg

Cockrell Hill • Illinois Ave. • Keist St. • Red Bird Ln. • Camp Wisdom Rd. • Johnson • Elam • Hawn Frwy • Murdock Rd. • Hutchins

Duncanville • Woodland Hills • Lyndon B. Lancaster • Thornton • Pleasant Run • Lancaster • Hutchins • Wintergreen • Dowdy • Wilmer

Cedar Hill • Mansfield Rd. • De Soto • Line • Parkerville • Belt Line • Malloy • Ferris

Lake Joe Pool • Wilson • Joe • Bear Creek Rd. • Glenn Heights • DALLAS COUNTY / ELLIS COUNTY • Ovilla • Red Oak • Ferris • Post Oak Rd. • Simmons R. • Trinity

Carrier Pkwy • Mountain Creek Lake • Naval Air Station • Jorgon Rd.

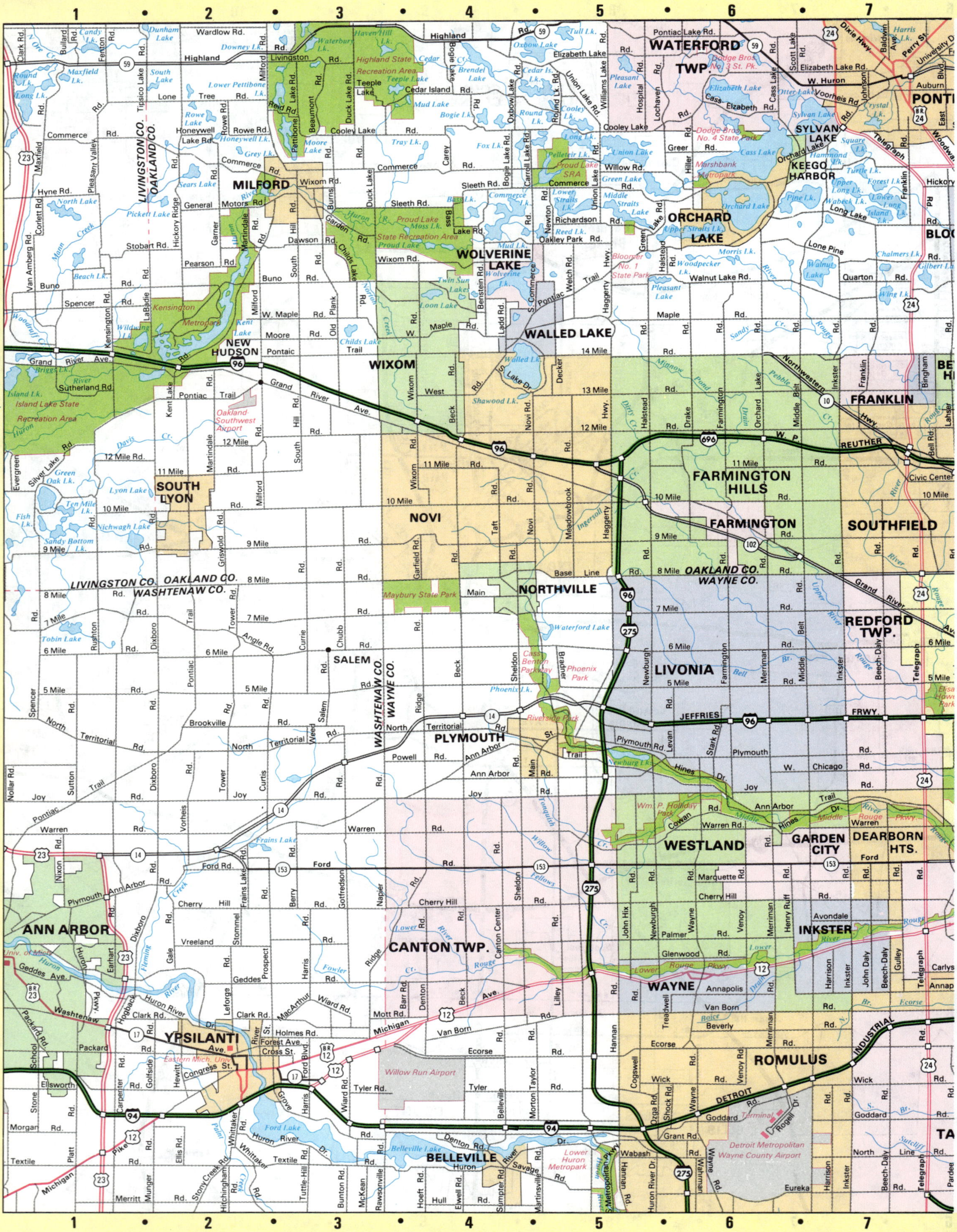
WATERFORD TWP
MILFORD
WOLVERINE LAKE
WALLED LAKE
WIXOM
NEW HUDSON
SOUTH LYON
NOVI
FARMINGTON HILLS
FARMINGTON
SOUTHFIELD
NORTHVILLE
LIVONIA
REDFORD TWP.
SALEM
PLYMOUTH
WESTLAND
GARDEN CITY
DEARBORN HTS.
ANN ARBOR
CANTON TWP.
INKSTER
WAYNE
YPSILANTI
ROMULUS
BELLEVILLE
Willow Run Airport
Detroit Metropolitan Wayne County Airport

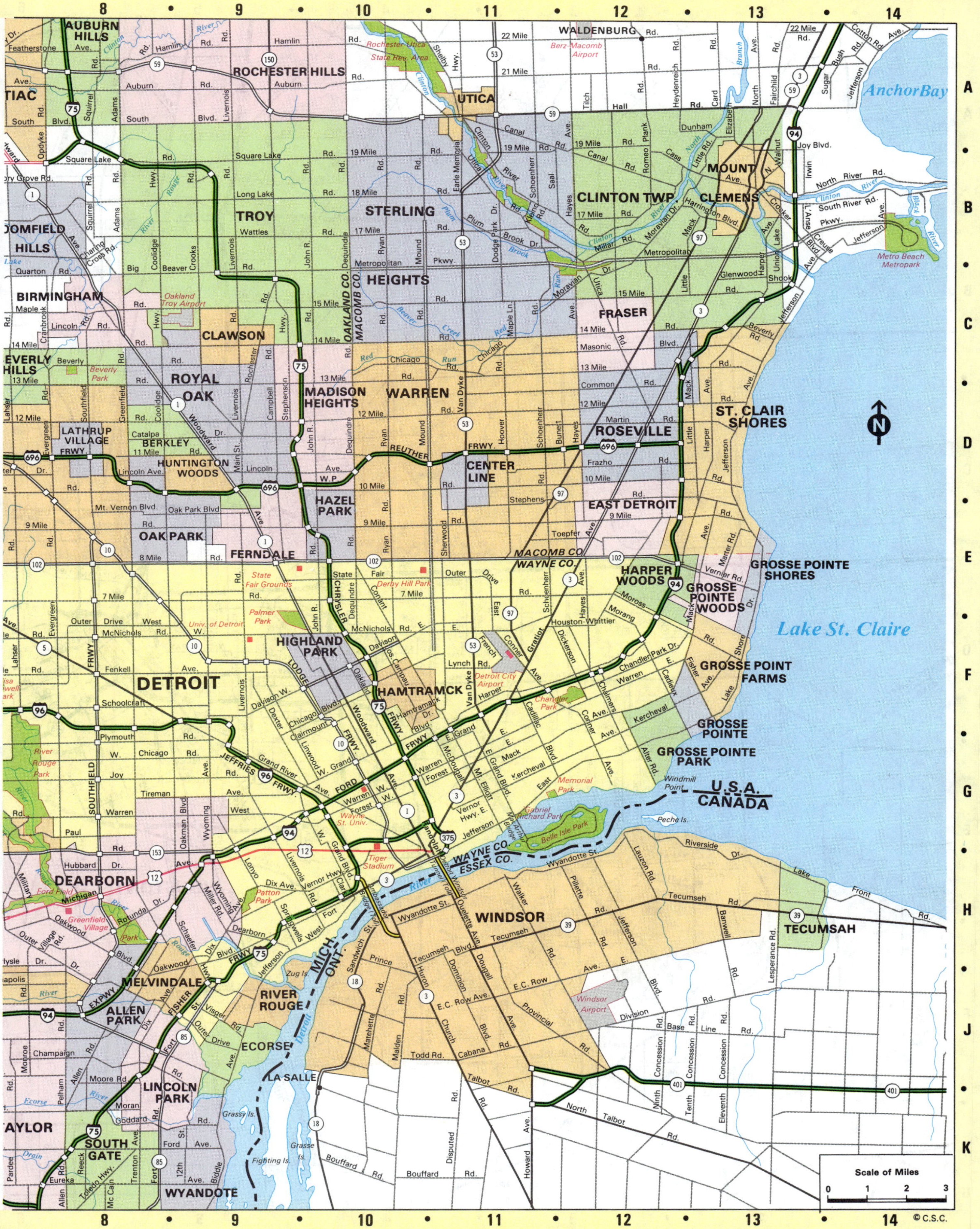

AnchorBay

AUBURN HILLS

ROCHESTER HILLS

UTICA

WALDENBURG

MOUNT CLEMENS

CLINTON TWP.

Metro Beach Metropark

TROY

STERLING HEIGHTS

BLOOMFIELD HILLS

BIRMINGHAM

CLAWSON

FRASER

ST. CLAIR SHORES

BEVERLY HILLS

ROYAL OAK

MADISON HEIGHTS

WARREN

ROSEVILLE

LATHRUP VILLAGE

BERKLEY

HUNTINGTON WOODS

CENTER LINE

OAK PARK

HAZEL PARK

FERNDALE

EAST DETROIT

HARPER WOODS

GROSSE POINTE SHORES

GROSSE POINTE WOODS

Lake St. Claire

HIGHLAND PARK

GROSSE POINT FARMS

DETROIT

HAMTRAMCK

GROSSE POINTE

GROSSE POINTE PARK

Windmill Point

U.S.A.
CANADA

Belle Isle Park

WAYNE CO.
ESSEX CO.

DEARBORN

Tiger Stadium

WINDSOR

TECUMSAH

MELVINDALE

ALLEN PARK

RIVER ROUGE

ECORSE

LA SALLE

Windsor Airport

LINCOLN PARK

TAYLOR

SOUTH GATE

WYANDOTE

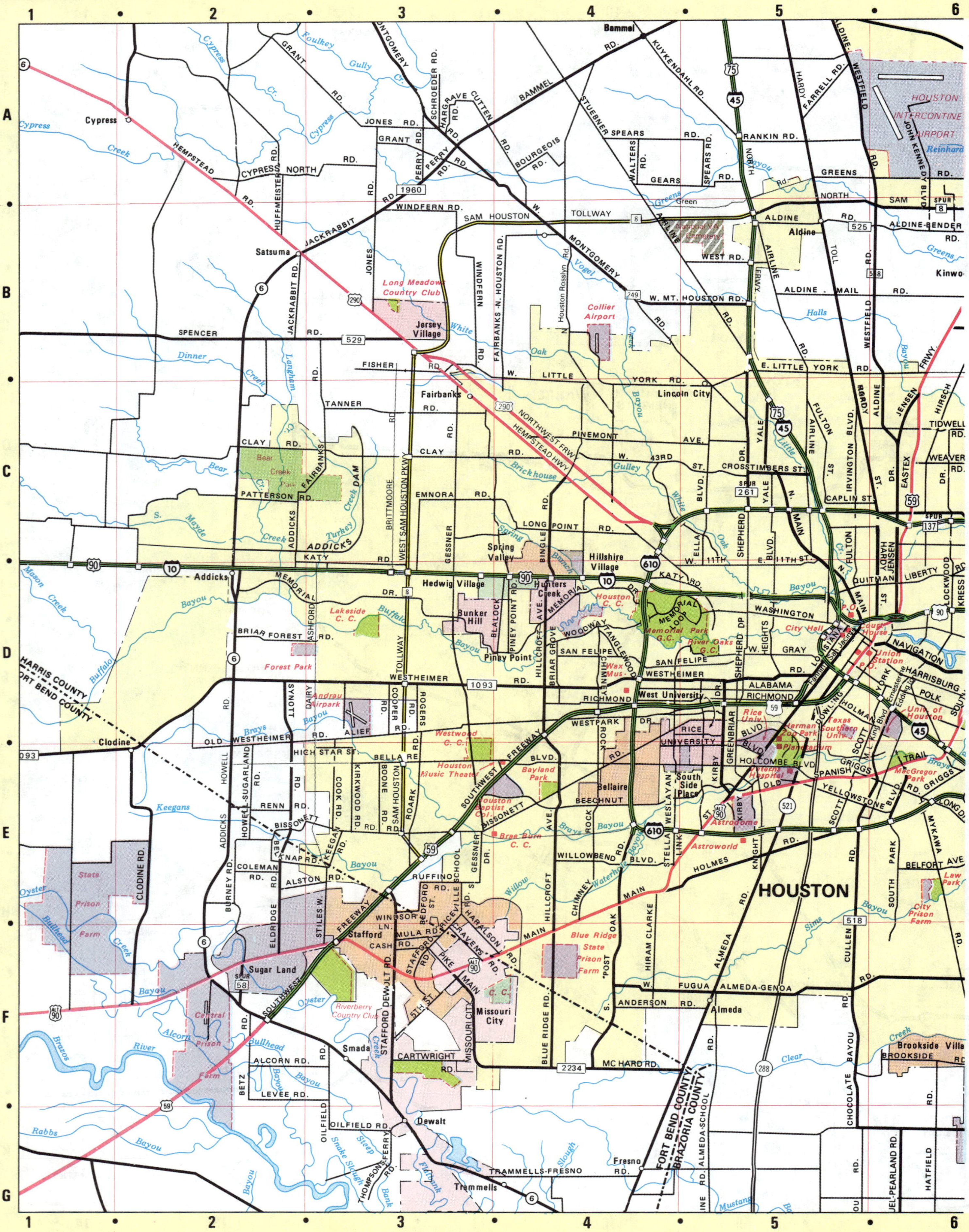

Cypress

Hempstead Rd.

Satsuma

Jersey Village

Long Meadow Country Club

Fairbanks

Bear Creek Park

Addicks

Katy

Hedwig Village

Hunters Creek

Bunker Hill

Piney Point

Spring Valley

Hillshire Village

Memorial Park

River Oaks G.C.

City Hall

Union Station

West University

Rice University

Bellaire

South Side Place

Astrodome

Astroworld

HOUSTON

Clodine

Alief

Houston Music Theater

Bayland Park

Brae Burn C.C.

Stafford

Sugar Land

Missouri City

Riverberry Country Club

Smada

Cartwright

Dewalt

Trammells

Fresno

Brookside Village

Houston Intercontinental Airport

Aldine

Collier Airport

Lincoln City

Harris County / Fort Bend County

Fort Bend County / Brazoria County

State Prison Farm

Central Prison Farm

Blue Ridge State Prison Farm

City Prison Farm

Almeda

Memorial Loop

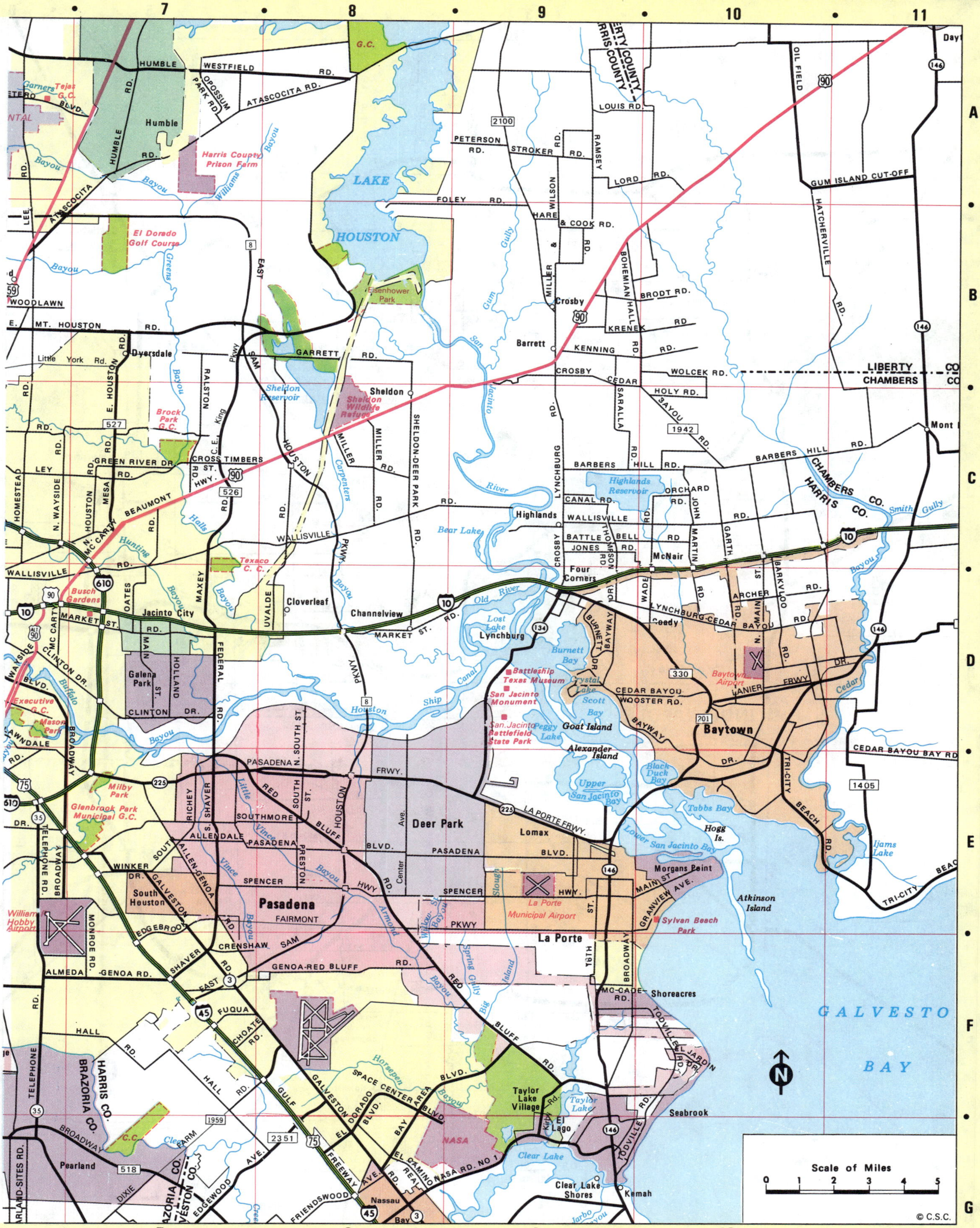

Scale of Miles
0 1 2 3 4 5

N

GALVESTON BAY

LAKE HOUSTON

Humble
Westfield Rd.
Atascocita Rd.
Opossum Park Rd.
Garners Tejas G.C.
Harris County Prison Farm
El Dorado Golf Course
Woodlawn
E. Mt. Houston Rd.
Dyersdale
Little York Rd.
Eisenhower Park
Garrett Rd.
Sheldon Reservoir
Sheldon Wildlife Refuge
Sheldon
Brock Park G.C.
Green River Dr.
Cross Timbers
Beaumont
Wallisville
Texaco C.C.
Cloverleaf
Busch Gardens
Jacinto City
Galena Park
Clinton
Executive G.C.
Mason Park
Lawndale
Milby Park
Glenbrook Park Municipal G.C.
Pasadena
South Houston
Fairmont
Winker
Williams Hobby Airport
Almeda-Genoa Rd.
Genoa-Red Bluff Rd.
Brazoria Co.
Harris Co.
Pearland
Nassau Bay
NASA
Clear Lake
Clear Lake Shores
Kemah
Taylor Lake Village
El Lago
Seabrook
Shoreacres
La Porte
La Porte Municipal Airport
Sylvan Beach Park
Morgans Point
Atkinson Island
Deer Park
Lomax
Pasadena Blvd.
Spencer Hwy.
San Jacinto Monument
San Jacinto Battlefield State Park
Battleship Texas Museum
Lynchburg
Goat Island
Alexander Island
Crystal Lake
Scott Bay
Burnett Bay
Black Duck Bay
Baytown
Baytown Airport
Upper San Jacinto Bay
Lower San Jacinto Bay
Tabbs Bay
Hogg Is.
Cedar Bayou
Wooster Rd.
Highlands
Wallisville
Highlands Reservoir
Four Corners
McNair
Barbers Hill
Crosby
Barrett
Kenning
Krenek
Liberty / Chambers Co.
Harris Co. / Chambers Co.
Peterson Rd.
Stroker Rd.
Foley Rd.
Louis Rd.
Ramsey Rd.
Lord Rd.
Oil Field
Gum Island Cut-Off
Hatcherville
Ijams Lake
Tri-City Beach
Cedar Bayou Bay Rd.
Taylor Lake
Horsepen Bayou
Space Center
Clear Creek
Mud Lake
Lost Lake
Old River
San Jacinto River
Buffalo Bayou
Greens Bayou
Carpenters Bayou

Routes: 59, 90, 610, 10, 8, 146, 225, 330, 134, 201, 1405, 1942, 1959, 2100, 2351, 518, 527, 526, 3, 35, 75, 45, 1, 525

1 · 2 · 3 · 4 · 5 · 6

W. 111TH ST.
Zionsville
334

421

116TH ST.

White

37

A — 465
HAMILTON CO.
MARION CO.
96TH ST.
69

65
52
86TH ST.
100
86TH ST.
Nora
Allisonville
Castleton
82ND ST.

B — Traders Point
79TH ST.
465
79TH ST.
Augusta
73RD ST.
Meridian Hills
Williams Creek
Ravenswood
71ST ST.
71ST ST.
100
465

New Augusta
62ND ST.
64TH ST.
North Crows Nest
Shore Acres
65TH ST.
65TH ST.
Eagle Creek Pk.
TOWNSHIP LINE RD.
DITCH RD.
FOX HILL DR.
Highland Country Club
Kessler
62ND ST.
FORT BENJAMIN HARRISON

C — 56TH ST.
56TH ST.
Rocky Ripple
KESSLER BLVD.
431
56TH ST.
Eagle Creek Reservoir
Little Eagle Creek
62ND
GUION RD.
Broadmoor Country Club
Spring Hills
Highwoods
State School For The Deaf
46TH ST.
Lawrence
PENDLETON PIKE
Eagle Creek Airport
Bob Shank Airport
Wynnedale
Woodstock
Butler University
State Fairgrounds
38TH ST.
67
36
100
Clermont
136
52
74
W. 38TH ST.
34TH ST.
LAFAYETTE RD.
HIGH SCHOOL
Marian College
30TH ST.
34TH ST.
30TH ST.
SHADELAND AVE.

D — Indianapolis Country Club
Big Eagle Creek
21ST ST.
Indianapolis Motor Speedway Museum
Indianapolis Motor Speedway
Coffin G.C.
South Grove G.C.
25TH ST.
MASSACHUSETTS AVE.
70
465
136
GEORGETOWN RD.
TIBBS BLVD.
16TH ST.
Bush Stadium
Benjamin Harrison Memorial
21ST ST.
16TH ST.
10TH ST.
ARLINGTON AVE.
EMERSON AVE.
Pleasant Run G.C.
Warren Park
Speedway
10TH ST.
War Memorial
I.U.P.U.I.
War Memorial
RURAL ST.
SHERMAN DR.
MICHIGAN ST.
NEW YORK ST.
INDIANAPOLIS
ROCKVILLE RD.
Indiana Univ. Medical Center
Indiana Univ. State Capitol
P.O.
NEW YORK ST.
WASHINGTON ST.
40
100

E — HENDRICKS COUNTY
MARION COUNTY
Tremont
36
465
40
Hoosier Dome
65
70
40
ENGLISH AVE.
ENGLISH AVE.
Ben Davis
Mickeyville
Morris ST.
WEST ST.
PROSPECT
SOUTHEASTERN
421
52
Bridgeport
Minnesota
Union Stock Yards
W. RAYMOND ST.
Beech Grove
Five Points
E. RAYMOND ST.
Indianapolis International Airport
GIRLS SCHOOL RD.
HIGH SCHOOL RD.
LYNHURST DR.
HOLT RD.
TIBBS RD.
Mars Hill
Maywood
MERIDIAN ST.
MADISON AVE.
Sarah Shank G.C.
Troy AVE.
KEYSTONE AVE.
FISHER RD.
MICHIGAN RD.
74

F — HANNA AVE.
Hanna Ave.
Univ. of Indianapolis
THOMPSON RD.
THOMPSON RD.
Edgewood
SHELBYVILLE RD.
Wanamaker
BRUSHWOOD
70
67
FLYNN RD.
MANN RD.
HARDING ST.
EAST ST.
MADISON AVE.
74
465
65
52
White River
37
EPLER RD.
Homecroft
N

G — Camby
CAMBY RD.
Antrim
Edgewood
7
REYNOLDS RD.
West Newton
MOORESVILLE RD.
SOUTHPORT RD.
SOUTH PORT RD.
STOP 11 RD.
MORGAN TOWN RD.
Glenns Valley
431
Southport
MARION COUNTY

Scale of Miles
0 5 1 2 3

© C.S.C.

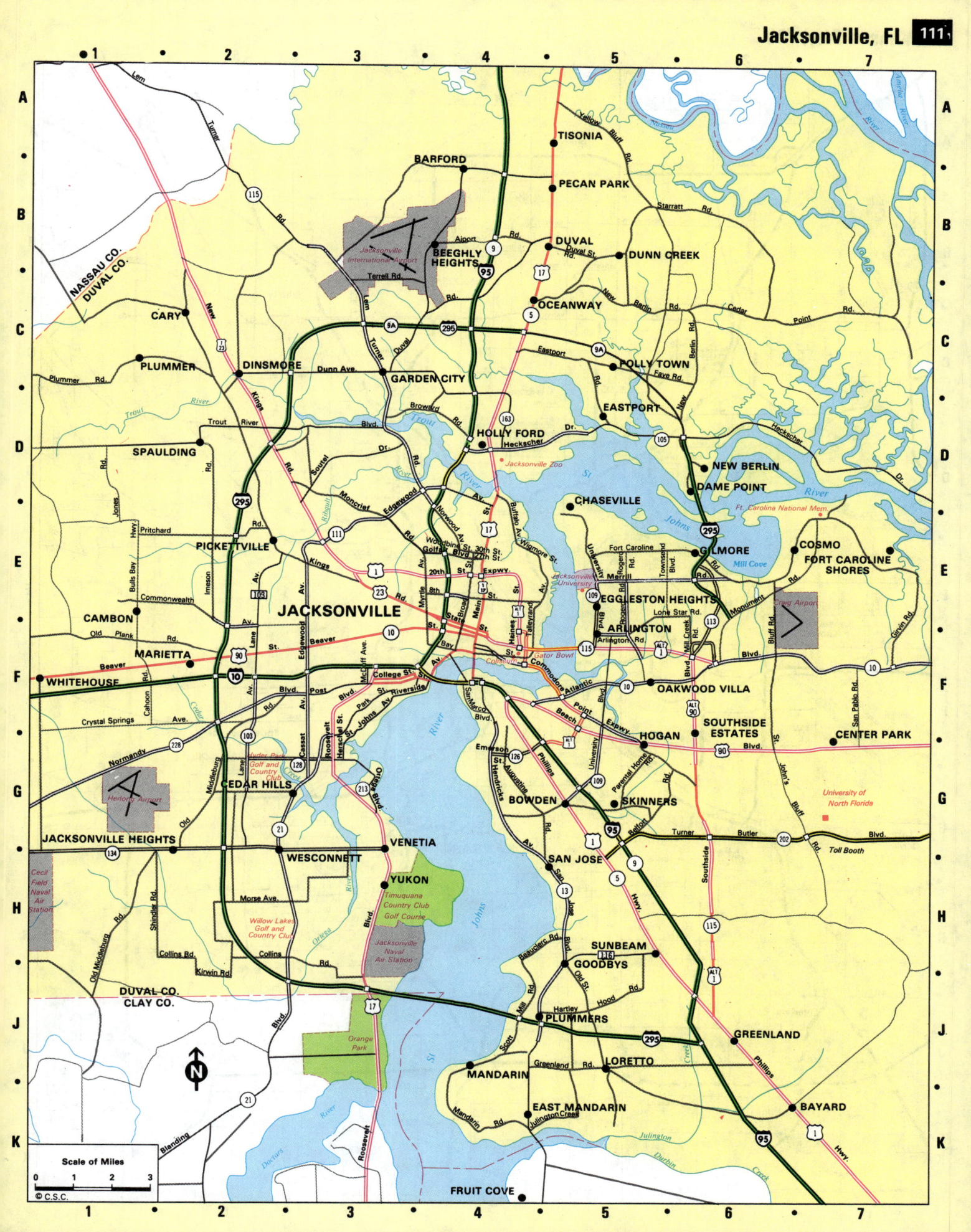

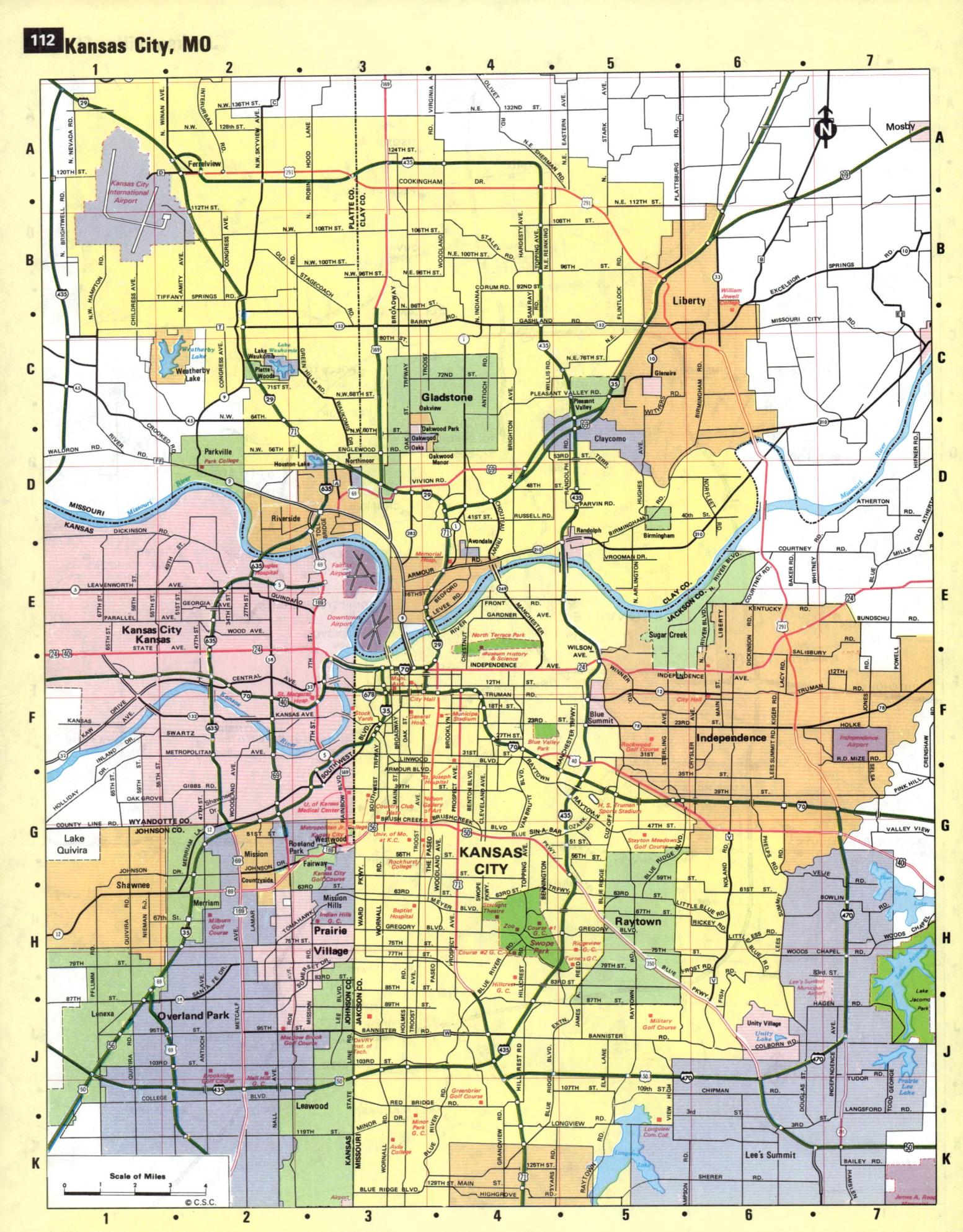

Scale of Miles
0 1 2 3 4

© C.S.C.

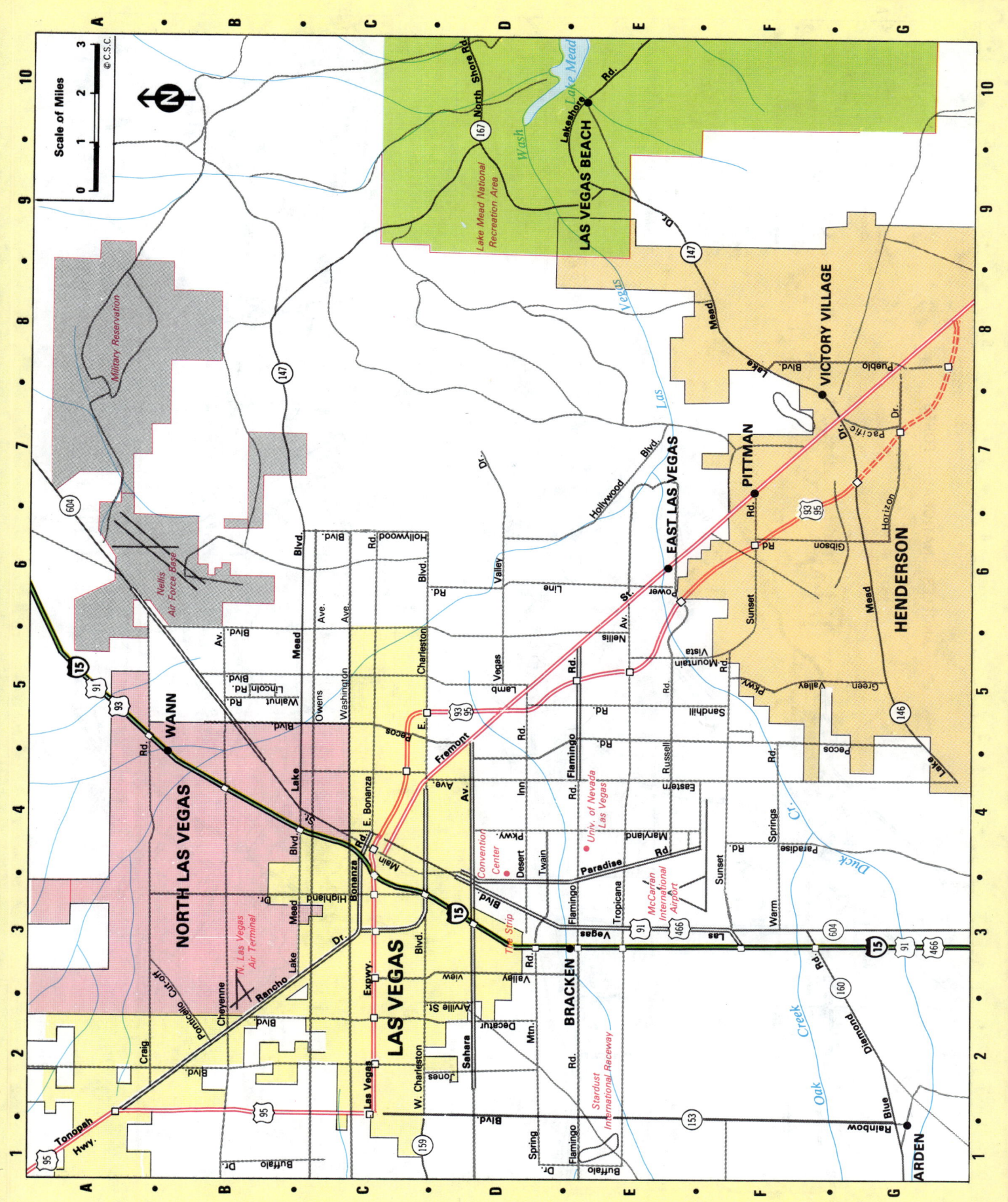

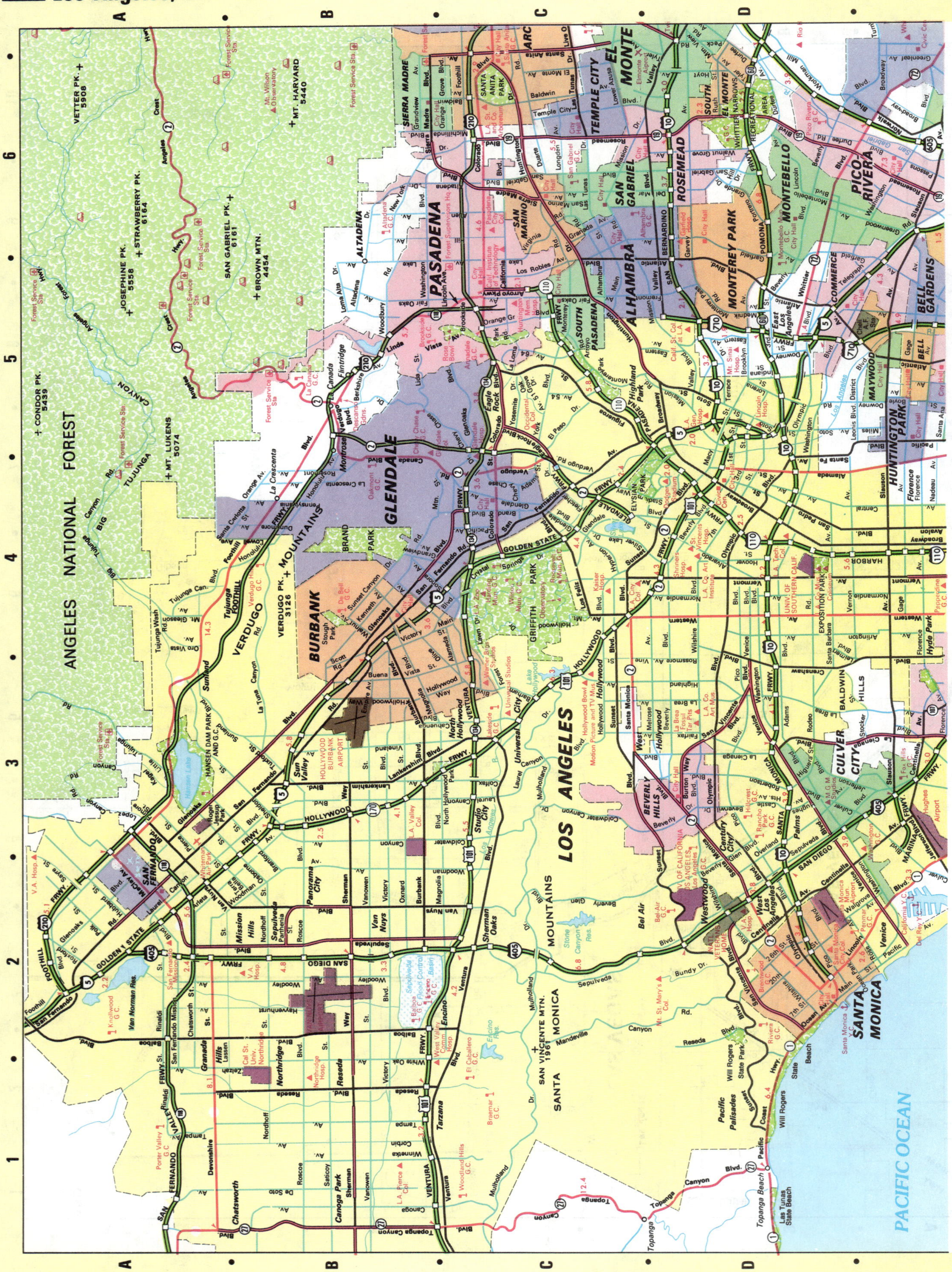

ANGELES NATIONAL FOREST

PASADENA

GLENDALE

BURBANK

SIERRA MADRE

TEMPLE CITY

EL MONTE

SOUTH EL MONTE

ROSEMEAD

SAN GABRIEL

ALHAMBRA

SAN MARINO

ALTADENA

SOUTH PASADENA

MONTEREY PARK

MONTEBELLO

PICO RIVERA

COMMERCE

BELL GARDENS

BELL

MAYWOOD

HUNTINGTON PARK

LOS ANGELES

SANTA MONICA MOUNTAINS

BEVERLY HILLS

CULVER CITY

BALDWIN HILLS

SANTA MONICA

PACIFIC PALISADES

SAN FERNANDO

Panorama City

Sherman Oaks

Van Nuys

Encino

Tarzana

Canoga Park

Northridge

Chatsworth

Reseda

PACIFIC OCEAN

VERDUGO PK. MOUNTAINS

GRIFFITH PARK

Hollywood

North Hollywood

Studio City

Universal City

VETTER PK. 5908

MT. WILSON Observatory

MT. HARVARD 5440

STRAWBERRY PK. 6164

JOSEPHINE PK. 5558

SAN GABRIEL PK. 6161

BROWN MTN. 4454

CONDOR PK. 5439

MT. LUKENS 5074

TUJUNGA

BIG TUJUNGA CANYON

HOLLYWOOD BURBANK AIRPORT

V.A. Hosp.

UNIV. OF SOUTHERN CALIFORNIA

EXPOSITION PARK

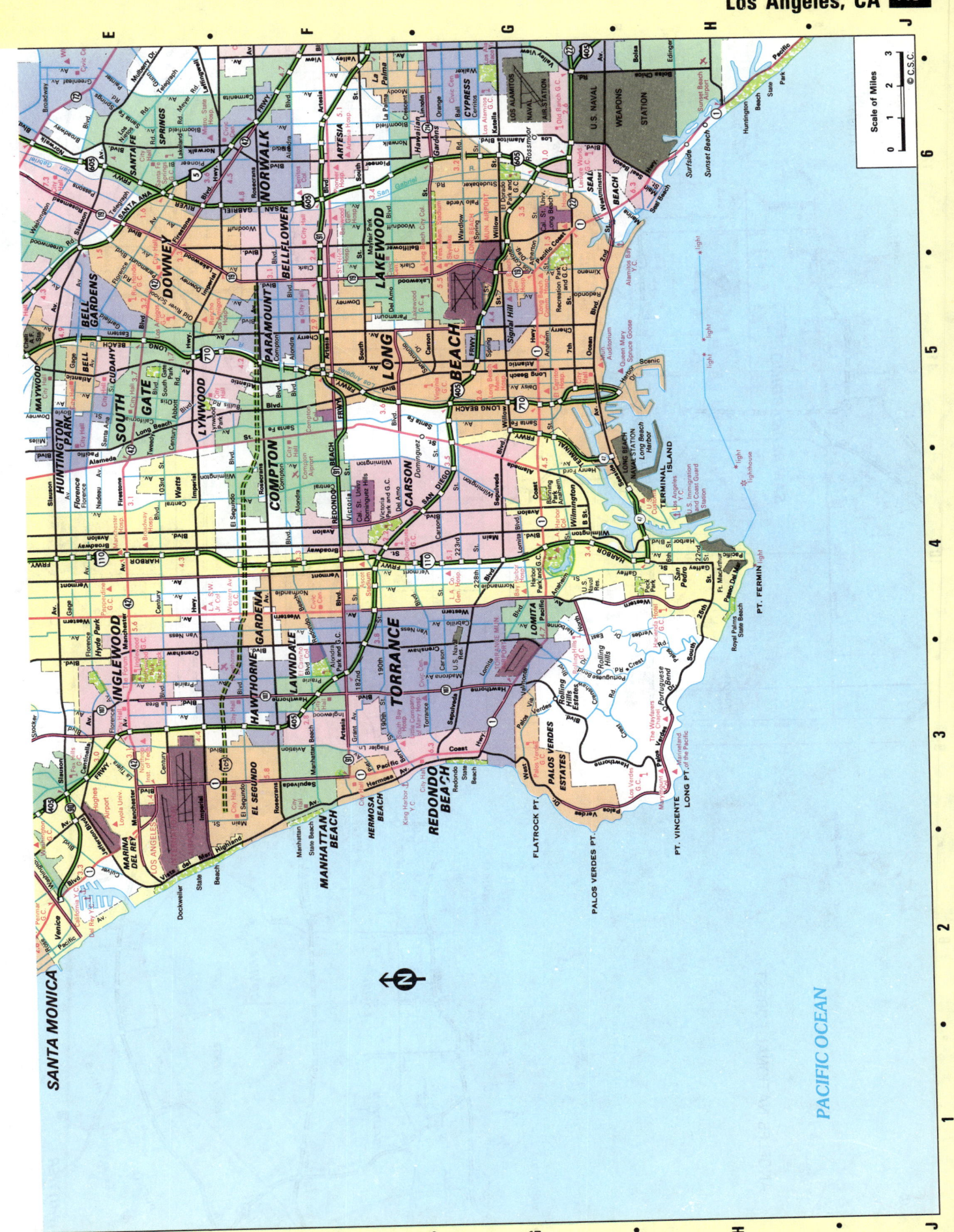

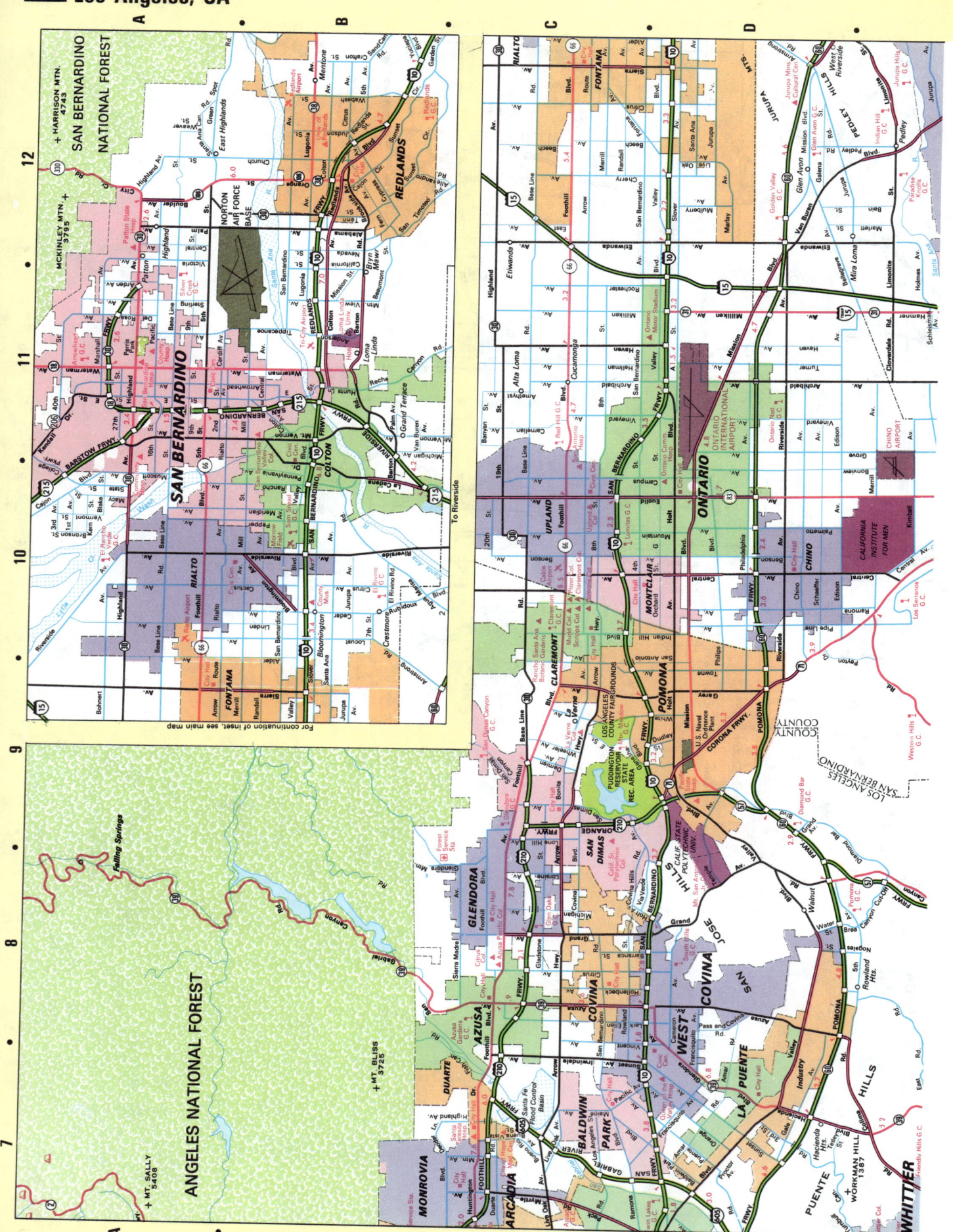

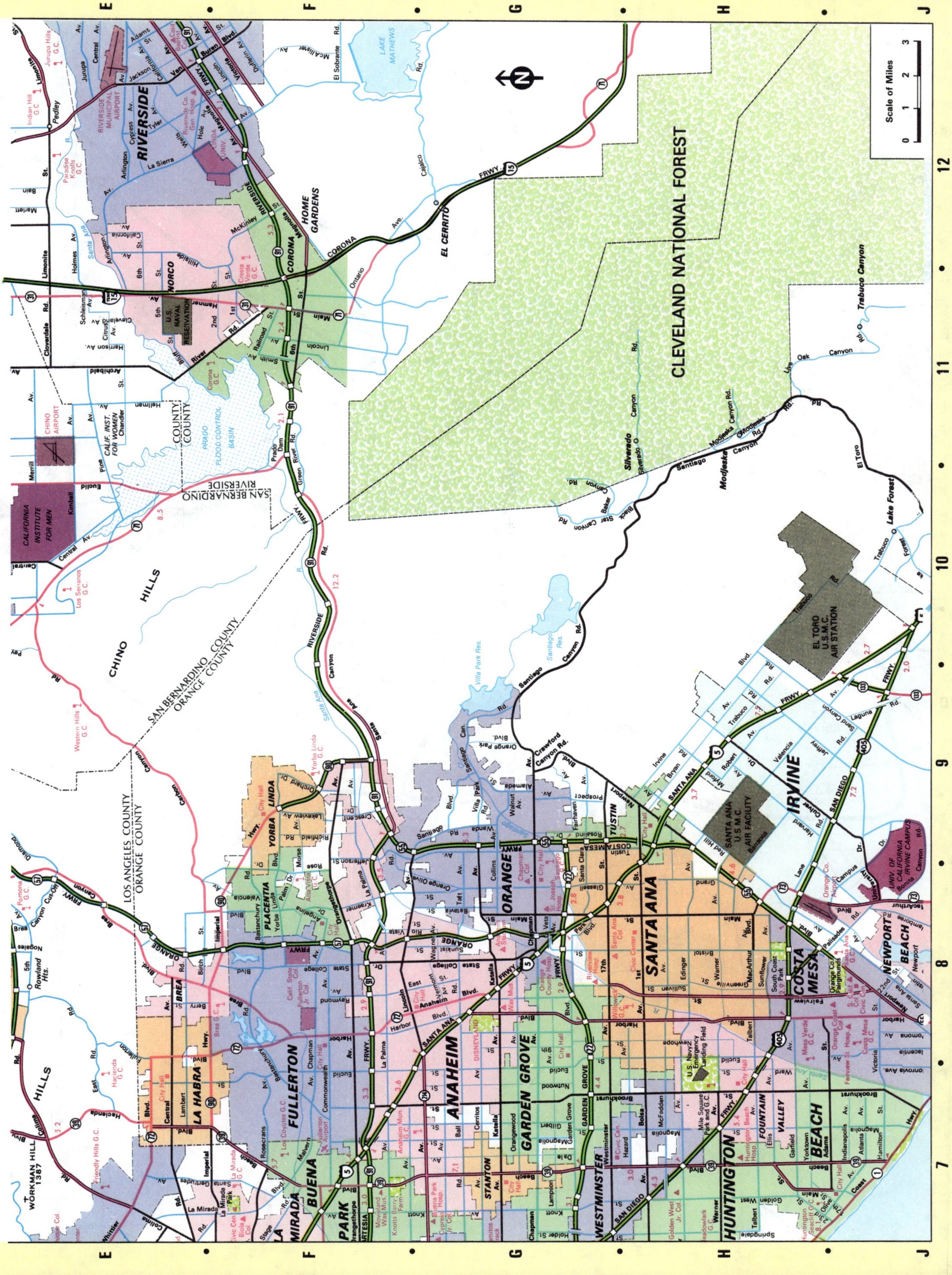

Scale of Miles
0 1 2 3

N

RIVERSIDE
Jurupa Hills G.C.
Indian Hill G.C.
Paradise Knolls G.C.
La Sierra
RIVERSIDE MUNICIPAL AIRPORT
UNIV.
NORCO
U.S. NAVAL RESERVATION
HOME GARDENS
CORONA
Cresta Verde G.C.
EL CERRITO
LAKE MATHEWS

CLEVELAND NATIONAL FOREST

CHINO AIRPORT
CALIF. INST. FOR WOMEN
CALIFORNIA INSTITUTE FOR MEN
PRADO FLOOD CONTROL BASIN
Prado Dam
Los Serranos G.C.
Western Hills G.C.

SAN BERNARDINO
RIVERSIDE
SAN BERNARDINO COUNTY
RIVERSIDE COUNTY

CHINO HILLS

Silverado
Modjeska Canyon
Santiago
Trabuco Canyon
Oak Canyon

LOS ANGELES COUNTY
ORANGE COUNTY

WORKMAN HILL 1387
HILLS
Pomona G.C.
Rowland Hts.
Diamond

YORBA LINDA
PLACENTIA
Yorba
Villa Park Res.
Santiago Res.
Orange Park
Crawford Canyon Rd.

Cleveland National Forest
El Toro
Lake Forest
Trabuco

EL TORO U.S.M.C. AIR STATION

IRVINE
SANTA ANA U.S.M.C. AIR FACILITY
UNIV. OF CALIFORNIA IRVINE CAMPUS

SANTA ANA
TUSTIN
ORANGE
COSTA MESA
NEWPORT BEACH

FULLERTON
Cal. State Univ.
Fullerton Jr. Col.
Fullerton Airport

BREA
Brea G.C.

LA HABRA

LA MIRADA
Friendly Hills G.C.
Los Coyotes C.C.

ANAHEIM
DISNEYLAND
Anaheim Mun.

BUENA PARK
Knott's Berry Farm

STANTON
GARDEN GROVE

WESTMINSTER
FOUNTAIN VALLEY
Mile Square Park and G.C.
U.S. Navy Seal Beach
Mesa Verde G.C.

HUNTINGTON BEACH
Huntington Beach G.C.

San Diego Frwy
Santa Ana Frwy
Riverside Frwy
Orange Frwy
Costa Mesa Frwy

1 2 3 4 5

A

State St.
Graybrook Rd.
Grant Line Rd.
Charlestown Rd.
Beechwood Av.
8TH ST.
Silver St.
Vekin St.
Vincennes St.
111
111
62
Slate Run Rd.
McCulloch
131
Emery Crossing Rd.
Eastern Blvd.
65
31E
Pike
Charlestown Pike
Hamburg Pike
62
3
RD.
Middle
Allison
Mullins La.
Utica
Pike
Chenoweth
71
Blankenbaker

New Albany
I-64
62
Spring
Main St.
62
Harrison Av.
Clarksville
Dutch
Spring St.
10TH
8TH
MAIN ST.
Jeffersonville
Springdale Dr.
Chippewa
62
INDIANA
KENTUCKY
Cox Park
Indian Hill Trail
Druid Hills
RD.
Hubbard
RD.
Westport

B

111
150
62
Shawnee Park
North
Western Pkwy.
Bank
Portland
264
150
River Park
Chestnut
18TH
MAIN
Market
St.
OHIO RIVER
Shippingport I.
George Rogers Clark Bridge
Kentucky-Indiana Bridge (Toll)
Sherman Minton Bridge
Riverside Pkwy.
J.F. Kennedy Mem. Bridge
Towhead I.
Bandman Park
River
Mellwood Av.
Story Av.
Frankfort
71
60
Brownsboro
42
Mockingbird Valley
Mockingbird Valley
Rolling Fields
Zorn Av.
1932
Matthews
Westport
Chenoweth La.

C

South Western Pkwy.
Commonwealth Park
Gibson
11TH
River Park
34TH
26TH
Broadway
Greenwood Ave.
Virginia
Kentucky St.
22ND
21ST
15TH
12TH
Hill St.
Oak
7TH
3RD
Broadway
150
BR 60
61
Liberty
Expwy.
31E
42
Breckenridge St.
Kentucky St.
Jackson
Preston
2ND
Campbell St.
Lexington
Payne
Logan
Barret
Winter Av.
Bardstown
Baxter
Grinstead
Cave Hill Cemetery
64
Grinstead
Lexington
Cherokee Park
Cherokee Pkwy.
Seneca Park
Alta Vista
Rock Creek
Bowman Field
Willis
Cannons La.
Broadfields
Big Springs G.C.
Dutchmans
Expwy.
155
264
31E

D

Bells La.
Algonquin Pkwy.
Wilson Rd.
2054
1931
264
Camp Ground Rd.
Cane Run Rd.
Millers La.
Dixie
1934
Ralph Av.
Shively
Central Blvd.
7TH
Winkler Av.
Av.
Churchill Downs
Longfield Av.
3RD
Park Dr.
North
Burnett
Shelby
Eastern
Goss Av.
864
ALT 60
Cave Hill Cemetery
Poplar Level
Louisville
Richmond Dr.
31E
Way
Parkway Village
Preston
Audobon Park
Audubon C.C.
Audubon Pkwy.
Trevilian Park
Trevilian
Zoological Gardens
Newburgh
Gardiner La.
Watterson
Henry
Goldsmith La.
264
Bashford Manor La.
West Buechel
Hikes La.
6 Mile

E

Rockford La.
Dixie
31W
60
BR 60
1931
Crums La.
Berry Blvd.
Henry
Taylor
264
1020
Bluegrass
1865
Hazelwood Av.
New Southern Av.
Cut
Woodlawn Av.
Watterson Expwy.
Crittenden Dr.
Crittenden La.
U.S. Navy Ordnance Plant
Standiford Field
Kentucky State Fair & Exposition Center
1631
Hwy.
Lynnview
Norton Av.
61
Indian Trail
Gilmore La.
Jennings La.
1703
Bishop
864
General Electric Appliance Park
Buechel
Bank Rd.
Shepherdsville
2052

F

Gagel Av.
Dixie
31W
Blanton Rd.
Church Rd.
1931
St. Andrews
Manslick Rd.
Palatka
Iroquis Park
3RD ST.
Kenwood Dr.
Southside Dr.
New Cut Rd.
907
Strawberry La.
Grade La.
National TPK.
Ford Car Plant
Crittenden Dr.
Fern Valley Rd.
1631
Preston Hwy.
Kentucky Turnpike
61
Poplar Level Rd.
864
Fegenbush
2052

N

G

Arnoldtown Rd.
St. Anthony Church Rd.
Outer Loop
1065
Brown Ausi...
Manslick
907
National TPK.
Minors
Minor Lane Hts
Outer Loop
65
Lick Branch Rd.
Preston Hwy.
1065
2052

Scale of Miles
0 1 2 3

© C.S.C.

Scale of Miles

MEMPHIS

TENNESSEE
MISSISSIPPI

TENNESSEE
ARKANSAS

Mississippi River

Wolf River

SHELBY CO.
CRITTENDEN CO.

SHELBY CO.
DE SOTO CO.

Arlington, Bolton, Gildfield, Brunswick, Spring Lake, Ellendale, Bartlett, Elmore Park, Pisgah, Fisherville, Cordova, Germantown, Forest Hill, Collierville, Bailey, Mineral Wells, Lucy, Woodstock, Raleigh, Egypt, Benjestown, Ramsey, Redman Point, St. Clair, Mound City, Blanton, Harvard, Gammon, West Memphis, Hulbert, Galet, Wyanoke, Lake View, Whitehaven, Oakville, Capleville, Plum Point

Memphis International Airport
Gen. DeWitt Spain Downtown Airport
Shelby County Airport
John F. Kennedy Park
Shelby Farms
Penal Farm
Meeman Shelby Forest State Park
Fuller State Park
McKellar Park
Audubon Park
Overton Park
Riverside Park

Interstate 40, 55, 240
Highways 51, 61, 64, 70, 72, 78, 79, 14, 1, 3

1 • 2 • 3 • 4 • 5 • 6

Map continues on this page A-2

Scale of Miles
0 1 2 3
© TRAKKER MAPS INC.

N

A

PALM BEACH COUNTY
INDIANTOWN RD 706
To Stuart
To Ft. Pierce
Jupiter
CENTER ST
Jupiter Inlet Colony
Jupiter Inlet
To Stuart
DONALD ROSS RD
HOOD RD
DIXIE HWY
Juno Beach
PROSPERITY FARMS RD
LOST TREE VILLAGE
Parkland
SAWGRASS EXPY
Coconut Creek
HILLSBORO EXIT 71
Deerfield Beach
NW 10 ST
FEDERAL HWY
OCEAN BLVD
Hillsboro Beach
SAMPLE RD 834
EXIT 69
COPANS RD
SAMPLE RD
DIXIE HWY
Lighthouse Point
Hillsboro Inlet

B
PGA BLVD
Palm Beach Gardens
North Palm Beach
MILITARY TRAIL
NORTH LAKE BLVD 809
Lake Park
BLUE HERON BLVD
Riviera Beach
West Palm Beach
WEST PALM JAI-ALAI
Mangonia Park
Coral Springs
Royal Palm Blvd
Margate
ATLANTIC BLVD
MARGATE BLVD 814
North Lauderdale
Pompano Beach
POMPANO BEACH AIRPARK
ATLANTIC BLVD
EXIT 67
TPK PLAZA
POMPANO RACE TRACK
CYPRESS CREEK
Fort Lauderdale
COMMERCIAL BLVD
Sea Ranch Lakes
Lauderdale-By-The-Sea
McNAB RD
Tamarac
COMMERCIAL BLVD
Lauderdale Lakes
Oakland Park
EXIT 62
Wilton Manors
OAKLAND PARK BLVD
SUNRISE BLVD
HUGH TAYLOR BIRCH STATE RECREATION AREA

C
LAKE WORTH
Royal Palm Beach
OKEECHOBEE BLVD 704
PALM BEACH KENNEL CLUB
BELVEDERE RD
PALM BEACH INTERNATIONAL AIRPORT
Glens Ridge
SOUTHERN BLVD 98
FLAGLER MUSEUM
Wellington
FOREST HILL BLVD
Greenacres City
Palm Springs
Lake Clarke Shores
Lake Worth
South Palm Beach
MARKHAM PARK
Davie
OAKLAND PARK BLVD
SUNRISE BLVD
Sunrise
Plantation
EXIT 58
BROWARD BLVD
Fort Lauderdale
SWIMMING HALL OF FAME
DAVIE BLVD
PORT EVERGLADES
CRUISE SHIPS
BEACH STATE RECREATION AREA

D
LOXAHATCHEE NATIONAL WILDLIFE REFUGE
Atlantis
PALM BEACH CO. AIRPORT
LANTANA RD
Lantana
HYPOLUXO RD
Hypoluxo
Manalapan
WEST RD
Ocean Ridge
Pembroke Pines
C.B. SMITH PARK
PINES BLVD
Miramar
MIRAMAR PKWY
PEMBROKE RD
HOMESTEAD EXTENSION
Cooper City
STIRLING RD
SHERIDAN ST
TAFT ST
Hollywood
HOLLYWOOD BLVD
NORTH PERRY AIRPORT
EXIT 49
EXIT 47
Pembroke Park
EXIT 47A
Hallandale
HALLANDALE BEACH BLVD
HOLLYWOOD DOG TRACK
GULFSTREAM PARK
Golden Beach

E
Golf
Beynton
Briny Breezes
Gulf Stream
WOOLBRIGHT RD
BOYNTON WEST RD
PALM BEACH COUNTY
BROWARD COUNTY
Carol City
Miami Gardens
OPA-LOCKA AIRPORT
Opa-locka
Hialeah Gardens
Medley
Pennsuco
North Miami Beach
IVES DAIRY RD
LEHMAN CSWY
GARDENS DR
North Miami Beach
HAULOVER BEACH PARK
North Bay Village
Bal Harbor
Biscayne Park
Indian Creek Village
Surfside
Miami Shores

F
Delray Beach
LINTON BLVD
Boca Raton
Highland Beach
CLINT MOORE RD
YAMATO RD
BOCA RATON MUNICIPAL AIRPORT
EXIT 75
PALMETTO PARK RD
Boca Raton
Hialeah
Miami Springs
Virginia Gardens
MIAMI INTERNATIONAL AIRPORT
AIRPORT EXPWY
DOLPHIN EXPWY
Miami
Miami Beach
JULIA TUTTLE CSWY
VENETIAN CSWY
BAYSIDE MARKETPLACE
CONVENTION CENTER
ORANGE BOWL
CRUISE SHIPS
MacARTHUR CSWY
Fisher Is.

G
Parkland
SAWGRASS EXPY
Coconut Creek
HILLSBORO BLVD
EXIT 71
Deerfield Beach
NW 10 ST
Map continues on this page G-5
Sweetwater
West Miami
Coral Gables
SCIENCE MUSEUM SPACE TRANSIT PLANETARIUM
MIAMI MARINE STADIUM
UNIVERSITY OF MIAMI
VIZCAYA
RICKENBACKER CSWY
SEAQUARIUM
Virginia Key
Key Biscayne
CRANDON BLVD
CAPE FLORIDA STATE PARK
LIGHTHOUSE
MATHESON HAMMOCK PARK
PARROT JUNGLE
KILLIAN
KENDALL
SUNSET DR

ATLANTIC OCEAN

Biscayne Bay

1 • 2 • 3 • 4 • 5 • 6

MEEKER
GERMANTOWN
COLGATE
WASHINGTON CO.
WAUKESHA CO.
MEQUIN
MEQUON
Dondes Bay
Granville
Swan
County Line
OZAUKEE CO.
MILWAUKEE CO.
BROWN DEER
RIVER HILLS
BAYSIDE
MENOMONEE FALLS
Plainview
Menomonee
Brown Deer
Bradley
Good Hope
Brown Deer Park
FOX POINT
LANNON
Good Hope
GLENDALE
WHITEFISH BAY
SUSSEX
W. Mill
Silver Spring
Mill
Range Line
Bender
W. Mill
Marcy
Lisbon
Silver Spring
Appleton
Hampton
Teutonia
SHOREWOOD
BUTLER
Capitol
Lisbon
Capitol
Villard
Keefe Av.
Edgewood
BROOKFIELD
Burleigh
Lisbon
Burleigh
University of Wisconsin (Milwaukee)
Lake Park
PEWAUKEE
DUPLAINVILLE
North
North
Sherman
McKinley Park
ELM GROVE
WAUWATOSA
Vliet
MILWAUKEE
City Hall
GOERKES CORNER
Watertown Plank
Wisconsin
Highland
Wells
Federal Bldg.
Blue Mound
Milwaukee County Zoo
Freeway
Stadium
Marquette Univ.
WAUKESHA
East-West
Greenfield
State Fair Park
Milwaukee County Stadium
Greenfield
WEST MILWAUKEE
Lake Michigan
NEW BERLIN
Lincoln
WEST ALLIS
National
Lincoln
SAINT FRANCIS
Lawnsdale
Oklahoma
Morgan
Holt
Morgan
Cleveland
Howard
Forest Home
Thompson
MUSKEGO
Airport
GREENFIELD
Edgerton
General Mitchell International Field
CUDAHY
Little Muskego Lake
College
Grobschmidt Park
Sheridan Park
VERNON
HALES CORNERS
Grange
GREENDALE
Rawson
Grant Park
BIG BEND
Whitnall Park
Root River Pkwy
College
OAK CREEK
SOUTH MILWAUKEE
Big Muskego Lake
Ryan
Drexel
Puetz
Bender Park
FRANKLIN
Oakwood
Rainbow Airport
Oakwood G.C.
Lake Michigan
WAUSHEKA CO.
RACINE CO.
MILWAUKEE CO.
RACINE CO.
TICHIGAN
Kee Nong Go Mong Lake
UNION CHURCH
Seven Mile
CADDY VISTA
Wind Lake
KNEELAND
Six Mile
HUSHER
Waubeesee Lake
Six Mile
TABOR
Tichigan Lake
Five and a Half Mile
CALEDONIA
BUENA PARK
RAYMOND
Five Mile
NORTH CAPE
THOMPSONVILLE

Scale of Miles
0   1   2   3

© C.S.C.

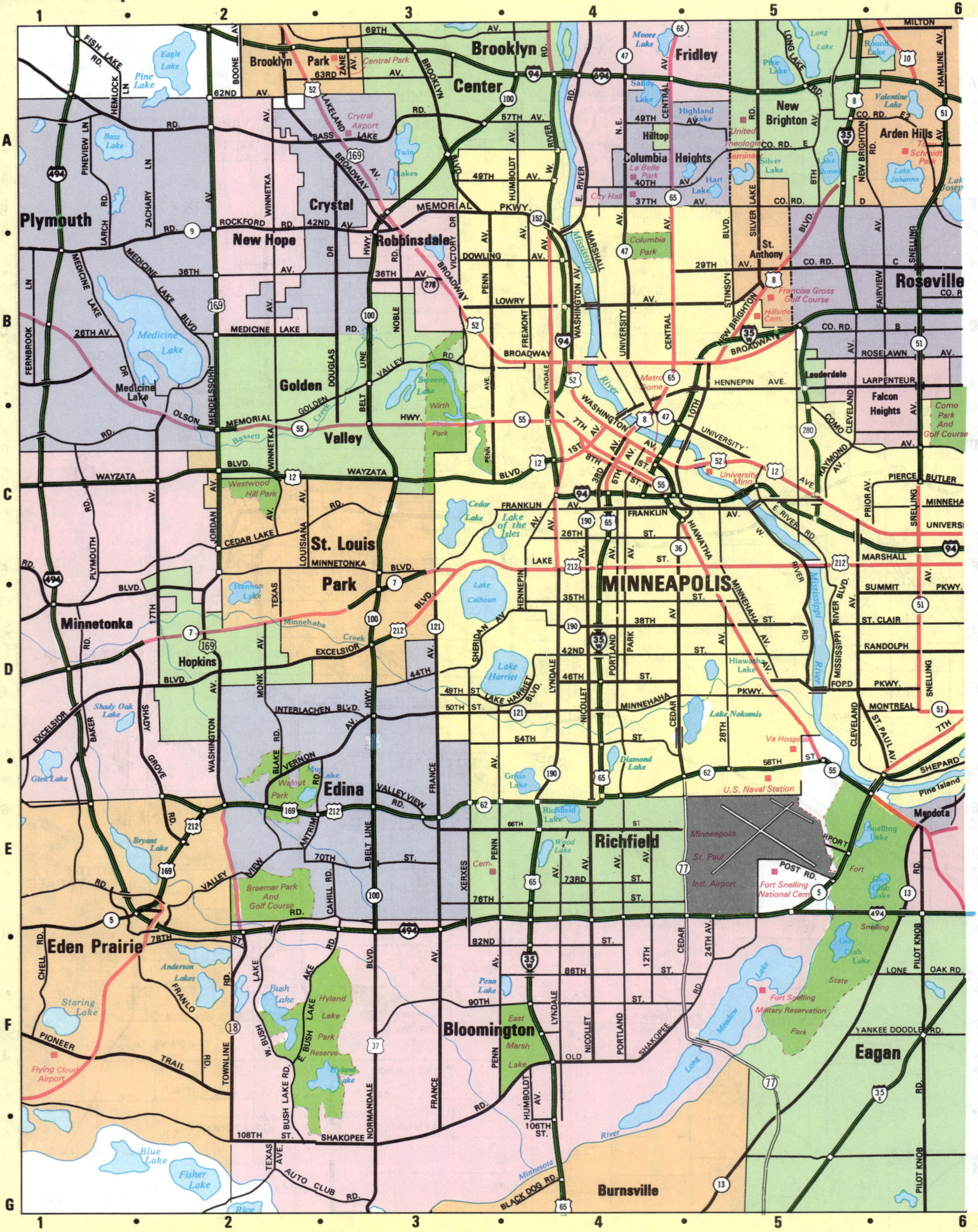

Plymouth

Brooklyn Park

Brooklyn Center

Fridley

New Brighton

Arden Hills

Crystal

New Hope

Robbinsdale

Hilltop

Columbia Heights

St. Anthony

Roseville

Lauderdale

Falcon Heights

Golden Valley

Medicine Lake

Wirth Park

Minnehaha

Westwood Hill Park

St. Louis Park

Cedar Lake

Lake of the Isles

MINNEAPOLIS

University of Minn.

Minnetonka

Hopkins

Lake Calhoun

Lake Harriet

Lake Nokomis

Edina

Walnut Park

Richfield

Richfield Lake

Diamond Lake

Grass Lake

U.S. Naval Station

Minneapolis St. Paul Intl. Airport

Fort Snelling National Cem.

Mendota

Eden Prairie

Braemar Park And Golf Course

Bush Lake

Hyland Lake Park Reserve

Bloomington

Fort Snelling Military Reservation

Eagan

Flying Cloud Airport

Staring Lake

Blue Lake

Fisher Lake

Burnsville

Como Park And Golf Course

6   7   8   9   10   11

CO. RD. 96

Snail Lake

Shoreview

Lexington

Victoria

Rice

McMenemy

Vadnais Heights

Lake Vadnais

Little Canada

Little Canada

Roselawn

Larpenteur

Arlington

Maryland

Como Park Golf Course

ST. PAUL

Pierce Butler

Minnehaha

University

Concordia Coll.

Dayton

Summit

Lexington

Mendota

Mendota Heights

Sunfish Lake

Rogers Lake

Highland Park Golf Course

Lilydale

West St. Paul

Thompson

South St. Paul

Southview Blvd.

Inver Grove

Heights

Yankee Doodle Rd.

70th

Lone

Diffley Rd.

Kohlman Lake

Gervais Lake

Maplewood

Frost

Larpenteur

Lake Phalen

Phalen Park Golf Course

Maryland

Minnehaha

Burns

Warner Blvd.

St. Paul Downtown Airport (Holman Field)

Mississippi

George St.

Annapolis

Butler

Charlton

Wentworth

Thompson

15th St.

9th

5th

Pigs Eye Lake

Burlington Rd.

Concord

So. St. Paul Municipal Airport

80th

College Tr.

Cuneen Tr.

Inver Grove Tr.

105th

White Bear Lake

Gem Lake

Birchwood

White Bear

Lake

Bellaire

North St. Paul

Silver Lake

Larpenteur

Beaver Lake

Minnehaha

McKnight

East Co. Line

Upper Afton

Lower Afton

Linwood Av.

Highwood

Carver Av.

Newport

Point Douglas

St. Paul Park

Hastings

66th St.

65th

70th

80th

100th St. S.

Mahtomedi

Willernie

Pine Springs

Lake De Montreville

Lake Jane

Sunfish Lake

Lake Elmo

Oakdale

Harvester

Minnehaha

Landfall

Hudson

Battle Creek Lake

Brookview

Markgrafs Lake

Powers Lake

Woodbury

Valley Creek

Steeple View Rd.

Lower Afton

Colby Lake

Bailey

Military

Tower

Dale

Radio

Glen

Woodlane

65th

70th

Cottage Grove

80th

Military

Afton

40th St. N.

30th St. N.

Eagle Point Lake

Lake Elmo

10th St.

40th St. S.

Keats

Manning

Dullwood Rd.

75th St. N.

36

Scale of Miles
0   1   2

N

© C.S.C.

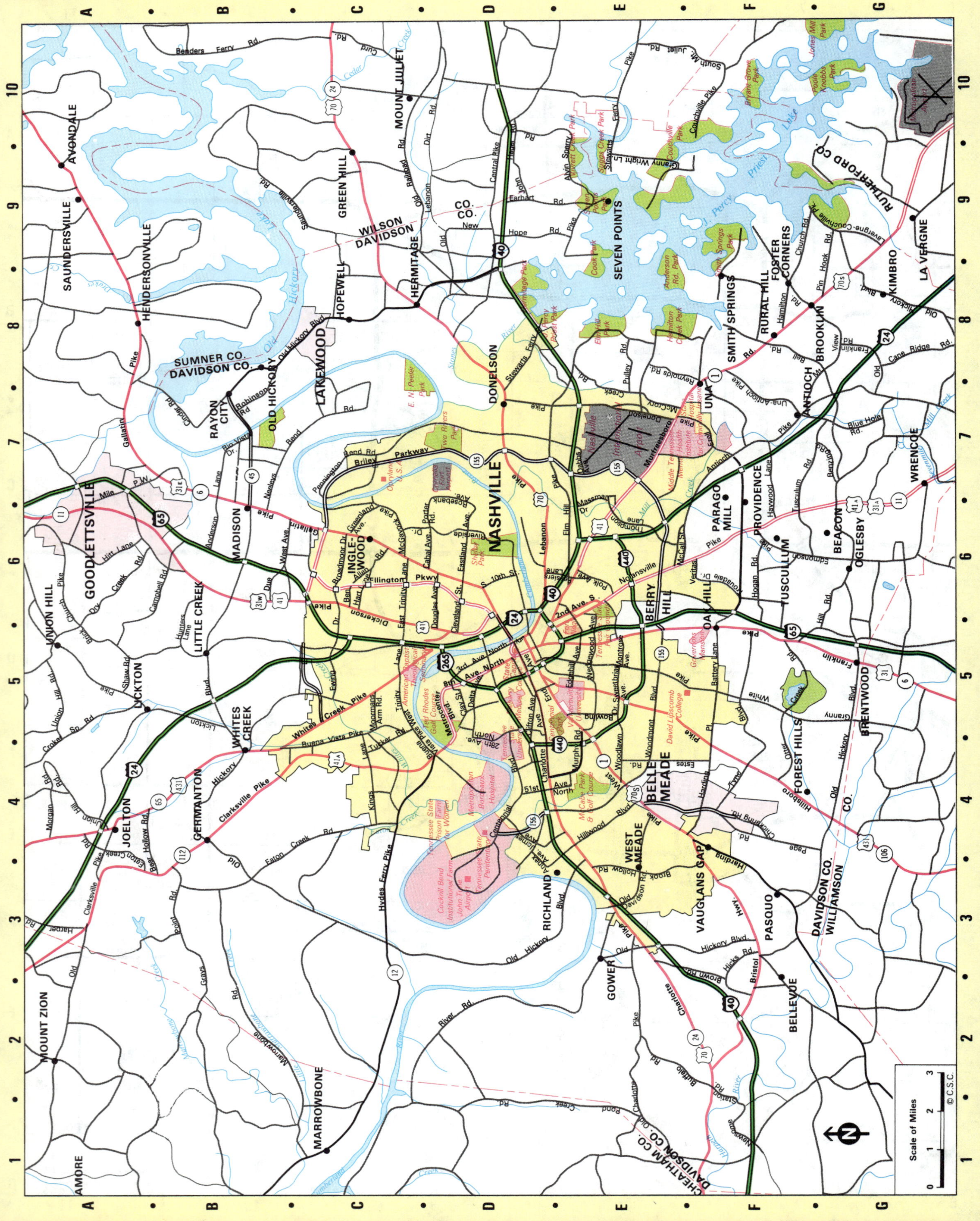

NASHVILLE

AVONDALE
SAUNDERSVILLE
HENDERSONVILLE
GREEN HILL
WILSON
DAVIDSON
MOUNT JULIET
HERMITAGE
CO. CO.
HOPEWELL
LAKEWOOD
SUMNER CO.
DAVIDSON CO.
RAYON CITY
OLD HICKORY
DONELSON
SEVEN POINTS
SMITH SPRINGS
RURAL HILL
FOSTER CORNERS
ANTIOCH
BROOKLYN
KIMBRO
LA VERGNE
RUTHERFORD CO.
UNA
GOODLETTSVILLE
MADISON
INGLE-WOOD
Briley Parkway
PARAGON MILL
PROVIDENCE
BEACON
OGLESBY
TUSCULUM
WRENCOE
UNION HILL
LITTLE CREEK
BERRY HILL
OAK HILL
DICKTON
WHITES CREEK
GERMANTOWN
JOELTON
RICHLAND
BELLE MEADE
WEST MEADE
VAUGLANS GAP
FOREST HILLS
BRENTWOOD
MOUNT ZION
MARROWBONE
GOWER
PASQUO
BELLEVUE
DAVIDSON CO.
WILLIAMSON CO.
CHEATHAM CO.
DAVIDSON CO.
AMORE

Scale of Miles
0 1 2 3
© C.S.C.

Scale of Miles
0 1 2 3
© C.S.C.

PARISH PARISH

NEW ORLEANS

ORLEANS PARISH

ST. BERNARD PARISH

ST. BERNARD PLAQUEMINES

National Aeronautics & Space Administration

Intracoastal Waterway

Chef Menteur Hwy.

Mirabeau Ave.

Paris Rd.

Bullard Rd.

Haynes Blvd.

Read Blvd.

Crowder Rd.

Downman Rd.

France Rd.

New Orleans Lakefront Airport

Pontchartrain Beach Amusement Park
Univ. of New Orleans

Pontchartrain Blvd.

Lakeshore Dr.

Robert E. Lee Blvd.

Marconi Ave.

Wisner Blvd.

City Park

Fair Grounds Racetrack

Elysian Fields Ave.

Franklin Ave.

St. Bernard Ave.

Paris Ave.

Esplanade Ave.

Canal St.

Tulane Ave.

Carrollton Ave.

Broad St.

Claiborne Ave.

Napoleon Ave.

Louisiana Ave.

Washington Ave.

Magazine St.

St. Charles Ave.

Louisiana Ave.

Jackson Ave.

Prytania St.

Loyola Ave.

Tulane Univ.

Xavier Univ.

Audubon Park

Broadway St.

ARABI

CHALMETTE

Chalmette Nat'l Hist. Park

Packenham Oaks (Versailles)

Pakenham Rd.

Volpe St.

Genie St.

Gen. Meyer Ave.

Madison Ave.

Gallier Dr.

French Quarter

U.S. Naval Air Station

Claude Ave.

Florida Ave.

ALGIERS

Patterson Dr.

Newton St.

Behrman Ave.

MERAUX

Woodland Dr.

GRETNA

HARVEY

Behrman Hwy.

Brechtel Park

Lakewood Country Club

Gen. De Gaulle Dr.

MacArthur Blvd.

Terry Pkwy.

Carol Sue Ave.

Fairfield Ave.

Cottonwood Dr.

Chassie Ave.

Manhattan Blvd.

Maplewood Dr.

Claire Ave.

Peters Rd.

Destrehan Rd.

Farmington Rd.

Derbigny St.

4th St.

16th St.

Lapalco Blvd.

MARRERO

WESTWEGO

Bank St.

Ames Blvd.

Barataria Rd.

Westwood Dr.

Ridgefield Rd.

ESTELLE

JEAN LAFITTE

Barataria Blvd.

Kenta Canal

CROWN POINT

CYPRESS GARDENS

POYDRAS

ST. BERNARD

CAERNARVON

ENGLISH TURN

SAINT CLAIR

BELLE CHASSE

SCARSDALE

STELLA

CONCESSION

Alvin Callender Field U.S. Naval Air Station

DALCOUR

CEDAR GROVE

AUGUSTA

OAKVILLE

BERTRANDVILLE

LIVE OAK

WILLS POINT

JESUIT BEND

Big Mar

Le Blanc Bayou

Tiger Ridge

ORLEANS PARISH

PLAQUEMINES PARISH
JEFFERSON PARISH

KENNER

Jefferson Downs

Williams Blvd.

Duncan Canal

New Orleans International Airport

ORLEANS PARISH
JEFFERSON PARISH

Lake Pontchartrain Causeway (Toll)

EAST END

METAIRIE

Bonnabel Blvd.

Bonnabel Canal

Causeway Blvd.

Metairie Country Club

Airline Hwy.

Esplanade Ave.

Suburban Canal

Veterans Memorial Blvd.

Transcontinental Dr.

Clearview Pkwy.

Central Ave.

Hickory Ave.

Lafrenier Park

Elmwood Canal

HARAHAN

BRIDGE CITY

AVONDALE

WAGGAMAN

WILLSWOOD

LIVE OAK MANOR

JEFFERSON HTS.

Jefferson Hwy.

Soniat Canal

Avondale Canal

AIRLINE PARK

DESTREHAN

ST. ROSE

AMA

LONE STAR

Walker Canal

JEFFERSON PARISH
ST. CHARLES PARISH

Lake Cataouatche

Couba Island

Lake Salvador

Bayou Couba

Mississippi River

Lake Pontchartrain

Lake

CHAPPAQUA
THORNWOOD
HAWTHORNE
MT. PLEASANT
EAST VIEW
POCANTICO HILL
ARCHVILLE
N. TARRYTOWN
TARRYTOWN
ELMSFORD
GREENBURGH
WHITE PLAINS
SCARSDALE
EASTCHESTER
TOWN OF MAMARONECK
LARCHMONT
NEW ROCHELLE
PELHAM
PELHAM MANOR
MOUNT VERNON
WESTCHESTER CO.
BRONX CO.
BRONX
IRVINGTON
ARDSLEY
DOBBS FERRY
HASTINGS-ON HUDSON
YONKERS
GRANDVIEW-ON HUDSON
PIERMONT
SPARKILL
PALISADES
UPPER NYACK
NYACK
S. NYACK
CENTRAL NYACK
VALLEY COTTAGE
CLARKSTOWN
BARDONIA
BLAUVELT
ORANGETOWN
ORANGEBURG
ROCKLEIGH
NORTHVALE
ALPINE
NORWOOD
CLOSTER
DEMAREST
CRESSKILL
TENAFLY
ENGLEWOOD
ENGLEWOOD CLIFFS
FORT LEE
RIVERDALE
BERGEN CO.
OLD TAPPAN
HARRINGTON PK.
HAWORTH
DUMONT
BERGENFIELD
TEANECK
LEONIA
PALISADES PK.
RIVER VALE
WESTWOOD
EMERSON
ORADELL
NEW MILFORD
RIVER EDGE
HACKENSACK
BOGOTA
RIDGEFIELD PK.
LITTLE FERRY
HILLCREST
SPRING VALLEY
NEW HEMPSTEAD
MT. IVY
PEARL RIVER
MONTVALE
PARK RIDGE
WOODCLIFF LAKE
HILLSDALE
WASHINGTON TWP
WESLEY HILLS
LADENTOWN
VIOLA
MONSEY
TALLMAN
AIRMONT
ROCKLAND CO.
UPPER SADDLE RIVER
SADDLE RIVER
HO-HO-KUS
RIDGEWOOD
PARAMUS
ROCHELLE PK.
MAYWOOD
SADDLE BROOK
LODI
HASBROUCK HTS.
TETERBORO
MOONACHIE
WOOD RIDGE
WALLINGTON
GARFIELD
ELMWOOD PARK
FAIR LAWN
GLEN ROCK
MIDLAND PARK
WALDWICK
ALLENDALE
RAMSEY
MAHWAH
SUFFERN
HILLBURN
RAMAPO
SLOATSBURG
TUXEDO PARK
ORANGE CO.
NEW YORK
NEW JERSEY
PASSAIC CO.
WYCKOFF
FRANKLIN LAKES
OAKLAND
NORTH HALEDON
HAWTHORNE
PROSPECT PK.
HALEDON
PATTERSON
WEST PATTERSON
BORO OF TOTOWA
WAYNE
WAYNE TWP.
LITTLE FALLS TWP.
CLIFTON
PASSAIC
ESSEX CO.
CEDAR GROVE
NORTH CALDWELL
WEST CALDWELL
FAIRFIELD
LINCOLN PARK
PEQUANNOCK
RIVERDALE
BORO OF BLOOMINGDALE
POMPTON LAKES
BORO OF WANAQUE
BORO OF RINGWOOD
ERSKINE
RINGWOOD
HEWITT
Hudson River
Tappan Zee
Tappan Zee Bridge
George Washington Bridge
Essex Co. Airport
Teterboro Airport
Ramapo Valley Airport

Scale of Miles

© C.S.C.

QUEENS

JAMAICA

SPRINGFIELD GDNS.

INWOOD

John F. Kennedy International Airport

GREAT NECK EST.

FLUSHING

COLLEGE POINT

La Guardia Airport

JACKSON HTS.

ASTORIA

LONG ISLAND CITY

GREEN POINT

MANHATTAN

RICHMOND HILL

OZONE PARK

FOREST HILLS

E. NEW YORK

CANARSIE

KINGS CO. QUEENS CO.

Gateway National Recreational Area

Floyd Bennett Field

BROOKLYN

FLATBUSH

BENSON HURST

CONEY ISLAND

Atlantic Ocean

NEW YORK

BAY RIDGE

KINGS CO. RICHMOND CO.

STATEN ISLAND

NEW BRIGHTON

CASTLETON CORNERS

DONGAN HILLS

NEW DORP

NEW DORP BEACH

GREAT KILLS

WILLOW BROOK

PORT RICHMOND

CHELSEA

BAYONNE

HUGUENOT PARK

HUGUENOT

MIDDLESEX CO. RICHMOND CO.

CROSSVILLE

CARTERET

PORT READING

SEWAREN

WOOD BRIDGE

PERTH AMBOY

AVENEL

RAHWAY

COLONIA

ISELIN

FORDS

JERSEY CITY

HOBOKEN

UNION CITY

WEEHAWKEN

WEST NEW YORK

NORTH BERGEN

SECAUCUS

EDGEWATER

CLIFFSIDE

FAIRVIEW

RIDGEFIELD

CARLSTADT

EAST RUTHERFORD

RUTHERFORD

LYNDHURST

NORTH ARLINGTON

KEARNY

HARRISON

E. NEWARK

NEWARK

Newark International Airport

ELIZABETH

LINDEN

BELLEVILLE

NUTLEY

BLOOMFIELD

GLEN RIDGE

MONTCLAIR

VERONA

WEST ORANGE

ROSELAND

LIVINGSTON TWP.

MILLBURN

MAPLEWOOD

EAST ORANGE

ORANGE

IRVINGTON

HILLSIDE TWP.

SPRINGFIELD TWP.

UNION TWP.

KENILWORTH

ROSELLE

ROSELLE PARK

BORO OF GARWOOD

CRANFORD

CLARK TWP.

WESTFIELD

BORO OF ROSELLE PARK

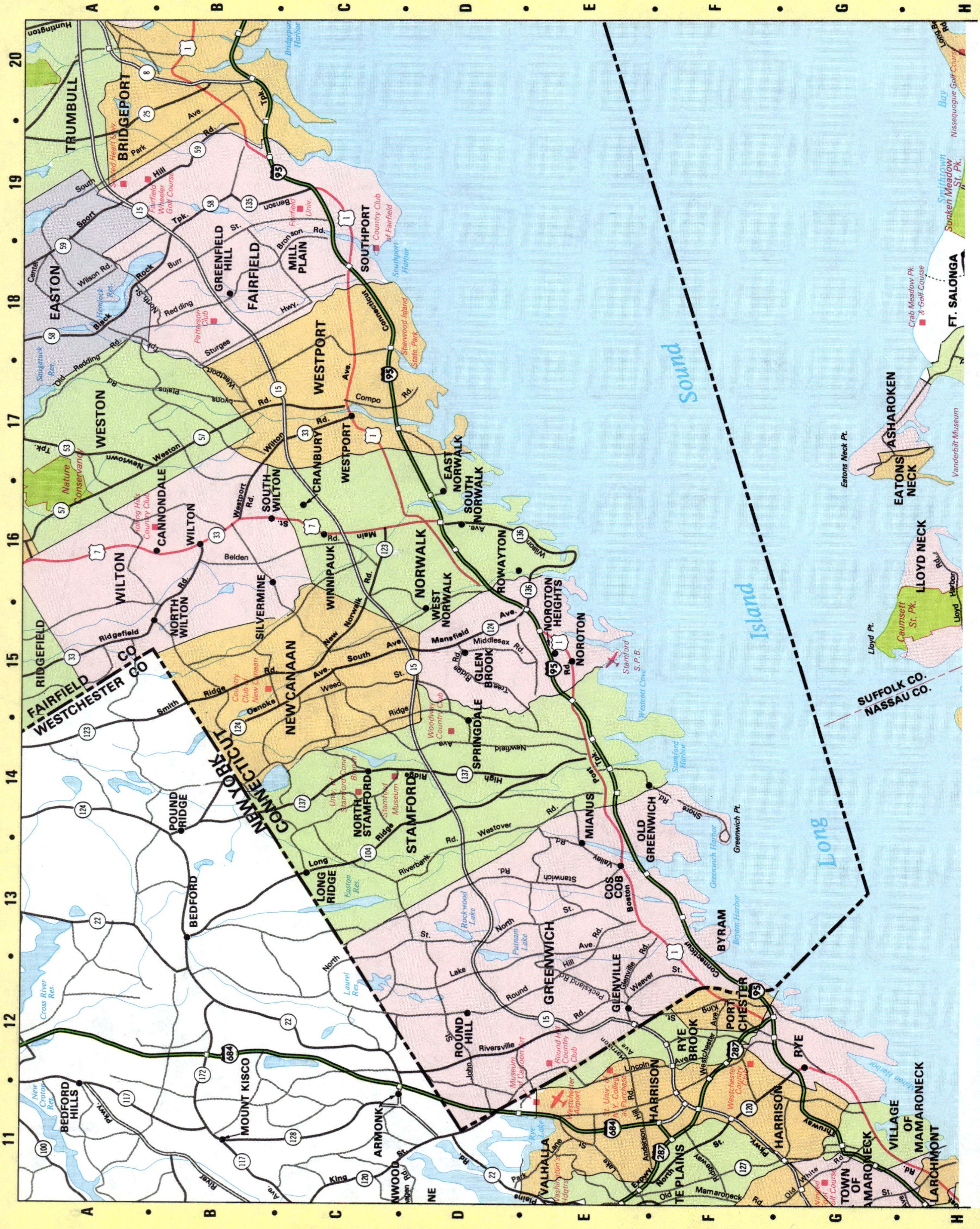
BRIDGEPORT
TRUMBULL
EASTON
FAIRFIELD
GREENFIELD HILL
MILL PLAIN
SOUTHPORT
WESTPORT
WESTON
CANNONDALE
WILTON
SOUTH WILTON
CRANBURY
EAST NORWALK
SOUTH NORWALK
ROWAYTON
WINNIPAUK
NORWALK
WEST NORWALK
NOROTON HEIGHTS
NOROTON
SILVERMINE
NORTH WILTON
RIDGEFIELD
NEW CANAAN
GLEN BROOK
SPRINGDALE
STAMFORD
NORTH STAMFORD
LONG RIDGE
POUND RIDGE
BEDFORD
MIANUS
OLD GREENWICH
COS COB
GREENWICH
GLENVILLE
BYRAM
PORT CHESTER
RYE BROOK
RYE
ROUND HILL
HARRISON
BEDFORD HILLS
MOUNT KISCO
ARMONK
VALHALLA
VILLAGE OF MAMARONECK
LARCHMONT
ASHAROKEN
EATONS NECK
LLOYD NECK
FT. SALONGA
FAIRFIELD CO
WESTCHESTER CO
NEW YORK
CONNECTICUT
SUFFOLK CO.
NASSAU CO.
Long Island Sound

Scale of Miles

© C.S.C.

VILLAGE OF THE BRANCH
SAN REMO
KINGS PARK
SMITHTOWN TWP.
HAUPPAUGE
CENTRAL ISLIP
N.Y. Inst. of Tech.
Carleton
Islip
ILSIP TWP.
BRENTWOOD
Brentwood
BRIGHT WATERS
BAY SHORE
Great Bay
SALTAIRE
Fire Island
Robert Moses Causeway
Captree State Park
OAK BEACH
Robert Moses State Park
Great South Bay
Fire Island Inlet
Atlantic Ocean

EAST NORTHPORT
CENTER PORT
HALESITE
MIDDLEVILLE
V.A. Hospital
Lakefield
COMMACK
Dix Hills Pk. & Golf Course
Deer Park Ave.
DEER PARK
BABYLON TWP.
Belmont Lake State Park
Republic
BABYLON
LINDENHURST
Bergen Pt. Golf Course

GREEN LAWN
ELWOOD
HUNTINGTON TWP.
Walt Whitman House
MELVILLE
WYANDANCH
Wellwood
COPIAGUE
AMITYVILLE
Oyster Bay

HUNTINGTON
COLD SPRING HARBOR
LLOYD HARBOR
Sagamore Hill Historic Site
LAUREL HOLLOW
WOODBURY
LOCUST GROVE
PLAINVIEW
OLD BETHPAGE
Bethpage St. Pk.
SOUTH FARMINGDALE
FARMINGDALE
St. Univ. of N.Y. Ag. & Tech College
MASSAPEQUA
MASSAPEQUA PK.
SEAFORD
South Oyster Bay

COVE NECK
OYSTER BAY
I. COVE
NORWICH
SYOSSET
MUTTONTOWN
Muttontown Preserve
HICKSVILLE
Jerusalem
BETHPAGE
Grumman Bethpage Airport
LEVITTOWN
WANTAGH
BELLMORE
MERRICK
East Bay
JONES IS.
MEADOW IS.

BAYVILLE
MILL NECK
MATINECOCK
UPPER BROOKVILLE
The Creek Club
OYSTER BAY
BROOKVILLE
Planting Fields
JERICHO
NEW CASSEL
EAST MEADOW
UNIONDALE
ROOSEVELT
Mitchel Field
FREEPORT
Middle Bay
Pt. Outlook

LATTINGTON
LOCUST VALLEY
GLEN COVE
SEA CLIFF
GLEN HEAD
OLD BROOKVILLE
ROSLYN HARBOR
OLD WESTBURY
Old Westbury
WESTBURY
Roosevelt Raceway
HEMPSTEAD
ROCKVILLE CENTER
BALDWIN
OCEANSIDE
BAY PARK
LIDO BEACH
BARNUM IS.

ROSLYN
ROSLYN HTS.
EAST HILLS
Eisenhower Park
Meadowbrook
MINEOLA
HEMPSTEAD
MALVERNE
LYNBROOK
EAST ROCKAWAY
HEWLETT BAY PARK
HEWLETT HARBOR
WOODS BURG
LONG BEACH
LIDO BEACH

MANHASSET
PORT WASHINGTON
FLOWER HILL
NORTH HILLS
SEARINGTON
WILLISTON PK.
NORTH NEW HYDE PARK
NEW HYDE PARK
GARDEN CITY
FLORAL PARK
ELMONT
VALLEY STREAM
HEWLETT
WOODMERE
CEDARHURST
INWOOD
ATLANTIC BEACH
Atlantic Beach Bridge

SANDS POINT
Sands Point Golf Course
MANORHAVEN
PORT WASHINGTON NORTH
KINGS POINT
PLANDOME
MANHASSET
GREAT NECK
EST. GARDENS
UNIVERSITY GARDENS
SADDLE ROCK
KENSINGTON
GREAT NECK
SUCCESS
NORTH HILLS
Lake Success
NASSAU CO.
QUEENS
JAMAICA
QUEENS VILLAGE
F. Kennedy International
EDGEMERE

WESTCHESTER CO.
BRONX CO.
BAYSIDE
SPRINGFIELD GDNS.

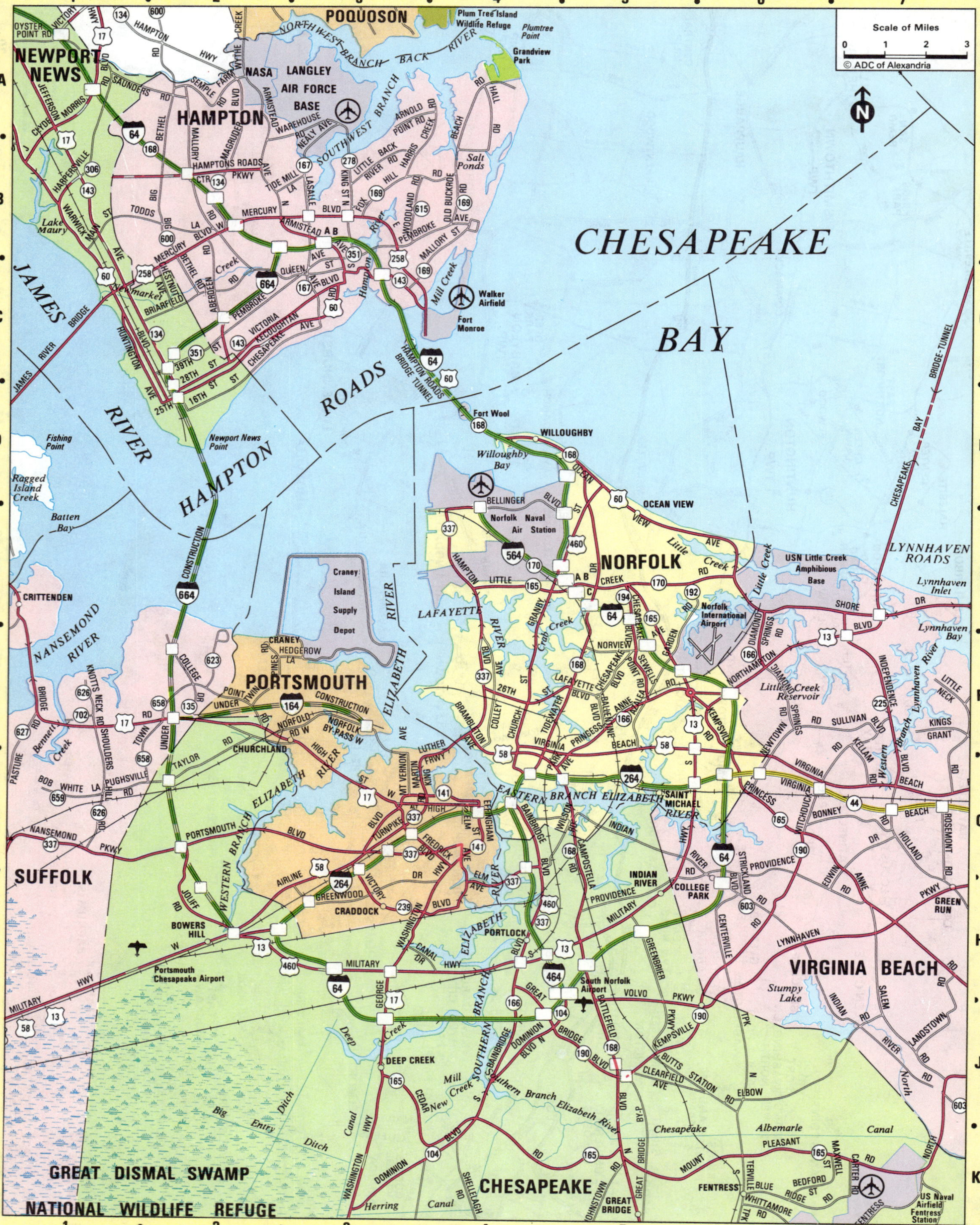

POQUOSON

Plum Tree Island
Wildlife Refuge

Plumtree
Point

Grandview
Park

NEWPORT
NEWS

NASA
LANGLEY
AIR FORCE
BASE

HAMPTON

Scale of Miles
0   1   2   3
© ADC of Alexandria

N

CHESAPEAKE

BAY

Walker
Airfield

Fort Monroe

Mill Creek

JAMES

RIVER

HAMPTON

ROADS

Fishing
Point

Newport News
Point

Ragged
Island Creek

Batten
Bay

Fort Wool

WILLOUGHBY

Willoughby
Bay

OCEAN VIEW

LYNNHAVEN
ROADS

Lynnhaven
Inlet

Lynnhaven
Bay

CRITTENDEN

Craney
Island
Supply
Depot

Norfolk Naval
Air Station

Bellinger

NORFOLK

USN Little Creek
Amphibious
Base

Little Creek

Little Creek
Reservoir

NANSEMOND

RIVER

Lafayette

RIVER

Norfolk
International Airport

Diamond
Springs

LITTLE
NECK

KINGS
GRANT

ELIZABETH

RIVER

PORTSMOUTH

CRANEY
HEDGEROW
LA

Churchland

Norview

Sewells

Little Creek

VIRGINIA

Newtown

Eastern Branch Elizabeth River

SAINT
MICHAEL

Indian River

College
Park

Bonney

Pughsville

Bowers
Hill

Greenwood

CRADDOCK

Washington

Portlock

South Norfolk
Airport

INDIAN RIVER

**VIRGINIA
BEACH**

Stumpy
Lake

Green
Run

SUFFOLK

Portsmouth
Chesapeake Airport

Deep
Creek

DEEP CREEK

Western Branch Elizabeth River

Southern Branch Elizabeth River

Dominion
Bridge

Clearfield

Elbow

GREAT DISMAL SWAMP

NATIONAL WILDLIFE REFUGE

Big
Entry
Ditch

Herring
Canal

CHESAPEAKE

Albemarle
Canal

MOUNT
PLEASANT

BLUE
RIDGE

FENTRESS

US Naval
Airfield
Fentress
Station

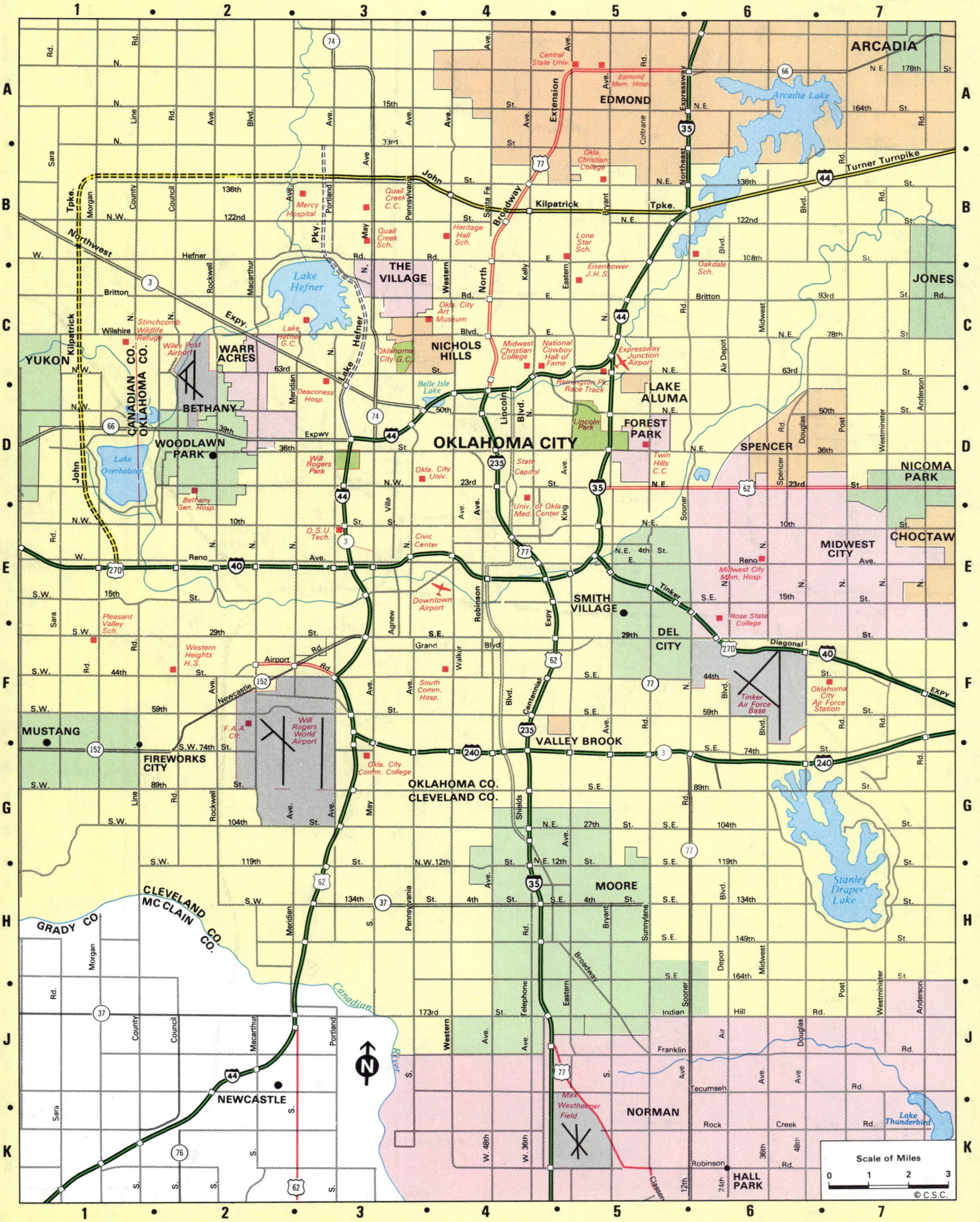

ARCADIA
Arcadia Lake
EDMOND
Central State Univ.
Edmond Mem. Hosp.
Okla. Christian College
Turner Turnpike
Kilpatrick Tpke.
John Kilpatrick Tpke.
Northwest Expy.
Quail Creek C.C.
Quail Creek Sch.
Mercy Hospital
Heritage Hall Sch.
Lone Star Sch.
Eisenhower J.H.S.
Oakdale Sch.
JONES
Lake Hefner
Lake Hefner Pkwy.
THE VILLAGE
Okla. City Art Museum
NICHOLS HILLS
Oklahoma City G.C.
Lake Hefner G.C.
Stinchcomb Wildlife Refuge
Wiley Post Airport
YUKON
WARR ACRES
BETHANY
CANADIAN CO.
OKLAHOMA CO.
Deaconess Hosp.
Belle Isle Lake
Midwest Christian College
National Cowboy Hall of Fame
Expressway Junction Airport
Remington Pk. Race Track
LAKE ALUMA
FOREST PARK
Lincoln Park
WOODLAWN PARK
Lake Overholser
OKLAHOMA CITY
Will Rogers Park
Okla. City Univ.
State Capitol
Univ. of Okla. Med. Center
Twin Hills C.C.
SPENCER
NICOMA PARK
Bethany Gen. Hosp.
O.S.U. Tech.
Civic Center
MIDWEST CITY
CHOCTAW
Downtown Airport
SMITH VILLAGE
Midwest City Mem. Hosp.
Rose State College
Pleasant Valley Sch.
Western Heights H.S.
DEL CITY
Tinker Diagonal Expy.
Tinker Air Force Base
Oklahoma City Air Force Station
South Comm. Hosp.
MUSTANG
F.A.A. Ctr.
Will Rogers World Airport
FIREWORKS CITY
VALLEY BROOK
Okla. City Comm. College
OKLAHOMA CO.
CLEVELAND CO.
Stanley Draper Lake
MOORE
CLEVELAND CO.
MC CLAIN CO.
GRADY CO.
Canadian River
NEWCASTLE
NORMAN
Max Westheimer Field
Lake Thunderbird
HALL PARK
Scale of Miles
0 1 2 3
© C.S.C.

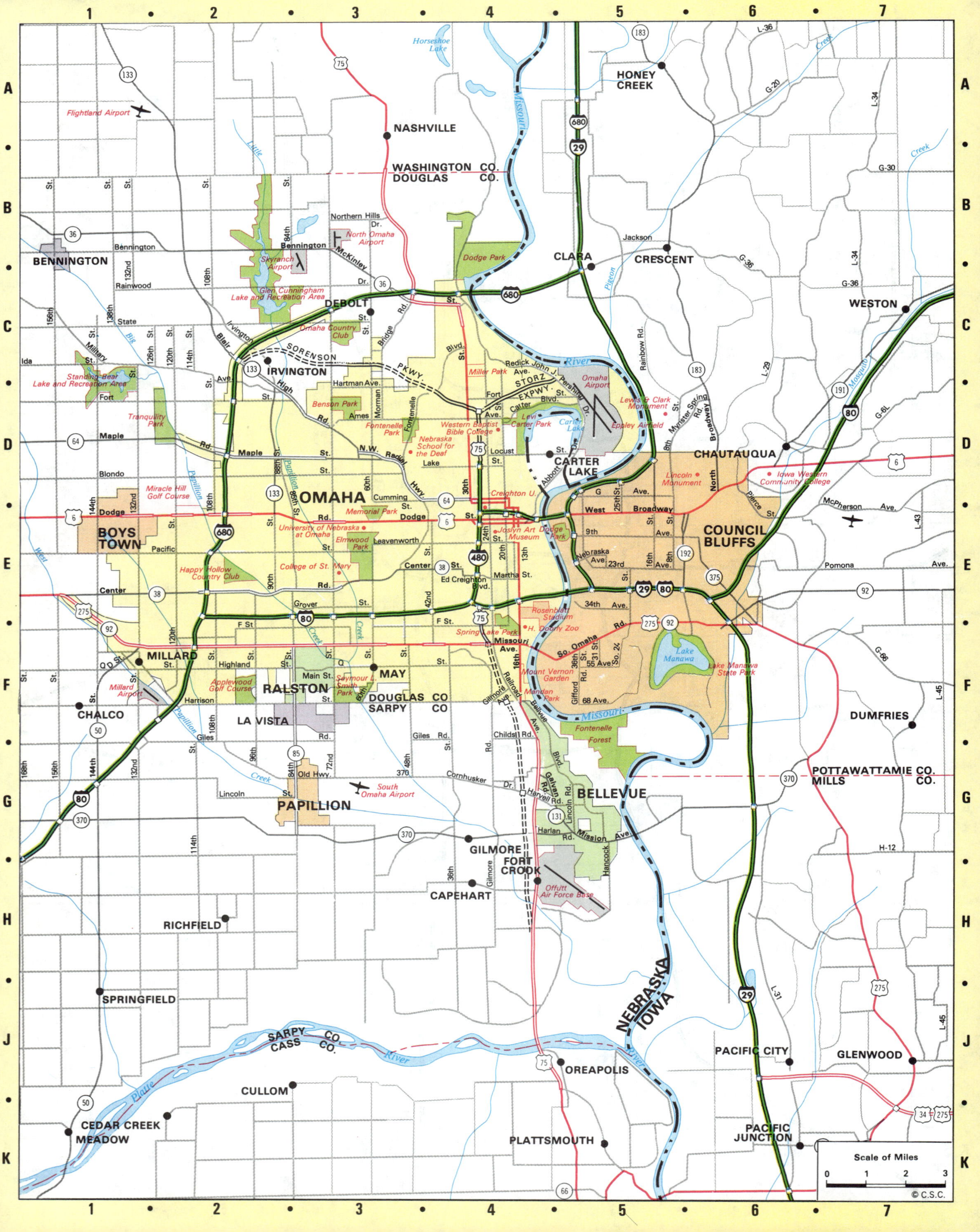
Flightland Airport
NASHVILLE
HONEY CREEK
WASHINGTON CO.
DOUGLAS CO.
Horseshoe Lake
Missouri
BENNINGTON
Bennington
Skyranch Airport
North Omaha Airport
Northern Hills Dr.
McKinley
Glen Cunningham Lake and Recreation Area
Dodge Park
CLARA
CRESCENT
Jackson
DEBOLT
Omaha Country Club
WESTON
Rainwood
State
Military
Ida
IRVINGTON
SORENSON PKWY.
Standing Bear Lake and Recreation Area
Tranquility Park
Benson Park
Hartman Ave.
Ames
Miller Park
Redick Ave.
John J. Pershing Dr.
STORZ EXPWY.
Omaha Airport
Eppley Airfield
Lewis & Clark Monument
Fontenelle Park
Western Baptist Bible College
Nebraska School for the Deaf
Levi Carter Park
Carter Lake
CARTER LAKE
CHAUTAUQUA
Maple
Blondo
N.W. Radial Hwy.
Lincoln Monument
Iowa Western Community College
Miracle Hill Golf Course
OMAHA
Creighton U.
Cumming
Dodge
BOYS TOWN
Pacific
Memorial Park
University of Nebraska at Omaha
Elmwood Park
Leavenworth
Joslyn Art Museum
Dodge Park
Broadway
West Broadway
McPherson Ave.
COUNCIL BLUFFS
Happy Hollow Country Club
College of St. Mary
Center
Ed Creighton Blvd.
Martha St.
Pomona Ave.
Grover
F St
Rosenblatt Stadium
H. Doorly Zoo
Spring Lake Park
Lake Manawa
Lake Manawa State Park
MILLARD
Millard Airport
Highland
Applewood Golf Course
RALSTON
MAY
Seymour L. Smith Park
Mount Vernon Garden
Mandan Park
DOUGLAS CO
SARPY CO
CHALCO
LA VISTA
Harrison
Giles Rd.
Fontenelle Forest
DUMFRIES
POTTAWATTAMIE CO.
MILLS CO.
South Omaha Airport
PAPILLION
Lincoln
BELLEVUE
Mission Ave.
GILMORE
FORT CROOK
Offutt Air Force Base
CAPEHART
RICHFIELD
SPRINGFIELD
NEBRASKA
IOWA
SARPY CO.
CASS CO.
Platte River
PACIFIC CITY
GLENWOOD
OREAPOLIS
CULLOM
CEDAR CREEK
MEADOW
PLATTSMOUTH
PACIFIC JUNCTION
Scale of Miles
0 1 2 3
© C.S.C.

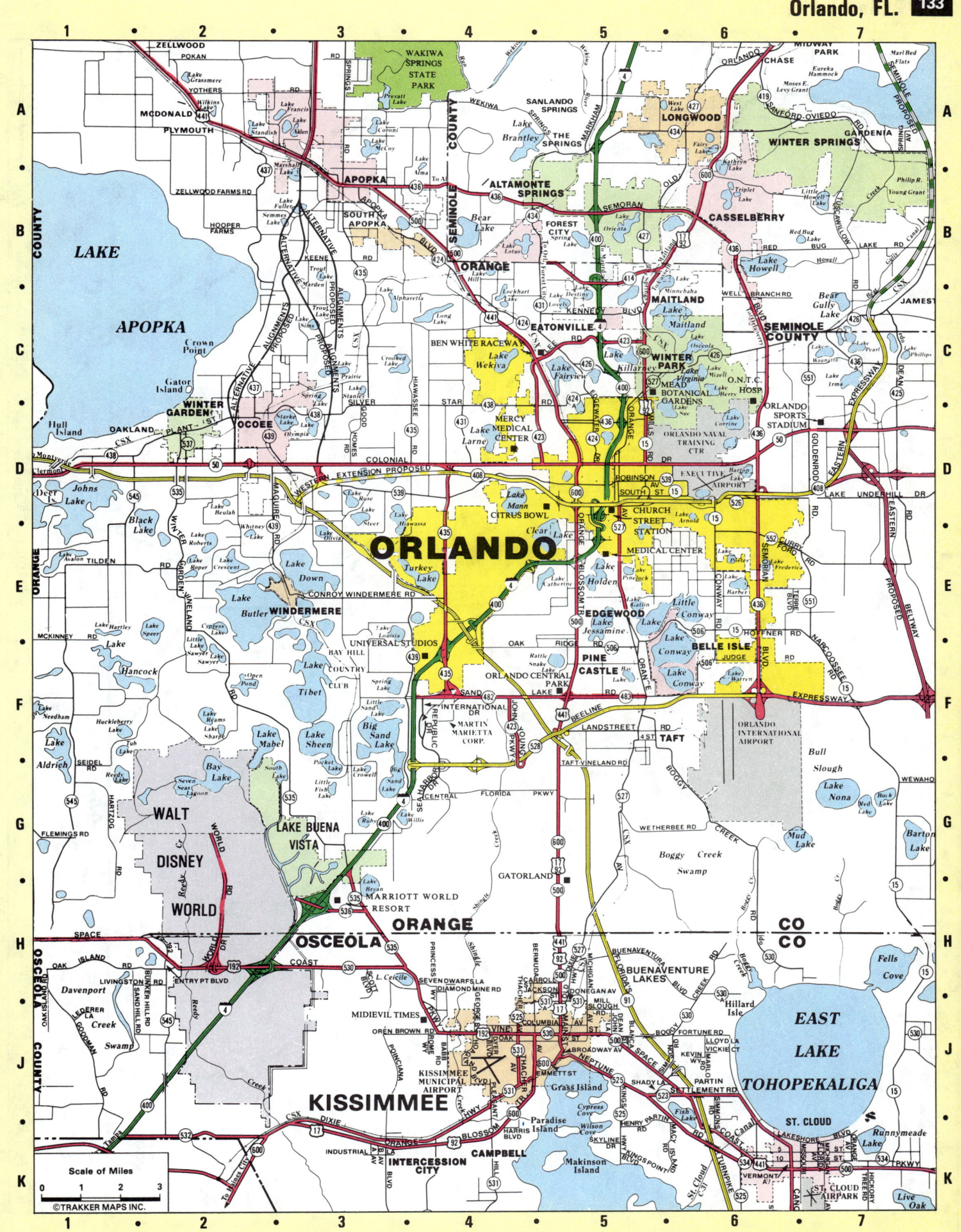

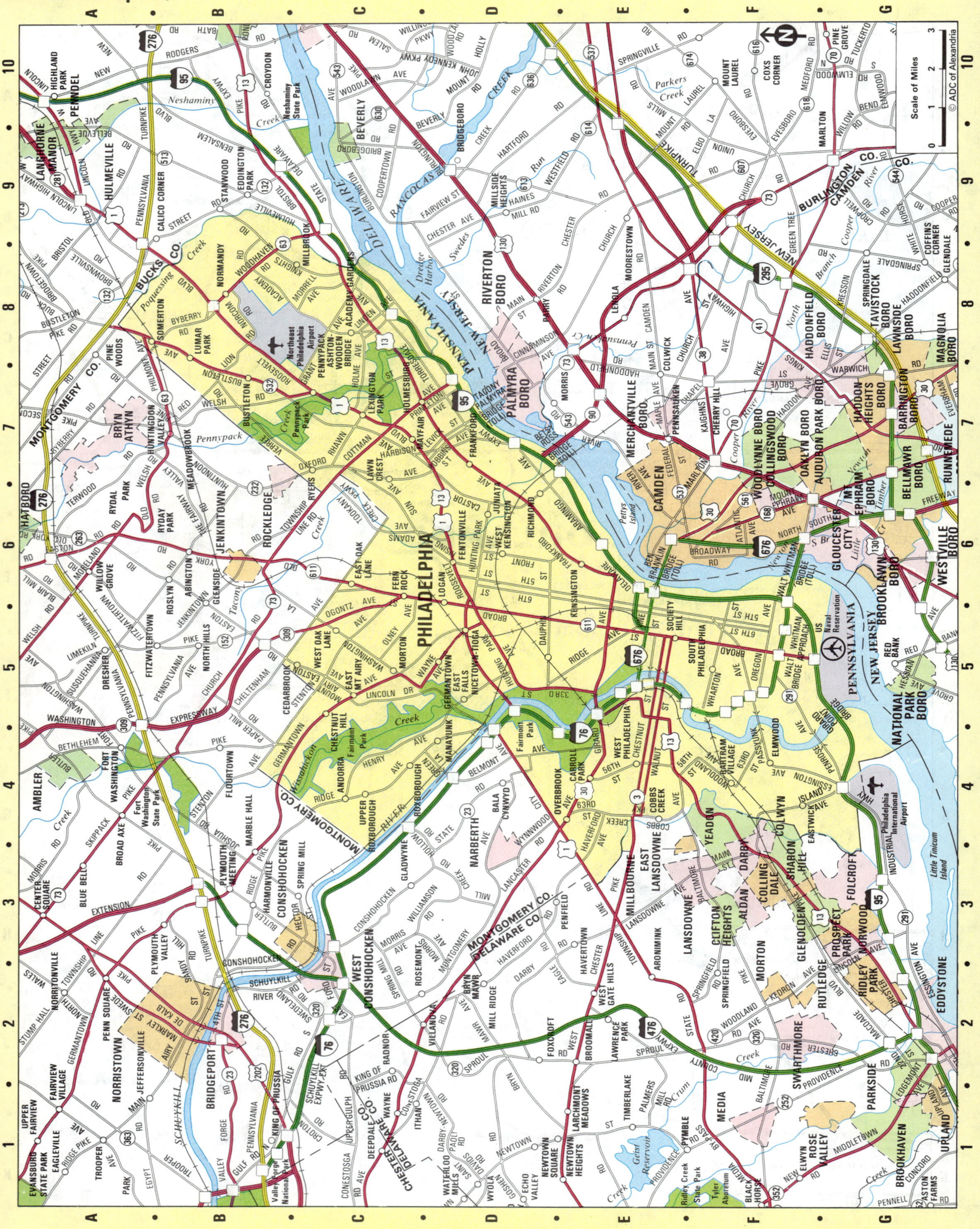

Scale of Miles

© ADC of Alexandria

Scale of Miles
0 1 2 3 4 5

N

Beardsley Canal
McMicken Dam Outlet Canal

DYNAMITE RD.
JOMAX RD.
Currys Corner
PINNACLE PEAK RD.
HAPPY VALLEY RD.
PINNACLE PEAK RD.
Deer Valley Airport
Adobe DEER VALLEY RD.
Scottsdale
Thunderbird Regional Pk.
BEARDSLEY RD.
BEARDSLEY RD.
Beardsley
89 93
Surprise
El Mirage
UNION HILLS RD.
UNION HILLS
Paradise City
BELL
Paradise Valley Park
American Inst. for Foreign Trade
GREENWAY RD.
GREENWAY
Turf Paradise Race Track
Moon Valley C.C.
Scottsdale Mun. Airport
THUNDERBIRD
Sun City
101
Youngstown
CACTUS
Cactus Pk.
North Mountain Park
Century C.C.
SHEA BLVD.
Peoria
PEORIA AVE.
Metro Center
DUNLAP
Glendale Com. Co.
Arizona Canal
Royal Palm Mobile Pk.
Paradise Valley
Luke Air Force Base
NORTHERN
Resthaven Pk. Cem.
Glendale
Squaw Peak Park
Paradise Valley C.C.
Scottsdale
Agua Fria
New River
GLENDALE AVE.
PHOENIX
LINCOLN
McDONALD DR.
BETHANY HOME RD.
Holiday Pk.
Grand Canyon Col.
Arizona Biltmore
CAMELBACK
Litchfield Park
Mun. G.C.
Grand
INDIAN SCHOOL
Eloso Pk.
THOMAS
V.A. Hospital
Enchanto Park
Phoenix J.C.C.
Arizona C.C.
State Fair Grounds
Heard Mus.
County Hospital
McDOWELL
MC DOWELL RD.
Papago Frwy.
Military Res.
Desert Botanical Gardens
Papago Park
10
State Capitol
Mun. Bldg.
Phoenix Greyhound Pk.
Zoological Park
Tempe Park
Goodyear
Avondale
Tolleson
VAN BUREN ST.
WASHINGTON ST.
BUCKEYE
Phoenix Litchfield Airfield
State Hospital
Sky Harbor Int'l Airport
143
Ariz. State Univ.
APACHE
UNIVERSITY
LOWER BUCKEYE RD.
Salt River
BROADWAY RD.
360
Tempe
SOUTHERN AVE.
Manzanita Speedway
Western Canal
Casey Abbott Semi-Regional Park
BASE LINE RD.
GUADALUPE RD.
ESTRELLA MOUNTAIN REGIONAL PARK
DOBBINS RD.
Laveen
Phoenix Police Academy
Thunderbird C.C.
Guadalupe
ELLIOT
Gila River
ELLIOT RD.
Las Ramadas Picnic Area
Kyrene
WARNER
ESTRELLA DR.
Stephen Mather Rd.
Buena Vista Rd.
TELEGRAPH PASS
Gila Valley Lookout
RAY
PHOENIX SOUTH MOUNTAIN PARK
International Harvester Proving Ground
Chandler
Highland
WILLIAMS
McCLINTOCK DR.
GILA
RIVER
PECOS RD.
MARICOPA CO. PINAL CO.
GILA RIVER INDIAN RESERVATION
Goodyear Air Force Mil. Field
PIMA FREEWAY
10

Pittsburgh, PA

West View

Bellevue

McKees Rocks

PITTSBURGH

Mt. Oliver

Brentwood

Baldwin

Castle Shannon

Whitehall

Bethel Park

Whitaker

West Homestead

Homestead

Sharpsburgh

Etna

Ben Avon

Avalon

Neville

Thornburg

Crafton

Ingram

Rosslyn Farms

Green Tree

Heidelburg

Dormont

Mt. Lebanon

Ohio River

Allegheny River

Monongahela River

Chartiers

Riverview Pk.

Highwood Cem.

Union Dale Cem.

Allegheny Gen. Hosp.

3 Rivers Stadium

Point Pk.

West End Park

Mt. Washington

Grandview Park

McKinley Pk.

St. Josephs Cem.

St. Geo. Cem.

South Side Cem.

St. Adalbert Cem.

Philips Park

Schenley Park

Carnegie-Mellon Univ.

University of Pittsburgh

Highland Park

Allegheny Cem.

Homewood Cem.

Frick Park

Calvary Cem.

St. Peters Roman Cath. Cem.

Brentwood Park

Allegheny County Airport

Mt. Lebanon Cem.

Mt. Lebanon Park

Scott Twnsp. Mun. Pk.

Kane Memorial Hosp.

Penn State Police

Carnegie Park

Mt. Olive Cem.

Dormont Pk.

Duquesne Univ. of the Allies

Mercy Hosp.

Rosalia Hosp.

Herron Hill Park

St. Francis Hosp.

Western Penn Hosp.

U.S. V.A. Hosp.

Mellon Park

St. Mary's Cem.

Ridgelawn Cem.

Hebrew Cem.

United Cem.

St. Alexanders Cem.

St. Philomena Cem.

St. John's Gen. Hosp.

Scale of Miles
0 .25 .5 .75 1 1.25

N

Portland, OR

Vancouver

Hayden Island

CLARK COUNTY / MULTNOMAH COUNTY

E. MILL PLAIN BLVD.

500

PEARSON FIELD

WASHINGTON
OREGON

5

Columbia River

Smith Lake

Columbia Slough

Exposition Center
Delta Park

Tomahawk Island

Portland Yacht Club

Delta Park

Tyee Yacht Club
Rose City Yacht Club
Columbia River Yacht Club

N. PORTLAND RD.

N. FESSENDEN ST.

Columbia Edgewater G. C.

N.E. MARINE RD.

PORTLAND INT'L AIRPORT

N. COLUMBIA BLVD.

N. PENINSULAR AVE.

Portland G. C.

GERTZ

N.E. SUNDERLAND AVE.

N. LOMBARD ST.

Portland Air Force Base

N. WILLAMETTE BLVD.

N. PORTSMOUTH AVE.

Riverside G. C.

Broadmoor G. C.

Colwood G. C.

Willamette River

Columbia Park

Univ. of Portland

N. DENVER AVE.

5

BYP 30

Peninsula Park

Alberta Park

N.E. LOMBARD ST.

N.E. COLUMBIA BLVD.

N.E. KILLINGSWORTH ST.

Forest

PORTLAND

30

Swan Island

N. PORTLAND AVE.

GREELEY AVE.

N. INTERSTATE

N. UNION AVE.

99E

N.E. FREMONT ST.

N.E. 33RD AVE.
N.E. 39TH
N.E. 42ND AVE.
ALAMEDA
N.E. 57TH AVE.
N.E. CULLY RD.

BLVD.

BR 30

Rose City G. C.

N.W. VAUGHN ST.

Fremont Bridge

Broadway Bridge

N.E. BROADWAY

N.E. HALSEY ST.

84

N.W. LOVEJOY AVE.

MacLeay Park

N.W. SKYLINE BLVD.

Washington Park

N.W. 23RD AVE.
N.W. 19TH AVE.

405

Memorial Coliseum

N.E.

N.E. GLISAN ST.

30

N.W. CORNELL RD.

N.W. ST. HELENS RD.

Zoological Gardens And Museum

Park

Portland State Univ.

E. BURNSIDE

Laurelhurst Park

S.E. STARK ST.

S.E. MORRISON ST.
S.E. BELMONT ST.

Mt. Tabor Park

26

JENKINS RD.

CORNELL RD.

N.W. BARNES RD.

W. HUMPHREY

MARKET

26

405

99E

S.E. HAWTHORNE BLVD.

Warner Pacific Coll.

CEDAR HILLS BLVD.

West Slope

S.W. BARNES RD.

8

Washington Park

S.W. VISTA AVE.

Council Crest

S.W. BROADWAY DR.

Univ. of Oregon Med. Sch.

Ross Island

S.E. DIVISION ST.

S.E. POWELL

26

CANYON

8

10

217

S.W. SHATTUCK RD.

S.W. FATTON RD.

Raleigh Hills

BEAVERTON - HILLSDALE RD.

10

Hillsdale

TERWILLIGER BLVD.

S.W. MACADAM AVE.

Ross Island Bridge

Hardtack Is.

S.E. 26TH AVE.
S.E. 39TH AVE.
S.E. 52ND AVE.

S.E. HOLGATE BLVD.

S.E. FOSTER RD.

S.E. HAROLD ST.

FARMINGTON RD.

SCHOLLS FERRY RD.

Beaverton

Gabriel Park

S.W. VERMONT ST.

FERRY RD.

99W

F.H. BALDOCK FWY.

Pioneer Park

Sellwood Pk.

Reed College

S.E. WOODSTOCK BLVD.

S.E. DUKE ST.

10

Metzger

S.W. MULTNOMAH BLVD.

Multnomah BLVD.

BYBEE BLVD.

S.E. 13TH AVE.
S.E. 11TH AVE.
S.E. TACOMA AVE.

Eastmoreland Golf Course

JOHNSON CREEK BLVD.

Kendall

WASHINGTON CO.
MULTNOMAH CO.

S.W. TAYLORS FERRY RD.

S.W. BARBUR BLVD.

F.H. BALDOCK FWY.

MC LOUGHLIN BLVD.

Waverly C.C.

99E

KING RD.

Tigard

PACIFIC HWY.

5

Portland Comm. College

S.W. BOONES FERRY RD.

KERR RD.

Tryon Creek State Park

TERWILLIGER BLVD.

Lewis & Clark College

RIVERSIDE DR.

HARRISON ST.

Milwaukie

224

217

210

BONITA RD.

COUNTRY CLUB RD.

Lake Oswego C.C.

Oak Grove

N. Clackamas Central Park

McLOUGHLIN RD.

OATFIELD RD.

KELLOGG CREEK

WEBSTER RD.

King City

CARMAN DR.

Lake Grove

Waluga Park

Oswego Lake

LAKE RD.

PORTLAND AVE.

Willamette River

WASHINGTON CO.
CLACKAMAS CO.

99W

Tualatin River

Durham

5

Lake Oswego

STAFFORD RD.

ROSEMONT RD.

43

Maryhurst College

Scale of Miles
0   .5   1   1.5

© C.S.C.

Raleigh, NC (top map)

DURHAM, SPRING HILL, PARKWOOD, GENLEE, NELSON, RESEARCH TRIANGLE PARK, DURHAM WAKE, MORRISVILLE, RALEIGH, LEESVILLE, BRANDON STATION, SIX FORKS, BAYLEAF, STONEBRIDGE, FALLS, WALKERS CROSSROADS, WAKE CROSSROADS, NEUSE, SIX FORKS CROSSROAD, NEW HOPE, MILBURNIE, BARCLAY DOWNS, PARKSIDE, KNIGHTDALE

RALEIGH-DURHAM INTERNATIONAL AIRPORT, WILLIAM B UMSTEAD STATE PARK, Lake Crabtree, Lake Crabtree County PK, Rex Hospital, Meredith Coll, St Marys Coll, Peace Coll, St Augustine Coll, NC State University, State Capitol, Shaw Univ, Dorthea Dix State Hospital, Lake Johnson, Lake Raleigh, Wake Memorial Hospital, Raleigh Comm Hospital, Med Ctr

GREEN LEVEL, CARY, MACGREGOR DOWNS, APEX, Luther Airstrip, Western Wake, FRIENDSHIP, CLOVERDALE, GARNER, GREENBRIER ESTATES, EMERALD VILLAGE

CHATHAM WAKE, WAKE COUNTY, DURHAM COUNTY, Crabtree Creek, Neuse River, Poplar Creek

Scale of Miles 0 1 2 3
© ADC of Alexandria

Rochester, NY (bottom map)

GRAND VIEW HEIGHTS, HILTON, CRESCENT BEACH, RIGNEY BLUFF, FOREST LAWN, OKLAHOMA BEACH, PARMA CENTER, NORTH GREECE, PARMA CORNERS, WEST GREECE, GREECE, IRONDEQUOIT, WEST WEBSTER, WEBSTER, UNION HILL, SPENCERPORT, SOUTH GREECE, OGDEN CENTER, ROSELAND, ROCHESTER, PENFIELD CENTER, GATE, PENFIELD, EAST PENFIELD, WEST WALWORTH, NORTH CHILI, CHILI CENTER, BRIGHTON, EAST ROCHESTER, PENFIELD, WEST CHILI, CRITTENDEN, PITTSFORD, FAIRPORT, WAYNEPORT

Lake Ontario, Irondequoit Bay, Genesee River

Durand Eastman Park, St Bernard's Seminary, Seneca Park, Edgerton Park, Webster Park, Intl Museum of Photography, Highland Park, Cobbs Hill Park, Ellison Park, Susan B. Anthony House, St Marys Hosp., Univ. of Rochester, Univ. of Rochester Med. Cen., Rochester-Monroe Co. Airport, Genesee Valley Park, Nazareth Coll. of Rochester

Scale of Miles 0 1 2 3
© C.S.C.

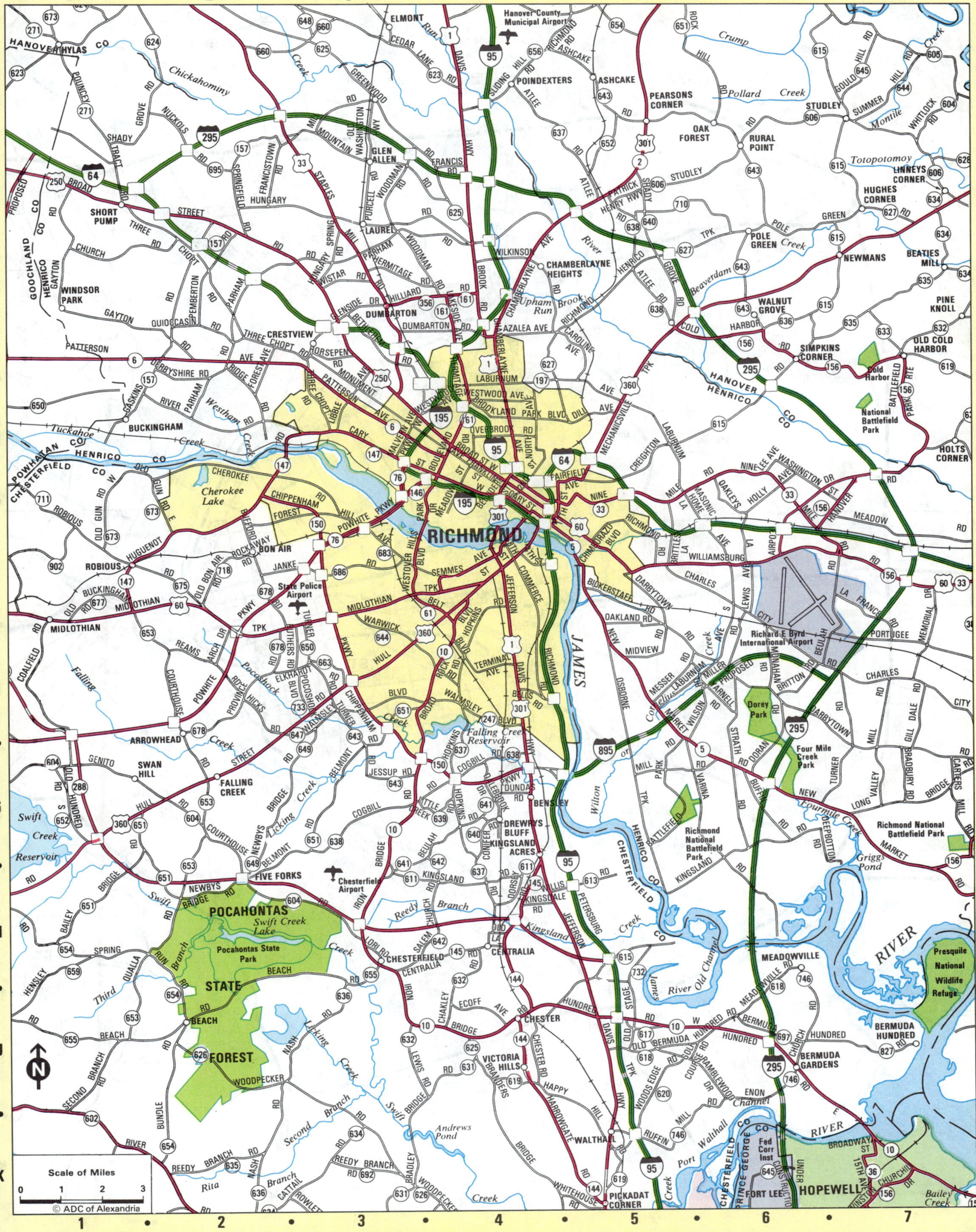
RICHMOND
JAMES
RIVER
Chickahominy
Hanover County Municipal Airport
Chesterfield Airport
State Police Airport
Richard E Byrd International Airport
POCAHONTAS STATE FOREST
Pocahontas State Park
Swift Creek Lake
Swift Creek Reservoir
Falling Creek Reservoir
Cherokee Lake
Dorey Park
Four Mile Creek Park
Richmond National Battlefield Park
National Battlefield Park
Presquile National Wildlife Refuge
Cold Harbor
HOPEWELL
FORT LEE
BERMUDA HUNDRED
CHESTER
CENTRALIA
CHESTERFIELD
MIDLOTHIAN
BON AIR
FIVE FORKS
SHORT PUMP
ELMONT
ASHCAKE
POINDEXTERS
GLEN ALLEN
LAUREL
DUMBARTON
CHAMBERLAYNE HEIGHTS
MECHANICSVILLE
HANOVER
HENRICO
GOOCHLAND
POWHATAN
PEARSONS CORNER
OAK FOREST
RURAL POINT
STUDLEY
LINNEYS CORNER
HUGHES CORNER
NEWMANS
BEATIES MILL
PINE KNOLL
OLD COLD HARBOR
POLE GREEN
WALNUT GROVE
SIMPKINS CORNER
HOLTS CORNER
WINDSOR PARK
CRESTVIEW
BUCKINGHAM
ROBIOUS
ARROWHEAD
SWAN HILL
FALLING CREEK
BENSLEY
DREWRYS BLUFF
KINGSLAND ACRES
MEADOWVILLE
BERMUDA GARDENS
VICTORIA HILLS
WALTHALL
PICKADAT CORNER
© ADC of Alexandria
Scale of Miles
0 1 2 3

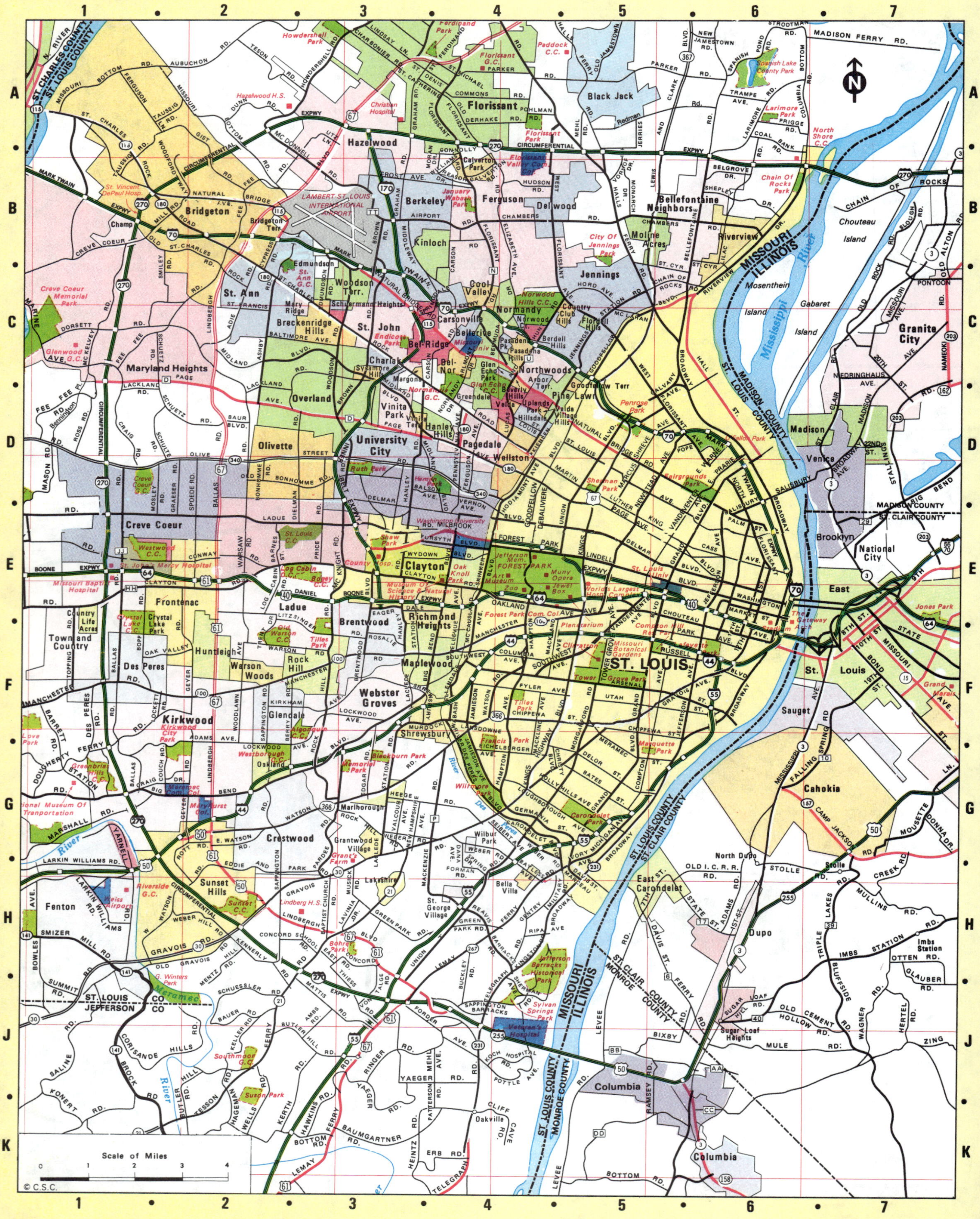

Scale of Miles

0 1 2 3 4

© C.S.C.

Sacramento, CA

Municipal Airport
Elkhorn
Line
99
70
RIO LINDA
NORTH HIGHLANDS
Elkhorn
Rd.
FOOTHILL FARMS
Greenback Ln.
ORANGEVALE
Ave.
VALLEY VIEW ACRES
ROBLA
McClellan Air Force Base
Roseville
Madison Ave.
FAIR OAK
Northridge C.C.
Manzanita
Sunset
Del Paso
Centro Rd.
Main Ave.
Ascot
Raley
Blvd.
Auburn
80
Winding Way
Hazel
Main
Ave.
El Paso
99
San Juan
Rd.
47th St.
Haggin Oaks G.C.
CARMICHAEL
Robertson
Fair Oaks Blvd.
Winding Way
Sunrise
50
El Dorado Hwy.
ALDER CREEK
16
Tule
Garden
Northgate
Truxel Rd.
Norwood
Rio Linda Blvd.
Del Paso
Auburn
Marconi Ave.
Del Paso Country Club
Walnut
El Camino Ave.
Garfield
Eastern
Coloma
Blvd.
C.M. Goethe Park
White Rock
NIMBUS
CITRUS
Carl Johnston Park
Highway
Discovery Park
Arden Way
El Camino
Howe
Fulton
Watt
Ancil Hoffman Park
RANCHO CORDOVA
Old Sacramento St. Hist. Park
Sacramento
160
Exposition Blvd.
California Exposition
Oaks
Arden
Fair
American River
Coloma Blvd.
WEST SACRAMENTO
State Capitol
9th
16th St.
21st St.
Capitol Ave.
SACRAMENTO
C St.
E St.
J St.
H St.
California St. Univ. at Sacramento
Folsom Blvd.
Old Placerville Rd.
Mather Air Force Base
Douglas Rd.
80
Greens Lake
ARLINGTON OAKS
Linden Rd.
Broadway
Land Park
Sutterville
Rd.
50
Broadway
12th Ave.
14th Ave.
Tahoe Park
Power Inn
Florin
PERKINS
ROSEMONT
Kiefer Blvd.
Bradshaw
Jackson
Mather
Blvd.
Excelsior
Rd.
16
Elk Grove
SOUTH PORT
Jefferson
Gregory
Blvd.
Fairy Tale Town
24th
Franklin
Fruitridge
Stockton
Expressway
Sacramento Army Depot
Perkins Rd.
Elder
Florin
Rd.
RIVERVIEW
Riverside
S. River Rd.
160
Sacramento Executive Airport
Florin
FLORIN
Creek Rd.
5
Meadowview Rd.
Gerber Rd.
99
Mack Rd.

N ↑

Scale of Miles
0 1 2 3

Antelope Island
WOODS CROSS
BOUNTIFUL
NORTH SALT LAKE
15
106
Orchard Dr.
Wasatch Bountiful Nat'l Forest
DAVIS COUNTY
SALT LAKE COUNTY
68
DAVIS CO.
SALT LAKE CO.
2400 N.
Beck St.
Canyon Rd.
Creek
City
215
Great Salt Lake
N. Point
Consolidated Drain
Google
Canal
4000 W. St.
Redwood Rd.
Salt Lake City International Airport
Jordan River
6th N. St.
Riverside Park
Victory Rd.
SALT LAKE CITY
City Cemetery
Fort Douglas Military Res.
80
North Temple
State Fair Ground
80
4th
Salt Palace
Utah State Capitol
University of Utah
Salt Pond
SALT LAKE CITY
172
Jordan Park
2nd
3rd
South Temple St.
Mount Olivet Cemetery
Wasatch
Pioneer Trail State Park
Hogle Zoo
Tailings Pond
13th South
WEST VALLEY
St.
Liberty Park
California Ave.
700 E.
9th E.
11th E.
Foothill Dr.
Bonneville Golf Course
202
21st South
201
West
2700
3100 South
Canal
Sugarhouse Park
186
80
80
201
171
215
WEST VALLEY CITY
9th W.
Main
2nd W.
3500 South
56th
4100 South
SOUTH SALT LAKE
Forest Dale Golf Course
Fairmont Park
Parley's Way
Salt Lake Country Club Golf Course
MAGNA
3600 W.
2700 W.
33rd
EAST MILLCREEK
111
266
68
181
39th South
9th
45th South
23rd East
Van
215
BACCHUS
4700 South
Utah
HOLLADAY
1300 South

N ↑

Scale of Miles
0 1 2 3

© C.S.C.

GREY FOREST

HELOTES

SHAVANO PARK

HOLLYWOOD PARK

HILL COUNTRY VILLAGE

LIVE OAK

WINDCREST

Camp Bullis Military Reservation

Univ. of Texas at San Antonio

San Antonio International Airport

CASTLE HILLS

LEON VALLEY

BALCONES HEIGHTS

OLMOS PARK

ALAMO HEIGHTS

TERRELL HILLS

KIRBY

S. Texas Medical Center

Brooke Army Medical Center

Fort Sam Houston

Trinity University

Alamo Stadium

St. Mary's University

Assumption Seminary

SAN ANTONIO

Our Lady of the Lake Coll.

San Fernando Cem.

The Alamo

Joe Freeman Coliseum

Martindale Army Airfield

MARTINEZ

GARDENDALE

CHINA GROVE

Lackland AFB

Kelly AFB

East Kelly AFB

Lackland Military Training Center

Lions Park

Pecan Valley G.C.

Southcross

San Antonio State Hospital

Brooks AFB

Stinson Field

E. Aviation Blvd.

MACDONA

MANGUS CORNER

VON ORMY

SOUTHTON

BUENA VISTA

Blue Wing

CASSIN

Mitchell Lake

Brauning Lake

ELMENDORF

SOMERSET

LOSOYA

THELMA

Medina River

San Antonio River

Scale of Miles
0   1   2   3

N

© C.S.C.

Pacific Ocean

San Diego Bay

Major labeled places:

- SOLANA BEACH
- DEL MAR
- SORRENTO
- SAN DIEGO
- MIRAMAR
- POWAY
- FERNBROOK
- SHADY DELL
- ROCK HAVEN
- EUCALYPTUS HILLS
- MORENO
- LAKESIDE FARMS
- LAKESIDE
- CARLTON HILLS
- SANTEE
- LAKEVIEW
- JOHNSTOWN
- WINTER GARDENS
- GLENVIEW
- LA JOLLA
- MISSION BEACH
- EL CAJON
- GROSSMONT
- MT. HELIX
- CALAVO GARDENS
- JAMACHA JUNCTION
- JAMACHA
- LA MESA
- SPRING VALLEY
- LEMON GROVE
- DICTIONARY HILL
- LA PRESA
- BALBOA PARK
- CORONADO
- NATIONAL CITY
- LINCOLN ACRES
- SUNNYSIDE
- BONITA
- LYNWOOD HILLS
- HARBOR SIDE
- CASTLE PARK
- CHULA VISTA
- OTAY
- IMPERIAL BEACH
- SAN YSIDRO
- OTAY MESA

Points of interest:

- Torrey Pines State Park
- University of California San Diego Campus
- Scripps Institute of Oceanography
- La Jolla Caves
- Pacific Beach
- Mission Bay
- Sea World Aquatic Park
- Ocean Beach
- Pointe Loma Coll.
- U.S. International Univ.
- Fort Rosecrans Nat'l Cem.
- U.S. Military Reservation
- Cabrillo Nat'l. Mon.
- North Island Naval Air Station
- U.S. Naval Amphibious Base
- Silver Strand State Beach
- Imperial Beach Naval Radio Station
- Imperial Beach Naval Air Station
- U.S. Immigration Detention Facility
- Brown Field
- Miramar Naval Air Station
- Miramar G.C.
- U.S. International Univ.
- U.S. Air Force Reservation
- Sycamore Canyon Annex
- Camp Elliott
- San Diego Mesa Coll.
- Montgomery Field
- Clairemont General Hosp.
- Univ. of San Diego
- U.S. Naval Recreational Facilities
- San Diego State Univ.
- Chollas Res.
- Murray Reservoir
- Gillespie Field
- Fletcher Hills G.C.
- Carlton Oaks G.C.
- San Diego International Airport
- San Diego Naval Station
- San Diego Naval Hospital
- Southwestern College
- Greg Rogers Pk.
- Sweetwater Reservoir
- Loveland Reservoir
- Upper Otay Reservoir
- Lower Otay Reservoir
- Lower Otay County Pk.
- Rancho Del City Airstrip
- Elmhurst Pk.
- San Vicente Reservoir
- Miramar Reservoir
- Powers Airport
- U.S.M.C. Base
- Naval Training Center
- Zoo
- Balboa Park

Scale of Miles
0 1 2 3

© C.S.C.

N

SAN PABLO BAY

OAKLAND

SAN FRANCISCO

Richmond

Berkeley

El Cerrito

Albany

Emeryville

Alameda

Concord

Walnut Creek

Pleasant Hill

Lafayette

Martinez

Benicia

Crockett

Rodeo

Hercules

Pinole

San Ramon

Dublin

Danville

Moraga

Piedmont

Pittsburg

Clyde

Avon

Pomona

San Rafael

Tiburon

Belvedere

Sausalito

Treasure Island

Yerba Buena Island

Angel Island State Park

Alcatraz Island

Brooks Is.

BRIONES REGIONAL PARK

WILDCAT CANYON REGIONAL PARK

TILDEN REGIONAL PARK

REDWOOD REGIONAL PARK

ANTHONY CHABOT REGIONAL PARK

ROBERT SIBLEY REGIONAL PARK

LAS TRAMPAS REGIONAL PARK

MT. DIABLO STATE PARK

STATE GAME REFUGE

U.S. NAVAL MAGAZINE PORT CHICAGO

ALVARADO PARK

GRIZZLY PEAK

Oakland Metropolitan International Airport

Oakland Bay Bridge (Toll)

Richmond-San Rafael Bridge (Toll)

San Francisco-Oakland Bay Bridge

Golden Gate Bridge (Toll)

U.C. Berkeley

Mills College

St. Mary's College

Lake Chabot

San Pablo Res.

Briones Res.

Upper San Leandro Res.

Candlestick Park

Hunters Point Naval Shipyard

Alameda Naval Air Station

Oakland Naval Supply Center

Golden Gate

Carquinez Strait

San Pablo Strait

Raccoon Strait

Sacramento River

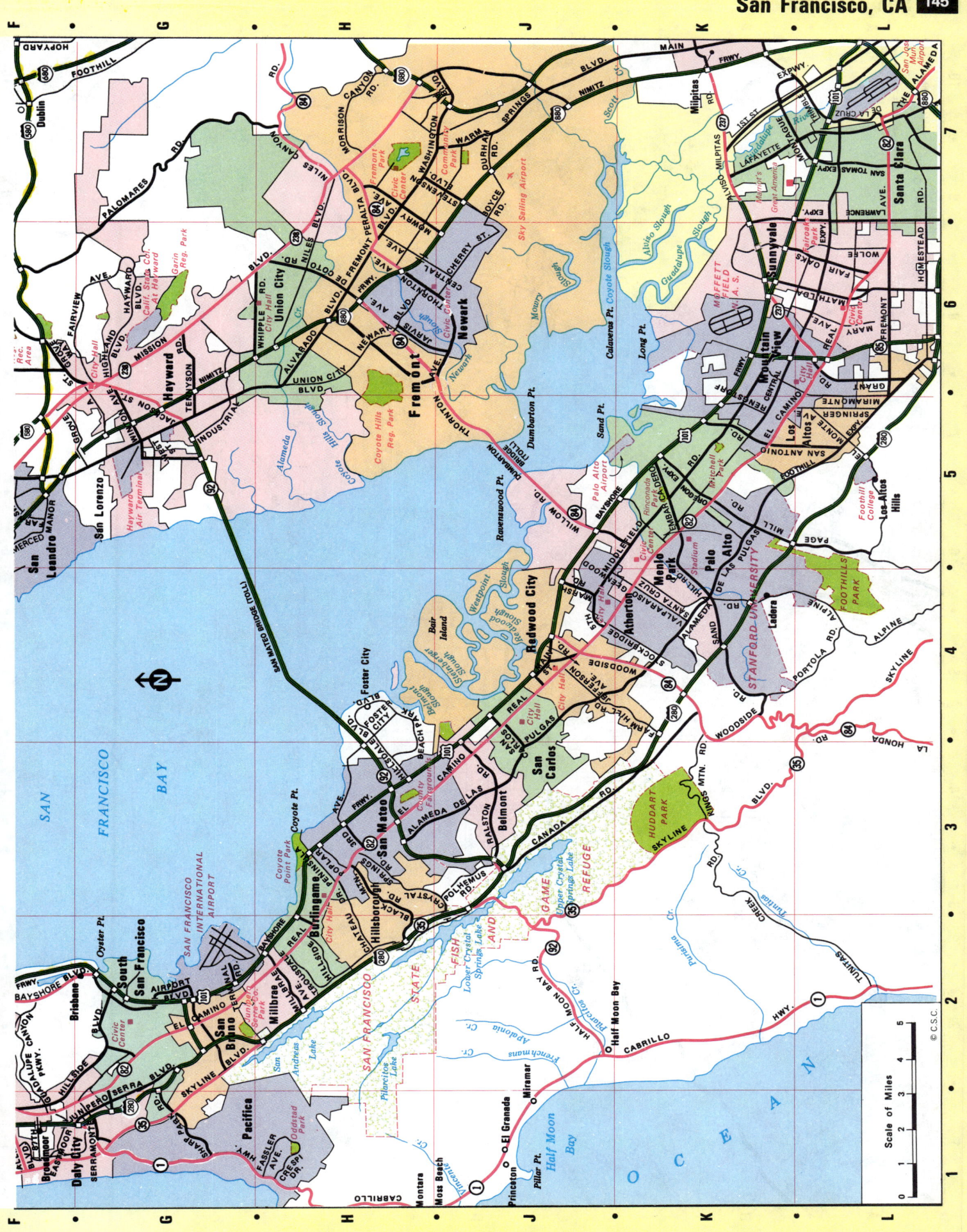

Scale of Miles

© C.S.C.

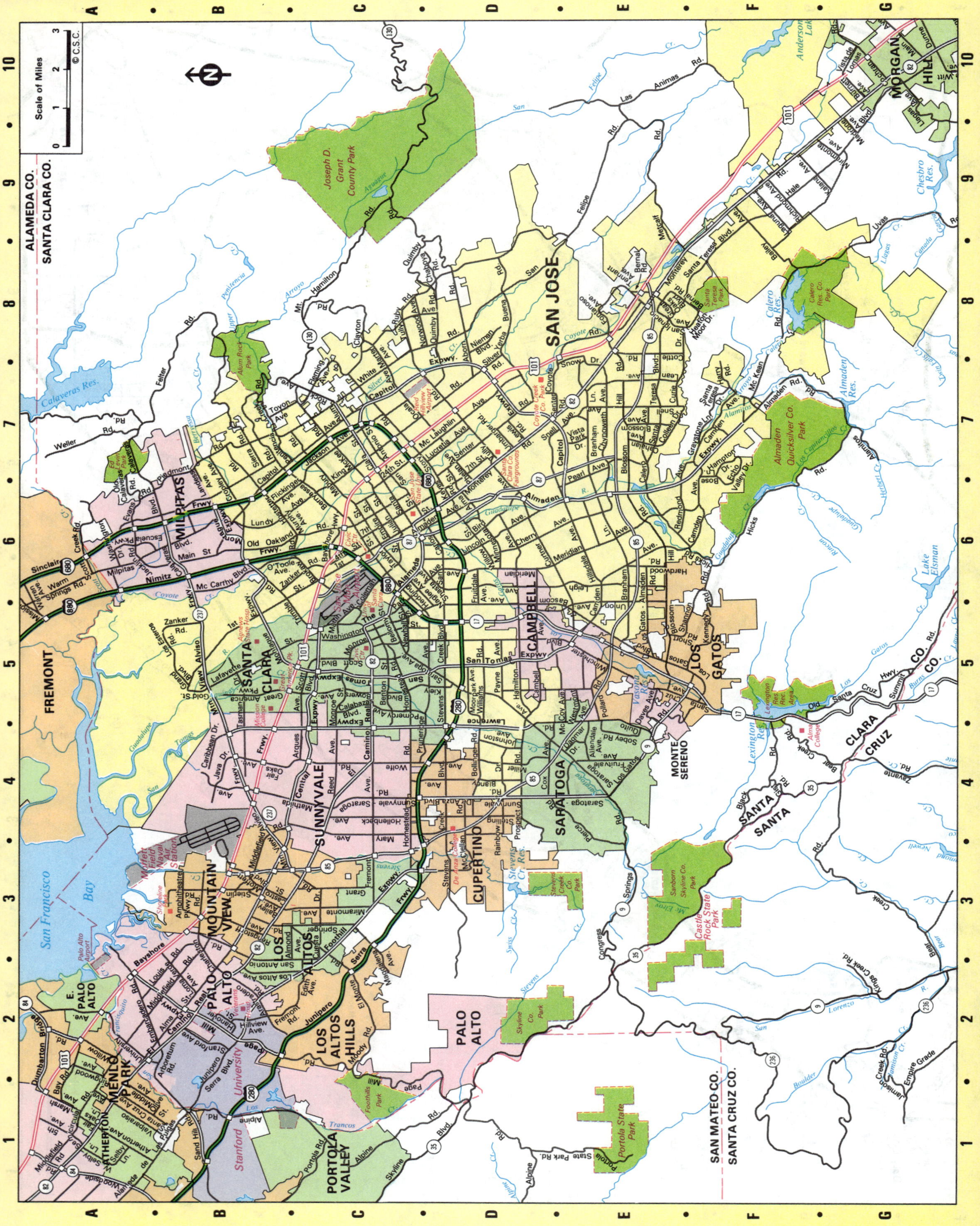

Scale of Miles

© C.S.C.

ALAMEDA CO.
SANTA CLARA CO.

Joseph D. Grant County Park

SAN JOSE

MORGAN HILL

Anderson Lake

Chesbro Res.

Calaveras Res.

Calero Res.

Almaden Quicksilver Co. Park

Almaden Res.

MILPITAS

FREMONT

SANTA CLARA

CAMPBELL

LOS GATOS

MONTE SERENO

SANTA CLARA CO.
SANTA CRUZ CO.

Lake Elsman

Lexington Res.

SUNNYVALE

CUPERTINO

SARATOGA

Castle Rock State Park

Sanborn Skyline Co. Park

MOUNTAIN VIEW

LOS ALTOS

Moffett Field Naval Air Station

San Francisco Bay

Palo Alto Airport

E. PALO ALTO

MENLO PARK

ATHERTON

PALO ALTO

LOS ALTOS HILLS

Stanford University

PALO ALTO

PORTOLA VALLEY

Skyline Co. Park

Portola State Park

SAN MATEO CO.
SANTA CRUZ CO.

Scale of Miles
0 1 2 3
© C.S.C.

Row A: KINGSTON · EDMONDS · LYNNWOOD · SEATTLE HEIGHTS · MALTBY · 196th Ave. S.W. · 524 · 99 · 5 · 405 · 527 · 9 · 522 · Filbert Rd. · Maltby Rd. · Fales Rd. · Echo Lake Rd. · Lost Lake Rd. · Main St. · 212th Ave. S.W. · WOODWAY · MOUNTLAKE TERRACE · BRIER · 228th St. S.W. · Canyon Park Rd. · 228th St. · Paradise Lake Rd. · Welch Rd.

Row B: Appletree Cove · Jefferson Pt. Rd. · Tulin Rd. · 104 · 220th St. · 84th Ave. · 9th Ave. · RICHMOND BEACH · RICHLAND HIGHLANDS · Beach N.E. · N. 175th St. · LAKE FOREST PARK · Ballinger Way · Brier Way · Locust Way · KENMORE · 522 · BOTHELL · 170th St. · Simonds Rd. N.E. · WOODINVILLE · Woodinville · 45th St. · 175th Ave. · Woodinville · Duvall · SNOHOMISH CO. KING CO. · Cottage Lake · Cottage Lake Ct.

Row C: Puget Sound · N · Carkeek Park · N. 145th St. · N. 130th St. · N. 105th St. · 1st Ave. · North · N.E. · 513 · St. Edwards State Park · Holmes Pt. Dr. N.E. · N.E. 132nd St. · JUANITA · N.E. 124th St. · N.E. 116th St. · Market St. N.E. · 100th Ave. N.E. · 202 · REDMOND · 116th Ave. · Novelty Hill Rd.

Row D: ROLLINGBAY · Murden Cove · Golden Gardens Park · Shilshole Bay · Seaview Ave. N.W. · Holman Rd. N.W. · 85th · 65th St. · 15th Ave. · Greenwood · Green Lake · Green Lake Park · Roosevelt · 35th Ave. N.E. · N.E. 65th St. · 99 · Lake City Way · Way · Sand Point Way · Magnusson Park · KIRKLAND · 908 · 405 · 132nd Ave. N.E. · 140th Ave. N.E. · Union Hill Rd. · 196th Ave. N.E. · 208th Ave. N.E. · 202 · 901 · Avondale · Market St. · Discovery Park · Gilman Ave. W. · 45th · 5 · N.E. Pacific St. · University of Washington

Row E: Seattle-Victoria Ferry · Seattle-Winslow Ferry · U.S. Naval Supply Depot · Thorndyke Ave. · Elliott Ave. · 15th Ave. W. · Queen Anne Ave. · Aurora · 10th Ave. · Madison · E. · Lake Union · Union Bay · Evergreen Point Floating Bridge · HUNTS PT. · 520 · 78th Ave. · 84th Ave. · 92nd Ave. · MEDINA · CLYDE HILL · 104th Ave. N.E. · Bellevue-Redmond · N.E. 8th St. · 134th Ave. N.E. · Northrup Rd. · Lake Sammamish · Inglewood Hill Rd. · Eagle Harbor · Shapser Forest Pk.

Row F: Country Club Rd. · Bremerton-Seattle Ferry · Alki Beach Park · Elliott Bay · SEATTLE · S.W. Admiral Way · S.W. · California Ave. S.W. · Fauntleroy Ave. S.W. · West Seattle Freeway · 99 · 4th Ave. S. · 23rd · Empire · Golden Ave. · E. Yesler Way · I-90 · Lake Washington Floating Bridge · Lake Washington · BEAUX ARTS · MERCER ISLAND · S.E. 40th St. · Seward Park · BELLEVUE · Kalthan Rd. · Phantom Lake · Newport Way · 168th Ave. · Pine Lake · S.E. 24th St. · 212th Ave. N.E. · Issaquah

Row G: Puget Sound · Lincoln Park · Vashon-Southworth Ferry · Fauntleroy-Vashon Ferry · SOUTHWORTH · VASHON HEIGHTS · 35th Ave. S.W. · Delridge Way · California Ave. S.W. · 900 · 5 · King Co. Airport · 15th Ave. S. · Rainier Ave. South · Empire Way · 167 · NEWCASTLE · N. 30th St. · New Castle Rd. · Coalfield Way · S.E. 36th Ave. · COALFIELD · Coalfield · 164th Ave. S.E. · Creek · ISSAQUAH · 90

Row H: Vashon Southworth Ferry · Ambaum Blvd. S.W. · 1st Ave. S.W. · Military Rd. · 509 · 99 · BURIEN · S.W. Barton · S.W. Henderson · 599 · 148th Ave. S.E. · 128th · BRYN MAWR · MAPLEWOOD · 169 · Coalfield-Issaquah Rd. · Issaquah-Hobart Rd. · 152nd St. · S.W. Holden · Des Moines · Renton-Issaquah Rd.

Row J: S.W. 168th St. · S.W. 176th St. · S.W. 196th St. · 204th St. S.W. · 91st Ave. S.W. · Vashon Island · NORMANDY PARK · Seattle Tacoma Intl. Airport · 518 · 99 · 188th St. · 509 · 5 · 181 · S. 180th St. · RENTON · Yelley Rd. · S.E. 192nd St. · 140th · 116th Ave. S.E. · 132nd Ave. S.E. · Lake Desire · Offer Lake · Petrovitsky Rd. · Cedar Grove Rd. · 18 · Lake Youngs

Row K: SOUTHWORTH · VASHON ISLAND · 131st · S.W. 232nd St. · 248th St. S.W. · PORTAGE · Tramp Harbor · Weitzel Rd. · Wick Rd. · DES MOINES · 516 · KENT · S. 200th St. · S. 216th St. · 212th St. · S. 228th St. · S.E. 240th St. · Pacific Hwy. · Kent · 167 · Kent-Kangley Rd. · S.E. 208th · S.E. 224th St. · 240th St. · S.E. 208th · North Rd. · 18 · MAURY ISLAND

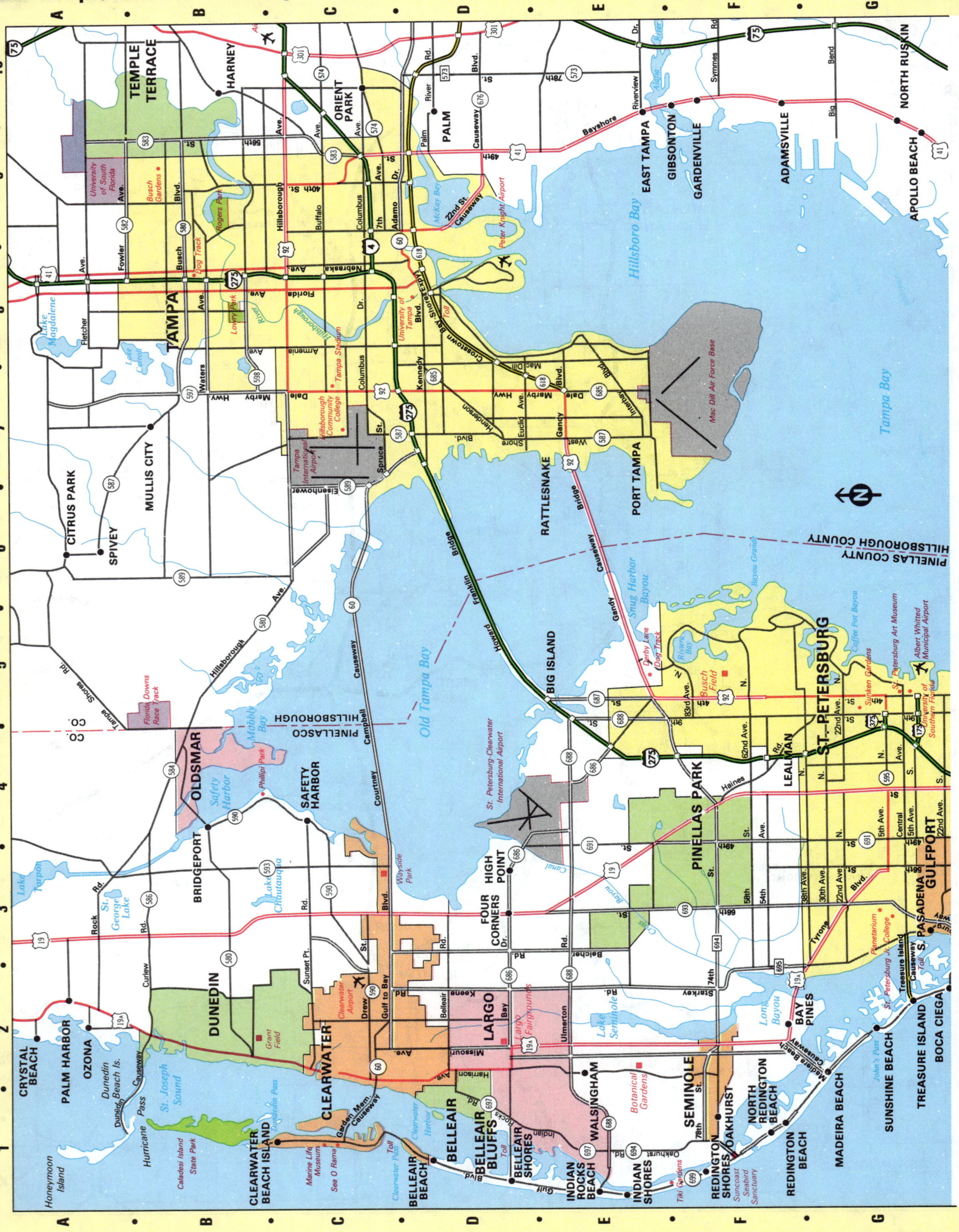

TEMPLE TERRACE, HARNEY, ORIENT PARK, PALM, EAST TAMPA, GIBSONTON, GARDENVILLE, ADAMSVILLE, NORTH RUSKIN, APOLLO BEACH, University of South Florida, Busch Gardens, Rogers Park, TAMPA, Lowry Park, Tampa Stadium, University of Tampa, Hillsborough Community College, Tampa International Airport, Peter Knight Airport, Mac Dill Air Force Base, CITRUS PARK, MULLIS CITY, SPIVEY, Lake Magdalene, Lake Carroll, PORT TAMPA, RATTLESNAKE, BIG ISLAND, Tampa Bay, Hillsboro Bay, Old Tampa Bay, PINELLAS COUNTY, HILLSBOROUGH COUNTY, ST. PETERSBURG, Albert Whitted Municipal Airport, St. Petersburg Art Museum, Sunken Gardens, University of Southern Florida, Busch Field, Derby Lane (Dog Track), Florida Downs Race Track, OLDSMAR, Safety Harbor, SAFETY HARBOR, BRIDGEPORT, Phillip Park, Mobbly Bay, St. Petersburg-Clearwater International Airport, PINELLAS PARK, LEALMAN, GULFPORT, PASADENA, CRYSTAL BEACH, PALM HARBOR, OZONA, DUNEDIN, St. Joseph Sound, St. George Lake, Lake Chautauqua, Grant Field, Clearwater Airport, CLEARWATER, FOUR CORNERS, HIGH POINT, Wayside Park, LARGO, Largo Fairgrounds, WALSINGHAM, SEMINOLE, Lake Seminole, OAKHURST, BAY PINES, Long Bayou, Boca Ciega Bay, St. Petersburg Jr. College, TREASURE ISLAND, BOCA CIEGA, Honeymoon Island, Caledesi Island State Park, Hurricane Pass, Dunedin Beach Is., Marine Life Museum, Sea O Rama, CLEARWATER BEACH ISLAND, BELLEAIR, BELLEAIR BEACH, BELLEAIR BLUFFS, BELLEAIR SHORES, INDIAN ROCKS BEACH, INDIAN SHORES, Botanical Gardens, Tiki Gardens, Suncoast Seabird Sanctuary, REDINGTON SHORES, NORTH REDINGTON BEACH, REDINGTON BEACH, MADEIRA BEACH, John's Pass, Madeira Beach, SUNSHINE BEACH, Planetarium, Snug Harbor Bayou, Coffee Pot Bayou, Bayou Grand, Riviera Bay

Route markers shown include: 75, 41, 92, 275, 60, 19, 19A, 580, 582, 583, 584, 585, 586, 587, 588, 589, 590, 593, 595, 597, 598, 301, 574, 573, 576, 618, 685, 686, 687, 688, 691, 693, 694, 695, 697, 699, 680, 301

Street labels include: Fletcher Ave., Fowler Ave., Busch Blvd., Hillsborough Ave., Buffalo Ave., Columbus Dr., Adamo Dr., Kennedy Blvd., Gandy Blvd., Dale Mabry Hwy., West Shore Blvd., Eisenhower Blvd., Hillsborough River, Crosstown Bay Shore Blvd., Bayshore, Riverview Rd., Symmes Rd., Big Bend, Nebraska Ave., Florida Ave., Armenia Ave., 22nd St. Causeway, 49th St., McKay Bay, Henderson, Euclid, Interbay Blvd., MacDill, Gandy Bridge, Howard Franklin Bridge, Courtney Campbell Causeway, Bayside Causeway, Gulf to Bay Blvd., Drew St., Keene Rd., Belcher Rd., Starkey Rd., Seminole Blvd., Ulmerton Rd., Missouri Ave., Harrison Ave., Central Ave., 4th St., 9th St., 16th St., 22nd Ave., 30th Ave., 38th Ave., 54th Ave., 62nd Ave., 83rd Ave., Tyrone Blvd., Pasadena Ave., Park St., Bay Pines Blvd., Oakhurst Rd., Walsingham Rd., Indian Rocks Rd., Gulf Blvd., Clearwater Mem. Causeway, Garden Mem. Causeway, Dunedin Causeway, Curlew Rd., Sunset Pt. Rd., Rock St., Tampa Shores Rd., Merby Rd., Waters Ave.

Grid reference letters A–G across top and bottom; numbers 1–10 along sides.

Scale of Miles
© C.S.C.

RUSKIN

GULF CITY

Gulf of Mexico

SUNSET BEACH
ST. PETERSBURG BEACH
PASS-A-GRILLE BEACH

TIERRA VERDE

Florida Presbyterian College
London Wax Museum
Aquatarium
St. Petersburg Beach
Boca Ciega Bay
Big Bayou
Country Club Way
Sunshine Pkwy. (Toll)
Pinellas Bayway Toll

JAYNES
TUCSON
SOUTH TUCSON
EMERY PARK
LITTLETOWN

Airport

University of Arizona
Randolph Park Municipal Golf Course
Davis-Monthan Air Force Base
Downtown Airport
Veterans Hospital
John F. Kennedy Park
Tucson International Airport

San Xavier Indian Reservation

Miracle Mile
Speedway Blvd.
Broadway
22nd St.
Ft. Lowell Rd.
Grant Rd.
Prince Rd.
Roger Rd.
Wetmore Rd.
River Rd.
Sunrise
Sabino Canyon Rd.
Skyline Dr.
Ina Rd.
Orange Grove Rd.
Cortaro Farms Rd.
Naranja Dr.
Lambert Ln.
Magee Rd.
Linda Vista Blvd.
Hardy Rd.
Overton Rd.

Tucson-Florence Hwy.
Casa Grande Hwy.
Tucson-Benson Hwy.
Tucson-Nogales Hwy.

Silverbell Rd.
La Cholla Blvd.
La Canada Dr.
Thornydale Rd.
Camino De Oeste
Shannon Rd.
Romero Rd.
Northnau Rd.
Campbell Ave.
Alvernon Way
Swan Rd.
Craycroft Rd.
Kolb Rd.
Wilmot Rd.
Pantano Rd.
Golf Links Rd.
Valencia Rd.
Irvington Rd.
Drexel Rd.
Hughes Access Rd.
Los Reales Rd.
Old Vail Rd.

Camino Del Cerro
El Camino
Sweet Water Dr.
Ruthrauff Rd.
Flowing Wells Rd.
Fairview Ave.
Grant Rd.
Ironwood Hill Dr.
W. Anklam Rd.
W. Speedway Blvd.
Marys
W. Congress
22nd St.
San Juan
36th St.
Ajo
Tucson Ajo Hwy.
De Oeste
Dakota
Valley Rd.
Cardinal Ave.
Mission Rd.
6th Ave.
12th Ave.
S. Park Ave.
Palo Verde Blvd.
Country Club Rd.
Fairland
Stray

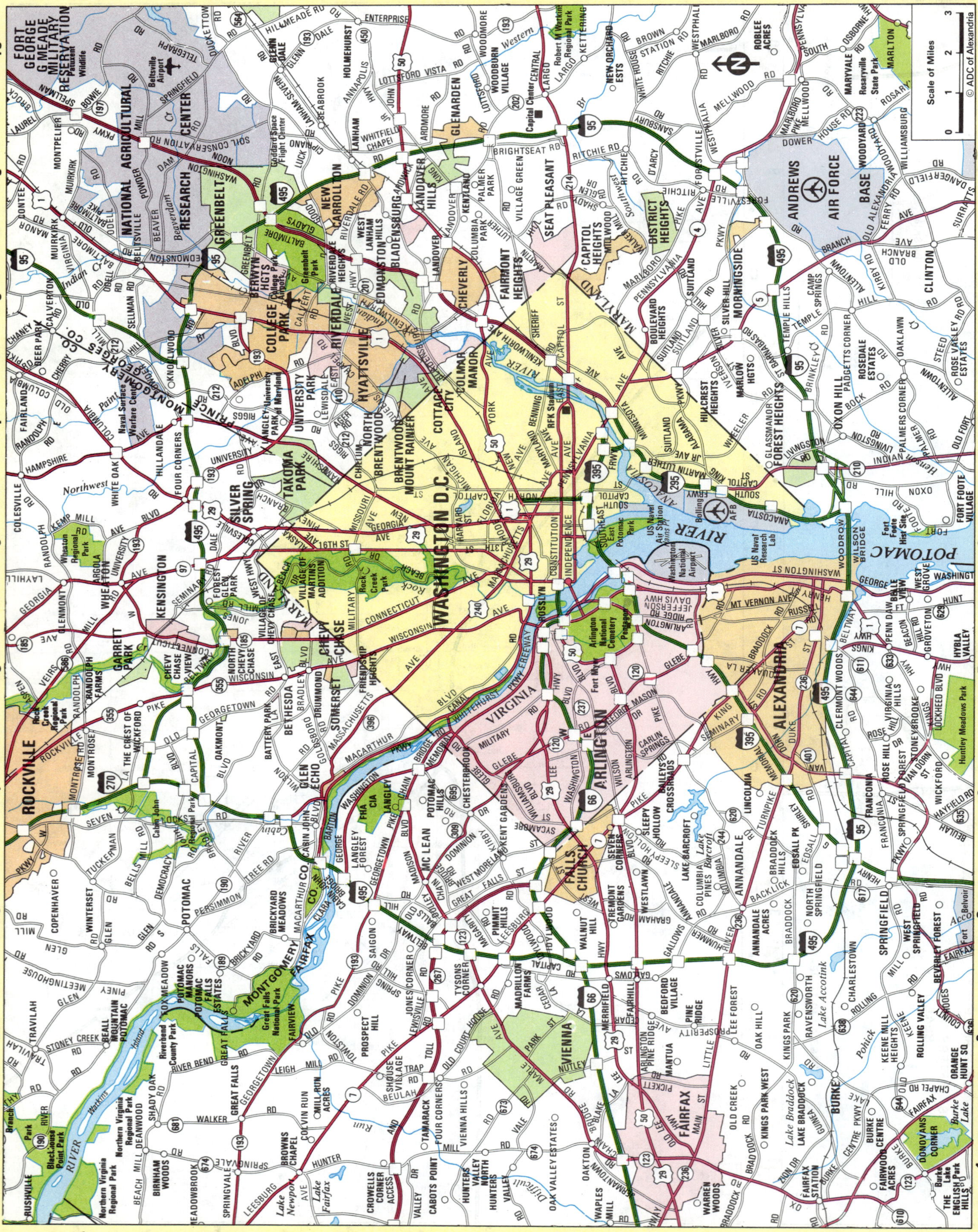
WASHINGTON D.C.
POTOMAC
RIVER
MARYLAND
VIRGINIA
ALEXANDRIA
ARLINGTON
FALLS CHURCH
FAIRFAX
VIENNA
ROCKVILLE
BETHESDA
SILVER SPRING
TAKOMA PARK
KENSINGTON
WHEATON
GREENBELT
COLLEGE PARK
HYATTSVILLE
RIVERDALE
ANDREWS AIR FORCE BASE
NATIONAL AGRICULTURAL RESEARCH CENTER
FORT GEORGE G MEADE MILITARY RESERVATION
MCLEAN
POTOMAC
SPRINGFIELD
ANNANDALE
BURKE
CLINTON
MORNINGSIDE
DISTRICT HEIGHTS
CAPITOL HEIGHTS
SEAT PLEASANT
CHEVERLY
LANDOVER HILLS
NEW CARROLLTON
CHEVY CHASE
GARRETT PARK
GLEN ECHO
SOMERSET
FRIENDSHIP HEIGHTS
MOUNT RAINIER
BRENTWOOD
NORTH BRENTWOOD
COTTAGE CITY
COLMAR MANOR
BLADENSBURG
EDMONSTON
UNIVERSITY PARK
BERWYN HEIGHTS
FOREST HEIGHTS
OXON HILL
MONTGOMERY
PRINCE GEORGES CO.
FAIRFAX CO.
Scale of Miles
© ADC of Alexandria
A
B
C
D
E
F
G
1
2
3
4
5
6
7
8
9
10

Scale of Miles
0 1 2 3
© C.S.C.

Scale of Miles
0 1 2 3
© C.S.C.

Grid letters (left/right): A B C D E F G H J K
Grid numbers (top/bottom): 2 3 4 5 6
Left inset grid: H J — 10 9 8 7 6 5 4 3 2 1

Left inset (St. Petersburg area)
RUSKIN
GULF CITY
SUNSET BEACH
ST. PETERSBURG BEACH
PASS-A-GRILLE BEACH
TIERRA VERDE
Gulf of Mexico
Big Bayou
Boca Ciega Bay
Lake Maggiore
Salt Creek
Gordon Wax Museum
Aquatarium
Florida Presbyterian College
Pinellas Bayway
Tall
St. Petersburg Beach Cswy.
Sunshine Skyway Pkwy. (Toll)
Country Club Way
6th St.
1st St.
4th
62nd Ave. S.
66th Ave. S.
Pinellas Pt. Dr.
22nd Ave. S.
34th St. S.
34th Ave. S.
19
682
679
693

Main map (Tucson)
Airport
N
Big
US 89
Tucson Florence Hwy.
Naranja Dr.
Lambert Ln.
Linda Vista Blvd.
Camino De Oesta
Thornydale Rd.
Magee Rd.
La Cholla
Overton Rd.
La Canada
Romero Rd.
Hardy Rd.
Magee
Sage St.
Northernau Rd.
89
Cortaro Farms Rd.
Casa Grande Hwy.
Silverbell Rd.
Ina Rd.
Skyline Dr.
Campbell Ave.
Del Sol
Alvernon Way
10
Orange Grove Rd.
Shannon Rd.
La Cholla
La Canada Rd.
River Rd.
Hacienda
Pontatoc Rd.
Swan
Craycroft
Sunrise
Sabino Canyon Rd.
Kolb Rd.
Snyder
JAYNES
Sunset Rd.
Camino Del Cerro
El Camino Del Cerro
Ruthrauff Rd.
Rillito Creek
Wetmore
Roger Rd.
Flowing Wells Rd.
Oracle Rd.
N. 1st Ave.
River Rd.
Cloud Rd.
Bear Canyon
Water
Sweet
El Morago Dr.
Miracle Mile
Fairview
Prince
Stone Ave.
Tucson
Fairview
Ironwood Hill Dr.
Ft. Lowell Rd.
Ft. Lowell
Dodge Blvd.
Grant Rd.
Tanque Verde
Wrightstown
Tucson
Gdret Rd.
Grant Rd.
Speedway
Campbell Blvd.
TUCSON
Speedway Blvd.
W. Speedway Blvd.
W. Anklam
Marvs Rd.
Greasewood
University of Arizona
Club
Alvernon
Wilmot
Pantano
Camino Seco
W. Congress
Broadway
Randolph Park Municipal Golf Course
Fairland
22nd St.
22nd
Shannon Rd.
San Juan
Davis-Monthan Air Force Base
Freeway
89
John F. Kennedy Park
10
36th St.
36th
Strav.
Golf Links Rd.
Escalante
Irvington
Lachola Blvd.
Aio
Veterans Hospital
Downtown Airport
Country Club Blvd.
Verde
Tucson-Benson Hwy.
Hwy. 86
SOUTH TUCSON
Irvington Rd.
Palo Verde Way
Alverson Way
Craycroft
Golf Links Rd.
LITTLETOWN
Tucson Aio
De Oeste Ave.
Dakota
Valley Rd.
Drexel
S. Park Ave.
EMERY PARK
Kolb Rd.
Old Vail Rd.
10
Valencia Rd.
12th
Valencia
Missiondale
Tucson International Airport
Los Reales Rd.
Cardinal
19
Mission Rd.
6th Ave.
Tucson-Nogales Hwy.
San Xavier Indian Reservation
Hughes
Access
San Xavier Indian Reservation
89
Wilmot
19

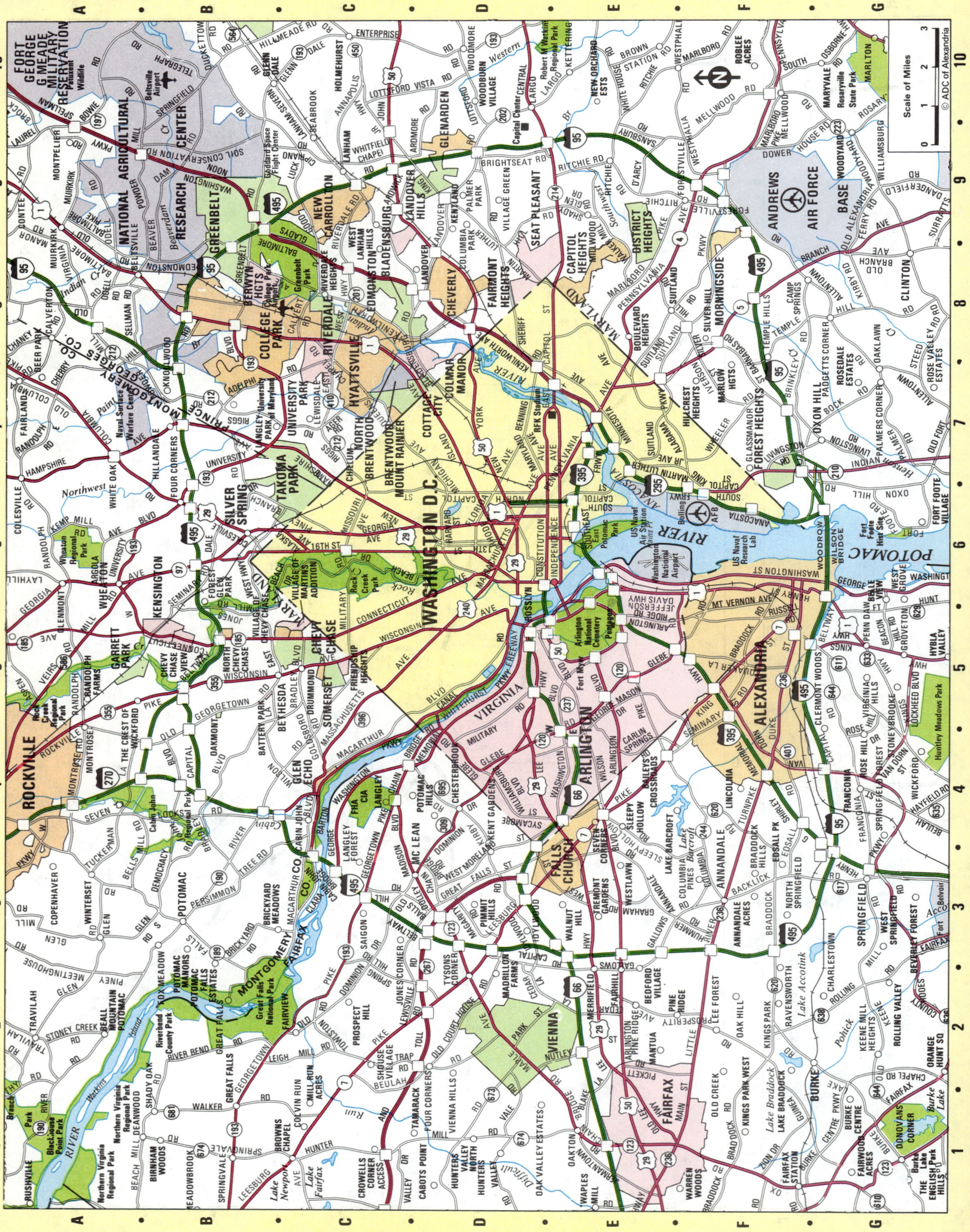
WASHINGTON D.C.
ARLINGTON
ALEXANDRIA
VIRGINIA
MARYLAND
ROCKVILLE
KENSINGTON
WHEATON
SILVER SPRING
TAKOMA PARK
BETHESDA
CHEVY CHASE
COLLEGE PARK
GREENBELT
HYATTSVILLE
RIVERDALE
NEW CARROLLTON
CHEVERLY
CAPITOL HEIGHTS
DISTRICT HEIGHTS
MORNINGSIDE
ANDREWS AIR FORCE BASE
FALLS CHURCH
ANNANDALE
SPRINGFIELD
FAIRFAX
VIENNA
MC LEAN
POTOMAC
GREAT FALLS
FRANCONIA
CLINTON
NATIONAL AGRICULTURAL RESEARCH CENTER
FORT GEORGE G MEADE MILITARY RESERVATION
POTOMAC RIVER
ANACOSTIA RIVER
Washington National Airport
Arlington National Cemetery
Rock Creek Park
Great Falls National Park
Scale of Miles
© ADC of Alexandria

INDEX
To The United States

Index to Canadian Cities and Towns on Pages 8-9.
Index to Mexican Cities and Towns on Page 11.

ALABAMA
Page 13

Population: 3,893,888
Capital: Montgomery
Land Area: 50,767 sq. mi.

Abanda E-6
Abbeville H-6
Action Pg. 92, J-4
Ada G-5
Adamsville D-4
Vicinity Pg. 92, C-2
Addison B-4
Akron E-3
Alabaster D-4
Albertville B-5
Alden Pg. 92, C-2
Aldrich D-4
Alexander City E-5
Aliceville E-2
Allgood C-5
Almond E-6
Altoona C-5
Andalusia H-4
Anderson A-4
Anniston C-5
Arab B-5
Arcus H-5
Ardilla H-6
Ardmore A-4
Argo D-5
Arkadelphia C-4
Arley C-4
Ashbury C-6
Ashford H-7
Ashland D-6
Ashville C-5
Athens A-4
Atmore J-3
Attalla C-5
Auburn F-6
Awin G-4
Axis J-2
Babbie H-5
Baileyton B-4
Bakerhill G-6
Ballplay C-6
Bangor C-4
Banks G-6
Bankston C-3
Barfield D-6
Barton A-3
Bass A-6
Batesville G-7
Bay Minette J-3
Bay View Pg. 92, D-2
Bayou LaBatre K-2
Bear Creek B-3
Beatrice G-3
Belgreen B-3
Belk D-3
Bellamy F-2
Belleville H-4
Benton F-4
Berry C-3
Bessemer D-4
Vicinity Pg. 92, H-2
Bessie Pg. 92, C-1
Big Cove B-5
Billingsley E-4
Birmingham D-4
Vicinity Pg. 92
Blacksher H-3
Blount Springs C-4
Blountsville C-4
Blue Mountain D-5
Bluff C-3
Boaz C-5
Bolinger G-2
Bon Secour K-3
Borden Springs C-6
Boyd F-2
Braggs G-4
Brantley H-5
Bremen C-4
Brent E-4
Brewton J-4
Bridgeport A-6
Brighton Pg. 92, G-2
Brilliant C-3
Brinn B-3
Brooklyn H-4
Brookside Pg. 92, C-3
Brooksville C-5
Brookwood D-3
Browns F-4
Brownsville Pg. 92, G-3
Brundidge G-6
Bryant A-6
Butler G-2
Bynum D-5
Cahaba Heights Pg. 92, G-6
Calera E-4
Calvert H-2
Camden G-4
Campbell G-3
Camphill E-6
Carbon Hill C-3
Cardiff Pg. 92, C-2
Carrollton D-2
Carrville F-6
Castleberry H-4
Catalpa G-6
Catherine F-3
Cedar Bluff B-6
Center Point C-4
Vicinity Pg. 92, C-6
Centre C-6
Centreville E-4
Chalkville Pg. 92, B-7
Chapel Pg. 92, H-5
Chase A-4
Chastang J-2
Chatom H-2
Chelsea D-5
Vicinity Pg. 92, J-7
Cherokee A-3
Chickasaw J-2
Childersburg D-5
Chrysler H-3
Citronelle H-2
Claiborne H-3
Clanton E-4
Claud F-5
Clayhatchee H-6
Clayton G-6
Cleveland C-5
Clinton E-2
Clio G-6
Clopton H-6
Cloverdale A-3
Coalburg Pg. 92, D-3
Cochrane E-2
Coden K-2
Coffeeville G-2
Collinsville B-6
Columbia H-7
Columbiana D-5
Consul F-3
Cooper E-5
Cordova C-4
Cottonwood J-6
Courtland B-4
Coxey A-4
Creola J-2
Crossville B-6
Cuba F-2
Cullman C-4
Cullomburg G-2
Dadeville E-6
Daleville H-6
Damascus H-4
Dancy E-2
Danville B-4
Daphne J-3
Dauphin Island K-2
Daviston E-6
Davisville F-6
Dawes J-2
Dayton F-3
Deans H-4
Deatsville F-5
Decatur B-4
Deer Park H-2
Dees K-2
Delta D-6
Demopolis E-3
Devenport G-5
Dill H-6
Divide Station Pg. 92, B-3
Dixie J-4
Dixon Mills G-2
Dixonville J-4
Docena Pg. 92, E-2
Dolomite Pg. 92, G-2
Dora C-4
Dothan H-7
Double Springs C-3
Dry Forks G-3
Dublin G-5
Duke C-6
Duncanville E-3
E. Brewton J-4
Eastern Valley Pg. 92, J-2
Easton E-6
Echola D-3
Eclectic F-6
Edgewater Pg. 92, E-2
Edwin G-6
Eight Mile J-2
Elamville H-6
Elba H-5
Elberta K-3
Elias E-5
Eliska H-3
Elmore F-5
Elrod D-3
Elvira Pg. 92, K-3
Emelle E-2
Enterprise H-5
Eoline E-4
Epes E-2
Equality E-5
Ethelsville D-2
Eufaula G-7
Eunola J-6
Eutaw E-3
Evergreen H-4
Ewell H-6
Fairfax E-7
Fairfield D-4
Vicinity Pg. 92, F-2
Fairhope K-2
Falkville B-4
Fatama G-4
Fayette D-2
Fieldstown Pg. 92, C-4
Flat Rock A-6
Flint City B-4
Flomaton J-4
Florala J-5
Florence A-3
Foley K-3
Forkland F-2
Forkville B-3
Fort Mitchell F-7
Fort Payne B-6
Fountain H-3
Francisco A-5
Frisco City H-3
Fruitdale H-2
Fulton G-3
Fultondale D-4
Vicinity Pg. 92, C-4
Gadsden C-6
Gainesville E-2
Gallant C-5
Gallion F-3
Gantt H-5
Gardendale C-4
Vicinity Pg. 92, B-5
Geiger E-2
Genery Pg. 92, K-3
Geneva J-5
Georgiana G-4
Geraldine B-5
Glencoe C-6
Goodwater E-5
Gordo D-3
Grand Bay K-2
Grants Mille Pg. 92, F-7
Graysville C-4
Vicinity Pg. 92, C-2
Green Bay H-5
Green Pond D-4
Greens Station Pg. 92, C-6
Greensboro E-3
Greenville G-5
Greenwood Pg. 92, K-2
Grove Hill G-3
Guin C-2
Gulf Shores K-3
Guntersville B-5
Gurly B-5
Hackleburg B-3
Haleyville B-3
Halsell F-2
Halsos Mill G-5
Hamilton B-2
Hammondville B-6
Hanceville C-4
Harpersville D-5
Harrisburg E-3
Hartford J-6
Hartselle B-4
Hatton B-3
Havana E-3
Hawk D-6
Hayneville F-4
Hazel Green A-5
Hazen F-4
Headland H-7
Helena D-4
Vicinity Pg. 92, K-4
Henagar B-6
Hobson City D-6
Hodges B-3
Hokes Bluff C-6
Hollis D-6
Hollywood A-6
Holt D-3
Holy Trinity F-7
Homewood D-4
Vicinity Pg. 92, F-4
Hoover D-4
Vicinity Pg. 92, H-4
Hueytown D-4
Vicinity Pg. 92, G-1
Hulaco B-4
Hunter F-5
Huntsville A-5
Hurtsboro F-6
Huxford H-3
Hybart G-3
Ider B-6
Ino H-5
Intercourse D-3
Irondale D-4
Vicinity Pg. 92, E-7
Ishkooda Pg. 92, G-3
Isney G-2
Jachin F-2
Jack H-5
Jackson H-3
Jacksonville C-6
Jasper C-4
Jefferson F-2
Jefferson Park Pg. 92, E-7
Jemison E-4
Jenkins Crossroads G-6
Jones F-4
Jones Chapel C-4
Kellerman D-4
Kelly's Crossroads E-5
Kellyton E-5
Kennedy D-3
Ketona Pg. 92, D-5
Kilgore Pg. 92, B-1
Kimberly C-4
Kimbrough G-3
Kinsey H-6
Kinston H-5
Knoxville E-3
Koenton H-2
La Place F-6
Lafayette E-6
Lanett E-6
Langdale E-7
Lawrenceville H-6
Leeds D-5
Leighton A-3
Letohatchee G-4
Lewisburg Pg. 92, D-4
Lexington A-3
Lillian K-3
Lin Crossing Pg. 92, B-2
Lincoln D-5
Lindbergh Pg. 92, C-1
Linden F-3
Lineville D-6
Lipscomb Pg. 92, H-3
Littleville B-3
Livingston F-3
Lockhart J-5
Lottie H-3
Louisville G-6
Lowndesboro F-5
Loxley K-3
Luverne G-5
Lyeffion H-4
Lynn C-3
Magnolia F-3
Malvern J-6
Maplesville E-4
Marbury E-5
Marion E-3
Marvyn F-6
Maytown Pg. 92, E-2
McCalla Pg. 92, J-1
McDade F-5
McIntosh H-2
McKenzie H-5
Mentone B-6
Meridianville A-5
Midfield Pg. 92, G-3
Midland City H-6
Midway G-4
Millbrook F-5
Millerville E-5
Millport D-2
Millry G-2
Mineral Springs Pg. 92, C-3
Mitchell F-6
Mobile J-2
Monroeville H-4
Monrovia $UP
Montevallo E-4
Montgomery F-5
Montrose K-2
Moores Bridge D-3
Mooresville B-4
Morgan Pg. 92, J-3
Morgan City B-5
Morris C-4
Morvin G-3
Moulton B-4
Moundville E-3
Mount Andrew G-6
Mount Olive E-5
Vicinity Pg. 92, B-4
Mount Vernon J-2
Mount Willing G-4
Mountain Brook D-4
Vicinity Pg. 92, F-5
Mulberry F-4
Mulga Pg. 92, E-1
Munford D-6
Muscle Shoals A-3
Muscoda Pg. 92, H-2
Nanafalia G-2
Natural Bridge C-3
New Brockton H-5
New Castle Pg. 92, B-5
New Hope B-5
Vicinity Pg. 92, J-6
New Lexington D-3
New Market A-5
Newburg B-3
Newsite E-6
Newton H-6
Newtonville D-3
Newville H-6
Normal A-5
Northport D-3
Notasulga F-6
Oak Grove D-4
Oakland B-4
Oakman C-3
Oakwood F-5
Odenville D-5
Ohatchee C-5
Omaha G-7
Oneonta C-5
Opelika E-6
Opp H-5
Overton Pg. 92, F-6
Owens Crossroads B-5
Oxford D-6
Oxmoor Pg. 92, G-3
Ozark H-6
Palmerdale C-4
Vicinity Pg. 92, A-7
Parrish C-4
Pelham D-4
Vicinity Pg. 92, D-4
Pell City D-5
Pennington F-2
Perdido J-3
Peterman H-3
Peterson D-3
Petersville A-3
Phil Campbell B-3
Phoenix City F-7
Pickensville D-2
Piedmont C-6
Pine Apple G-4
Pine Grove C-6
Pine Hill G-3
Pinson Pg. 92, B-6
Pisgah B-6
Plantersville F-4
Pleasant Grove D-2
Vicinity Pg. 92, F-1
Prattville F-5
Priceville B-4
Prichard J-2
Pt. Clear K-2
Rabun J-3
Rainbow City C-5
Rainsville B-6
Ranburne D-6
Range H-3
Red Bay B-2
Red Level H-4
Reece City C-5
Reform D-3
Repton H-3
Republic Pg. 92, D-3
Riley G-4
River Falls H-5
River View J-4
Roanoke E-6
Robertsdale K-3
Robinwood Pg. 92, C-5
Rockdale D-6
Rockford E-5
Rocky Ridge Pg. 92, H-5
Roebuck Plaza Pg. 92, D-7
Rogersville A-3
Rome H-5
Romulus E-3
Russellville B-3
Rutledge G-5
Saco G-6
Safford F-3
Saint Elmo K-2
Salitpa G-2
Samson H-5
Sanford H-5
Santuck E-5
Saraland J-2
Sardis F-4
Satsuma J-2
Sayre Pg. 92, A-2
Scottsboro B-5
Seale F-7
Section B-5
Selma F-4
Shannon Pg. 92, H-3
Shawmut E-7
Sheffield A-3
Shelby E-5
Shepardville G-4
Shorter F-6
Silver Hill K-3
Simcoe B-4
Sipsey C-4
Sledge F-3
Slocomb H-6
Smiths F-7
Smut Eye G-6
Snead C-5
Snowdoun F-5
Somerville B-4
Southside C-5
Spring Hill H-6
Springville C-5
Sprott E-3
Spruce Pine B-3
Stafford D-2
Steele C-5
Stevenson A-6
Stewartville E-5
Stockton J-3
Sulligent C-2
Sumiton C-4
Summerdale K-3
Sunflower H-2
Suttle F-4
Sweet Water G-3
Sylacauga E-5
Sylvan Springs Pg. 92, E-1
Sylvania B-6
Talladega D-5
Tallasee F-6
Tarrant City Pg. 92, D-5
Tensaw H-3
Terese G-7
Theodore K-2
Thomaston F-3
Thomasville G-3
Thorsby E-4
Three Notch G-6
Tibbie H-2
Town Creek B-4
Toxey G-2
Trinity B-4
Troy G-5
Trussville D-5
Tuscaloosa D-3
Tuscumbia A-3
Tuskegee F-6
Union E-3
Union Grove E-5
Vicinity Pg. 92, D-1
Union Springs G-6
Uniontown F-3
Uriah H-3
Valley Head B-6
Vance E-3
Vernon C-2
Vestavia Hills D-4
Vicinity Pg. 92, G-5
Victoria H-6
Vidette G-5
Village Springs C-5
Vineland G-3
Vinemont B-4
Wadley E-6
Wagarville H-2
Walker Chapel Pg. 92, C-4
Walnut Grove C-5
Walnut Hill E-6
Warrior C-4
Weaver C-6
Wedowee D-6
Wenonah Pg. 92, G-3
West Blockton D-4
West Point B-4
Wetumpka F-5
Whatley G-3
Whiteoak B-2
Whitson D-3
Wicksburg H-6
Wilburn C-4
Wilmer J-2
Wilton E-4
Windham Springs D-3
Winfield C-3
Wing J-4
Winterboro D-5
Woodville B-5
Wren B-3
Yantley F-2
Yarbo H-2
York F-2
Zip City A-3

ALASKA
Page 14

Population: 401,851
Capital: Juneau
Land Area: 570,883 sq. mi.

Akhiok F-5
Akolmiut D-4
Akulurak D-4
Akutan F-2
Alakanuk C-4
Alaktak A-7
Aleknagik E-4
Alice Arm H-10
Allakaket C-6
Ambler B-6
Anartuvuk Pass B-7
Anchorage E-6
Inset Map B-2
Anderson D-7
Angoon G-9
Aniak D-4
Anvik D-5
Arctic Village C-8
Atka H-8
Atkasuk A-6
Attu H-5
Baranof G-9
Barrow A-7
Beaver C-7
Beechey Pt A-7
Bethel D-4
Bettles C-7
Big Delta D-7
Big Port Walter G-9
Black D-4
Brevig Mission B-4
Buckland C-5
Candle C-5
Cantwell D-7
Cape Romanzof D-3
Cape Yakataga F-8
Caro C-7
Chalkyitsik C-8
Chatanika D-7
Chenik F-5
Chevak D-4
Chickaloon E-7
Inset Map A-2
Chicken D-8
Chignik F-4
Chitina E-7
Christian C-8
Christochina E-7
Chugiak B-2
Circle C-8
Circle Hot Springs D-8
Clarks Pt E-5
College D-7
Copper Center E-7
Cordova E-7
Craig H-9
Crooked Creek D-5
Deadhorse B-7
Deering B-5
Delta Junction D-7
Dillingham E-4
Donnelly D-7
Dot Lake D-8
Douglas G-9
Dutch Harbor F-2
Eagle D-8
Eagle River E-6
Inset Map B-2
Edna Bay H-9
Eek E-4
Egavic C-5
Elfin Cove G-9
Emmonak C-4
English Bay F-6
Eureka D-7
Fairbanks D-7
False Pass F-3
Farewell D-6
Flat D-5
Fort Yukon C-8
Gakona E-7
Galena C-6
Gambell C-3
Glen Alps E-6
Glennallen E-7
Golovin C-5
Goodnews Bay E-4
Gordon B-8
Grayling D-5
Gulkana E-7
Gustavus G-9
Haines F-9
Hawk Inlet G-9
Healy D-7
Homer E-6
Inset Map C-1
Hoonah G-9
Hooper Bay D-3
Hope E-6
Inset Map B-2
Houston A-2
Hughes C-6
Huslia C-6
Hydaburg H-9
Itulilick E-5
Juneau G-9
Kachemak E-6
Kake G-9
Kaktovik B-8
Kalla C-6
Kaltag C-5
Karluk F-5
Kashegelok E-5
Kasilof E-6
Inset Map B-1
Kaskanak E-5
Katalla F-7
Kenai B-1
Ketchikan H-10
Kiana B-5
Kinegnak E-4
King Cove F-3
King Salmon F-5
Kipnuk E-4
Kivalina B-5
Klawock H-9
Knik B-2
Kobuk C-6
Kodiak F-6
Kokrines C-6
Koliganek E-5
Kotlick C-4
Kotzebue B-5
Koyuk C-5
Koyukuk C-5
Kuliuk F-5
Kwethluk D-4
Kwigillingok E-4
Larsen Bay F-5
Latouche F-7
Levelock E-5
Lime Village E-5
Livengood C-7
Long D-6
Lower Tonsina E-7
Manley Hot Springs D-6
Manokotak E-4
McCarthy E-8
McGrath D-5
McKinley Park D-7
Medfra D-6
Mekoryuk D-3
Mentasta Lake E-7
Metlakata H-10
Minto D-7
Moose Pass B-2
Mount Edgecumber G-9
Mountain Village D-4
Naknek F-5
Napakiak D-4
Napaskiak E-4
Nenana D-7
New Stuyahok E-5
Newhalen E-5
Nikolai D-6
Nikolski F-1
Noatak B-5
Nogamut E-5
Nome C-4
Nondalton E-5
Noorvik B-5
North Pole D-7
Northeast Cape C-4
Northway E-8
Nulato C-5
Old Harbor F-5
Ooliktok A-7
Ouzinkie F-6
Palmer E-7
Inset Map A-2
Pedro Bay E-5
Pelican G-9
Perryville F-4
Petersburg E-6
Pilgrim Springs C-4
Pilot Point F-4
Inset Map D-4
Platinum E-4
Point Hope A-5
Point Lay A-5
Porcupine F-9
Port Alexander G-9
Port Lions F-5
Portlock F-6
Prudhoe Bay B-8
Quinhagak E-4
Rampart C-7
Rampart House C-8
Richardson D-7
Ruby C-6
Russian Mission D-4
Sagwon B-7
Salchaket D-7
Sand Pt F-4
Saroonga C-3
Selawik B-5
Seward E-6
Inset Map C-2
Shageluk D-5
Shaktoolik C-5
Shishmaref B-4
Shungnak B-6
Sinuk C-4
Sitka G-9
Skagway F-9
Sleetmute D-5
Soldotna E-6
Inset Map B-1
Squaw Harbor G-3
St. George E-2
St. Marys D-4
St. Michael C-5
St. Paul E-2
Stebbins C-4
Stevens Village C-7
Stony River D-5
Stuyahok D-5
Susitna B-2
Takotna D-5
Talkeetna E-7
Inset Map A-1
Tanalian Pt E-5
Tanana C-6
Tatitlek E-7
Teller C-4
Tetlin E-8
Tetlin Junction E-8
Togiak E-4
Tok D-8
Toksook Bay D-4
Tonsina E-7
Tuluksak D-4
Tununak D-4
Tyonek E-6
Inset Map B-1
Ugashik F-5
Umiat B-7
Unalakleet C-5
Unalaska F-2
Valdez E-7
Venetie C-8

ALASKA

ARIZONA
Pages 16-17

Population: 2,718,215
Capital: Phoenix
Land Area: 113,508 sq. mi.

ARKANSAS
Page 15

Population: 2,286,435
Capital: Little Rock
Land Area: 52,078 sq. mi.

CALIFORNIA
Pages 18-21

Population: 23,667,902
Capital: Sacramento
Land Area: 156,299 sq. mi.

COLORADO
Pages 22-23
Population: 2,889,964
Capital: Denver
Land Area: 103,595 sq. mi.

ILLINOIS

INDIANA

INDIANA
Pages 34-35

Population: 5,490,224
Capital: Indianapolis
Land Area: 35,932 sq. mi.

INDIANA

IOWA
Page 36

Population: 2,913,808
Capital: Des Moines
Land Area: 55,965 sq. mi.

IOWA

MAINE

MARYLAND
Pages 42-43

Population: 4,216,975
Capital: Annapolis
Land Area: 9,837 sq. mi.

MASSACHUSETTS

MASSACHUSETTS
Pages 24-25

Population: 5,737,037
Capital: Boston
Land Area: 7,824 sq. mi.

MASSACHUSETTS

MICHIGAN

MISSISSIPPI

MISSOURI

MONTANA
Page 51

Population: 786,690
Capital: Helena
Land Area: 145,398 sq.mi.

NEBRASKA
Pages 52-53

Population: 1,569,825
Capital: Lincoln
Land Area: 76,664 sq. mi.

Syracuse H-12
Table Rock H-12
Tarnov F-10
Taylor E-8
Tecumseh H-12
Tekamah E-12
Terrytown D-2
Thayer G-10
Thedford E-6
Thurston E-12
Tilden E-10
Tobias H-11
Trenton H-6
Trumbull G-9
Tryon E-6
Uehling E-12
Ulysses G-11
Unadilla G-12
Upland H-8
Valentine C-7
Valley F-12
Valparaiso G-11
Venango G-4
Verdel C-10
Verdigre D-10
Verdon J-13
Waco G-10
Wahoo F-12
Wakefield D-11
Wallace G-5
Walthill E-12
Wauneta H-5
Wausa D-10
Waverly G-12
Wayne D-11
Weeping Water G-12
Weissert F-8
Wellfleet G-6
West Point E-11
Western H-11
Westerville F-8
Whitman D-5
Whitney C-3
Wilber H-11
Wilcox H-8
Willow Island G-7
Wilsonville H-7
Winnebago D-12
Winnetoon D-9
Winside E-11
Winslow F-12
Wisner E-11
Wolbach F-9
Wood Lake C-7
Wood River G-9
Wymore J-12
Wynot C-11
York G-10

NEVADA
Page 54

Population: 800,493
Capital: Carson City
Land Area: 109,893 sq. mi.

Adaven F-5
Alamo G-5
Arden Pg. 113, G-1
Ash Springs G-5
Austin D-4
Babbitt E-2
Baker E-6
Battle Mountain C-4
Beatty H-4
Beowawe C-4
Blue Diamond J-5
Boulder City J-6
Bracken Pg. 113, E-3
Bunkerville H-6
Cactus Springs H-5
Cal Nev Ari J-6
Caliente G-6
Carlin C-5
Carp G-6
Carson City E-1
Carver's E-3
Caselton F-6
Cherry Creek D-6
Coaldale F-3
Cold Spring D-3
Contact A-6
Crescent Valley C-4
Currant E-5
Currie C-6
Deeth B-5
Duckwater E-5
Dyer F-3
Eagle Picher Mine C-2
East Ely E-6
East Las Vegas Pg. 113, E-6
Elko C-5
Ely E-6
Empire C-2
Eureka D-5
Fallon D-2
Fernley D-2
Frenchman E-3
Gabbs E-3
Gerlach C-2
Glendale H-6
Golconda B-3
Gold Point G-3
Goldfield G-3
Goodsprings J-5
Halleck B-5
Hawthorne E-2
Henderson J-6
Vicinity Pg. 113, G-6
Hiko G-5
Imlay C-3
Indian Springs H-5
Ione E-3
Jack Creek B-5
Jackpot A-6
Jarbridge A-5
Jean J-5
Jiggs C-5
Kimberly E-5
Lage's D-6
Lamoille C-5
Las Vegas J-5
Vicinity Pg. 113
Las Vegas Beach Pg. 113, E-9
Lee C-5
Lida G-3
Lovelock C-2
Lund E-6
Luning F-3
Major's Place E-6
McDermitt A-3
McGill D-6
Mercury H-5
Mesquite H-6
Midas B-4
Middle Gate E-3
Mill City C-3
Mina F-3
Moapa H-6
Montello B-6
Mountain City A-5
Nelson J-6
Nixon D-2
North Las Vegas J-6
Vicinity Pg. 113, B-3
Nyala F-5
Oasis B-6
Oreana C-3
Orovada B-3
Overton H-6
Owyhee A-5
Panaca G-6
Paradise Valley B-3
Pioche F-6
Pittman Pg. 113, F-7
Preston E-6
Rachel G-5
Reno D-1
Round Mt. E-4
Ruby Valley C-5
Ruth E-5
Sandy J-5
Schurz E-2
Scotty's Jct. G-4
Searchlight K-6
Shantytown C-5
Silver City D-2
Silver Peak F-3
Silver Springs D-2
Sloan J-5
Sparks D-2
Sulphur B-2
Sutcliffe D-1
Thousand Springs B-6
Tonopah F-3
Tuscarora B-4
Unionville C-3
Ursine F-6
Valmy C-4
Victory Village Pg. 113, F-8
Virginia City D-2
Wadsworth D-2
Warm Springs F-4
Weed Heights E-2
Wellington E-2
Wells B-6
Winnemucca B-3
Yerington E-2

NEW HAMPSHIRE
Page 55

Population: 920,610
Capital: Concord
Land Area: 8,993 sq. mi.

Albany E-6
Allenstown H-6
Alstead H-3
Alton G-6
Alton Bay G-6
Amherst J-5
Andover G-5
Antrim J-4
Ashland F-5
Ashuelot K-3
Atkinson J-6
Auburn J-6
Barnstead H-6
Bartlett E-6
Bath E-4
Bayside J-7
Bedford J-5
Belmont G-5
Bennington J-4
Berlin D-6
Bethlehem D-5
Boscawen H-5
Bow Center H-5
Bradford H-4
Brentwood J-6
Bretton Woods E-5
Bridgewater G-5
Bristol G-5
Brookfield G-6
Brookline K-5
Canaan G-4
Canaan Center F-4
Candia J-6
Carroll D-5
Cascade D-6
Center Conway E-6
Center Ossipee F-6
Charlestown H-3
Cheever F-4
Chester J-6
Chesterfield J-3
Chichester H-5
Chocorua F-6
Cilleyville G-4
Claremont G-4
Coburn G-6
Cold River H-3
Colebrook B-5
Columbia B-5
Concord H-5
Contoocook H-5
Conway E-6
Coos Junction D-5
Cornish City G-3
Cornish Flat G-3
Crystal C-6
Danbury G-5
Davisville H-5
Derry J-6
Derry Village J-6
Dixville B-6
Dorchester F-4
Dover H-7
Drewsville H-3
Dublin J-4
Dummer C-6
Durham H-7
East Alton G-6
East Barrington H-6
East Grafton G-4
East Hebron F-5
East Kingston J-6
East Lempster H-3
East Madison F-6
Easton E-5
Eaton Center F-6
Effingham Falls F-6
Elkins G-4
Epping J-6
Epsom H-6
Epsom Four Corners H-6
Errol C-6
Exeter J-7
Fabyan D-5
Farmington G-7
Fish Market G-4
Francestown J-4
Franconia D-5
Franklin G-5
Freedom F-6
Fremont J-6
Gerrish H-5
Gilford G-6
Gilmans Corner F-4
Gilmanton G-6
Gilsum J-4
Glen E-6
Glen House D-6
Glendale G-5
Goffs Falls J-5
Goffstown J-5
Gorham D-6
Goshen H-4
Gossville H-6
Grafton G-4
Grantham G-4
Greenfield J-4
Greenville K-4
Groton F-4
Groveton C-5
Guild G-4
Guildhall C-5
Hampton J-7
Hampton Beach J-7
Hancock J-4
Hanover F-4
Hanover Center F-4
Harts Location E-6
Haverhill E-4
Hebron F-4
Henniker H-5
Hillsborough H-4
Hinsdale J-3
Hooksett H-6
Hopkinton H-5
Hoyts Corner H-4
Hudson K-6
Jackson D-6
Jaffrey J-4
James City H-6
Jefferson D-5
Jefferson Highlands D-5
Keene J-3
Kensington J-7
Kidderville B-5
Kingston J-6
Laconia G-5
Lancaster D-5
Laskey Corner G-7
Leavitts Hill H-6
Lebanon G-4
Lincoln E-5
Lisbon E-4
Little Boars Head J-7
Littleton D-5
Loudon H-5
Lower Shaker Village G-4
Lower Village J-3
Lyme F-4
Lyme Center F-4
Madbury H-7
Madison F-6
Manchester J-5
Marlborough J-4
Marlow H-4
Martin J-6
Mason K-5
Meadows D-5
Meredith F-5
Meriden G-3
Merrimack J-5
Milan C-6
Milford J-5
Milton G-6
Mirror Lake F-6
Monroe D-4
Mont Vernon J-5
Moultonborough F-6
Moultonville F-6
Mount Sunapee H-4
Munsonville J-4
Nashua K-5
New Durham G-6
New Hampton G-5
New Ipswich K-4
New London G-4
New Rye H-6
Newbury H-4
Newfields J-7
Newington H-7
Newmarket J-7
Newport H-4
Newton J-7
North Chatham D-6
North Conway E-6
North Grantham G-4
North Groton F-5
North Haverhill E-4
North Rochester H-6
North Sandwich F-6
North Stratford C-5
North Sutton H-4
North Wakefield G-6
North Woodstock E-5
Northfield G-5
Northumberland C-5
Northwood H-6
Orford F-4
Orfordville F-4
Ossipee F-6
Otterville G-4
Pages Corner H-5
Parker J-5
Pearls Corner H-5
Pelham K-6
Pembroke H-5
Penacook H-5
Peterborough J-4
Pinardville J-5
Pittsburg B-6
Pittsfield H-6
Plainfield G-3
Plaistow J-6
Plymouth F-5
Portsmouth H-7
Potter Place G-4
Province Lake F-7
Randolph D-6
Raymond J-6
Redstone E-6
Richmond K-3
Rindge K-4
Riverton D-5
Rochester H-6
Rollinsford H-7
Rumney F-5
Rye J-7
Rye Beach J-7
Salem J-6
Salisbury H-5
Sanbornton G-5
Sanbornville G-7
Sandwich F-6
Seabrook Beach J-7
Sharon J-4
Shelburne D-6
Somersworth H-7
South Acworth H-4
South Cornish G-3
South Danbury G-5
South Stoddard J-4
South Weare J-5
Spofford J-3
Springfield G-4
Squantum J-4
Stark C-6
Stewartstown B-6
Stoddard H-4
Stratford C-5
Stratham J-7
Sunapee G-4
Surry J-3
Sutton H-4
Swiftwater E-4
Tamworth F-6
Temple J-4
Thornton F-5
Tilton G-5
Trapshire H-3
Troy J-4
Tuftonboro F-6
Twin Mountain D-5
Union G-6
Wakefield G-7
Wallis Sands J-7
Walpole J-3
Warner H-5
Warren F-4
Washington H-4
Weare J-5
Wendell H-4
Wentworth F-4
Wentworths Location B-6
West Campton F-5
West Lebanon F-4
West Milan C-6
West Ossipee F-6
West Rindge K-4
West Rumney F-5
West Stewartstown B-5
West Swanzey J-4
Westmoreland J-3
Westville J-6
Willey House E-5
Wilton J-5
Winchester J-3
Windsor H-4
Winnisquam G-5
Wolfeboro G-6
Wonalancet F-6
Woodman F-7
Woodsville E-4

NEW JERSEY
Pages 56-57

Population: 7,364,823
Capital: Trenton
Land Area: 7,468 sq. mi.

Absecon M-6
Adelphia H-7
Allamuchy C-5
Allendale Pg. 126, D-4
Allentown H-6
Alloway M-2
Alpha E-3
Alpine B-6
Vicinity Pg. 126, F-7
Andover C-5
Asbury Park G-8
Atlantic City N-7
Atlantic Highlands F-8
Atsion K-5
Audubon K-4
Vicinity Pg. 134, E-8
Audubon Park Pg. 134, F-7
Avalon P-5
Avenel Pg. 127, P-1
Baptistown F-4
Barnegat K-8
Barnegat Light K-8
Barrington Pg. 134, G-7
Bay Head H-8
Bay Point N-3
Bayonne E-8
Vicinity Pg. 127, M-4
Beach Haven M-7
Beachwood J-7
Bedminster E-5
Beesley Pt. N-5
Belleplain N-4
Belleville D-7
Vicinity Pg. 127, J-3
Bellmawr K-3
Vicinity Pg. 134, G-7
Belmar H-8
Belvidere D-3
Bergenfield C-8
Vicinity Pg. 126, F-6
Berlin K-4
Vicinity Pg. 134, G-10
Bernardsville D-6
Beverly H-4
Vicinity Pg. 134, C-10
Blairstown C-4
Blawenburg F-5
Bloomfield D-7
Vicinity Pg. 127, J-3
Bloomingdale C-7
Vicinity Pg. 126, D-1
Bloomsbury E-3
Boonton C-7
Bordentown H-5
Bound Brook F-6
Bradley Beach H-8
Branchville B-5
Bridgeboro Pg. 134, D-9
Bridgeport K-2
Vicinity Pg. 134, G-4
Bridgeton M-2
Brielle H-8
Brigantine N-6
Broadway D-4
Brooklawn Pg. 134, G-6
Browns Mills J-6
Budd Lake C-5
Buena M-4
Burlington H-4
Vicinity Pg. 134, B-11
Butler C-7
Buttzville D-4
Caldwell Pg. 127, H-1
Califon E-5
Camden J-3
Vicinity Pg. 134, E-6
Cape May Q-4
Cape May Court House Q-4
Carls Corner M-3
Carneys Pt. L-1
Carteret E-6
Vicinity Pg. 127, P-2
Cassville H-7
Cedar Bridge K-7
Cedar Grove J-8
Vicinity Pg. 126, G-2
Cedarville N-3
Centerton M-3
Vicinity Pg. 134, C-10
Chatham D-6
Chatsworth K-6
Cherry Hill J-4
Vicinity Pg. 134, E-8
Chesilhurst K-4
Chester D-5
Cinnaminson J-4
Vicinity Pg. 134, C-9
Clark Pg. 127, N-1
Clarksburg H-6
Clarksville G-5
Clayton L-3
Clermont P-5
Cliffside Park Pg. 127, J-6
Clifton D-8
Vicinity Pg. 126, H-3
Clinton E-4
Closter Pg. 126, E-7
Coffins Corner Pg. 134, G-9
Colesville A-5
Collingswood J-3
Vicinity Pg. 134, F-7
Colonia Pg. 127, P-1
Colts Neck G-7
Columbus H-5
Colwick Pg. 134, E-8
Corbin City N-5
Coxs Corner Pg. 134, F-10
Cranbury G-6
Cranford Pg. 127, M-1
Cresskill B-6
Vicinity Pg. 126, F-7
Crestwood Village J-7
Croton F-4
Cumberland N-4
Deacons J-5
Vicinity Pg. 134, C-11
Deerfield M-3
Delaware C-3
Denville C-6
Dividing Creek N-3
Dover C-6
Dumont Pg. 126, F-6
Dunellen E-6
East Orange D-7
Vicinity Pg. 127, J-3
East Rutherford Pg. 127, H-4
East Vineland M-4
Eatontown G-8
Edgewater Park J-4
Edinburg G-5
Edison F-6
Egg Harbor M-6
Elizabeth E-7
Vicinity Pg. 127, M-3
Elmer L-3
Elmwood Park Pg. 126, G-4
Elwood M-5
Emerson Pg. 126, E-6
Englewood C-9
Vicinity Pg. 126, G-7
Englewood Cliffs A-6
Vicinity Pg. 126, B-1
Englishtown G-7
Estell Manor N-5
Everittstown E-4
Ewingville G-5
Fair Haven G-8
Vicinity Pg. 126, G-1
Fair Lawn C-8
Vicinity Pg. 126, F-4
Fairmount D-5
Fairton N-3
Farmingdale H-7
Flemington F-4
Florham Park D-7
Folsom L-4
Vicinity Pg. 127, Q-1
Forked River K-8
Fort Dix J-6
Fort Lee D-9
Vicinity Pg. 126, H-6
Four Mile F-6
Franklin B-6
Franklin Lakes Pg. 126, D-3
Franklinville L-3
Fredon C-5
Freehold G-7
Freewood Acres H-7
Frenchtown F-4
Garfield C-8
Vicinity Pg. 126, G-4
Garwood Pg. 127, M-1
Gibbsboro K-4
Vicinity Pg. 134, F-9
Gilford Park J-8
Glassboro L-3
Glen Gardner E-4
Vicinity Pg. 134, F-8
Glen Rock Pg. 126, E-4
Glendale Pg. 134, G-8
Glenwood A-6
Gloucester City K-3
Vicinity Pg. 134, G-6
Gouldtown M-3
Great Meadows D-4
Green Bank K-6
Guttenberg Pg. 127, J-5
Hackensack C-8
Vicinity Pg. 126, G-6
Hackettstown D-4
Haddon Heights Pg. 134, G-7
Haddonfield K-4
Vicinity Pg. 134, F-8
Hainesburg C-4
Haledon C-7
Vicinity Pg. 126, F-3
Hamburg B-6
Hamilton Sq. G-6
Hammonton L-5
Hampton E-4
Hanover D-6
Harmony D-3
Harrington Park Pg. 126, E-6
Harrison Pg. 127, K-4
Harrisonville L-1
Harvey Cedars L-8
Hasbrouck Hts Pg. 126, G-5
Hawthorne C-8
Vicinity Pg. 126, F-3
Helmetta G-7
Hewitt A-6
Vicinity Pg. 126, B-1
High Bridge E-4
Highland Park F-7
Highlands F-9
Hightstown G-6
Hillsdale B-6
Vicinity Pg. 126, D-5
Ho-Ho-Kus Pg. 126, E-4
Hoboken D-8
Vicinity Pg. 127, K-5
Holmdel G-7
Hopatcong C-5
Hope C-4
Hopewell F-5
Hurdtown C-6
Irvington D-7
Vicinity Pg. 127, L-2
Iselin Pg. 127, P-1
Island Heights J-8
J-3myra Pg. 134, D-7
Jamesburg G-6
Jersey City D-8
Vicinity Pg. 127, L-5
Johnsonburg C-4
Keansburg F-8
Kearny D-8
Vicinity Pg. 127, K-4
Kenilworth E-7
Keyport F-8
Kinnelon C-6
Vicinity Pg. 134, F-9
Kresson Pg. 134, G-10
Lafayette B-5
Lakehurst J-7
Lakeside B-7
Lakewood H-7
Lambertville G-4
Larisons Cor. F-4
Laurence Harbor F-7
Lavallette J-8
Lawnside Pg. 134, G-8
Lawrence G-5
Lebanon E-5
Lenola E-4
Vicinity Pg. 134, D-9
Liberty Cor. E-6
Lincoln Park C-7
Vicinity Pg. 126, F-1
Linden E-7
Vicinity Pg. 127, N-2
Lindenwold K-4
Vicinity Pg. 134, G-9
Linwood N-6
Little Egg Harbor M-7
Little Falls Pg. 126, G-2
Little Ferry Pg. 126, H-5
Livingston Pg. 127, J-1
Lodi Pg. 126, G-4
Long Branch G-9
Long Valley D-5
Longport N-6
Lumberton J-5
Lyndhurst Pg. 127, J-4
Madison D-6
Magnolia F-4
Vicinity Pg. 134, G-8
Mahwah A-6
Vicinity Pg. 126, C-4
Manahawkin L-7
Manalapan G-6
Manasquan H-8
Mantoloking J-8
Manville F-6
Maple Shade J-3
Maplewood Pg. 127, K-2
Marcella C-6
Margate City N-6
Marlboro G-7
Marlton E-4
Vicinity Pg. 134, F-10
Marshallville N-5
Matawan F-7
Maurice River P-4
Mays Landing M-5
Maywood Pg. 126, G-5
McAfee B-6
Medford J-5
Medford Lakes K-5
Mendham D-6
Merchantville Pg. 134, E-7
Metuchen E-7
Mickleton K-3
Vicinity Pg. 134, G-6
Midland Park Pg. 126, E-4
Milford E-3
Millside Heights Pg. 134, D-9
Millstone F-6
Milltown F-6
Millville N-3
Monmouth Jct. G-6
Monroe G-6
Montague A-5
Montvale Pg. 126, D-5
Montville C-7
Moorestown J-4
Vicinity Pg. 134, E-8
Morris Pg. 134, E-7
Morris Plains D-6
Morristown D-6
Morrisville E-3
Vicinity Pg. 134, D-8
Mt. Arlington C-6
Mt. Ephraim Pg. 134, G-6
Mt. Holly J-5
Mt. Laurel Pg. 134, F-10
Mullica Hill L-3
National Park K-3
Vicinity Pg. 134, G-5
Neptune H-8
Neshanic F-5
Netcong C-5
New Brunswick F-6
New Egypt J-6
New Gretna E-6
New Providence E-6
New Rochelle Pg. 126, G-5
Newark D-8
Vicinity Pg. 127, K-3
Newfield M-4
Newfoundland B-6
Newton B-5
North Arlington Pg. 127, J-4
North Bergen Pg. 127, J-6
North Caldwell Pg. 126, G-2
North Cape May Q-4
North Dennis P-4
North Haledon C-7
Vicinity Pg. 126, F-3
North Wildwood Q-5
Northfield N-6
Northvale Pg. 126, D-7
Norwood C-9
Vicinity Pg. 127, E-7
Nutley D-8
Vicinity Pg. 127, H-3
Oakland Pg. 126, D-2
Oaklyn Pg. 134, F-7
Ocean City N-6
Ocean Gate J-8
Oceanport G-8
Ogdensburg B-5
Old Bridge F-7
Old Tappan C-8
Vicinity Pg. 126, D-6
Oldwick E-5
Oradell Pg. 126, F-6
Orange D-7
Vicinity Pg. 127, K-2
Oxford D-4
Palisades Park Pg. 126, H-6
Paramus C-8
Vicinity Pg. 126, F-5
Park Ridge Pg. 126, D-5
Parsippany-Troy Hill D-6
Passaic D-8
Vicinity Pg. 126, H-4
Paterson C-7
Patterson B-6
Vicinity Pg. 126, F-3
Paulsboro K-2
Peapack E-5
Pemberton J-5
Pennington G-5
Penns Grove L-2
Pennsauken E-3
Vicinity Pg. 134, E-7
Pennsville L-1
Penny Pot M-5
Pequannock Pg. 126, F-1
Perth Amboy F-7
Vicinity Pg. 127, Q-2
Phillipsburg E-3
Pine Beach Pg. 126, H-1
Pine Hill K-4
Vicinity Pg. 134, G-9
Pitman L-3
Pittstown E-4
Plainfield E-6
Plainsboro G-6
Pleasantville N-6
Pole Tavern L-3
Pomona M-6
Pompton Lakes C-7
Vicinity Pg. 126, D-1
Pompton Plains B-6
Vicinity Pg. 126, E-1
Port Elizabeth N-4
Port Norris P-4
Port Reading Pg. 127, P-2
Port Republic M-6
Princeton G-5
Princeton Jct. G-6
Prospect Park C-8
Pt. Pleasant H-8
Pt. Pleasant Beach H-8
Quinton M-2
Rahway E-7
Vicinity Pg. 127, N-2
Ramsey Pg. 126, C-4
Raritan E-5
Readington E-5
Reaville F-5
Red Bank G-8
Vicinity Pg. 134, G-5
Red Lion K-5
Ridgefield Pg. 127, H-6
Ridgefield Park Pg. 126, G-6
Ridgewood C-8
Vicinity Pg. 126, E-4
Ringwood B-7
Vicinity Pg. 126, B-2
Rio Grande Q-4
River Vale B-6
Vicinity Pg. 126, E-6
Riverdale C-7
Vicinity Pg. 134, C-9
Riverside J-4
Riverton J-4
Vicinity Pg. 134, D-8
Robertsville G-7
Rock Leigh Pg. 126, E-7
Rockaway C-6
Rocky Hill F-5
Roosevelt H-6
Roseland Pg. 127, H-1
Roselle E-7
Vicinity Pg. 127, M-2
Roselle Park E-7
Vicinity Pg. 127, M-2
Ross Corners B-5
Rumson G-8
Runnemede K-3
Vicinity Pg. 134, G-7
Rutherford Pg. 127, H-4
Saddle Brook Pg. 126, G-5

NEW JERSEY

NEW MEXICO
Page 62

Population: 1,302,894
Capital: Santa Fe
Land Area: 121,335 sq. mi.

NEW YORK
Pages 58-61

Population: 17,558,072
Capital: Albany
Land Area: 47,377 sq. mi.

NORTH CAROLINA

NORTH DAKOTA
Page 63

Population: 652,717
Capital: Bismarck
Land Area: 69,300 sq. mi.

OHIO

OHIO
Pages 66-67

Population: 10,797,630
Capital: Columbus
Land Area: 41,004 sq. mi.

OKLAHOMA
Pages 68-69

Population: 3,025,487
Capital: Oklahoma City
Land Area: 68,655 sq. mi.

RHODE ISLAND
Page 25

Population: 947,154
Capital: Providence
Land Area: 1,055 sq. mi.

SOUTH CAROLINA
Pages 64-65

Population: 3,121,820
Capital: Columbia
Land Area: 30,203 sq. mi.

SOUTH DAKOTA
Page 74

Population: 690,768
Capital: Pierre
Land Area: 75,952 sq. mi.

SOUTH DAKOTA

TENNESSEE
Pages 38-39
Population: 4,591,120
Capital: Nashville
Land Area: 41,155 sq. mi.

TEXAS
Pages 75-79
Population: 14,229,191
Capital: Austin
Land Area: 262,017 sq. mi.

TEXAS

Perrin F-12
Perry J-13
Perryton A-9
Petersburg E-8
Petrolia E-12
Pettus N-12
Petty E-15
Pflugerville K-13
Phalba G-15
Pharr S-12
Phillips B-7
Pilot Point F-13
Pine Mills G-16
Pinehurst K-17
Pineland J-17
Pioneer H-11
Pipecreek L-11
Pittsburg F-16
Placedo N-14
Plains F-6
Plano F-14
Vicinity Pg. 105, A-10
Plantersville K-15
Plata L-4
Pleasanton N-12
Point Comfort N-14
Pollok J-16
Ponder F-13
Ponta H-16
Pontotoc K-11
Poolville F-12
Port O' Connor N-14
Port Aransas P-13
Port Arthur L-17
Port Bolivar L-16
Port Isabel S-13
Port Lavaca N-14
Port Mansfield R-13
Port Neches L-17
Porter L-16
Portland P-13
Posey F-8
Post F-8
Poteet N-11
Poth M-12
Pottsboro E-14
Pottsville H-12
Powderly E-15
Powell H-14
Poynor H-15
Prairie Dell K-13
Prairie Hill H-14
Prairie Lea L-13
Prairie View L-15
Premont Q-12
Presidio L-4
Priddy H-11
Princeton F-14
Pritchett G-16
Proctor H-12
Prosper F-14
Purmela J-12
Putnam G-11
Pyote H-5
Quail C-9
Quanah D-10
Queen City F-17
Quemado N-9
Quinlan G-14
Quitaque D-8
Quitman G-15
Rachal R-12
Ralls E-8
Ramirez Q-12
Randado Q-11
Randlett Charlie E-12
Randolph F-14
Ranger G-11
Rankin J-7
Ratcliff J-16
Ravenna E-14
Rayland E-10
Raymondville R-12
Raywood L-17
Reagan J-14
Realitos Q-11
Red Oak G-13
Red Oak Pg. 105, G-9
Red Springs E-10
Redford M-4
Reese Vill. E-7
Refugio P-13
Reklaw H-16
Reno E-15
Retta Pg. 104, G-4
Rhome F-13
Ricardo Q-12
Rice H-14
Richardson F-13
Vicinity Pg. 105, A-9
Richland G-14
Richland Hills Pg. 104, C-4
Richland Springs J-11
Richmond L-15
Richwood M-16
Ridge J-14
Riesel J-13
Ringgold E-12
Rio Grande City R-11
Rio Vista H-13
Riomendina M-11
Rios Q-12
Rising Star H-11
River Oaks Pg. 104, D-2
Riverside K-15
Riviera Q-12
Roans Prairie K-15
Robbins J-15
Robert Lee H-9
Robinson H-13
Robstown P-13
Roby G-9
Rochelle J-11
Rochester F-10
Rock Island M-14
Rockdale K-14
Rockland J-17
Rockport P-13
Rocksprings L-9
Rockwood J-10
Roganville K-17
Rogers K-13
Roma R-10
Romayor K-16
Roosevelt K-9
Ropesville F-7
Rosanky L-13
Roscoe G-9
Rosebud J-14
Rosenberg M-15
Rosevine J-17
Rosser G-14
Rotan G-9
Round Mountain K-12
Round Rock K-13
Round Top L-14
Rowena H-9
Roxton E-15
Royalty J-6
Rule F-10
Runge M-12
Rusk H-16
Rye K-16
Sabinal M-10
Sacul H-16
Sadler E-14
Sagerton F-10
Saginaw G-13
Vicinity Pg. 104, C-2
Saint Hedwig M-12
Saint Jo E-13
Salado J-13
Salt Falt H-3
Samnorwood C-9
San Angelo J-9
San Antonio M-12
Vicinity Pg. 142
San Augustine H-17
San Benito S-13
San Diego P-12
San Elizario H-1
San Felipe L-14
San Gabriel K-13
San Isidro R-11
San Juan R-12
San Marcus L-12
San Patricio P-12
San Perlita R-13
San Saba J-11
San Ygnacio Q-10
Sanderson L-6
Sandia P-12
Sanford B-8
Sanger F-13
Sansom Park Pg. 104, C-2
Santa Anna H-11
Santa Elena R-12
Santa Fe L-15
Santa Maria S-12
Santa Rosa S-12
Saragosa J-5
Saratoga K-17
Sarita Q-12
Satsuma Pg. 108, B-2
Savoy E-14
Schertz M-12
Schulenburg L-14
Scotland E-11
Scottsville G-17
Scranton G-11
Seabrook L-16
Vicinity Pg. 109, G-10
Seadrift N-14
Seagraves F-6
Sealy L-14
Sebastian R-13
Sebastopol K-16
Segovia K-10
Seguin M-12
Seminole G-6
Seven Points G-14
Seymour E-11
Shafter L-4
Shallowater E-7
Shamrock C-9
Shannon F-12
Shavano Park Pg. 142, A-4
Sheffield K-7
Shelbyville H-17
Sheldon L-16
Vicinity Pg. 109, C-8
Sheridan M-14
Sherman F-14
Sherwood J-9
Shiner M-13
Shiro K-15
Shoreacres Pg. 109, F-10
Sidney H-11
Sierra Blanca J-3
Silsbee K-17
Silver H-9
Silverton D-8
Simms F-16
Singleton K-15
Sinton P-13
Sisterdale L-11
Sivells Bend E-13
Skellytown B-8
Skidmore P-12
Slaton F-8
Slidell F-13
Slocum H-16
Smada Pg. 108, F-3
Smiley M-13
Smyer E-7
Snook K-14
Snyder G-8
Socorro H-1
Somerset M-11
Vicinity Pg. 142, J-1
Somerville K-14
Sonora K-9
Sour Lake L-17
South Bend F-11
South Houston Pg. 109, E-7
South Padre Island S-13
South Plains D-8
Southlake Pg. 104, B-5
Southland F-7
Southton Pg. 142, H-6
Spade E-7
Spanish Fort E-12
Speaks M-14
Spearman B-8
Spicewood K-12
Splendora L-16
Spofford M-9
Spring L-15
Spring Branch L-11
Spring Valley Pg. 108, C-3
Springlake D-7
Springtown F-12
Spur F-9
Spurger K-17
Stafford M-15
Vicinity Pg. 108, F-3
Stamford F-10
Stanton H-7
Star J-12
Stephenville H-12
Sterling City H-8
Stinnett B-8
Stockdale M-12
Stoneburg E-12
Stoneham K-15
Stonwall L-11
Stowell L-16
Stratford A-7
Strawn G-11
Streetman H-14
Study Butte M-5
Sudan E-7
Sugar Land L-15
Vicinity Pg. 108, F-2
Sullivan City S-11
Sulphur Sprs. F-15
Summerfield D-6
Sumner E-15
Sundown F-6
Sunray B-8
Sunset F-13
Sutherland Springs M-12
Sweeny M-15
Sweetwater G-9
Swenson F-9
Swenson F-9
Taft P-13
Tahoka F-7
Talco F-16
Talpa H-10
Tankersley J-9
Tarpley M-10
Tarzan G-7
Tatum G-17
Taylor K-13
Taylor Lake Village Pg. 109, F-9
Teague H-14
Telegraph K-9
Telephone E-15
Telferner N-14
Tell D-9
Temple J-13
Tenaha H-17
Tenneseee Colony H-15
Tennyson H-9
Terlingua M-5
Terrell G-14
Terrell Hills Pg. 142, D-5
Texarkana F-17
Texas City M-16
Texhoma A-8
Texico D-6
Texline A-6
Thackerville E-13
Thalia E-10
The Grove J-13
The Woodlands L-15
Thelma Pg. 142, K-5
Thomaston M-13
Thorndale K-13
Thornton J-14
Thorp Spring G-12
Thrall K-13
Three Rivers N-12
Throckmorton F-10
Tilden N-11
Timpson H-17
Tioga F-13
Tira F-15
Tivoli N-14
Toco E-15
Tolar G-12
Tomball K-15
Tool H-14
Topsey J-12
Tornillo H-1
Toyah J-5
Trammells Pg. 108, G-4
Trent G-10
Trenton F-14
Trickham H-11
Trinidad H-15
Trinity J-15
Troup H-16
Troy J-13
Tucker H-15
Tuleta N-13
Tulia D-7
Turkey D-9
Turnertown H-16
Tuscola H-10
Twin Sisters L-12
Twitty C-9
Tye G-10
Tyler G-16
Tynan P-12
Umbarger C-7
Unity E-15
Universal City M-12
University Park Pg. 105, C-9
Utopia M-10
Uvalde M-10
Valentine K-4
Valera H-10
Valley Mills H-13
Valley Spring K-11
Valley View F-13
Van G-15
Van Alstyne F-14
Van Horn J-3
Van Vleck M-15
Vancourt J-9
Vanderbilt N-14
Vanderpool L-10
Vashti E-12
Vealmoor G-8
Vega C-7
Venus G-13
Vera E-10
Vernon E-11
Victoria N-13
Vidor L-17
Village Mills K-17
Vincent G-8
Voca J-11
Von Ormy Pg. 142, H-2
Voss H-10
Votaw K-17
Waco H-13
Wadsworth N-15
Waelder L-13
Waka A-9
Wake Village E-17
Wall J-9
Waller L-15
Wallis L-14
Walnut Sprs. H-13
Warda L-13
Warren K-17
Washington K-15
Waskom G-17
Water Valley H-9
Watson K-12
Watsonville Pg. 104, F-5
Waxahachie G-14
Wayside D-8
Weatherford G-12
Weaver F-15
Webster M-16
Vicinity Pg. 109, G-8
Weches J-16
Weesatche N-13
Weimar L-14
Weinort F-10
Welch F-7
Wellington D-9
Wellman F-7
Wells J-16
Weslaco S-12
West H-13
West Columbia M-15
West Orange K-17
West Point L-13
Westbrook G-8
Westfield L-15
Westhoff M-13
Westlake Pg. 104, A-4
Westover F-11
Westworth Pg. 104, D-2
Wharton M-15
Wheeler C-9
Wheeler G-15
Wheelock K-14
White Deer C-8
Whiteface E-6
Whiteflat E-9
Whitehouse G-15
Whitesboro E-13
Whitewright F-14
Whitharral E-7
Whitney H-13
Whittsett N-12
Wichita Falls E-12
Wickett H-5
Wiergate J-18
Wildorado C-7
Wildwood K-17
Wilkinson F-16
Willow City K-11
Wills Point G-15
Wilmer Pg. 105, F-10
Wilson F-8
Wimberly L-12
Winchell J-11
Windcrest Pg. 142, C-7
Windhorst E-12
Windom F-15
Winfield F-16
Wingate H-9
Wink H-5
Winnie L-17
Winnsboro F-15
Winona G-16
Winters H-9
Wolfe City F-15
Wolfforth F-7
Woodlake J-16
Woodland Hills Pg. 105, F-8
Woodlawn G-17
Woodsboro P-13
Woodson F-11
Woodville K-17
Woodward N-10
Wortham H-14
Yoakum M-13
Yorktown M-13
Zavalla J-17
Zephyr H-11
Zorn L-12

UTAH

Pages 80-81

Population: 1,461,037
Capital: Salt Lake City
Land Area: 82,073 sq. mi.

Abraham H-4
Adamsville K-4
Alpine F-5
Alta F-6
Altamont F-8
Alton L-4
American Fork F-5
Aneth M-9
Angle K-5
Annabella J-5
Antimony K-5
Arcadia F-8
Aurora J-5
Austin J-5
Axtell H-5
Bacchus Pg. 141, K-2
Bear River City D-5
Beaver K-4
Benjamin F-5
Beryl K-2
Bicknell K-5
Birdseye G-6
Black Rock J-4
Blanding L-9
Blue Cr. C-4
Bluebell F-8
Bluff L-9
Bluffdale F-5
Bonanza G-9
Boneta F-7
Boulder K-6
Bountiful E-5
Vicinity Pg. 141, F-6
Brian Head L-4
Bridgeland F-8
Brigham City D-5
Bryce Canyon L-4
Burmester E-4
Burrville J-5
Cannonville L-4
Carbonville G-7
Castle Dale H-7
Castle Rock E-6
Cave C-5
Cedar City L-3
Cedar Creek C-3
Cedar Fort F-5
Cedar Springs D-4
Cedarview F-8
Center Creek F-6
Centerfield H-5
Centerville E-5
Central J-5
Central L-2
Charleston F-6
Chester H-5
Circleville K-4
Cisco J-9
Clarkston C-5
Clawson H-6
Clear Creek C-3
Clearcreek G-6
Clearfield E-5
Cleveland H-7
Clinton D-5
Clover F-4
Coalville E-6
Colton G-7
Corinne D-5
Cornish C-5
Cove Fort J-4
Crescent Jct. J-8
Croydon E-6
Delle E-4
Delta H-4
Deseret H-4
Desert Mound L-3
Dividend G-5
Draper F-5
Duchesne F-8
Dugway F-4
East Carbon City H-8
East Mill Creek Pg. 141, J-7
Eastland L-9
Echo E-6
Elberta G-5
Elmo H-7
Elsinore J-5
Emery J-6
Enoch L-3
Enterprise L-2
Ephraim H-6
Escalante L-5
Etna D-2
Eureka G-5
Fairfield F-5
Fairview G-6
Farmington E-5
Faust F-4
Fayette H-5
Ferron H-6
Fillmore H-5
Fish Springs G-3
Flowell H-4
Fort Duchesne F-8
Fountain Green G-5
Francis F-6
Freedom G-5
Fremont J-6
Fremont Jct. J-6
Fruit Heights E-5
Fruitland F-7
Fry Canyon L-8
Gandy G-2
Garden City C-6
Garrison H-2
Geneva F-5
Genola G-5
Glendale L-4
Glenwood J-5
Goshen G-5
Grantsville E-4
Green Lake E-9
Green River H-8
Greenville K-4
Greenwich J-5
Greenwood H-4
Grouse Creek C-2
Gunlock L-2
Gunnison H-5
Gusher F-8
Hamilton Fort L-3
Hanksville K-7
Hanna F-7
Harrisville D-5
Hatch L-4
Hatton J-4
Heber City F-6
Helper G-7
Henefer E-6
Henrieville L-5
Hiawatha H-6
Hinckley H-4
Holden H-5
Holladay F-5
Vicinity Pg. 141, K-7
Honeyville D-4
Hot Springs D-5
Howell C-4
Hoytsville E-6
Huntington H-7
Huntsville D-6
Hurricane M-3
Hyde Park C-5
Hyrum D-5
Indianola G-6
Ioka F-8
Iron Springs L-3
Ivins M-2
Jensen F-9
Jericho G-5
Joseph J-4
Junction K-4
Kamas F-6
Kanab M-4
Kanarraville L-3
Kanosh J-4
Kaysville E-5
Kelton D-4
Kenilworth G-7
Kimball Jct. E-6
Kingston K-5
Knolls E-3
Koosharem J-5
La Sal K-9
La Sal Jct. K-9
La Verkin L-3
Lake Pt. Jct. E-4
Lake Shore F-5
Lake View F-5
Laketown C-6
Lapoint F-8
Leamington H-5
Leeds L-3
Leeton F-8
Lehi F-5
Leota F-9
Levan G-5
Lewiston C-5
Loa J-6
Logan D-5
Long Valley Jct. L-4
Low E-3
Lucin D-2
Lund K-3
Lyman J-6
Lynndyl G-4
Maeser F-9
Magna F-5
Vicinity Pg. 141, J-2
Manderfield J-4
Manila E-8
Manti H-6
Mantua D-5
Mapleton F-6
Marion E-6
Marysvale J-4
Mayfield H-6
Meadow J-4
Meadowville C-6
Mendon D-5
Mexican Hat M-8
Midvale E-5
Midway F-6
Milburn G-6
Milford J-3
Mills H-5
Minersville K-3
Moab J-9
Modena K-2
Molen H-6
Mona G-5
Monarch F-8
Monroe J-5
Montezuma Creek M-9
Monticello K-9
Moore H-6
Morgan E-5
Moroni G-6
Mountain Home F-7
Mt. Carmel L-4
Mt. Carmel Jct. L-4
Mt. Emmons F-7
Mt. Pleasant G-6
Murray E-5
Myton F-8
N. Logan C-6
N. Salt Lake F-5
Vicinity Pg. 141, F-5
Naples F-9
Neola F-8
Nephi G-5
New Harmony L-3
Newcastle L-2
Newton C-5
Oak City H-5
Oakley E-6
Oasis H-4
Ogden D-5
Orangeville H-6
Orderville L-4
Orem F-6
Ouray F-9
Panguitch K-4
Paradise D-5
Paragonah K-4
Park City E-6
Park Valley C-3
Parowan K-4
Payson G-5
Peoa E-6
Perry Willard D-5
Pigeon Hollow Jct. H-6
Pine Valley L-2
Pintura L-3
Plain City D-5
Pleasant Grove F-6
Pleasant View D-5
Plymouth C-5
Portage C-5
Porterville E-6
Price G-7
Providence D-5
Provo F-6
Randolph D-6
Redmond H-5
Richfield J-5
Richmond C-5
Riverdale D-5
Riverton F-5
Rockville M-3
Roosevelt F-8
Rosette C-3
Rowley Jct. E-4
Roy E-5
Ruby's Inn L-4
Saint George M-3
Saint John Sta. F-4
Salem G-5
Salina H-5
Salt Lake City F-4
Vicinity Pg. 141
Sandy F-5
Santa Clara M-2
Santaquin G-5
Scipio H-5
Scofield G-6
Sevier J-4
Shivwits M-2
Sigurd J-5
Silver City G-5
Smithfield C-5
Smyths J-3
Snowville C-4
Soldier Summit G-7
South Jordan F-5
South Ogden D-5
South Salt Lake E-5
Vicinity Pg. 141, J-5
Spanish Fork F-6
Spring City H-6
Spring Lake G-5
Springdale M-3
Springville F-6
Sterling H-6
Stockton F-4
Summit K-3
Summit Pt. K-9
Sunnyside G-8
Sunset E-5
Sutherland H-4
Syracuse E-5
Tabiona F-7
Talmage F-7
Teasdale K-6
Terrace D-6
Thistle G-6
Thompson H-9
Tooele F-4
Toquerville L-3
Torrey K-6
Tremonton D-5
Tropic L-5
Trout Cr. G-2
Tucker G-6
Upalco F-8
Uvada L-2
Venice J-5
Vernal F-9
Veyo L-2
Virgin M-3
W. Valley City E-5
Wahsatch D-6
Wales H-5
Wanship E-6
Washington M-3
Washington Terrace D-5
Wellington G-7
Wellsville D-5
Wendover E-2
West Jordan F-5
West Point D-4
West Valley City F-5
Vicinity Pg. 141, J-4
Whiterocks F-8
Widtsoe Jct. K-5
Woodruff D-6
Woods Cross E-5
Vicinity Pg. 141, F-5
Woodside H-8
Zane K-2

VERMONT

Page 55

Population: 511,456
Capital: Montpelier
Land Area: 9,273 sq. mi.

Addison E-1
Albany C-3
Alburg B-1
Arlington J-1
Ascutney G-3
Averill B-5
Bakersfield B-2
Barnard F-3
Barnet D-4
Barre E-3
Barton C-4
Bellows Falls H-3
Bennington J-1
Bethel F-3
Bloomfield C-5
Bomoseen G-1
Bondville H-2
Bradford E-4
Brandon F-2
Brattleboro J-3
Bridgewater Cors. G-3
Bridport E-1
Bristol E-1
Broadford Cen. E-3
Brunswick Sprs. C-5
Burlington D-1
Cambridge J-1
Cambridgeport H-3
Canaan B-5
Castleton G-1
Charlotte D-1
Chelsea E-3
Chester H-3
Chester Depot H-3
Chimney Cor. C-2
Concord D-4
Cornwall E-1
Danby G-2
Dorset H-1
E. Barnet D-4
E. Berkshire B-2
E. Braintree E-3
E. Brookfield E-3
E. Burke C-4
E. Calais D-3
E. Dorset H-2
E. Fairfield C-2
E. Granville E-2
E. Hardwick D-3
E. Haven C-4
Eden C-3
Eden Mills C-3
Enosburg Falls B-2
Essex Jct. D-2
Fair Haven G-1
Fairfax C-2
Ferrisburg E-1
Franklin B-2
Gassetts H-3
Gaysville F-3
Glover C-4
Grafton H-3
Grand Isle C-1
Granville E-2
Groton E-4
Guilford J-3
Hancock F-2
Hardwick D-3
Heartwellville J-2
Hinesburg D-2
Holland B-4
Hubbardton F-1
Hyde Park C-3
Irasburg B-3
Irasville E-2
Island Pond C-4
Jacksonville J-2
Jamaica H-2
Jay B-3
Jeffersonville C-2
Johnson C-3
Lake Elmore C-3
Leicester F-2
Londonderry H-2
Lowell B-3
Ludlow G-2
Lunenberg D-5
Lyndon D-4
Lyndonville C-4
Maidstone C-5
Manchester H-2
Manchester Cen. H-2
Marlboro J-2
Marshfield D-3
Middlebury E-1
Middletown Sprs. G-1
Mill Village E-3

VIRGINIA
Pages 82-83
Population: 5,346,818
Capital: Richmond
Land Area: 39,703 sq. mi.

WASHINGTON
Pages 84-85
Population: 4,132,156
Capital: Olympia
Land Area: 66,511 sq. mi.

WEST VIRGINIA
Pages 82-83
Population: 1,949,644
Capital: Charleston
Land Area: 24,119 sq. mi.

WEST VIRGINIA

WISCONSIN
Pages 86-87

Population: 4,705,767
Capital: Madison
Land Area: 54,426 sq. mi.

WYOMING
Pages 88-89

Population: 469,559
Capital: Cheyenne
Land Area: 96,989 sq. mi.

VACATION DESTINATIONS

including Scenic Drives;
National Parks and Monuments;
Historic Villages; and Resorts

NORTHWEST

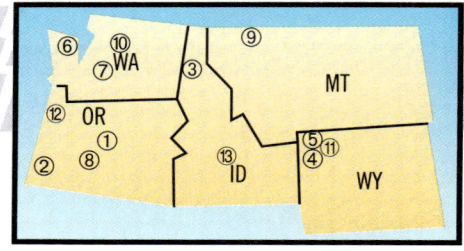

SCENIC DRIVES

▼1
Century Drive
Cascades Lakes Area, OR

This 100-mile tour begins at Bend, OR, on the banks of the Deschutes River. In the shadow of the Oregon Cascade Mountains, Bend is a year-round recreation center for fishing, hiking, boating, camping, and snow skiing. Amid high meadows and sparkling lakes that reflect snow-capped peaks, the route follows OR 46, west from US 97, crossing pathways used by early explorers, trappers, and hunters. In Deschutes National Forest, acres of pines captivate with their variations in size, density, and color. Ascending the rise at Bachelor Butte Wayside, you will have a magnificent view of Three Sisters and Broken Top peaks. This is the gateway to the Cascades Lakes Country where dormant volcanic peaks dominate the skyline. South is Dutchman Flat, a pumice desert surrounded by lush forest. Rising from the flatlands, motorists are greeted by summer wildflowers in a glade leading to Todd Lake, one of many alpine lakes in the region. Roosevelt elk, coyotes, and mink can be seen along the route. There are also numerous fishing spots—particularly good for trout, steelhead, and salmon.
*Deschutes Nat'l Forest, 1645 Hwy 20 East, Bend, OR 97701, **503/388-2715***

▼2
Coastal Cascades
Brookings–Bandon, OR (US 101)

Skirting the coastline from Santa Barbara, CA, to Olympia, WA, legendary US 101 offers more than a thousand miles of natural and man-made wonders. The 113 miles from Brookings to Bandon of this remarkable road follow the rugged coastline, taking motorists past green inland valleys and clear mountain lakes. Brookings, known as "Home of the Winter Flowers" because of its annual Azalea Festival, boasts beautiful beaches, charming art galleries, and seafood-brimming restaurants. The spectacular drive north to Bandon takes you past broad beaches and shifting sand dunes that hide glistening lakes. Kiteflying, crabbing, beachcombing, and fishing are the most popular shore activities. Storm-watching in winter draws spectators to witness crashing waves. Historic Oldtown, numerous gift and antique shops, and a cheddar cheese factory are in coastal Bandon, which also hosts a late September Cranberry Festival. Rock hounds often find agate, jasper, and other semiprecious stones along the beach. Eastbound via Rtes 42

and 138 are the Wildlife Safari in Winston, a drive-through wildlife preserve, and skiing at Diamond Lake.
*Tourism Division, 775 Summer St NE, Salem, OR 97310, **503/378-3451, 800/547-7842***

▼3
Idaho Escape
Lake Coeur d'Alene Area, ID

Idaho's northern panhandle is becoming a favorite destination because of its mountainous terrain, lava beds, sand dunes, ice caves, evergreen forests, and more than 2000 lakes. Following I-90 east from Coeur d'Alene, you'll enter the primitive woodlands of Coeur d'Alene National Forest, dominated by moderately steep to rugged mountains. At Old Mission State Park south of I-90, you can view Idaho's oldest standing building—a beautifully preserved church built by a Jesuit Missionary in the 1850s. Rte 3 runs south from I-90 winding through fertile farmlands and wooded foothills and near the Coeur d'Alene River—good for trout fishing in summer and fall. Farther south at St. Maries is the world's highest navigable river, the St. Joe. West of St. Maries, stretching for 6000 acres, are

the rolling hills of Heyburn State Park, bordering the shores of Chatcolet Lake. The year-round recreation center has camping, hiking, picnicking, swimming, and boating in summer; and cross-country skiing, snowmobiling, and ice fishing in winter. Two miles inside the park on Rte 5 is a splendid view of the St. Joe River.
*Idaho Travel Council, 700 W State St, State House Mail, Boise, ID 83720-2700, **208/334-2470***

Boardman State Park, OR

Sparks Lake, OR

Photo: State of Oregon Travel Information Section

NATIONAL PARKS & MONUMENTS

Grand Teton
Nat'l Park, WY

Soaring more than a mile above the sagebrush flats of Jackson Hole, the Teton Range is relatively young geologically and, therefore, extremely rugged. Trips down the Snake River are popular with experienced canoeists, although wet suits are advised. Over 200 miles of trails are maintained for hikers. Because of the mountains' ruggedness, mountaineering is a popular activity here. Experienced climbers need only register with park rangers. It is strongly suggested that novices be led by the park's experienced climb-tour leaders. Roads vary from paved to primitive. Major roads are cleared during winter. Numerous nature programs are offered. Five campgrounds are operated by the National Park Service from June to September.

Supt, Grand Teton Nat'l Park, PO Drawer 170, Moose, WY 83012, **307/733-2880**

Yellowstone
Nat'l Park, WY

In 1872 Congress withdrew "from settlement, occupancy, or sale" 3472 square miles of land in northwest Wyoming to create the world's first national park. Yellowstone is also the largest and best-known park in the continental U.S. The Old Faithful geyser, which still spews thousands of gallons of thundering water with each eruption, remains the most popular attraction. At Mammoth Hot Springs, mineral-laden waters flowing from deep within the earth have created tiers of ragged stone terraces. More than 700,000 gallons of water pour out daily, carrying an estimated two tons of limestone. The more than 1000 miles of hiking trails range from easy to challenging. Rangers suggest hikers either talk continuously or wear bells to scare off the timid, but extremely dangerous, bears. Campsites are available first-come, first-served. Sites are usually full by noon during the summer.

Yellowstone Nat'l Park, PO Box 168, Yellowstone, WY 82190, **307/344-7381**

Olympic
Nat'l Park, WA

From Alpine-like meadows to thick rain forests and from towering mountains to the rugged Pacific coastline, Olympic National Park is a study in diverse habitats. The climate near sea level is cool in summer and warm in winter, but torrential rains (especially between October and March) often last for days. US 101 is the principal through route for motorists, and numerous spurs give access to the park's most scenic areas. There are a variety of hiking trails, some taking as much as a week or more to travel. Licenses are not required for fishing, but Washington State punchcards are needed to fish for steelhead and salmon. A number of motels, cabins, and campsites are within the park. The park is open all year, but parts of the high country (and backcountry, including campsites) are often closed by snow from late September through June.

Supt, Olympic Nat'l Park, 600 E Park Ave, Port Angeles, WA 98362, **206/452-4501, ext 230**

Mt. Rainier
Nat'l Park, WA

More than 2500 annual visitors climb the 14,410-foot summit of Mount Rainier. However, less strenuous activities are also rewarding in this scenic park. The Wonderland Trail that circles the gleaming mountain is a 90-mile challenge to hikers and takes about two weeks. No license is needed to fish park waters, but some fishing is prohibited. There are five modest campgrounds, but only the camp at Sunshine Point is open all year. Except for the roads from Nisqually Entrance to Paradise (WA 706), most roads are closed by snow from late November to June or July. Of the three Visitor Information Centers, only the one at Longmire is open year round. Park personnel warn visitors about the dangers of bears, glaciers, and avalanches.

Supt, Mt Rainier Nat'l Park, Ashford, WA 98304-9051, **206/569-2211**

Crater Lake
Nat'l Park, OR

Volcanic peaks, evergreen forests, and rolling mountains surround this lake high in the Cascades Range. Formed by a dormant volcano, this is the deepest lake in the U.S. (1932 feet). Although the area is blanketed by snow much of the year, heat from the summer sun, stored in the water, retards ice formation. Many park roads are closed by late fall due to snow, but OR 62, from the west and south, is open year round. The park road to the lake is kept open if possible. Backpacking trails require a permit. Guided boat tours are offered in summer. Accommodations are available. May through October camping is allowed at more than 200 campsites.

Crater Lake Nat'l Park, PO Box 7, Hwy 62, Crater Lake, OR 97604, **503/594-2211**

Glacier
Nat'l Park, MT

Lofty mountain ranges and ice-cold lakes in glacial valleys make this park a true elixir of the spirit. In summer, rangers conduct interpretive walks, hikes, and campfire talks. Other activities include fishing, boating, and horseback riding. Known for hiking, Glacier has nearly 750 miles of trails. Wildlife includes black and grizzly bears. Upon arrival visitors should obtain information on backcountry travel and safety. Auto campgrounds are first-come, first-served. Permits are required to camp in the backcountry. Most roads are not plowed during winter and are popular for cross-country skiing and snowshoeing.

Supt, Glacier Nat'l Park, W Glacier, MT 59936, **406/888-5441**

Grand Teton National Park, WY

179

HISTORIC VILLAGES

Pioneer Village
Cashmere, WA

This community restoration honors those pioneers who, after the Civil War, endured hardships, loneliness, and danger to move the frontier across the Rocky Mountains and open the Far West. Authentic, primarily log-walled, structures gathered throughout Chelan Country have been reassembled as a late 19th-century northwestern outpost. There are primitive medical facilities, barber and millinery shops, and the post office. Included in the village are a smithy, a gold assayer's office, a general store, a one-room schoolhouse, a print shop, and early family cabins that show broad-axe and dovetailing log construction techniques. The museum collection of historical artifacts from 9000 years ago up to the arrival of white pioneers details the rich culture of the Indian tribes who lived along this river basin.
Pioneer Village, Chelan Hist Soc Cottage, PO Box 22, Cashmere, WA 98815, **509/782-3230**

Old Trail Town
Cody, WY

The Old West lives on at this historic location, where Buffalo Bill and his associates surveyed the first town site of Cody City in 1895. Old Trail Town consists of 25 buildings, dating from 1879 to 1900, plus 100 horse-drawn vehicles, and memorabilia of the Wyoming frontier. Visit the "hole in the wall" cabin, a popular rendezvous for Butch Cassidy and the Sundance Kid; inspect bullet holes in the doors of the Rivers Saloon, a favorite watering hole for cowboys and gold miners; and view the cabin where Indian scout Curly lived until his death in 1923. Other structures include a livery barn, a post office, a school, and blacksmith shops. The Trail Town Cemetery is the final resting place for such notables as John "Jeremiah" Johnson and buffalo hunter Jim White. Be sure to visit the Buffalo Bill Historical Center.
Old Trail Town, PO Box 696, Cody, WY 82414, **307/587-5302**

Salishan Lodge, Gleneden Beach, OR

RESORTS

Salishan Lodge
Gleneden Beach, OR

Seals drifting with the tide, seagulls diving for fish, and crabs scurrying along the beach can all be seen at Salishan Lodge, a rustic resort hugging the shore of Siletz Bay on the Oregon coast. White sand beaches and wooded hiking and jogging trails lure guests. Winding nature trails lace the resort's 750-acre woodland. The 200 rooms are in modern two-story villas of native wood. Each room has a wood-burning fireplace; balcony overlooking the 18-hole golf course, forest, or bay; and a covered walkway connecting it to the main lodge. The lodge houses an art gallery and several restaurants. Diners can choose from a candlelit table for two or a patio barbecue.
Salishan Lodge, PO Box 118, Gleneden Beach, OR 97388, **503/764-3600, 800/452-2300**

Sun Valley Lodge & Inn
Sun Valley, ID

Since the mid-1930s when Averell Harriman, chairman of the board of Union Pacific Railroad, first sought the ideal ski center to attract people to his railroad, the Sun Valley area has become a world-famous mecca for winter sports enthusiasts. Today there are 64 ski runs on Baldy and Dollar/Elkhorn. Novices should not be intimidated by the runs as a ski school provides expert instruction. Summer attractions include 4 golf courses, 3 hydrotherapy pools, 2 Olympic-sized pools, and nearly 50 tennis courts. Nearby stables offer hayrides, fox hunts, dressage clinics, and sleigh rides. The lodge and surrounding buildings are chalets with steeply sloping roofs. The paneled rooms have mock fireplaces. At the Trail Creek Cabin a horse-drawn sleigh transports guests to the secluded restaurant for a feast of hearty American fare.
Sun Valley Co, Sun Valley, ID 83353, **208/622-4111**

Old Trail Town, Cody, WY

SOUTHWEST

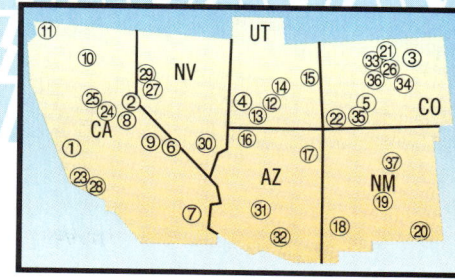

Spectacular Shores

Big Sur–Monterey, CA (CA 1)

Hugging a rugged coastline of forbidding cliffs that plunge to sheltered coves and secluded beaches, CA 1 is perhaps the most famous and scenic road in America. Drive through sun-dappled clearings in the 400,000-acre Los Padres National Forest, past the crashing surf of Big Sur, or search for precious stones on the beach at Jade Cove. You'll pass the Point Sur Lighthouse and Bixby Creek Bridge, rising 285 feet above the gaping canyon below. Farther north is Point Lobos, known for its jagged rocks and Monterey cypress. On a curving beach at the foot of rolling hills sits Carmel—named for the Spanish friars who first settled there. This village abounds with flower gardens, art galleries, and homes bordered by cypress-lined avenues. The Seventeen Mile Drive to Pacific Grove takes you past the rocky, flower-edged shoreline. Picnicking and seal-watching are popular at Cypress Point Lookout and at Seal and Bird Rocks. From Pacific Grove Gate, take Ocean View Boulevard along Monterey Bay where red-roofed, white stucco houses overlook sugar loaf beaches and an emerald harbor. In winter, monarch butterflies migrate to Pacific Grove, often referred to as "Butterfly Town USA."
Convention & Visitors Bureau, PO Box 1770, Monterey, CA 93940, **408/649-1770**

Tahoe Trail

Around Lake Tahoe, CA/NV

Lake Tahoe's water is 99.7% pure, and its 72 miles of shoreline are some of the most dramatic in America. Bisected by the California/Nevada state line, the mountain lake is 6225 feet above sea level and more than 1600 feet deep. The lake is rimmed with paved roads, and to best enjoy the view, leave South Lake Tahoe following NV 89 west into national forest lands. The Pope-Baldwin Recreation Area features miles of alpine beach as well as the Historic Estates Tour through mansions built over 100 years ago. NV 89 climbs north past a lateral moraine formed by ice-age glaciers. Take in the view from Eagle Point State Campgrounds. Bliss State Park is next, followed by the beaches of Meeks Bay. Travel east on NV 28, where many of the hotel/casinos are as well as the Ponderosa Ranch which is the site of the television western *Bonanza* and which offers horseback riding, gift shops, and an amusement park. From Incline Village, the road heads south along the east shore through pine and fir forests intersecting

with NV 50. A right turn brings you to Cave Rock, Zephyr Cove, and the Heavenly Valley Tram, which is 2000 feet above the sparkling lake.
Lake Tahoe Visitors Authority, PO Box 16299, S Lake Tahoe, CA 96151, **800/AT-TAHOE**

Colorado Climb

Mount Evans, CO

Above the foothills of the Rocky Mountains nearly three miles above sea level, Mount Evans boasts what is believed to be the world's highest highway. Following I-70 west from Denver to Bergen Park, you've already ascended 7500 feet. Past Bergen Park, CO 103 twists and turns through pine and aspen forests, revealing glimpses of distant snow-capped peaks—including Pike's Peak. Echo Lake, the last chance for food and drink before the summit, is ideal for a picnic, but it is not unusual to find snow in June, even when mile-high Denver is basking in 90°F. Follow CO 5 from Echo Lake for the final 4000-foot climb to the top, a 14-mile trip. Summit Lake lies about 1000 feet from the crest—where the water is always bone-chilling. The final stretch is the steepest. Vegetation is unable to grow in this Arctic-like wasteland. The road becomes a series of switchbacks, finally reducing itself to a beaten dirt trail. The road is open from mid-June to October. Check local weather conditions beforehand.
Colorado Div of Wildlife, 6060 Broadway, Denver, CO 80216, **303/297-1192; 303/639-1111** *(road conditions);* **303/398-3964** *(Nat'l Weather Service)*

Cedar Splendor

Cedar City Area, UT

Spectacular early morning vistas are common in southern Utah, a veritable palace of regal red rocks, massive granite monoliths, and cavernous canyonlands. Beginning in Cedar City, home of the Utah Shakespearean Festival and the heart of Utah's Color Country, the columns, statuary, and bluffs have provided the backdrop for countless Hollywood classics. Take I-15 south to Kolob Canyon in the northwest corner of Zion National Park. Crimson canyons and wind-worn cliffs vie for attention, and diversions include camping, fishing, swimming, and rock hunting. Head back north on I-15, then east on Hwy 14 to Strawberry Point, where the 8000-foot-high rock formations in the chasm change colors because of light variations throughout the day and with each season and are said to resemble thrones, cathedrals, and temples. Eight miles north of nearby Navajo Lake on Hwy 143 is Cedar Breaks National Monument, multi-hued natural amphitheater rising over 10,000 feet, surrounded by lava beds and bristlecone pines—the oldest known living trees on earth. Return to Cedar City and catch a Shakespearean performance under the stars.
Utah Travel Council, 300 N State St, Salt Lake City, UT 84114, **801/538-1030**

Colorado Color

San Juan Mountains Area, CO

US 550 is also known as the "Million Dollar Highway," partly because of the low-grade ore that intermittently flecks its surface, but more so because of its views—green valleys, abysmal canyons, and glistening lakes bordered by towering snow-capped peaks. The region is best known as the southern terminus of the historic Silverton railroad, which still labors through the spectacular San Juan Mountains. The road parallels the narrow-gauge tracks following one of the old toll road routes where ore was removed by pack mules. Continuing north, you'll pass through historic mining sites. At Silverton, there's a still-thriving mining center complete with reconstructions of businesses and home-

Durango/Silverton Narrow Gauge R.R., CO.

Photo: Denver & Colorado Convention & Visitors Bureau

181

Death Valley National Monument, CA/NV

Photo: National Park Service

steads and a three-story jail now home to the Historical Society Museum. The Navajo Trail from Durango along US 160 takes you through forests of ponderosa pine, juniper, and gambel oak. The La Plata Mountains rise majestically to the north, and the waving hayfields of the Mancos Valley stretch to the south. The imposing escarpment looming to the southwest is the Mesa Verde ("green table"), site of primitive Indian dwellings at Mesa Verde National Park where a 20-mile scenic drive takes you from the base of the mesa to the ruins at Chapin Mesa.
Colorado Tourism Board, 1625 Broadway, Suite 1700, Denver, CA 80202, 303/592-5510

NATIONAL PARKS & MONUMENTS

▼
6

Death Valley
Nat'l Monument, CA/NV

Despite the harsh environment and furnace-like heat that bakes the valley half the year, more than 900 species of plants live in the park. The roots of some extend down more than 60 feet in search of water. In the late 1800s the famous 20-mule teams hauled out mined borax (used for cleansing and water softening) from Death Valley. This is also the lowest point in North America (282 feet below sea level). Because of the valley's size and the distance between major features, an automobile is essential. Fuel is available only at Furnace Creek, Scotty's Castle, and Stovepipe Wells. The park has nine campgrounds, but only those at Furnace Creek, Mesquite Spring, and Wildrose are open year round. Nearby, the Furnace Creek Inn and Stovepipe Wells offer choice accommodations. Carry at least one gallon of water per person per day when leaving populated areas.
Supt, Death Valley Nat'l Monument, Box 579, Death Valley, CA 92328, 619/786-2331

▼
7

Joshua Tree
Nat'l Monument, CA

The arid ecosystems of the Colorado and Mohave deserts unite in this monument that encompasses some of the most interesting geological displays found in California's deserts. The monument is named for the Joshua Tree, a picturesque plant that looks like a cross between a cactus and a pine. The desert area is made up of a series of mountains (up to 6000 feet) separated by flat valleys abundant with wild plants and animals. Visitor centers, ranger stations, and wayside exhibits are found along main roads. The monument is about 140 miles east of Los Angeles. Nine campgrounds are available, but visitors must bring water and firewood. Walks, hikes, and campfire talks are conducted by rangers on weekends in spring and fall. Officials warn visitors about the dangers of poisonous rattlers, spiders, and abandoned mine shafts. Carry a water supply in your car.
Supt, Joshua Tree Nat'l Monument, 74485 Nat'l Monument Dr, Twenty-nine Palms, CA 92277, 619/367-7511

Joshua Tree National Monument, CA

Bryce Canyon National Park, UT

Carlsbad Caverns National Park, NM

11

Redwood
Nat'l Park, CA

Along northern California's Pacific coastline from north of Eureka to just south of the Oregon border, Redwood National Park protects the giant trees from the area's highly active timber companies. These trees (the tallest plants on earth) form a canopy hundreds of feet above the forest floor, creating a cathedral-like presence. Although temperatures are always mild, sea breezes can bring dangerous amounts of rain during winter. Reservations are necessary in summer. For motorists, US 101 runs the length of the park, providing excellent views of the tall trees as well as of the Pacific shoreline.
Redwood Nat'l Park, 1111 2nd St, Crescent City, CA 95531, **707/464-6101**

12

Bryce Canyon
Nat'l Park, UT

The beautiful columns and spires of the canyon were formed by geological faults and gradual erosion. The native Indian name for the area means "rocks standing like men in a bowl-shaped canyon." Spectacular hiking trails run through the principal areas, and 24 miles of roads lead to many of the best spots including Fairyland View, Sunset Point, Inspiration Point, Bryce Point, and Paria View. Cabins are available at Bryce Canyon Lodge from May to October. One campsite is open for use year round.
Supt, Bryce Canyon Nat'l Park, Bryce Canyon, UT 84717, **801/834-5322**

8

Yosemite
Nat'l Park, CA

A number of the grandest sights in America are in Yosemite National Park: majestic rock mountains such as El Capitan, Half Dome, and the Sentinel Rock; famous waterfalls such as the Yosemite Falls and Bridalveil Fall; and spectacular scenic drives such as the one through Tioga Pass. Footpaths and paved walkways are scattered throughout the park—two of the most popular (both short) are at Bridalveil Fall and Lower Yosemite Fall. Camping and backpacking in the backcountry are by permit only. Reservations are required in Yosemite Valley auto campgrounds year round.
Supt, Yosemite Nat'l Park, PO Box 577, CA 95389, **209/372-0264**

Gila Cliff Dwelling National Monument, NM

9

Sequoia & Kings Canyon
Nat'l Park, CA

These two contiguous parks in central California are truly the lands of giants. Their huge sequoia trees are the largest living things in the world, the only survivors of the giant trees that once flourished before the last great ice age. On the eastern boundary of Sequoia National Park is Mt. Whitney, highest peak in the U.S. outside of Alaska. Both parks are accessible only from the west, along CA 180 from Fresno and CA 198 from Visalia. No roads cross the east-west width of the parks. Numerous campgrounds are open from June 1 until October; some are open year round.
Sequoia and Kings Canyon Nat'l Parks, PO Box 789, Three Rivers, CA 93271, **209/561-3314**

10

Lassen Volcanic
Nat'l Park, CA

If you enjoy mountains and lakes, head for this park—it has 50 wilderness lakes and almost as many soaring peaks. Containing more than 160 square miles, the park is dominated by Lassen Peak, a 10,000-foot volcano last active around 1914. The park contains vast coniferous forests and a spectacular variety of wildlife. There are self-guided hiking trails and a scenic drive that half encircles Lassen Peak. Seven campgrounds and five picnic areas are along Lassen Park Road. Non-powered boats may be used on all but a handful of lakes. There are no boat rental facilities. Overnight accommodations are at Drakesbad Guest Ranch from mid-June to mid-September.
Lassen Volcanic Nat'l Park, PO Box 100, Mineral, CA 96063-0100, **916/595-4444**

Redwood National Park, CA

Petrified Forest National Park, AZ

Photo: Dale Schicketanz

Arches
Nat'l Park, UT

In southeastern Utah's red rock country, Arches National Park boasts the world's largest collection of natural bridges. The smallest have a three-foot opening (minimal distance to be considered a natural bridge). However, Landscape Arch is nearly 306 feet from base to base. The park can only be entered off US 191 near Moab. A visitor center near the entrance provides information and permits. Popular in spring and summer is the guided two-hour Fiery Furnace walk through white rock formations. The limited campsites near Skyline Arch are more popular in spring and fall, when the mercury is not as likely to rise above 100°F.
Supt, Arches Nat'l Park, PO 907, Moab, UT 84532,
801/259-8161

Gila Cliff Dwellings
Nat'l Monument, NM

The oldest Indian ruins in this monument were constructed about A.D. 100-400; others, about a thousand years ago. By A.D. 1300, the Mogollon Indians had abandoned the area entirely. Why they left or where they went is not known. A 44-mile drive heads north from Silver City on NM 15. The national monument is virtually surrounded by the Gila National Forest and Wilderness Area. Hiking, horseback riding, and camping are popular activities. Tours of the Indian homes, most built in natural caves, are available.
Gila Cliff Dwellings Nat'l Monument, Rte 11, Box 100, Silver City, NM 88061, **505/536-9344**

Zion
Nat'l Park, UT

This park's most famous attraction is Zion Canyon, formed by the Virgin River. A 13-mile round-trip drive takes visitors past the canyon and a number of landmarks including the Sentinel, Court of the Patriarchs, Mountain of the Sun, and the Great White Throne. A popular folklife festival held each September features pioneer crafts and vittles, storytelling, and children's games. South and Watchman campgrounds have unreserved sites year round; more primitive sites are elsewhere (camping permits from visitor centers). Cabins are operated by Zion Lodge with reservations usually necessary in summer.
T.W. Recreational Services, PO Box 400, Cedar City UT 84721, **801/586-7686**
Zion Nat'l Park, Springdale, UT 84767, **801/772-3256**

Grand Canyon
Nat'l Park, AZ

The most spectacular section of the world-famous chasm is in this national park. At one point the canyon is 18 miles wide and about one mile deep. The north rim averages about 1200 feet higher than the south and is usually closed because of heavy snows except during summer. Facilities are along both rims because crossing the canyon requires a drive in excess of 200 miles. However, strong hikers can cross via a 20-mile route on the Kaibab Trail. Campgrounds are first-come, first-served. Mule trips are available for persons over age 12 and weighing less than 200 pounds. Scenic flights originate daily from Grand Canyon National Airport.
Supt, Grand Canyon Nat'l Park, PO Box 129, Grand Canyon, AZ 86023, **602/638-7888**

Salinas, Pueblo Missions
Nat'l Monument, NM

On a ridge atop Chupadera Mesa in central New Mexico stand the ruins of an Indian pueblo and two massive 17th-century Franciscan missions. The people of Gran Quivira (they called it Cueloze) lived in an area where two Indian cultures, the Mogollon and Anasazi, met and blended. The earliest Spanish explorers in the area entered the Salinas Valley near the end of the 16th century. A walk through the Indian and Spanish ruins begins at the information center. The monument includes the Abo Ruins and the Quarai Ruins. The nearby Mountaineer Headquarters has exhibits with an audio-visual presentation.
Supt, Salinas Nat'l Monument, PO Box 496, Mountainair, NM 87036, **505/847-2585**

Capitol Reef
Nat'l Park, UT

This park lies in southern Utah's slickrock country where water has cut monoliths, arches, and canyons out of a sandstone and shale desert. The park was named for one of its high ridges that resembles the dome of the U.S. Capitol. Much of the park is still a wilderness area. The Fremont Indians lived there 1000 years ago, and many tribal rock drawings remain. There are no services in the park, but two campsites are open year round. Backpacking is by permit. Carry sufficient water, and avoid camping in ditches.
Capitol Reef Nat'l Park, Hwy 24, Capitol Reef, UT 84775, **801/425-3791**

Petrified Forest
Nat'l Park, AZ

This park is noted for its petrified wood, prehistoric animal fossils, Indian ruins, rock formations, and desert landscapes—especially the Painted Desert. Long Logs Trail takes visitors past the park's largest collection of petrified wood and the Agate House ruins—a partially reconstructed building of petrified wood. The trail offers views of fossil-rich badlands and desert wildlife. There are no developed campsites, but camping is allowed by permit in certain wilderness areas. Overnight accommodations are in nearby towns.
Petrified Forest Nat'l Park, PO Box 2217, Petrified Forest Nat'l Park, AZ 86028, **602/524-6228**

Carlsbad Caverns
Nat'l Park, NM

Carlsbad Cavern is the largest of about 70 caves preserved beneath the harsh, rugged land of the nearly 47,000-acre national park. At sunset in summer, as many as 5000 bats a minute can be seen flying out of the caverns. The intricate patterns of water-dripped limestone remain awe-inspiring. The centuries-long process has formed what seem to be colorful hanging "curtains" of rock along the cave's walls. Self-guided tours are permitted. Walnut Canyon and the Capitan Reef Escarpment, aboveground, are approachable by car. Marked trails are near the cavern entrance and Walnut Canyon. Only a restaurant and gift shop are in the park, but lodgings and camping are nearby.
Supt, Carlsbad Caverns Nat'l Park, 3225 Nat'l Parks Hwy, Carlsbad, NM 88220, **505/785-2233**

Rocky Mountain
Nat'l Park, CO

The grandeur of high mountains and alpine valleys, crystal-clear lakes and sparkling mountain streams is most abundant in this national park in north central Colorado. One-third of the area is above the tree line where frozen tundra predominates. There are no lodgings in the park, but rooms are available in nearby towns. The five campgrounds are filled to capacity early each summer day. More than 300 miles of magnificent hiking trails are more rewarding than the limited road system, although US 34 (Trail Ridge Road) is one of the great Alpine drives in the U.S. It is frequently closed in winter. In summer, horses with guides can be hired in or around the park, but horses are permitted only on designated trails. Alpine and Moraine Park visitor centers are open summer months only.
Supt, Rocky Mt Nat'l Park, Estes Park, CO 80517,
303/586-2371

Mesa Verde
Nat'l Park, CO

Near the Ute and Navajo Indian reservations is the majestic plateau of Mesa Verde, site of extensive prehistoric Indian ruins. About 1300 years ago, American Indians built mesa-top villages and later great cities of stone in the cliffs of Mesa Verde. Before Columbus discovered America, the Anasazi Indians had abandoned their homes, which were not found until after the Civil War. The multi-room dwellings rise four stories and are made of talus stones with pinon pines as roof beams. These pre-Columbian cliff dwellings are a "don't miss" attraction. There are free ranger-guided tours of two ruins in summer, one in winter. Wetherill Mesa now is open to private vehicles and has an interpretive loop of early ruins. Wetherill is open from late May to early September. Other roads in the park are open year round, weather permitting. A lookout point at 8572 feet offers views of four states. Camping is permitted only at the 500-site Morefield Campground. Lodgings are available at the 150-room Far View Lodge.
ARA Mesa Verde Co, PO Box 277, Mancos, CO 81328,
303/529-4421

HISTORIC VILLAGES

Solvang
Solvang, CA

You could easily believe you were on a street in Copenhagen. Instead, you have discovered the Danish capital of America—Solvang (Sun Valley) tucked away in Santa Ynez Valley. Founded more than 70 years ago by Danish clergymen and settled by Danish immigrants, this village abounds in Scandinavian flavor. Danish can still be heard in homes, churches, and on the streets. If you visit during Danish Days (third week of September), you can have an *aebleskiver* breakfast (fried dough rolled into a small ball, with juice and coffee) served on the street and still take in the roving singers and folk dancers in Old World Danish costumes. Competition is fierce among the bakers, who woo you with breads, pastries, cookies, and cakes. Danish recipes are featured at the restaurants where smorgasbords include marinated herring, wilted cucumbers, and red cabbage and meatballs. For a taste of Denmark, you need to know only one Danish word—Solvang.
Solvang Convention and Visitor Bureau, 1571 Mission Drive, PO Box 70, Solvang, CA 93464, **805/688-3317**

Columbia State Historic Park
Columbia, CA

"Gold! Gold!" When James Marshall exclaimed those words in January 1848 he sparked an extraordinary movement in American history—the gold rush. Boomtowns sprang up overnight in the Sierra Nevada hills drawing prospectors in quest of the mother lode. Far from being a ghost town, Columbia is alive with the sounds, sights, and activity of yesteryear. The 21 restored buildings include a harness shop, a restaurant, antique shops, a barbershop, and an old-fashioned candy store. Year-round activities feature craft demonstrations, old mine tours, stagecoach rides, plays at the Fallon Theatre, and films and exhibits about the town's history. No visit is complete without panning for gold. Some visitors have returned home with a shiny nugget or two. Highlights in surrounding Tuolomne County include Yosemite National Park, Railtown 1897 Historical Park, and scenic rivers and lakes where fishing, camping, boating, and hot air ballooning are found.
Columbia State Historic Park, PO Box 151, Columbia, CA 95310, **209/532-4301**

Durango, Colorado

Photo: Steve Pierce

Old Sacramento Sutter's Fort
Sacramento, CA

Old Sacramento was a strategic mid-19th-century headquarters for Wells Fargo & Co. and the earliest Western Union facility, a central staging area for the gold prospecting forty-niners, and the starting point for the western branch of the transcontinental railway. A four-square-block restoration along the Sacramento River contains the California State Railroad Museum and the 1870 Central Pacific Railroad Passenger Depot, a train buff's paradise. (Steam train rides along a six-mile route on summer weekends.) Other displays and buildings include the original Wells Fargo and Western Union offices in the B.F. Hastings Museum/Building; well-stocked period shops, such as the Huntington-Hopkins Hardware Store; the Old Eagle Theater; and, from the era of barge traffic, a Jack London-style waterfront along the river. The earliest non-Indian settlement in California's Great Central Valley is nearby Sutter's Fort, founded in 1839 by John Augustus Sutter. With help from Indians, his small party built a crude fort of sun-cured adobe to protect the soon-to-boom community, later named Sacramento. Today, Sutter Fort State Historic Park is a restored and recreated frontier outpost with blacksmiths, cooks and candlemakers, carpenters and coopers, all in period dress, talking period language, and living an 1840 pioneer's life down to authentic menus.
Sacramento District State Parks, 101 J St, Sacramento, CA 95814, **916/445-4209**

Central City
Central City, CO

The fabled poem "Face On The Barroom Floor" is interpreted in the elegant Teller House hotel. In its 19th-century heyday, this so-called "richest square mile on earth" was substantially larger than Denver. To honor a visit by President Grant, community fathers paved part of main street in solid silver. No precious metals gild the streets today, but the town and surrounding Gilpin County yield a wealth of vintage honky-tonk saloons, period museums and exhibits, mine tours, ghost-mine camps, good restaurants and shops, and authentically refurbished Victorian lodgings. During summer, the splendid, heavy-stone 1878 Opera House offers major musical and theatrical productions. Central City also hosts an annual summer Ragtime and Traditional Jazz Festival and an adult soapbox derby called the Gravity Grand Prix. Nearby are challenging backcountry aspen trails for hiking and horseback riding, plus six campground facilities—all at an altitude of 8000 feet.
Central City Chamber of Commerce, PO Box 249, Central City, CO 80427, **303/582-5251**

Virginia City
Virginia City, NV

To this day the Comstock Lode, discovered in 1859, remains the world's record for gold and silver—an incredible $400 million in ore. These mineral deposits have been said to be largely responsible for financing the Union Army's triumph in the Civil War and for subsidizing a substantial portion of the development of San Francisco. Although this tiny community, self-styled "the liveliest ghost town in the West," is a shadow of its former self, it remains a repository of old boardwalks, 22 saloons, and many Victorian mansions constructed by suddenly wealthy miners. In 1875, a wind-shipped conflagration virtually flattened the town, but it quickly re-emerged as one finds it today. An incredible network of some 750 miles of mining tunnels is an underground attraction. In recent years, about 100 hotel rooms and RV hookups have been built here. Virginia City offers hiking, swimming, tennis, and dirt biking; arts, crafts, and antiques; plus a singular curiosity in September—the Virginia City International Camel Races.
Chamber of Commerce, Box 464, Virginia City, NV 89440, **702/847-0311**

San Ysidro Ranch
Montecito, CA

In the foothills of the Santa Ynez Mountains are the storybook cottages of the San Ysidro Ranch. Ronald Coleman's hideaway for friends, the resort has been refurbished, and the cottages now blend modern amenities with old-fashioned comfort. Antiques, overstuffed love seats, oriental rugs, and brass beds fill the cozy cottages. Some have private Jacuzzis set into redwood decks. Hikers and horseback riders explore the 550 acres on well-marked trails. Swimmers enjoy poolside barbecues and cocktails. The three tennis courts overlook the Pacific Ocean on one side and the mountains on the other. In the 1880s the ranch was the site of a Franciscan mission, and two of the original buildings remain. The former wine cellar is now the Plow and Angel Bar; what once was a fruit-packing house is now the dining room.
San Ysidro Ranch, 900 San Ysidro Ln, Montecito, CA 93108, **805/969-5046, 800/368-6788**

Harrah's Reno
Reno, NV

A bingo parlor in 1937, Harrah's has evolved into a quality resort and world famous casino. The 24-story, 566-room highrise in downtown Reno, while best known for its gaming and cabaret, also offers other activities. The rooms feature contemporary decor with plush furnishings and black-out curtains for total privacy day or night. When the sun is shining, which it mostly does, a swim in the outdoor pool is refreshing. Dining choices range from the elegant Steak House, Travel-Holiday magazine award winner, and Cafe Andreotti to the Skyway Buffet and Garden Room.
Harrah's Reno, PO Box 10, Reno, NV 89504, **702/786-3232, 800/648-3773**

Caesars Palace
Las Vegas, NV

With its marble statues, cascading fountains, and palatial courtyards, Caesars Palace is more than a casino. The 1600 rooms and suites are large and plush. The new Villa Suites are done

The Broadmoor Hotel, Colorado Springs, CO

The Wigwam, Litchfield Park, AZ

The Wigwam, Litchfield Park, AZ

Loews Ventana
Canyon Resort
Tucson, AZ

If ever a resort was designed to harmonize with its environment, it is the luxurious Ventana Canyon. The 94-acre resort is nestled among 300-

The Arizona Biltmore
Phoenix, AZ

Quality service, food, and accommodations have over the last three decades earned this elegant resort (opened in 1929) consecutive five-star Mobil ratings elevating it to a category all by itself. Built by a protege of Frank Lloyd Wright, the architecture itself is worth noting. Many of the rooms and suites have patios overlooking the famous Cataline-tile pool or the luxurious garden. The 39-acre garden intersperses palm trees and flowering cacti with fruit-bearing citrus trees. The Orangerie is noted for its seafood and fresh game selections. A climate-controlled glass wine room has a fine selection of domestic and imported labels. Guests have their choice of 12 lighted outdoor tennis courts, jogging trails or three pools. Overworked muscles can be soothed by a massage at the Biltmore Health and Fitness Center.
The Arizona Biltmore, 2400 Missouri Ave, Phoenix, AZ 85016, **602/955-6600, 800/950-0086**

Sheraton Tucson
El Conquistador
Tucson, AZ

The Santa Catalina Mountains provide a breathtaking backdrop for this 440-room resort amid towering palms, sparkling fountains, and cascading waterfalls. A 45-hole championship golf course, 31 lighted tennis courts, riding stables, and, of course, 4 outdoor swimming pools are just a few of the many amenities. Catering to hearty appetites are the diverse menus in four outstanding restaurants. The Last Territory offers mesquite-grilled entrees and features a live country-western band. The Sundance Cafe serves three meals a day from its selection of American and Southwestern favorites. Dos Locos Cantina features live mariachi music and savory Mexican cuisine; at night, it becomes a lively disco. The White Dove Restaurant provides more opulent surroundings. Recognized for its award-winning service, the resort has won Four Stars from Mobil Guide and Four Diamonds from AAA.
Sheraton Tucson El Conquistador, 10000 N Oracle Road, Tucson, AZ 85737, **602/742-7000**

in art deco style. Each suite has a computerized Jacuzzi, goldplated bath fixtures, marble floors, and a personal captain. Guests can relax on the tennis courts or in one of two pools. The Olympic-sized pool in the lush Garden of the Gods is made of Carrara marble. The second pool caters to ardent sunbathers—three "lounging islands" are continuously washed by cool, refreshing water. Guests can take in a movie at the Omnimax Theatre with its "sensaround" audio system or shop. At night, Caesars Palace comes alive with big-name entertainers, boxing matches, and tennis tournaments at The Circus Maximus Showroom. Thirsty patrons can enjoy an aperitif at Cleopatra's Barge—a floating entertainment lounge. There are six restaurants including the elegant Palace Court. Tropical plants, fine art, and antique furnishings create the atmosphere of a private palazzo. A stained glass dome retracts to unveil the star-studded Nevada sky.
Caesars Palace, 3570 Las Vegas Blvd S, Las Vegas, NV 89109, **702/731-7110, 800/634-6661**

year-old giant saguaro cacti in foothills of the Santa Catalina Mountains. Nearby is the beautiful Sabino Canyon, part of the Coronado National Forest. There are 366 guest rooms and 26 suites, each with mini-bar, stocked refrigerator, and private terrace. First-class recreational facilities include an 18-hole PGA golf course with driving range and putting green. Two heated swimming pools have adjacent hot tubs. A tennis club features 10 lighted courts, and a health spa offers such body-pampering amenities as sauna, steam room, whirlpool, mirrored aerobics room with ballet bar, weight-training equipment, and massage therapy. Outdoors, there are picnic areas, a signposted nature trail, an 18-station par course jogging track, and a croquet court. Horseback riding is nearby, and skiing (in season) is about a one hour drive. Dining opportunities range from the elegant Ventana to the "contemporary cowboy" ambience of the Flying V Bar & Grill. The resort has earned the AAA 4-Diamond and Mobil 4-Star awards for excellence.
Loews Ventana Canyon Resort, 7000 N Resort Dr, Tucson, AZ 85725, **602/299-2020, 800/223-0888**

187

C Lazy U Ranch
Granby, CO

If you've always wanted your own horse and a ride on the range in Big Sky country, come to this ranch resort overlooking the Continental Divide at 8300 feet above sea level. Guests are matched with one of the 145 horses, which is then theirs for a week of trail riding, breakfast rides, and instruction in the ring. Children perform in a "shodeo"—a horse show on Saturday. The A-frame lodge houses six rooms. The other 32 rooms are in cottages with wood-burning fireplaces. The C Lazy U Ranch also has an outdoor pool, two tennis courts, and a skeet range. Don't forget your waders—the ranch supplies everything else for anglers. After a vigorous game of racquetball in a glass court, unknot those muscles in the sauna or whirlpool. Family-style dinners in the lodge or outdoor cookouts allow guests to recap the day over hearty fare. In winter, the ranch lures guests with miles of machine-groomed trails, tubing, snowshoeing, ice skating, and sleigh rides.
C Lazy U Ranch, PO Box 379, Granby, CO 80446, **303/887-3344**

The Broadmoor Hotel
Colorado Springs, CO

With its pink, Mediterranean-style buildings, red tile roofs, and location, the Broadmoor is often called the "Riviera of the Rockies." The original hotel was opened in 1918; the 144-room Broadmoor South, in 1961; and the 150-room Broadmoor West, in 1976. The hotel maintains a European flavor in its restaurants—the Golden Bee and the Penrose Room. Three 18-hole golf courses are at the foot of Cheyenne Mountain. The Broadmoor World Arena building, often open to the public for skating, has hosted world figure skating championships, ice hockey games, and other sporting events. Three heated swimming pools, including one on the Lake Terrace, provide year-round swimming. A fitness center offers the finest in modern equipment. There are 16 tennis courts, 4 of which are covered by a heated, illuminated bubble for winter play. Pikes Peak is nearby.
The Broadmoor, Lake Circle, PO Box 1439, Colorado Springs, CA 80906, **800/634-7711**

Tamarron Resort
Durango, CO

Situated 7500 feet above sea level in the protected valley of the San Juan Mountains, this resort offers hands-on experiences. Fish for trout in clear-running streams, shoot the rapids in a raft or kayak, or horseback ride to a naturally-formed cave. Milder adventures include bus or jeep tours along old stagecoach trails to abandoned mining towns. A 45-minute helicopter ride provides an eagle's perspective of jewel-like hidden lakes. The resort also offers golf, swimming, tennis, and platform tennis. Skiers find challenges on the slopes of Purgatory or on well-groomed Nordic trails. Guests stay in rustic rooms and suites in the inn. After a day of activities in the crisp mountain air, appetites can be satisfied at Remington's, an elegant restaurant, or at the informal San Juan Club, popular with the après-ski crowd.
Tamarron Resort, PO Box 3131, Durango, CO 81302, **303/259-2000, 800/678-1000**

Keystone Lodge
Keystone, CO

As the strains of music float through sunlit pines, guests are lured to the 100-seat Keystone Pavilion where the summer-long Keystone Music Festival features the 90-piece National Repertory Orchestra and the acclaimed Summit Brass. The comfortable rooms have a lounging area and bedroom loft. Rough-hewn pine log condos have one to three bedrooms, full kitchens, and flagstone fireplaces. Colorado mornings are crisp, clear, and perfect for tennis on one of the 14 courts at the John Gardiner Tennis Club. Earlybird golfers can get in a round of golf on the 18-hole course. The nearby Arapaho National Forest awaits backpackers, rock climbers, and horseback riders—all outfitted by the lodge. For anglers, there is good fishing—for brook, brown, and rainbow trout. A swim, sauna, or Jacuzzi will invigorate tired muscles. Food is served in twelve different settings. The skiing season lasts nine months here, and guests often ski in short-sleeve shirts in June. A $15 million expansion has added a six-person gondola that whisks skiers to the pristine summit of North Peak. It's the resort's third ski mountain with 200 acres of challenging runs, new chairlifts, and ski village.
Keystone Resort, Box 38, Keystone, CO 80435, **303/468-4242**

Rancho Encantado
Santa Fe, NM

Santa Fe, steeped in Indian lore and Spanish traditions and the home of a thriving artist's colony and superb opera company, also is the home of Rancho Encantado—the enchanted ranch. Accommodations, ranging from 22 ranch rooms to 36 condominiums, feature a southwestern motif—Navajo rugs, wood-burning adobe fireplaces, red tile floors and sun porches overlooking desert gardens. The climate is perfect for hiking, tennis (two courts), swimming, or soaking in the hot tub. A natural-wood portal provides shade from the intense sunshine. Horseback rides in the desert are also available. The restaurant in the Main Lodge serves a diversity of cuisines.
Rancho Encantado, Rte 4, Box 57C, Santa Fe, NM 87501, **505/982-3537**

Sheraton Tucson El Conquistador, Tucson, AZ

MIDWEST

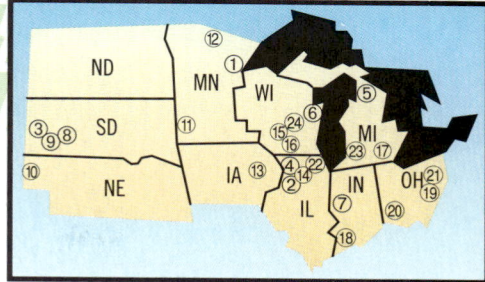

SCENIC DRIVES

▼1
Superior's Skyway
Duluth, MN (Skyline Parkway)

This 27-mile drive rises 600 feet above Duluth and not only offers spectacular views of bay, harbor, and river, but is a national hawk watch area. Birch-filled ravines, tumbling brooks, placid ponds, and blue-gray cliffs abound on this twisting trail. Views of ocean-bound ships on Lake Superior and snaking ore trains are common. Minnesota Point, the seven-mile peninsula that extends across the lake toward the Wisconsin shore, is Duluth's playground. Artists, photographers, and naturalists enjoy its gently rolling dunes and sandy flats, while swimmers and sunbathers flock to its fine beaches. From the parkway, you look down on a progressive city boasting contemporary architecture, a new convention and entertainment complex, a 25-acre zoo, and a host of historic museums.
Minnesota Office of Tourism, 375 Jackson St, Suite 250, St Paul, MN 55101, **612/296-5029, 800/657-3700**

▼2
Spoon River Valley
Galesburg/Havana Area, IL

A rich bounty awaits motorists who take the Knox County and the Spoon River Scenic Drives. Tour dozens of small, out-of-the-way towns on these two adjoining drives. On the Knox County Scenic Drive, visit the Wolfe Covered Bridge—the state's oldest—and see the birthplace of Carl Sandburg. Rewards come not only in the pastoral splendor of the rolling farmland of western Illinois, but also in meeting friendly, down-to-earth farm folk and in reaping the rich harvest of the land. The scenic inspiration for Edgar Lee Master's classic verse, *Spoon River Anthology*, is the locale for the second drive, 65 miles long. Picnic areas abound in parks along the marked route that parallels the historic river and signs direct you through Ellisville, Mt. Pisgah, and Babylon Bend, ending at Lewistown. Autumn is enchanting here, ablaze with color and festivities. During the festivals, residents dress in period costumes and provide demonstrations of early crafts. In towns along the route there are art and antique shows, old mills and churches, and an endless variety of scrumptious homemade cooking.
Galesburg Area Chamber of Commerce, PO Box 631, Galesburg, IL 61402-0631, **309/343-1194**

▼3
Iron Mountain Road
Black Hills, SD

It is impossible to speed on this winding mountain road, and many people drive slowly to take in the breathtaking views. Connecting Custer State Park and Mount Rushmore National Memorial in the Black Hills, US 16A was an engineer's nightmare when first designed in the 1930s. Climbing through tall ponderosa pines, it arrives at the top of Iron Mountain in a series of hairpin turns, dizzying switchbacks, and hardrock tunnels. The tunnels were designed to have their openings frame Mount Rushmore, some 17 miles distant. Another view of this world-famous monolith and the surrounding territory is afforded from Norbeck Lookout at the mountain's summit. Other equally scenic roads in the Black Hills include the Needles Hwy (US 87), Rimrock West Hwy 44, Boulder Canyon Dr, Palmer Gultch Rd, and Spearfish Canyon Dr.
Div of Tourism, 711 Wells Ave, Pierre, SD 57501, **605/773-3301, 800/843-1930**

Covered Bridge, Parke Country, IN

▼4
Riverside Roadway
The Great River Road, IA/IL

This 75-mile drive stretches along the Mississippi River from Dubuque, IA, to Rock Island, IL. It is part of the Great River Road, which hugs the banks of the "Big Muddy" for some 3000 miles from Minnesota to the Gulf of Mexico, and offers travelers the best route to explore the Mississippi River Valley. A picturesque starting point is Dubuque, IA, where you can board the Fenelon Place Incline Railway—a cable car that takes you up steep bluffs, 300 feet high, for a view across the river. Nearby Crystal Lake Cave features rare underground geological formations adjacent to an ultra-clear lake. At Galena, visit the home of former president Ulysses S. Grant and other historic buildings, such as an elegant 1859 Victorian mansion and a Civil War "Steamboat Gothic" estate. Board an old paddlewheeler at the Rhododendron Showboat Museum in Clinton, IA, which displays artifacts and specimens of Indian lore. The former home of the Sauk and Fox Indian nations is on the grounds of Black Hawk State Park at Rock Island, IL, and Arsenal Island.
Mississippi River Pkway Comm, Pioneer Bldg, Suite 1513, 336 Robert St, St Paul, MN 55107, **612/224-9903**

▼5
Michigan's Majesty
Mackinaw City–Paradise, MI

While Michigan may be one of the most industrialized states, it is also one of the most beautiful boasting more than 36,000 miles of rivers and streams, and 11,000 inland lakes. At Mackinaw City on the northern tip of the Lower Peninsula you can see the sun rise over Lake Huron and set over Lake Michigan. The Mackinac Bridge, one of the longest suspension bridges in the

Mackinac Bridge, MI

world, stretches for five miles to unite the Upper and Lower Peninsulas of Michigan. Crossing the Straits of Mackinac via the "Mighty Mac," you'll come upon the historic port of St. Ignace where Father Marquette, the Jesuit Missionary and explorer, settled more than 300 years ago; a 52-acre memorial depicts his life and adventures. US 2W will lead you along the southern shore of the Upper Peninsula, past Lake Michigan's deep blue waters, through the thick woodlands of the Hiawatha National Forest—inspiration for Longfellow's famous poem. Pointe Aux Chenes (Point of Oaks) is a popular spot with swimmers and picnickers. Rte 117 north takes you to Rte 28 east and Soo Junction where visitors can explore Tahquamenon State Falls Park via a train and boat tour. Newberry, via Rte 123 north, is a popular winter destination for tobogganers and cross-country skiers, and the well-stocked Tahquamenon River near Paradise is a favorite fishing spot.

Michigan Travel Bureau, Box 30226, Lansing, MI 48909, **800/5432-YES**

Wisconsin Waterfronts
Door County Peninsula, WI

Famous for fall foliage, quaint villages, fish boils, and 250 miles of shoreline, Door County, north of Green Bay on the "thumb of Wisconsin," often is dubbed "Cape Cod of the Midwest." WI 57 and 42 crisscross the peninsula, and motorists often spend days exploring the area. In Sturgeon Bay there is a narrated boat tour of the shipyards. North of Valmy via WI 57 and east on Clark Lake Road is Whitefish Dunes State Park and Cave Point County Park. Lake Michigan waves have created natural caves that may be explored during a stroll along the beach. North on WI 57 is Baileys Harbor, the oldest village in Door County and one of the best harbors on the east shore. In late May, 4000 acres of apple and cherry blossoms delicately color the scenic peninsula. Hwy Q takes you to Ridges Sanctuary, noted for its wild plants. Follow Hwy Q to the water's edge and cross a narrow strip of land to tour the Cana Island Lighthouse, built in 1851. Return to WI 57 and continue north to Sister Bay. North of Sister Bay is Ellison Bay, Gills Rock, and Northport. Ferry service is offered to Washington Island off the tip of the Door Peninsula. South of Sister Bay along the Green Bay side of the peninsula the waterfront villages of Ephraim, Fish Creek, and Egg Harbor offer galleries, boutiques, and summer stock theater.

Chamber of Commerce, Green Bay Rd, PO Box 406, Sturgeon Bay, WI 54235, **414/743-4456,** **800/52-RELAX**

Covered Bridges
Parke County, IN

Hoosiers quickly tell you that New England doesn't have a monopoly on covered bridges. In fact, there are no fewer than 33 in Parke County alone. These rust-colored enclosures protect bridges from the ravages of weather and time. The bridges attract tourists—1,000,000 during the 10-day Covered Bridge Festival during early October—and these visitors have spawned a thriving arts and crafts industry. You'll find tiny shops and studios where you can shop for quilts, handmade furniture, pottery, antiques, a whole range of arts and crafts, and country foodstuffs. Four separate covered bridge tours guide you around the county. Most tours start at Rockville, the county seat, with its handsome courthouse built of red sandstone. Nearby is Billie Creek, a recreated turn-of-the-century village and farmstead where costumed guides demonstrate old-time crafts. Other county highlights include Bridgeton, with a double-span bridge built in 1868, and a dam and grist mill that is one of the most photographed spots in the county; Marshall, a small farming community with an old-fashioned soda fountain at Spencer's Corner Barn; and Rosedale, where the Civic Center is packed with crafts people. Festivals include the Maple Fair; Quilt Show; and Sorghum-Cider Fair.

Parke County Convention and Visitors Bureau, Box 165, Rockville, IN 47872, **317/569-5226**

NATIONAL PARKS & MONUMENTS

Badlands
Nat'l Park, SD

The Badlands are a wonderland of strange, colorful spires and pinnacles, massive buttes, and deep gorges. In 1968, 133,000 acres within the Pine Ridge Indian Reservation were added to the national park. At the same time, nearly 65,000 acres were set aside as a wilderness area protected from roads or other kinds of development. Bison, Rocky Mountain bighorn sheep, prairie dogs, and other Great Plains wildlife roam the park. It is wonderful for backpacking, but stay alert for prairie rattlers. Contact a ranger before camping in the backcountry. Cabins, meals, and souvenirs available at Cedar Pass Lodge mid-April through October.

Badlands Nat'l Park, PO Box 6, Interior, SD 57750, **605/433-5361**

Wind Cave
Nat'l Park, SD

Although this 28,292-acre park is a sanctuary for bison, mule deer, prairie dogs, and birds and also preserves the flora of the virgin prairie, most visitors are attracted by the 51-plus miles of twisting passageways in Wind Cave. Named for the stiff breeze that still blows out of the entrance, the cave has at least a thousand passageways yet to be explored. Rangers lead cave tours several times daily. Mt. Rushmore National Memorial is north via SD 87.

Wind Cave Nat'l Park, RR 1, Box 190-WCNP, Hot Springs, SD 57747, **605/745-4600**

Scotts Bluff
Nat'l Monument, NE

Rising 800 feet above the valley around it, Scotts Bluff once was part of the ancient High Plains that are now almost eroded. The North Platte Valley, of which Scotts Bluff is the dominant natural feature, has been a human migration corridor for years. Well-worn traces of the famous Oregon Trail are still visible within the park. The summit can be reached by car. Grand vistas overlook Chimney Rock National Historic Site, Laramie Peak, and the Oregon Trail approach to Mitchell Pass. Open year around. Museum on site.

Scotts Bluff Nat'l Monument, PO Box 27, Gehring, NE 69341-0027, **308/436-4340**

Badlands National Park, SD

Voyageurs National Park, MN

Photo: Ron Schmid

11

Pipestone

Nat'l Monument, MN

Long before the first white man reached the northern plains, Indians of many tribes traveled up to 1000 miles to reach the pipestone quarries of southwestern Minnesota. Traditionally, this was a sacred place where all Indians could quarry in peace. Many 19th-century settlers made it a point to visit this famous quarry where Indians found the raw materials for peace pipes. In addition to exhibits covering geology, history, archeology, and the pipestone crafts, there are some lovely trails. A small stand of virgin prairie survives. The small park is adjacent to the north side of the city of Pipestone.

Supt, Pipestone Nat'l Monument, Box 727, Pipestone, MN 56164, **507/825-5464**

12

Voyageurs

Nat'l Park, MN

Practically adjacent to the Quetico and Boundary Waters Canoe Area, this park is a boater's paradise. In fact, watercraft must be used for travel within the park; automobiles are parked at the entrance. Resorts just outside the park rent boats, canoes, and other equipment. The park is renowned for challenging walleye, northern pike, and largemouth bass fishing (with many fish of trophy size) as well as for ice fishing. Fishing in Minnesota requires a state license; visitors fishing on the Canadian side must have an Ontario license. The park is home to the rare eastern timber wolf, and black bears are common to the entire region. Nearby International Falls is a houseboater's Avalon, with a half dozen or so fleet owners renting out these self-contained luxury craft. About 125 boat-in primitive camp-

sites are scattered throughout the park. Private and public campsites, as well as motels and rooms are outside the park.

Voyageurs Nat'l Park, HCR9 Box 600, International Falls, MN 56649, **218/283-9821**

HISTORIC VILLAGES

13

Amana Colonies

Amana, IA

Since the seven Amana colonies were founded in 1854, farming has been their principal activity. The rich northeastern Iowa River Valley soil has provided abundant yields of corn, soybeans, alfalfa, oats, and beef cattle. The original 800 Amana

settlers, escaped persecution and pursued a visionary faith called the Community of the True Inspirationalists. Part of their adopted lifestyle embraced the concept of communal enterprises: a blend of brotherhood and economics with each individual contributing what he or she did best. The result was an extraordinary variety of finely-crafted 19th-century pioneer furniture, clocks, embroidery, calico dresses, hand-loomed woolen items, whole-grained cereals, Westphalia-style smoked meats, wines of German character, and exceptional baked offerings. These early Amana traditions continue to be the Amana trademark of excellence. Awaiting today's visitor is a first-hand sampling of all of these goods, combined with historic buildings; numerous museums, including the significant Museum of Amana History; and tempting regional restaurants.

Amana Colonies Convention and Visitors Bureau, PO Box 303, Amana, IA 52203, **800/245-5465**

14

Historic Bishop Hill

Bishop Hill, IL

Hardy, industrious Swedes, driven from their homeland by religious persecution, created this charming community in the prairie heartland. Today, the village enjoys National Landmark status and offers quiet, tree-lined streets, well-preserved historic buildings, craft studios, antique and gift shops, Swedish inspired eateries, and colorful festivals. More than a dozen original buildings remain, including the Steeple Building, which houses a museum tracing the settlement and restoration of the colony. The Colony Church, with black walnut pews—separate sections for the men and the women—has

Henry Ford Museum & Greenfield Village, Dearborn, MI

Photo: The Edison Institute, Henry Ford Museum

Historic Bishop Hill, Bishop Hill, IL

Photo: Mike Michaelson

wood and wrought-iron chandeliers, copies of brass chandeliers colonists remembered in Swedish cathedrals. Over 90 paintings of Olof Krans, whose austere canvases capture the harsh life of the prairies and whose stern-faced portraits depict many of Bishop Hill's founders, are exhibited at the Bishop Hill Museum. Special events include: *Jorbruksdagarna*, an agricultural festival with harvesting demonstrations, crafts, and games (September); *Julmarknad*, a Christmas market featuring decorations, gifts, and Swedish foods (November); and Lucia Nights, the traditional Swedish festival of lights (December).
Bishop Hill State Historical Site, PO Box D, Bishop Hill, IL 61419, **309/927-3345**

15

Little Norway
Blue Mounds, WI

The tiny village of Mount Horeb reflects its Norwegian heritage with an annual Kafe Stu (July), featuring traditional Norwegian foods served by costumed villagers, and in shops selling imported arts and crafts, foodstuffs, crystal, porcelain, and linens. Nearby is Little Norway, an outdoor museum (also known as Nissedahle, "Valley of the Elves") that includes an outstanding collection of Norse antiques at the homestead of an early Norwegian settler. The homestead site includes a log cabin, barns, and sheds, all dating from 1856. Inside the buildings are the arts and crafts of these Norwegian pioneers. Also on the grounds is the Norway Building, a replica of a *Stavekirke*, a 12th-century Norwegian church. Nearby are the strikingly beautiful crystalline formations of Cave on the Mounds (with 18 underground rooms).
Little Norway, 3575 Hwy J G North, Blue Mounds, WI 53517, **608/437-8211**

16

Little Switzerland
New Glarus, WI

This small community is spiced with the festivals, singing, dancing, and folklore of Switzerland. Chalet-style buildings sport flower boxes; shops sell lace, embroidery, cheese, and Landjaeger sausages favored by Swiss hunters; and yodelers perform. Founded in 1845 by 108 emigrants from the Canton of Glarus, the village has retained its Swiss flavor and customs. The main preservator is the Swiss Historical Village, site of a replica pioneer village. Exhibits include log cabins, a log church, a one-room schoolhouse, and other structures. Attractions also include the Chalet of the Golden Fleece (a museum displaying more than 3000 Swiss items); the historic Swiss paintings in Puempel's Tavern; the Little Switzerland Festival and Heidi Drama (late June); and the Alpine Festival and Wilhelm Tell Drama.
NEWTAP, Box 713B, New Glarus, WI 53574, **608/527-2095**

17

Henry Ford Museum & Greenfield Village
Dearborn, MI

This 240-acre outdoor museum demonstrates the effects of the Industrial Revolution on everyday life: the cast-iron stove that replaced the fireplace; mass-produced furniture; and the incandescent lighting devices that supplanted the kerosene lamp. Included is Edison's actual Menlo Park laboratory. The Henry Ford Museum houses the country's finest collections of cars, airplanes, steam engines, and power machinery. Visitors can compare crude wooden plows to modern tractor plows and the rail cars and stagecoaches of yesteryear to the sleek cars and aircraft of today. The Automobile in American Life exhibit includes a 1946 diner, a 1950s drive-in theater, and a 1960s motel guest room.
Henry Ford Museum & Greenfield Village, 20900 Oakwood Blvd, Dearborn, MI 48121, **313/271-1620**

18

New Harmony
New Harmony, IN

In 1814 the Harmony Society formed of Lutheran Separatists from Wurttemberg, Germany, purchased 30,000 acres on the banks of the Wabash. From 1814 to 1824, the Harmonists perfected a cosmopolitan and efficient community. In 1825, a Scottish intellectual, Robert Owen, bought New Harmony and invited scientists, writers, and educators to participate in his utopian dream. Owen sold his venture in 1828. Today, New Harmony includes 12 exhibition buildings and other exhibits, such as a recreated labyrinthian network of hedges symbolizing the choices taken during life. The Roofless Church and the acclaimed Atheneum continue the radical tradition of this town.
Historic New Harmony, PO Box 579, New Harmony, IN 47631, **812/682-4474**

19

Schoenbrunn Village
New Philadelphia, OH

In 1772, David Zeisberger established a Moravian missionary village in Schoenbrunn, Ohio's first planned settlement. This German Protestant sect believed in pacifism and neutrality and converted Indians by persuading them that peace and order reap greater rewards than hostility. Ten years later, 96 of the Christian Indians were massacred, having been accused of assisting the British against the American militia. During the war, the 60 log and clapboard houses of Schoenbrunn were abandoned, and some were destroyed. The Ohio State Historical Society acquired the site in 1923 and the first cabin was reconstructed in 1927. Today, the village consists of 17 structures, plus a cemetery, and 2 1/2 acres of planted fields.
Schoenbrunn Village, PO Box 129, New Philadelphia, OH 44663, **216/339-3636**

Caesar's Creek Pioneer Village, Waynesville, OH

Amana Colonies, Amana, IA

Caesar's Creek Pioneer Village

Waynesville, OH

When the U.S. Corps of Engineers was constructing a flood-control dam on Caesar's Creek near Waynesville, they discovered log homes built by Quaker settlers in the early 1800s. Local residents began relocating and restoring the structures. Only one house from 1807 is on its original site; the other buildings have been assembled around it to recreate a 19th-century pioneer settlement. The Quaker village contains five homes, a general store, a schoolhouse, a Quaker meeting house, a log smokehouse, accessory buildings, and farming exhibits. Work on the restoration continues. Caesar Creek Lake, formed by the dam, is now a popular vacation spot.
*Caesar's Creek Pioneer Village, 3999 Pioneer Village Rd, Waynesville, OH 45068, **513/897-1120***

Swiss/Amish Village

Sugarcreek, OH

Authentic Swiss costumes, stone-tossing, Swiss wrestling, and polka-bands are a few of the annual late-September festival attractions that celebrate the heritage of this "little Switzerland of Ohio."

Many residents are direct descendants of immigrants whose influence is manifest in the community's architecture, customs, and some 17 varieties of Swiss cheese. The prosperous farm country is also home to America's largest concentration of Amish. Of special interest is the Alpine Historical Museum highlighting early village, farm, and Amish traditions. The region abounds in craft and specialty shops, Amish restaurants, and comfortable accommodations.
*Tuscarawas Co. Convention & Visitors Bureau, PO Box 926, New Philadelphia, OH 44663, **216/364-5453***

RESORTS

Marriott's Lincolnshire Resort

Lincolnshire, IL

Situated 35 miles northwest of downtown Chicago is one of the most complete resorts in northern Illinois. Within its self-contained world of recreation and rejuvenation is an 18-hole championship golf course, a private lake with sail- and paddleboats available in summer, cross-country skiing in winter, and an indoor tennis/racquetball complex, a fully-equipped health club, and the award-winning Marriott's Lincolnshire Theatre. The Lincolnshire provides for business travelers with extensive meeting space, an audio-visual staff, and secretarial services. You can relax in the sauna or spa and then dine at the King's Wharf or Fairfield Inn restaurants. Fine movies or premiere sporting events are available on the in-room cable television system.
*Marriott's Lincolnshire Resort, 10 Marriott Dr, Lincolnshire, IL 60069, **708/634-0100***

Point West Inn

Macatawa, MI

On a peninsula between Lake Michigan and Lake Macatawa, Point West Inn is a year-round resort combining the elegance of a country inn with the expertise and service of a big-city hotel. Swimming, sailing and fishing are obvious choices for recreation, but Point West also features tennis, golf, and tours of area wineries. And Point West visitors are granted membership privileges at the nearby Holland Tennis Club. Other highlights in neighboring Holland include a 200-year-old windmill and the annual Tulip Time Festival. The inn itself is host to the annual Oz Festival in June (Oz author L. Frank Baum lived in Macatawa). Point West is also a favorite for business meetings.
*Point West Inn, Box 36, Macatawa, MI 49434, **616/335-5894***

Heidel House Resort

Green Lake, WI

This resort is on the shores of Wisconsin's Green Lake and sometimes on the lake itself! No, it isn't sinking—the part of the resort that floats is a large party boat, punningly named "Yachts of Fun." Green Lake, Wisconsin's deepest inland lake is also known for its muskie, lake trout, and white bass fishing. If you prefer your recreation on dry land, Tuscumbria is across the street. For vacationing couples, the resort's Pump House is a charming cottage. Groups find it fun to rent Grey Rock Mansion, a seven-bedroom mansion. Of special note is the Fondue Chalet, featuring the Swiss specialty and authentic Swiss decor. Heidel House keeps humming during winter months: Green Lake is an ice fishing paradise, and the neighboring countryside is crisscrossed with Nordic ski trails.
*Heidel House Resort, 643 Illinois Ave, Green Lake, WI 54941, **414/294-3344, 800/444-2812***

Heidel House, Green Lake, WI

SOUTH CENTRAL

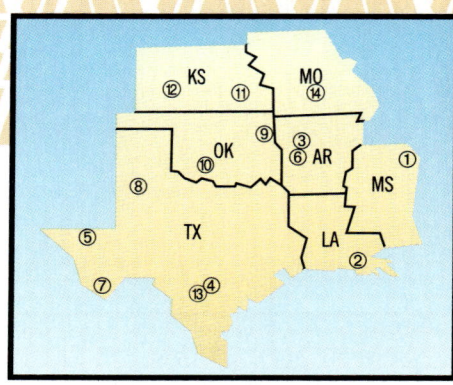

SCENIC DRIVES

Ancient Interstate

*Natchez Trace Parkway,
MS/AL/TN*

Originally an Indian trail, the Natchez Trace Parkway is a modern two-lane recreational road that roughly follows the route of the Old Natchez Trace between Natchez, MS, and Nashville, TN. About 430 miles of the proposed 445-mile-long parkway are complete. The parkway takes the traveler past Indian mounds and sites, historical landmarks, nature trails, and recreation areas. In many places it is possible to walk sections of the old trace. Markers indicate points of interest, such as Mount Locust north of Natchez, a rural plantation home restored to its 1810 appearance. Cypress Swamp, north of Jackson, MS, is a nature trail through a typical cypress-water tupelo swamp in an old bend of the Pearl River. Parkway headquarters and visitor center are five miles north of Tupelo. Facilities include a museum room depicting the history of the area and a 12-minute audio-visual orientation program. Park rangers are on hand to provide information and answer questions.
Supt, Natchez Trace Pkwy, RR 1, NT-143, Tupelo, MS 38801, **601/680-4000**

Bayou Backcountry

*Lafayette, LA–
New Orleans, LA*

While US 90 may not be the fastest route from Lafayette to New Orleans, it offers interesting diversions. Driving south from Lafayette, you'll pass through the rustic town of St. Martinville—site of Longfellow-Evangeline Commemorative Area and the Acadian House Museum—and New Iberia, with the white-pillared splendor of Shadows-on-the-Teche, an antebellum plantation. The landscape is painted with blossoming azaleas, camellias, and massive oaks draped with Spanish moss. Also in New Iberia is the oldest operating rice mill in America. Continuing south along US 90, you'll arrive at the colorful seaport of Morgan City on the banks of the winding Atchafalaya River. Swamp Gardens, location of the first Tarzan movie (1917), is the attraction here and is accessible via numerous tour boats. The wafting, salt-filled breezes of Houma-Terrebonne (the Good Earth) signal your arrival at the Gulf of Mexico.
Office of Tourism, PO Box 94291, Capitol Station, Baton Rouge, LA 70804, **504/342-8119**

Ozark Odyssey

Near Ozark Mountains, AR

The Arkansas River cuts a wide valley between rising bluffs in the shadow of the Ozark Mountains. Hwy 7 runs north of the river and, for breathtaking beauty, it makes little difference what time of year you make the drive. From Russellville, follow Hwy 7 north to Dover in the foothills of the Ozarks and browse through antique shops and flea markets. Continuing north, you'll pass great forest lands bordered by the majestic mountains. Nature lovers, backpackers, and photographers may enjoy a sidetrip to Fort Douglas, site of a large natural bridge, and to Haw Creek Falls, an area of rugged terrain and churning waters on the Big Piney River. Some of the rural, gravel-lined roads off Hwy 7 may be less than perfect, but the ruggedly beautiful landscape makes the detour worthwhile.
Dept of Parks & Tourism, 1 Capitol Mall, Little Rock, AR 72201, **501/682-1511, 501/682-7777, 800/482-8999, 800/642-8383**

South Texas Sojourn

San Antonio Area, TX

San Antonio is home to the "Cradle of Texas Liberty"—the Alamo—and also the launching spot for a scenic and storied drive through southern Texas. Leaving San Antonio, follow I-35 north to FM 3009 and turn left, which leads to Natural Bridge Caverns, an underground tangle of rock formations and caves that reach a depth of 250 feet and stretch for more than a mile beneath Texas ranch country. Continuing north on I-35, you'll pass through New Braunfels, settled in 1845 by German immigrants. Highlights

Cypress Lake, Lafayette, LA

include a preserved and restored immigrant village and a "Wurstfest" celebration each November. Head north on River Road from New Braunfels along the Guadalupe River to Rte 32 at Sattler. A northwest tack on Rte 32 and three miles west on Rte 1623 at the Blanco River brings you to the site of 120-million-year-old footprints of a massive brontosaurus. From Blanco, travel north on US 281 to Johnson City and the working ranch that was known as the Texas White House during Lyndon B. Johnson's administration. Also at the LBJ National Historical Park are the former president's birthplace and grave. The last leg of this drive runs west on US 290 to Fredericksburg, also settled by German immigrants shortly after New Braunfels.
Visitor Info Ctr, 317 Alamo Plaza, San Antonio, TX 78209, **512/270-8748, 800/447-3372**

NATIONAL PARKS & MONUMENTS

Guadalupe Mountains

Nat'l Park, TX

Just southwest of Carlsbad Caverns National Park, the Guadalupe Mountains stand like an island in the desert, watching over the most extensive fossil-reef complex in the world: Much of the park was covered by an enormous sea hundreds of millions of years ago. Some 80 miles of often rugged trails are available to hardy hikers and backpackers, but note that this is rattlesnake country. Motorists can catch spectacular views of El Capitan and Guadalupe Peak, the highest point in Texas, from US 62–180. Campgrounds are near the Visitors Center Headquarters and in the Dog Canyon area; hotel and motel accommodations are at least 30 miles away.
Supt, Guadalupe Mountains National Park, HC 60, Box 400 Salt Flat, TX 79847, **915/828-3251**

Hot Springs

Nat'l Park, AR

Situated in the small Zig Zag mountains southwest of Little Rock, Hot Springs is rich in history. In the early 1900s, huge, ornate buildings were constructed (in an area now known as Bathhouse Row) to cater to healthseekers anxious to soak in the "waters of the Ouachita." Although the tradition of mineral baths has declined, many people still enjoy the relaxing, warm waters from the springs. With a favorable

194

climate year round, Hot Springs is popular with horseback riders, boaters, anglers, and hikers. Scenic drives lead to views of woodlands and distant mountains and to the nearby city of Hot Springs. There are more than 40 springs along the lower slopes of Hot Springs Mountain. At the source, the average water temperature is 143°F.
Hot Springs Convention and Visitors Bureau, Hot Springs Nat'l Park, 134 Convention Blvd, Hot Springs, AR 71901, **800/543-BATH**

Big Bend
Nat'l Park, TX

The southern boundary of this park and its international boundary between the U.S. and Mexico are formed by the Rio Grande and three major canyons cut by it. This rocky wilderness was once home to freely roaming dinosaurs, and now more than 1000 plants and trees (from cacti to pine) dot the stark landscape. The river borders the park for 107 miles, and trips down the Rio Grande can be made by obtaining a free permit at any ranger station; river-running equipment can be rented west of the park. Lodgings are provided by National Parks Concessions, Inc. Guided horseback tours can also be arranged. All campgrounds, improved and primitive, are available on a first-come basis. Park officials recommend carrying snakebite kits.
Supt, Big Bend Nat'l Park, TX 79834, **915/477-2251**

HISTORIC VILLAGES

The Ranching Heritage Center
Lubbock, TX

Have you ever wondered what life was really like in the Old West? Well, strap on your chaps and step back in time as you visit 33 restored structures representing various aspects and time periods in the history of the ranching industry in Texas and the Southwest. The oldest building is from South Texas in the 1830s. Also included are a one-room schoolhouse, a blacksmith shop, a bunkhouse, ranch headquarters, a train depot, a carriage house, and several types of windmills. During special events and on summer weekends, volunteers demonstrate activities such as soap making, baking, horseshoeing, furniture construction, and quilt making. Throughout the year, visitors may tour the ranch site.
Museum of Texas Tech University, PO Box 43191, Lubbock, TX 79409, **806/742-2442**

Tsa-La-Gi, Tahlequah, OK

Tsa-La-Gi
Tahlequah, OK

For America's noble, early 19th-century Cherokee Indians, the infamous yearlong forced march—the "Trail of Tears"—in 1838 was a holocaust of heartbreak, blizzards, disease, and hunger. More than 4000 died in the cruelly-administered federal effort to relocate the Cherokee Nation from their native southeastern domains to the wilderness of northeastern Oklahoma. Before the Civil War, they established Tahlequah as their capital; built a public school system; established seminaries; and sent top scholars off to America's most historic town. Tahlequah still serves as the tribal center. Highlights include the Cherokee Heritage Center; the Cherokee National Museum; performances of a dramatic pageant, "Trail of Tears," at an outdoor amphitheater; and the recreated 17th-century working village of Tsa-La-Gi, all of which eloquently demonstrate the triumphant dignity of the Cherokee culture.
Cherokee Nat'l Hist Soc, PO Box 515, Tahlequah, OK 74465, **918/456-6007**

Indian City, USA
Anadarko, OK

An authentic restoration of Indian dwellings and the recreation of a way of life, Indian City is on the site of the massacre of the Tonkawa Indians by a band of Shawnees and other mercenaries during the Civil War. Planned and constructed under the supervision of the University of Oklahoma's Department of Anthropology, the dwellings are set in seven separate mock villages representing seven different tribes. The authentic Indian homes range from simple "wickiups" to familiar conical tepees to elaborate multi-story pueblos. Numerous artifacts illustrate the American Indian's ancient way of life. Tours are conducted by Indian guides. Dancers perform for most tours, and a Plains Indian Ceremonial is conducted many Saturday nights. A museum and campground are also on the premises.
Indian City, USA, PO Box 695, Anadarko, OK 73005, **405/247-5661**

Old Cowtown Museum
Wichita, KS

You may think that you're on the set of a frontier movie, but this isn't Hollywood—the buildings are real. You are on location in historic Wichita. The 36 restored structures depict the pioneer period from 1865–1880. Strolling through this quaint village back into history, you can't help but marvel at the painstaking detail rendered in the authentic decor, furnishings, and artifacts. Your journey will take you through rustic homes, a blacksmith's forge, harness and saddle shop, a corner drugstore, a saloon, and an old jail. Costumed characters populate the streets during summer weekends, and the Old Sedgwick County Fair is the big attraction in October. A Victorian Christmas is recreated on six consecutive evenings after Thanksgiving.
Old Cowtown Museum, 1871 Sim Park Dr, Wichita, KS 67203, **316/264-0671**

Boxley Valley, Ozark National Forest

Dodge City

Dodge City, KS

The Earp and Masterson brothers, Doc Holliday, Wild Bill Hickok, Buffalo Bill, Big Bill Tilghman, Shoot-Em-Up Ike, One-Eyed Jake, Toothless Neil are part of a seemingly endless legacy of this most infamous of all six-shooter communities at the top of the 1000-mile Santa Fe Trail. Five distinctly American terms originated in this rootin' tootin' town: "stinker" (buffalo hunters); "joint" (saloon); "stiff" (rigid corpse); "red light district" (from visiting railroad workers who left their lanterns in front of brothels); and "cooler" (the first official jail). Another of Dodge's grim realities was Boot Hill—a lonely bluff where gunfight losers were unceremoniously buried with their boots on. Kansas' number one tourist attraction is the combination of Boot Hill Cemetery and a replica of 1875 Front Street, both in today's downtown community. Here, one can find stagecoach rides, High Noon boardwalk gunfight showdowns, Miss Kitty's Long Branch Saloon, historic buildings and sites, small museums, shops, and assorted period-related amusements.

Dodge City Area Chamber of Commerce, Box 939, Dodge City, KS 67801, **316/337-3119**

The Marriott's Tan-Tar-A Resort

Osage Beach, MO

Tan-Tar-A means "one who moves swiftly," and that saying applies to this resort, which has grown from 12 cottages in 1960 to over 930 rooms, suites, and villas spread over 420 acres on the shores of the Lake of the Ozarks. On this shimmering lake you can water-ski and sail or just relax while sunbathing and fishing. For vacationing linksmen, Tan-Tar-A offers 27 holes of championship-quality golf, plus a staff of PGA professionals. There are six outdoor courts and an indoor sports center with all-weather tennis and racquetball courts. Other activities include bowling, billiards, miniature golf, canoeing, five pools and exciting Broadway-style shows at the Mainstage Theatre. Tan-Tar-A is also known as "The Honeymoon Capital of the Midwest." All of this, plus shops and 20 tempting restaurants and lounges on a wooded lakeshore make this a perennially popular resort.

Marriott's Tan-Tar-A Resort, State Rd KK, Osage Beach, MO 65065, **314/348-3131, 800/228-9290**

RESORTS

Plaza San Antonio

San Antonio, TX

With its red tile roof, sun-drenched climate, tranquil courtyards, and splashing fountains, the Plaza San Antonio captures the spirit of 19th century Spain. Each of the 250 rooms has its own private balcony overlooking the outdoor pool and terraced gardens. The hotel is within walking distance of the historic district, which is noted for its Victorian mansions and for the Alamo. Nearby is Riverfront, dotted with shops and outdoor cafes. The hotel offers tennis (two lighted courts), plus an exercise room and sauna. Restaurants include the casually elegant Anaqua and The Restoration Pub, a German home with fireplaces and pedimented porches, built in the 1850s and renovated as a tavern. Light lunches or snacks are served in a garden setting at the Palm Terrace or the Arbor. Three historic homes on the premises have been modernized and now host meetings, banquets, and receptions.

Plaza San Antonio, 555 S Alamo, San Antonio, TX 78205, **512/229-1000, 800/421-1172**

Ozark Mountains, AR

NORTHEAST

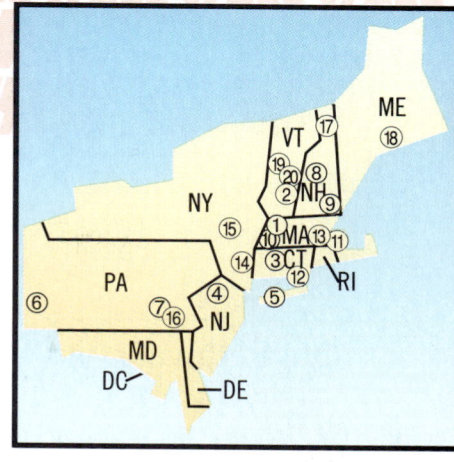

SCENIC DRIVES

1

Highway of History

Mohawk Trail, MA

Following a path originally blazed by the Pocumtuch Indians in 1663, Rte 2 stretches for 63 miles from the Massachusetts-New York line to Miller Falls on the Connecticut River. From the Mohawk Trail Concert Series at Charlemont in summer to superb downhill and cross-country skiing in winter, the trail is an avenue to more than 100 attractions—all cloaked in the seasonal beauty of the Berkshire Hills and the Connecticut Valley. Browse in antique shops, art galleries, country stores, flea markets, street fairs, and craft shows or take in a play at a summer theatre in Williamstown. Natural wonders abound along this route including the views from Mount Greylock, the Bridge of Flowers in Greenfield, and a natural bridge in North Adams with 30-foot marble walls attesting to thousands of years of erosion.
Chamber of Commerce, 69 Main St, N Adams, MA 01247, **413/663-3735**

2

Vermont Vistas

Woodstock, VT

This 155-mile tour of the Ottauquechee Valley, is particularly recommended for viewing fall foliage. Take US 4 east from Woodstock to White River Junction—the spot to sample local maple syrup and other goodies confected from Vermont's famous sweetener, as well as to shop for fine woolen products. Take US 5 north to East Thetford, continue on VT 113 past the rustic cottages of tiny Post Mills and Chelsea to VT 110, and then head north to Barre. The Rock of Ages (exit 6, I-89) is the site of the world's largest granite quarry; a train ride through the excavation is available in summer. US 302 leads you to Montpelier, where the Wood Art Gallery at Vermont College exhibits more than 250 paintings by Thomas Watterman Wood and works by American artists from the 1920s and 1930s. The Vermont State House is Doric and Corinthian architecture, crowned with a 14-carat gold-leaf dome. Take US 2 west to Middlesex and then VT 100 south to Stockbridge. The landscape is dotted with white-steepled churches, weathered red barns, and green meadows, against a backdrop of snow-capped mountains. VT 107 east takes you to VT 12 south back to Woodstock.
Travel Div, 134 State St, Montpelier, VT 05602, **802/828-3236**

3

Yankee Country

Hartford Area, CT

This river city, filled with parks, historic museums, and colonial mansions, is the point of departure for a 90-mile excursion through woodlands, hills, and meadows. You'll be wooed by roadside offerings as you navigate rural byways flanked by stone walls dating to the colonial period. Follow I-91 north to exit 45 at Warehouse Point, home of the Connecticut Electric Railway Trolley Museum. Take Rtes 140 and 75 west to Rte 20, and go west to Riverton where Lambert Hitchcock's 19th-century furniture is displayed at the Hitchcock Museum. West River Road heads south through People's State Forest and into Pleasant Valley to a 680 acre wildlife sanctuary. Follow Rte 181 south to Rte 44 and go east to Avon, home of the Farmington Valley Arts Center. This stone building, an explosives warehouse in the revolutionary war, houses an art gallery and artists' studios. Return to Rte 44 east, and then follow Rte 10 south to Rte 4 east. Here in Farmington you can visit the colonial Stanley-Whitman House and the Hill-Stead Museum, decorated with French impressionist paintings and treasures from around the world. Rte 4 will take you back to Hartford and to the homes of Mark Twain and Harriet Beecher Stowe. Stop at the Noah Webster House in West Hartford.
Dept. of Economic Dev, 210 Washington St, Hartford CT 06106, **800/243-1685, 800/842-7492** *(in CT),* **203/566-3977, -3385**

HISTORIC VILLAGES

4

Waterloo Village

Stanhope, NJ

Armaments for Washington's Continental Army were forged in these steep Sussex County hills not far from the Delaware Water Gap. And not long after that, Waterloo became a key lock-and-plane terminal along the old Morris Canal, northern New Jersey's first bulk-freight transportation system. Today, this restored village recalls its days as a bustling early 19th-century inland port. Surviving is a still-operational 1790 blacksmith shop, a gristmill and sawmill, and a general store stocked with reproduced period crafts. The church, in continuous use for 120 years, holds Sunday services, and more than 15 other early buildings include inns, taverns, an ironmaster's mansion, an apothecary, herb-drying rooms, broom and cabinet shops, a weaving barn, and a pottery shed. Seasonal events include antique and arts festivals and a renowned summer music festival.
Waterloo Foundation for the Arts, Inc, Waterloo Village, Stanhope, NJ 07874, **201/347-0900**

Old Sturbridge Village, Sturbridge, MA

Old Bethpage

Bethpage, NY

Almost in the shadows of the skyscrapers of Manhattan a smithy works at his anvil, and a schoolmarm teaches the three Rs in a primitive schoolhouse at a skillfully assembled working model of a typical early 19th-century farm village. Throughout the year are seasonal fairs, holiday celebrations, militia drills, temperance meetings, period dances, music, and parades. The setting includes authentically furnished houses, a schoolhouse, a tavern, barns, farm animals, era shops, an operating blacksmith, and carpentry shops. Actually, Old Bethpage never existed as a single community. Restoration has brought together historic structures from various parts of Long Island to establish this vintage composite.
Old Bethpage Village Restoration, Nassau County, Dept of Recreation & Parks, Round Swamp Road, Old Bethpage, NY 11804, **516/420-5281**

6

Old Economy Village

Ambridge, PA

In 1804, the Harmonists came from Germany, seeking religious and societal freedom. In 1824, they established the village of Economy along the Ohio River in Western Pennsylvania. Although the Pietist society at Economy, the longest-lived of three Harmonist towns in the U.S., was dissolved in 1905, Old Economy Village still thrives as an example of an immigrant communal settlement. The core of the village remains, including the large Feast Hall, used for meetings and communal meals; the Great House, the home of Harmonist leader and prophet George Rapp; and the cabinetmaker's; the tailor's; the cobbler's; and other shops. Costumed guides roam the 6.7 acres, answering questions and taking on the roles of actual Harmonist followers. These volunteers also give periodic demonstrations of traditional pioneer tasks.
The Harmonie Assn, Inc, 14th & Church Sts, Ambridge, PA 15003, **412/266-4500**

7

Lancaster County

Lancaster, PA

Delicious shoofly pie, snitz and knepp, funnel cakes, and other specialties are reasons enough to visit this center of Pennsylvania Dutch culture. The region was settled in the late 17th and early 18th centuries by fundamentalist Amish and Mennonite pioneers, the descendants of whom are known as "the plain people." The term "Dutch" is misleading and is a colonial adaptation of "Deutsche," referring to the area's predominant German ancestry. Aside from the ethnic foods of this rural retreat, one finds an unmechanized, brotherly way of life, time-removed customs, one-room schoolhouses, unadorned dress, and farming and transportation methods much as they have been for centuries. Lancaster County abounds in farmer's markets, historic homes open for public tours, covered bridges, hex signs, folk art and crafts, and lodgings. An excellent way to enjoy "the Lancaster experience" is via one of several Amish farm tours with a guide to explain this deeply religious way of life. Because of the literal Biblical restriction forbidding "graven images," visitors are asked not to snap people-pictures without permission.
Pennsylvania Dutch Convention & Visitors Bureau, 501 Greenfield Rd, Lancaster, PA 17601, **717/299-8901**

8

Shaker Village

Canterbury, NH

Englishwoman founder Mother Ann Lee and her tiny handful of "Shaking Quakers" first reached New England shores in 1774. The Shakers were seeking freedom for their religion and for their utopian beliefs. By 1792, this industrious Shaker colony, which held all goods in common, was established 30 miles north of Concord, NH. In its peak years, Canterbury Shakers numbered some 400 and had earned international renown for their simple, yet functional, building, furniture, and handicraft designs. Today, 22 of the colony's still-standing buildings and 600 acres of its field, woodlot, and waterway systems have been pre-served. Resident Shaker sisters guide visitors through five historically furnished buildings. Daily attendance is restricted to a few hundred to maintain the site's striking tranquility. Special events include craft demonstrations, heritage workshops, a series of Shaker-related art exhibits, children's programs, and meals. Friday evening candlelit tour/dinners in the Creamery Restaurant feature authentic Shaker menus.
Canterbury Shaker Village Inc, 288 Shaker Rd, Canterbury, NH 03224, **603/783-9511**

9

Strawbery Banke

Portsmouth, NH

This little-known, but historic, New England seaport dates back to 1623. Since 1957 the populace has created a 10-acre waterfront outdoor museum and cultural resource, incorporating some 42 restored architectural treasures dating from 1695. Some houses have been simply preserved and adapted for modern use; others are educational exhibits covering archaeology, traditional trades, and the evolution of architectural styles and construction techniques spanning four centuries of New England history. Year-round activities include workshops and historical games for kids, vintage songs and stories, and period decoration projects. There are symposiums on historic gardens, clinics on restoring old houses, seminar-workshops on boatbuilding, instruction on watercoloring and other historic art forms, craft fairs, seasonal events, and programs for the whole family.
Strawbery Banke, PO Box 300, Portsmouth, NH 03802-0300, **603/433-1100**

Photo: Clay Nolen
Old Bethpage, Bethpage, NY

Old Sturbridge Village, Sturbridge, MA

Hancock Shaker Village
Pittsfield, MA

Located in the hills of western Massachusetts, this restored 18th-century village depicts the farm life and crafts of the Shakers, America's oldest surviving religious communal sect. The "City of Peace" dates back to 1790 and was the third of 19 Shaker communities. This landmark provided a home for Shakers until 1960. With 20 restored buildings and 1000 acres of rolling farm and woodland, the "City of Peace" is now a popular attraction. The most interesting building is the Round Stone Barn, erected in 1826. Its efficient shape allowed farm workers to water and feed cattle in a simple circular operation around the perimeter, leaving center space for hay and grain storage. In other exhibits, crafts people reproduce Shaker wooden and tin goods, furniture, and confections. Visitors participate in special cooking, dancing, and farming workshops and demonstrations.

Hancock Shaker Village, PO Box 898, Pittsfield, MA 01202, ***413/443-0188***

Plimoth Plantation
Plymouth, MA

Pilgrims who survived the first terrible seasons in this most historic of all colonial American settlements endured what they would always remember as "The Starving Time." Their slender supply of food was shared by stragglers from outposts along the coast and with the Indians who later helped save them. Meanwhile, their spring planting was a disaster. Before their first year was over, half of them had died. Based on extensive research, today's recreated plantation conjures the stark original 17th-century colony, complete with 1627-vintage timber houses, furnishings, farm animals, and a replica of the Mayflower. A museum staff is trained to "impersonate" such known pilgrims as Miles Standish and William Bradford, as well as seamen who crossed the Atlantic in subsequent years to establish the first surviving English colony in the New World. They dress in period clothing, perform typical daily routines of the era, and speak in the Elizabethan language of Shakespeare.

Plimoth Plantation, PO Box 1620, Plymouth, MA 02360, ***508/746-1622***

Mystic Seaport, Mystic, CT

Photo: Claire White Peterson

Mystic Seaport
Mystic, CT

America's proud and unique sailing heritage is enshrined at this 37-acre preserve of maritime history. That bygone shipbuilding, whaling, and trading-port life is captured amidst the large sailing vessels moored here, scores of small craft prototypes, museum exhibits, and the complex of more than 60 mid-19th-century buildings, lofts, sheds, chapels, and taverns of waterfront New England. Several hundred interpreter-guides are on hand, many over 70 years of age with sea water in their veins and an intimate understanding of nautical traditions. There are many kinds of adult handicraft courses, scores of demonstrations, strollers singing sea shanties, an elaborate planetarium that offers celestial navigation instruction, open fireplace cooking, and seafood festivals.

Mystic Seaport Museum, Inc, PO Box 6000, Mystic, CT 06355, ***203/572-0711***

Old Sturbridge Village
Sturbridge, MA

At Sturbridge Village you can immerse yourself in an early American dining experience employing hearth cooking techniques, authentic preparations and kitchenware. It's one of many historical adventures offered in this living-history museum that recreates a rural New England 1830s village, a functioning community authentic to the smallest detail. Visitors are transported to the early 19th century amid 200 acres of period structures including meeting houses; water-powered grist, saw, and wool-carding mills; a district school; tin, blacksmith, and pottery shops; shoe shop, law office, bank, general store, and a working farm complete with livestock. Preparations for Thanksgiving include a turkey shoot and hearth cooking. All "recipes" are taken from period texts; turkeys are roasted in tin-reflector ovens; and a full traditional dinner is served in the Bullard Tavern.

Old Sturbridge Village, 1 Old Sturbridge Village Rd, Sturbridge, MA 01566, ***508/347-3362***. *The hearing-impaired can call the Telecommunications Device for the Deaf (TDD) number,* ***508/347-5383***

The Woodstock Inn & Resort, Woodstock, VT

RESORTS

▼ 14

Mohonk Mountain House
New Paltz, NY

In time, Mohonk Mountain House may well be a century removed; in distance, less than 100 miles north of New York City. This imposing 280-room mansion commands peace, and, in keeping with the 19th-century atmosphere, the rooms have period furnishings, and many have wood-burning fireplaces. Originally built by Quakers, the resort is a National Historic Landmark. The steep, rugged terrain of the 2000-acre estate is best traversed by hiking, horseback riding, or horse-drawn carriages. More than 128 outdoor gazebos provide places to rest and observe the countryside. The clean mountain air can also be taken in on the 9-hole

The Balsams Grand Resort Hotel, Dixville Notch, NH

golf course, on six tennis courts, or on the lake—swimming, boating, and fishing are popular. In winter, the sports change to ice skating on the frozen lake, cross-country skiing or snow shoeing on well-marked trails, and sleigh rides through the woods.
Mohonk Mountain House, 1000 Mountain Rest Rd, Mohonk Lake, New Paltz, NY 12561, **914/255-1000**

▼ 15

Otesaga Hotel
Cooperstown, NY

The Baseball Hall of Fame should be enough to lure you to historic Cooperstown, New York, at the foot of Lake Otsego near the Susquehanna River. There is also the lure of a charming Georgian inn, the Otesaga Hotel, with verandas offering lake and mountain views. Sailing, boating, and fishing are just steps away on Lake Otsego. Swimmers can float lazily in the lake or heated pool. The first tee of an 18-hole championship golf course is just 100 yards from the hotel. Two tennis courts are on the grounds. In addition to the baseball museum, Cooperstown is noted for the Fenimore Museum, known for its collection of American folk art as well as extensive memorabilia of James Fenimore Cooper, the author of *The Last of the Mohicans*.
The Otesaga Hotel, Lake St, PO Box 311, Cooperstown, NY 13326, **607/547-9931**

▼ 16

Lancaster Host Golf Resort & Conference Center
Lancaster, PA

Located on 225 acres in the heart of Pennsylvania Dutch Country, this resort offers 330 deluxe rooms. A variety of cuisines, with a selection of meal plans, is available. Activities include 27 holes of PGA championship golf, and tennis on eight outdoor and four indoor courts. This self-contained resort offers supervised activities for children of all ages and extensive conference facilities. In Lancaster County, Amish horse-and-buggies share roads with automobiles. Attractions include the Fulton Opera House, opened in 1852, and the Pennsylvania Farm Museum of Landis Valley.
Lancaster Host Golf Resort & Conference Center, 2300 Lincoln Hwy E, Lancaster, PA 17602, **717/299-5500, 800/233-0121**

The Balsams Grand Resort Hotel, Dixville Notch, NH

The Balsams
Dixville Notch, NH

This grand resort hotel in northern New Hampshire pioneered the American Plan concept in hotels and resorts. The plan has been expanded so that a single rate covers virtually everything the resort has to offer, including golf, tennis, water sports, trout fishing, hiking with a natural history guide in the 15,000-acre private estate, skiing (downhill and cross-country), and ice skating. Hot toddies, a crackling fire, and live entertainment warm winter evenings. Nestled between a lake and the snow-capped White Mountains, The Balsams resembles a castle in the Swiss alps.

The Balsams, Grand Resort Hotel, Dixville Notch, NH 03576, **603/255-3400**

Asticou Inn
Northeast Harbor, ME

In the rugged wilderness of Acadia National Park, the Asticou Inn has been part of Maine's vacation heritage for over 100 years. Overlooking Northeast Harbor on Mt. Desert Island, the inn is a short sail from Somes Sound, the only natural fjord in North America. The four-story rambling inn has many cozy rooms and guest houses with kitchen facilities. The Northeast Harbor Golf Club welcomes Asticou guests, and there are three other nearby courses. Grounds are beautifully landscaped and invite strolling—especially through the lovely formal gardens. Miles of mountain trails and carriage roads await the more adventuresome.

Asticou Inn, Northeast Harbor, ME 04662, **207/276-3344**

Basin Harbor Club
Vergennes, VT

Along with crisp mountain air and dense woods, this resort offers guests a chance to photograph Champ, the "Loch Ness" monster of Lake Champlain who reportedly has been seen, but never captured. The Basin Harbor Club, which celebrated its centennial in 1986, accommodates guests in two main buildings and 77 cottages. Secluded lakeview cottages with wildflower gardens are ideal for honeymooners or families. Water sports range from sailing to waterskiing. There is an Olympic-sized heated pool, five tennis courts, and an 18-hole golf course. Nearby is a 3200-foot airstrip. Convention facilities provide a unique business retreat.

Basin Harbor Club, Vergennes, VT 05491, **802/475-2311, 800/622-4000**

Otesaga Hotel, Cooperstown, NY

Acadia National Park, ME

Photo: David Bodson

The Woodstock Inn & Resort
Woodstock, VT

Covered bridges, steeple bells cast by Paul Revere, and a landmark village lure guests to this resort in Vermont. The Woodstock Inn, a three-story colonial style resort, opened in 1969, but the site has been occupied by village inns since 1793. The 143 rooms are decorated in an early American style with handmade Vermont furniture and colorful quilts. Contemporary attractions include the Woodstock Country Club with its 18-hole golf course and indoor sports center. Nearby are hiking, horseback riding and fishing in the Ottauquechee River. Antique shopping, photographing, or simply admiring the region's fabled, fall foliage are popular diversions. The area is known to skiers as the home of Suicide Six ski area. Cross-country skiers are not neglected—47 miles of trails provide views of the Green Mountains. Other winter activities include snowshoeing and moonlight sleigh rides.

The Woodstock Inn & Resort, 14 The Green, Woodstock, VT 05091, **800/448-7900, 802/457-1100**

SOUTHEAST

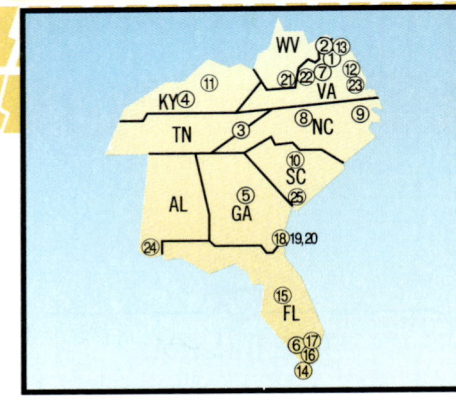

SCENIC DRIVES

1

Appalachian Adventure
Skyline Drive, VA

Winding its way for 105 miles along the peaks of the Blue Ridge Mountains through Shenandoah National Park, Skyline Drive is a nature lover's road. The slow speed limit allows you to appreciate the wild forest flowers, twisting vines, and trout-brimming streams. More than 100 species of trees display their fall colors. Enjoy a roadside picnic at any of 75 scenic overlooks. More than 500 miles of trails include the Appalachian Trail. Numerous parking overlooks with views of the Piedmont and Shenandoah Valley make frequent stops irresistible.

Supt, Shenandoah Nat'l Park, Rt 4, Box 348, Luray, VA 22835, **703/999-2266**

2

Hill Country
Harpers Ferry, WV

With an average elevation of 1500 feet, West Virginia deserves its title as the Mountain State. The rolling ridges of the Appalachian Mountains provide many opportunities to view the region's spectacular scenery. Driving west on Rte 340 from Harpers Ferry, the road winds past battlefields, ruins, and buildings that date back to the Civil War. Today, the heavily wooded countryside dotted with placid lakes is tranquil and peaceful. South on Rte 220, spelunkers will delight in seeing the longest ribbon stalactite in the world at Smoke Hole Caverns. Continuing south on Rte 28 is the southern branch of the Potomac River.

Its pastoral setting contrasts sharply with the breathtaking escarpment of the Seneca Rocks—a massive formation of Tuscarora sandstone rising 960 feet, yet only 15 feet wide at the top! Rock climbers may ascend the face. A tame pathway also leads to the top. Spruce Knob (4863 feet) is further south on Rte 28 and offers a panorama of nine mountain ranges from its observation tower, but beware: The misshapen spruce trees are evidence of the severity of the winds at this exposed peak.

W.V. Dept of Tourism, 2101 Washington St E, Charleston, WV 25305, **304/348-2286, 800/225-5982**

NATIONAL PARKS AND MONUMENTS

3

Great Smoky Mountains
Nat'l Park, TN/NC

Half in Tennessee, half in North Carolina, this park preserves the world's finest example of an

unspoiled temperate deciduous forest. Some 800 square miles of peaks and open valleys are covered with more than 1400 types of flowering plants. "Smoky" refers to the smoke-like haze blanketing the mountains. Some log cabins and barns have been restored to their pioneer-era condition and are open to visitors. Rental horses are available (except in winter) with riding permitted on designated trails. There are 10 campgrounds.

Supt, Great Smoky Mts Nat'l Park, Gatlinburg, TN 37738, **615/436-5615**

4

Mammoth Cave
Nat'l Park, KY

The appeal of this 52,000-acre park is the enormous limestone cave beneath the surface. More than 300 miles of twisting passageways have been mapped. From the up-reaching stalagmites and sturdily hanging stalactites to the onyx pillars, the world's longest cave has some of the most original sights you'll ever see. Guided cave trips are daily. Cave temperature is a constant 54°F. Walking is generally easy, but there are many steps to negotiate. Riverboat cruises are offered on the Green River. Above ground trails include areas with poisonous snakes.

Supt, Mammoth Cave Nat'l Park, Mammoth Cave, KY 42259, **502/758-2328**

Photo: T. Shirakawa

Skyline Drive, VA

Blackwater Falls, WV

Photo: W. Va. Gov's. Office of ECD, Crdit, Gerald S. Ratiff

Everglades National Park, FL

▼5
Ocmulgee
Nat'l Monument, GA

For more than 10,000 years people have sought their livelihood where the Ocmulgee River passes from the red clay land of the rolling piedmont to the sandy flat lands of the coastal plain. The area is noted for the relics of Indian mound builders who lived here. The visitor center houses a major archeological museum. Tours leave the museum for the Earthlodge, a restored ceremonial building with an original floor 1000 years old. The Temple Mound Drive leads to the three largest mounds as well as to the site of the British Colonial Trading Post. Opelofa Nature Trail leads past swamp and forest ecosystems along Walnut Creek.

Ocmulgee Nat'l Monument, 1207 Emery Hwy, Macon, GA 31201, **912/752-8257**

▼6
Everglades
Nat'l Park, FL

The Everglades are the only subtropical wilderness in the U.S. The lifeblood of the area is a freshwater river 50 miles wide but only a few inches deep. The national park acreage is only part of this watery expanse. The park is home and protector to many rare or threatened species such as the American crocodile, the Florida panther, and the great white heron. The Main Visitor Center is about 10 miles southwest of

Florida City (on S.R. 9336), Florida. Camping reservations are accepted for winter months only, when a fee is charged. The park contains numerous marked canoe trails. The Gulf Coast Ranger Station offers boat tours year round.

Supt, Everglades Nat'l Park, PO Box 279, Homestead, FL 33030, **305/247-6211, 305/242-7700**

▼7
Shenandoah
Nat'l Park, VA

The national park runs along both sides of the Skyline Drive and is worth exploring, especially in fall when the nearly 100 varieties of trees burst into their annual chromatic splendor. Numerous campgrounds are scattered throughout the park. More than 500 miles of trails, some of them used heavily, are available to hikers. Park visitor centers can be found at Miles 4.6 and 51. Open March to November.

Supt, Shenandoah Nat'l Park, Rt 4, Box 348, Luray, VA 22835, **703/999-2266**

Ocmulgee National Monument, GA

HISTORIC VILLAGES

▼ 8

Old Salem

Winston-Salem, NC

Founded in 1766 by members of the Moravian Church, this restored congregation town is peopled by costumed guides and includes hand-hewn buildings (many from the 18th century), such as a tobacco shop, bakery, boys' school, firehouse, tavern, shoemaker's shop, and a number of private residences. The Home Moravian Church Sanctuary, still in use, was built in 1800. Also on the grounds is the Museum of Early Southern Decorative Arts, presenting art objects from the Old South in 19 period rooms and six galleries. Other historic points of interest in Winston-Salem include historic Bethabara Park, site of the first Moravian settlement in North Carolina.

Old Salem, Inc, Drawer F, Salem Station, Winston-Salem, NC 27108, **919/721-7300**

▼ 9

Historic Bath

Bath, NC

Founded in 1705, Bath is a vibrant crossroads of mid-Atlantic colonial history. Among its earliest inhabitants were men of great refinement and wealth as well as notorious pirate Edward Teach, better known as Blackbeard. Farms and tobacco plantations prospered as did local merchants. Most of present-day Bath exists within its original quarter-square-mile where a historically-designated district of preserved and restored vintage structures includes the state's oldest surviving church and one of its oldest residences. Sailing and other watersport enthusiasts are attracted by the warm waters of the famous Hatteras Inner and Outer Banks region. A visitor's center offers brochures and an introductory film. The Bath Guest House provides sumptuous southern-style breakfasts as well as offering guests the use of bicycles.

Historic Bath, PO Box 148, Bath, NC 27808, **919/923-3971**

Historic Camden

Camden, SC

Fever for independence was not universal in upper South Carolina, but little support for the British came from this oldest inland settlement of 1750 Irish Quakers. Consequently, General Cornwallis made the town the final stronghold before the ultimate British defeat at Yorktown.

When the redcoats abruptly departed Camden in 1781, left behind was a unique collection of swords, muskets, coins, cannon balls, and cooking utensils, plus six small surrounding forts and substantial remains of the old community. The historic district recreates this period, with detailed dioramas, restored log cabins filled with antique museum pieces, and the Joseph Kershaw mansion taken over as Cornwallis' headquarters. Much of the area offers hiking trails, with historic markers; fort sites; and picnic areas.

Historic Camden, Box 710, Camden, SC 29020, **803/432-9841**

Shakertown

Harrodsburg, KY

Each time we use a flat broom, a wooden clothes pin, a circular saw, or a washing machine, we can thank the inventive Shakers. This religious sect believed in farsighted notions of racial and sexual equality, staunch pacifism, scientific agriculture and experimental farming, and total celibacy. This historic village preserves 30 original 19th-century buildings. A self-guided tour enables visitors to see 40 rooms of Shaker furnishings in the Centre Family House and watch broommakers, joiners, coopers, spinners, weavers, and quilters carrying on their trades. You can also sleep in authentic Shaker lodgings. More than 80 guest rooms are furnished with traditional hand-woven rugs, curtains, and Shaker furniture reproductions. Shaker meals are offered in a restored dining room.

Shakertown at Pleasant Hill, 3500 Lexington Rd, Harrodsburg, KY 40330, **606/734-5411**

Williamsburg, VA

Colonial Williamsburg
Williamsburg, VA

From 1699 to 1780, Williamburg served as the capital of the Virginia Colony. In 1926 John D. Rockefeller and others began restoring a large part of the original town to its 18th-century condition. More than 170 acres have been preserved, including 88 buildings and 90 acres of gardens and greens. In addition, 50 other major buildings have been rebuilt according to exhaustive research, making this the largest and most comprehensive 18th-century restoration project in the U.S. Using tools and methods that were common in the 18th century, craftsmen create goods ranging from ragpaper books to elegant wooden cabinets. Exhibits include more than 225 period rooms, 20 craft shops with live demonstrations, the Abby Aldrich Rockefeller Folk Art Center, and the 650-acre Carter's Grove Plantation nearby.
The Colonial Williamsburg Foundation, PO Box 1776, Williamsburg, VA 23187, **804/229-1000, 800/HISTORY**

Alexandria
Alexandria, VA

This ancient seaport, founded in 1749 by Scottish landowner John Alexander has restored and preserved more than 2000 18th- and 19th-century buildings. Old Town Alexandria presents examples of Georgian, Federal, Greek Revival, and Victorian styles. Supported by interpretive exhibits, are lyceums, taverns, an athenaeum, and an 18th-century town hall and market square; a Presbyterian meeting house with the Tomb of the Unknown Revolutionary Soldier; the George Washington National Masonic Memorial; and old Fort Ward—now an outstanding Civil War museum with an adjoining 45-acre park, outdoor amphitheater, and picnic area. Annual events include historical observances, concert series, a popular Scottish Games and Gathering of the Clans Festival, and a second-to-none Washington Birthday bash.
Alexandria Conv & Vis Bureau, 221 King St, Alexandria VA 22314, **703/838-4200;** *24-hour taped message on special events,* **703/838-5005**

RESORTS

Hawk's Cay
Duck Key, FL

Hawk's Cay is a 60-acre West-Indies-style resort in the Florida Keys. Renovated extensively in 1989, it boasts a landscaped tennis garden, two ocean-side Jacuzzis, four restaurants, and 20 new suites with private balconies. Three charter boats transport anglers to some of the best game fishing in the world. Four miles from Hawk's Cay is the largest barrier reef in America, teeming with snapper, grouper, yellowtail, and mackerel. Deeper waters are home for dolphin, marlin, and tuna. A unique Starter's Program for adults offers basic instruction in scuba diving, fishing, and tennis. Students can then do their "homework" on a sailboat, in or under the water, or on the two clay tennis courts or six hard courts. Sombrero Golf Course is nearby.
Hawk's Cay, Mile Marker 61, Marathon Duck Key, FL 33050, **305/743-7000, 800/432-2242** *FL,* **800/327-7775**

Walt Disney World
Lake Buena Vista, FL

Near Orlando in central Florida is a dream world offering more amusements, attractions, rides, shopping, sporting facilities, lodgings, and restaurants than any resort anywhere. Walt Disney World opened in 1971 and has never stopped growing. It encompasses such unique attractions as the Magic Kingdom, which includes Adventureland, Frontierland, Liberty Square, Tomorrowland, Mickey's Starland, and Fantasyland; Epcot Center, with Future World and World Showcase; Typhoon Lagoon Water Park; and Disney-MGM Studio Theme Park, with adventures in front of and behind the camera. Don't miss out on Disney Village Marketplace, River Country, Discovery Island and other sights. Not only does Disney provide the fun, but it also provides on its own property lodgings and facilities to suit families, campers, conventioneers, and budget-conscious travelers. There are 19 hotels, a campground and vacation villas totaling 17,260 vacation accommodations. Plan on staying a minimum of four to five days just to see the top attactions.
Walt Disney World Guest Information, PO Box 10,040, Lake Buena Vista, FL 32830, **407-824-4321**

Fontainebleau Hilton Resort & Spa
Miami Beach, FL

Like the phoenix, the mythical bird that rose from ashes, the Fontainebleau has risen from a state of neglect and disrepair to re-establish itself as one of the most glamourous resorts in America. The rooms have been redone in a Caribbean decor with overstuffed chairs, plush carpeting, and ornamental fireplaces. The redesigned lobby provides a view of the ocean and a rock grotto. The grotto, with its own cascading waterfall, surrounds an enormous free-form swimming pool. Lush tropical trees around the perimeter provide shade. Other temptations include three outdoor whirlpools, two 18-hole golf courses, and a bi-level tennis complex with seven lighted courts. Water sports, pursued off the private 300-foot-wide beach, include windsurfing and sailing. Chartered fishing boats take anglers in search of Atlantic sport fish.
Fontainbleau Hilton Resort & Spa, 4441 Collins Ave, Miami Beach, FL 33140, **305/538-2000**

Fountainebleau, Miami Beach, FL

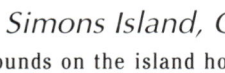

King & Prince Beach Resort

St. Simons Island, GA

History abounds on the island home of this Spanish colonial-style hotel and adjacent villas. The hotel is furnished with antiques, stained glass, and chandeliers. The villas, with kitchen facilities, offer a view of the sunrise over the Atlantic. History buffs will enjoy trips to nearby Fort Frederica, a British Fort built in 1736; to a lighthouse built in 1870; or to Christ Church, where Charles Wesley preached in 1736. More vigorous activities can be pursued on four tennis courts, in an indoor pool, or aboard a rental sailboat. A major expansion added 55 ocean view rooms, an indoor pool, gift shop, and convention facilities.

The King & Prince Resort, PO Box 798, St. Simons Island, GA 31522, **912/638-3631, 800/342-0212**

The Breakers

Palm Beach, FL

Architecture buffs will be attracted to this Italian Renaissance-style resort. The lobby and ballrooms are adorned with Flemish tapestries, frescoes, marble, and gilt. The large, luxurious rooms overlook the ocean or the gardens. The Florentine Dining Room specializes in continental cuisine. The wine collection, awarded for its diversity and quality, contains over 500 vintages. For those who need a spot of fresh air, there is a private beach to explore, two 18-hole golf courses, 20 tennis courts, scuba, snorkeling, and a heated outdoor pool.

The Breakers, 1 S County Rd, Palm Beach, FL 33480, **407/655-6611**

The Greenbrier, White Sulphur Springs, WV

The Cloister

Sea Island, GA

This plantation-style resort revives the Tara spirit with its expanse of lawn, beautiful gardens, and 10,000 acres of swaying palms and moss-covered oaks. The Cloister pampers its guests with top-notch service and a variety of accommodations. Besides the main building, there are beachfront villas and cottages. The beach, five miles long, is considered one of the finest on the east coast. Golfers are challenged by 36 holes divided into four distinct nines. Tennis buffs improve their game on the 18 clay courts or with lessons by a staff of pros. Other activities include skeet shooting, miniature golf, wind surfing, sailing, biking, swimming in two outdoor pools, and horseback riding.

The Cloister, Sea Island, GA 31561, **912/638-3611, 800/SEA ISLA**

Villas by the Sea

Jekyll Island, GA

Looking for a secluded villa, overlooking 1800 feet of Atlantic beachfront? This island resort offers it all. Each villa has a full kitchen, but many guests prefer to dine in the resort's restaurant or at one of 10 other on the island. A year-round pool competes with the ocean surf. Attractions on Jekyll Island include Summer Waves water park, three 18-hole golf courses and one 9-hole course, and eight lighted outdoor tennis courts, 13 clay tennis courts and one indoor court, miles of nature trails for cyclists and hikers, and musicals at an outdoor amphitheater during the summer.

Villas by the Sea, 1175 N Beachview Dr, Jekyll Island, GA 31527, **912/635-2521**

The Greenbrier

White Sulphur Springs, WV

The Greenbrier, built in 1778, is one of the most famous grand old resorts in America. The rooms, 650 in all with no two alike, are in the main building or in guest houses. Horse-drawn carriages transport guests over the grounds and past the Spring House, a landmark for the "curative" waters of White Sulphur Springs. Outdoor enthusiasts will find activities from golf to tennis, swimming, hiking, and fishing. The spa offers massages, saunas, and mineral baths. The Greenbrier, winner of many culinary awards, started its own cooking school in 1981. An artist's colony "on the hill" sells pottery and other handcrafted items.

The Greenbrier White Sulphur Springs, Station A, WV 24986, **800/624-6070**

King & Prince, St. Simons Island, GA

The Homestead
Hot Springs, VA

If George Washington and Thomas Jefferson were alive to stroll this 16,000-acre estate, they would still be satisfied with the traditional elegance. Afternoon tea in the Great Hall is accompanied by a string orchestra. The 600 rooms are all comfortable and some even sport spiral staircases leading to bedrooms. Facilities include three 18-hole golf courses, a trout stream, graded walks and paths, and four skeet and trap shooting fields. After a strenuous ride on a horse from the resort's own livery, soak in the naturally-heated mineral water pool. An indoor and outdoor pool and 19 tennis courts are also available. Winter sports enthusiasts can do figure eights on the Olympic-sized ice skating rink or perfect their stem turns on the downhill runs.
*The Homestead, Hot Springs, VA 24445, **800/542-5734** VA, **800/336-5771***

The Tides Lodge
Irvington, VA

The Tides Lodge is an intimate resort on a private 175-acre peninsula. Golfers may choose from 45 holes. After a dip in a freshwater or saltwater pool, eat at the poolside sandwich bar. Tennis (there is even one lighted court), sailing, and canoeing are popular. The informal Binnacle restaurant overlooks the marina, while the Royal Stewart is more formal. The perfect way to end the day is a twilight or moonlight cruise aboard one of the Lodge's two yachts.
*The Tides Lodge, PO Box 309, Irvington, VA 22480, **800/24-TIDES, 800/446-5660** VA*

Marriott's Grand Hotel
Point Clear, AL

Watching the sunset over Mobile Bay while sipping a mint julep has become synonymous with this grand resort. The 307 rooms have recently been renovated with ceiling fans, plush sitting rooms, and views of the bay, marina, or lagoon. The Lakewood Golf Club has two challenging 18-hole courses and PGA instructors. The resort's 53-foot yacht, complete with crew, is available for deep-sea fishing. The grand scale of this southern resort includes a 750,000-gallon swimming pool and a 40-slip marina. Trail riding offered by the hotel livery allows guests to slip away. Other diversions include 10 tennis courts and a sauna.
*Marriott's Grand Hotel, Scenic Route 98, Point Clear, AL 36564, **800/228-9290, 800/268-8181** (from Canada)*

Palmetto Dunes Resort
Hilton Head Island, SC

Palmetto Dunes Resort, on 1800 acres in the center of the island, accommodates guests in two hotels or in private villas. The Hyatt offers 479 rooms and 31 suites, with entertainment provided at its nightclub, Club Indigo. The Mariner's Inn offers rooms surrounding a central courtyard that contains an outdoor pool and groupings of tropical trees and flowers. Outdoor sports are almost a science here—four golf courses are the site of many tournaments. The Rod Laver Tennis Center has its 25 courts (six lighted) and staff of pros. The more adventuresome can explore the eight-mile lagoon system in a canoe or paddleboat. You can also relax and leave the driving to the captain of the Adventure, a tour boat specializing in nature, dinner, or moonlight cruises. Fishermen will be pleased to know that the day's catch is broiled over mesquite and served for dinner at the Pisces Restaurant.
*Palmetto Dunes Resort, Hyatt Circle, Hilton Head Island, SC 29918, **803/785-1234, 800/228-9000***

Homestead, Hot Springs, VA

208 Telephone Area Code Time Zone

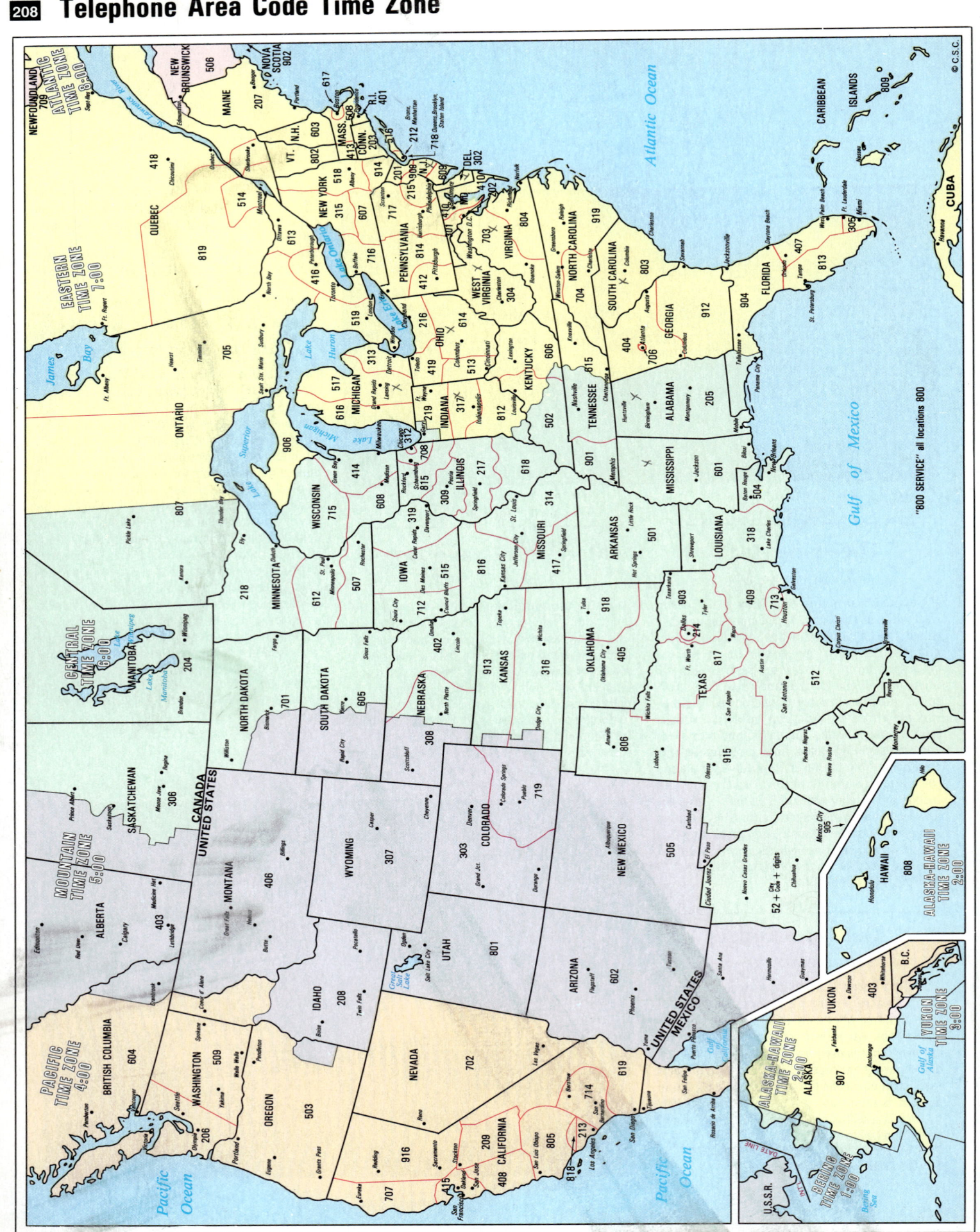